PITTSBURGH THEOLOGICAL MONOGRAPH SERIES

General Editor

DIKRAN Y. HADIDIAN

1

RHETORICAL CRITICISM

Essays In Honor of James Muilenburg

RHETORICAL CRITICISM

Essays In Honor of James Muilenburg

Edited by

JARED J. JACKSON

PITTSBURGH THEOLOGICAL SEMINARY

and

MARTIN KESSLER

STATE UNIVERSITY OF NEW YORK

AT ALBANY

THE PICKWICK PRESS

PITTSBURGH, PENNSYLVANIA

Library of Congress Cataloging in Publication Data

Rhetorical criticism.

    (Pittsburgh theological monograph series; no. 1)
    Includes bibliographical references.
    CONTENTS: Introduction: Anderson, B. W. The new
frontier of rhetorical criticism; a tribute to James
Muilenburg.--Pentateuch: Kessler, M. Rhetorical criticism of Genesis 7. Kikawada, I. M. The shape of
Genesis 11:1-9. Hamlin, J. E. The liberator's ordeal;
a study of Exodus 4:1-9.--Former prophets: Rose, A. S.
The "principles" of divine election; wisdom in 1 Samuel,
16. Ritterspach, A. D. Rhetorical criticism and the
Song of Hannah. Ridout, G. The rape of Tamar.--
Miscellanea biblica: Gottwald, N. K. Were the early
Israelites pastoral nomads? March, W. E. Laken: its
functions and meanings. Ball, I. J. Additions to a
bibliography of James Muilenburg's writings (p.   )
    1. Bible. O.T.--Addresses, essays, lectures.
2. Muilenburg, James. 3. Muilenburg, James--Bibli-
ography. I. Muilenburg, James. II. Jackson, Jared
Judd, 1930-   ed. III. Kessler, Martin, 1927-
ed. IV. Series.
BS1192.R48   809'.935'22   74-22493

ISBN 0-915138-00-X
Library of Congress Card Number 74-22493
Copyright © 1974 by The Pickwick Press
5001 Baum Boulevard
Pittsburgh, Pennsylvania 15213
and
Jared J. Jackson

PREFACE

The following essays by some of the younger students of Professor James Muilenburg are devoted to the ongoing pursuit of his major interests and contributions to the study of the Hebrew Bible, and are offered to him in honor of his 78th birthday, 1 June 1974, in the hope that he will recognize something of the inspiration which he has given to us all, and to the world of biblical scholarship.

Most of the readers of these pages need no introduction to the life and work of James Muilenburg, but all will be grateful, as we are, to Professor B. W. Anderson for his masterful Introduction, which not only sets Dr. Muilenburg's lifework within its proper setting in contemporary biblical scholarship, but serves as well to invite readers to sample these essays in rhetorical criticism, with which most of these studies deal. It is a matter of particular satisfaction to us that Dr. Anderson was one of the editors of the first Festschrift offered to Dr. Muilenburg, and we wish to thank him for his kindness in finding time in the midst of a demanding schedule to introduce this book.

Our thanks are also due to Dikran Y. Hadidian for accepting this book as the first in the new series of Pittsburgh Theological Monograph Series of which he is the General Editor.

Acknowledgements would not be complete without an expression of our gratitude to the many persons who typed and retyped the papers, including charts and Greek and Hebrew script, accurately and without complaint. We say "thank you" to them all, especially to Kathy A. Herrin, Dorothy M. Fleming and Laura Kruk, without whose skill and patience the book would never have appeared.

Generally, the abbreviations used throughout are those utilized in the publications of the Society of Biblical Literature (see JBL Supplement, vol. 90 [1971] 67-76).

April, 1974   The Editors

P.S. After this manuscript was submitted to the printer the sad news of Dr. James Muilenburg's death (May 10, 1974) reached us hence our hope to present him with a copy on his 78th birthday, June 1, 1974, was regretfully unfulfilled.

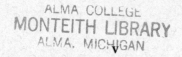

with affection and love
James M. [illegible]

CONTENTS

INTRODUCTION

The New Frontier of Rhetorical Criticism

A Tribute to James Muilenburg

Bernhard W. Anderson

Princeton Theological Seminary

The invitation to write the introduction to this volume provides a welcome opportunity to join with other students of James Muilenburg in offering a tribute to our teacher, whom we honor as a creative and dynamic interpreter of Israel's faith and one of the greatest Old Testament teachers and scholars of the past generation. This is actually the second Muilenburg Festschrift. The first, Israel's Prophetic Heritage,[1] was presented to him in 1962, just prior to his retirement from Union Theological Seminary in New York City. The present Festschrift differs from the former in two respects: without exception the essays have been written by his students (other than those who contributed to the first volume); and the contributions reflect the impact of the "rhetorical criticism" which he advocated in his presidential address to the Society of Biblical Literature in 1968.[2] In this monumental address, which represented the crowning climax of his career, he pressed the frontier of biblical studies into new regions which will be explored further in years to come.

It is fitting that this volume is published under the aegis of Pittsburgh Theological Seminary, where the bulk of his personal library is now deposited in Barbour Library with his name on the bookplates of each book. On May 10, 1966 Dr. Muilenburg gave the commencement address to the graduating class of the seminary. His text, according to his own translation and arrangement, was taken from the prophecy of Second Isaiah which he knows and loves so well:

> Behold, the former things have already come to pass,
>   now I tell you of new things.
>
> From now on I am causing you to listen to new things,
>   hidden things which you have not known.
> They are created now, not long ago;
>   before today you have never heard them.
>
> Remember not the former things,
>   nor consider the days of old.
> Behold, I am doing a new thing;
>   it is springing forth, don't you realize it?
>
> Sing to the Lord a new song,
>   his praise from the ends of the earth.
> (Isa. 42:9-10; 43:18-19)

---

[1] Israel's Prophetic Heritage: Essays in Honor of James Muilenburg (eds. Bernhard W. Anderson and Walter Harrelson; New York: Harper, 1962).

[2] "Form Criticism and Beyond," JBL 88 (1969) 1-18.

The theme of the sermon, relevant not only to his immediate audience but to all who are sensitive to the interior meaning of Israel's scriptures, was that "Our God is the innovating God," who leads into new paths and new frontiers. "The man who is free," he said, "knows that life is always open, open to new possibilities, open to the unprecedented, open to God and history. He will not stay put in any status quo ante, indeed in any status at all, for time and history do not allow it."[3]

Dr. Muilenburg's scholarly writings also are animated by the inability to "stay put in any status quo ante," and this is eminently true of his presidential address in which he advocated "Form Criticism and Beyond," the "beyond" being rhetorical criticism of Israel's scriptures. It should be realized, however, that his advocacy of rhetorical criticism, while representing a creative thrust into a new frontier, was actually a sharpening of concerns that had been present from the very beginning of his scholarly career. Indeed, in this time when biblical critics   ersing with literary critics in the field of the humanities, it i.   ᴍembering that he began his teaching career at the University of ᴺebraska (1920-1923) as an instructor in English composition, where he wrote a book dealing with specimens of biblical literature. His encounter with Hermann Gunkel, however, transformed his literary interest in the Bible. He was deeply influenced, as he has told me in correspondence, by the volume on The Oriental Literatures in the Kultur der Gegenwart series, in which Gunkel presented a sketch of what he considered to be a proper literary history of Israel. And while teaching at Mount Holyoke he was granted a sabbatical for study at Marburg, Germany (1929-1930), which provided him with the opportunity to visit several universities, especially the University of Halle where Gunkel was teaching. He attended Gunkel's seminar, visited him in his home, and read many of his works, including The Legends of Genesis. In his presidential address Dr. Muilenburg paid a very high tribute to Gunkel. "It is not too much to say," he stated, "that Gunkel has never been excelled in his ability to portray the spirit which animated the biblical writers, and he did not hesitate either in his lectures or in his seminars to draw upon the events of contemporary history or the experiences of the common man to explicate the interior meaning of a pericope."[4] Muilenburg's students undoubtedly would testify that this is an overstatement, for Gunkel's grasp of the meaning of Israel's scriptures was too much under the influence of the presuppositions of the Religionsgeschichtlicheschule. When it comes to grasping the interior, theological dimensions of Israel's faith, James Muilenburg is unexcelled, as those who have experienced his demanding and sensitive scholarship and the charismatic power of his teaching know.

His emphasis upon rhetorical criticism could easily be misunderstood if it is not seen in the context of his whole scholarly career. Since it was my privilege to be his first student to go into graduate study, and since I have kept in close touch with him through the subsequent years, it may be helpful for me to review the three phases of his career: his years at Pacific School of Religion (1936-1945), his period at Union Theological Seminary (1945-1963), and his very active "retirement" at San Anselmo

---

[3] Sermon, "The Innovating God," May 10, 1966. I am grateful to Dr. Muilenburg for providing me with a copy.

[4] "Form Criticism and Beyond," 2.

Theological Seminary (1963-1969). In retrospect each of these phases was characterized by different accents, each of which represents an important dimension of his presidential address. His continuous concern through his whole career, however, has been to give an exposition of Israel's historical faith which belongs essentially to the witness of the Christian community. As a scholar he has always been a churchman.

James Muilenburg began his career in theological education at Pacific School of Religion when new theological winds, emanating from Europe, were sweeping across the United States, though their intensity had diminished considerably by the time they reached the West. In those days Old Testament scholarship was still under the domination of the Wellhausen school which, supported by an analysis of the "sources" of the Pentateuch, advocated a unilinear, evolutionary interpretation of Israel's history. This view had been popularized by the writings of Harry Emerson Fosdick, minister of Riverside Church in New York City, whose radio sermons were heard nationally. Fosdick's books, such as The Modern Use of the Bible (1924) and A Guide to Understanding the Bible (1938), had a liberating effect upon many college students who were dissatisfied with a naive view of Scripture. This was the prevailing atmosphere when I entered Pacific School of Religion in 1936, the first year of Dr. Muilenburg's career in theological education. I remember that right away we were plunged into the problem of the Pentateuch in his course on Introduction to the Old Testament. One of our assignments was to go through the Pentateuch and mark with colored pencils the four sources (J,E,D,P) according to the diagrammatic analysis given in S.R. Driver's Introduction to the Literature of the Old Testament. The other assignment was to write a paper on "The Composition of the Pentateuch," an assignment-- as I came to learn--that was given annually to generations of students at Pacific School of Religion and, later, at Union Theological Seminary. Muilenburg's teaching, however, exploded the constricting framework of the Wellhausen view. This occurred, first of all, because of his intuitive penetration into the dimensions of Israel's experience of the reality of God in her history and his ability to dramatize the scriptural story so that students were drawn into it personally. And, secondly, he was profoundly influenced by Gunkel's Gattungsforschung--a word that is emblazoned on my memory from those days. In a course on Jeremiah, I became aware of the principles of interpretation which later were articulated as "rhetorical criticism:" the isolation of a discrete literary unit, the analysis of its structure and balance, and the attention to key words and motifs. Yet what stands out most in my memory from those years is his profound exposition of Yahweh's revelation in historical events and the eschatological import of that revelation. Students found themselves caught in the creative tension between James Muilenburg, an Old Testament teacher who was sympathetic with some aspects of "neo-orthodoxy," and C. C. McCown, a New Testament teacher who fervently advocated a "naturalistic" interpretation of Scripture.[5]

When Dr. Muilenburg moved to Union Theological Seminary in 1945, he found himself on the crest of the so-called Biblical Theology Movement. He approved

---

[5] See Harland E. Hogue, Christian Seed in Western Soil: Pacific School of Religion through a Century (Berkeley, California: Pacific School of Religion, 1965), chap. 8, "World War II and its Aftermath."

of the church's demand for a biblical theology and made his own contribution
to the movement, although expressing his qualifications. "The task of the
biblical theologian," he said during this period, "is a precarious one;"
for Israel's scriptures, having come out of life, resist any simple sche-
matization. In this respect, he confessed that he was a "liberal," profoundly indebted to historical criticism. One of the primary characteristics
of biblical faith, he never wearied of saying, is "the historical character of revelation"--"Israel's sense of the eventfulness of life and of
God's activity in history;" and it is to liberalism, he said, that we owe
this insight. It is essential, therefore, for the biblical critic to understand the historical setting in which words were spoken and to appreciate
how those words were shaped in concrete social situations.[6]

Consistent with these historical concerns, he championed even more
vigorously the method of form criticism, as evidenced by some of his writings from this period.[7] Like Gunkel, Muilenburg never repudiated in
principle the method of source criticism, but he shifted the emphasis
to a method which he believed to be more fruitful in understanding the
relation of scripture to the life of the people. He spoke appreciatively
of "the gains of form criticism." The task of the form critic, he said,
is not only to identify the Gattungen but "to restore them to their original spokenness (Gesprochenheit), for they must be heard in order to be
understood or made contemporary."[8] Yet even when he wrote those words in
1960, he was not unaware of the excesses and exaggerations of the method,
evident in the reduction of literary units to "mere snippets" or the
unduly heavy emphasis upon cultic provenance or Near Eastern parallels.
His reservations about the omnicompetence of the form-critical method
were surely nourished by his work on Second Isaiah for the Interpreter's
Bible (1956). His masterful commentary, which was severely reduced from
notes that could have extended it several times in length, displays
disagreement with form critics who divide the material into small units,
thereby confusing strophes with independent poems, and it evinces a fine
sensitivity to rhetorical and structural features of the poetry. It was
from Gunkel that he gained an appreciation of the forms and patterns in
Hebrew literary composition; and this interest, always evident in his
teaching and writing from the first, became more prominent,[9] though not
excluding other interests ranging from archaeology to biblical theology.

---

[6] See his essay, "Is There a Biblical Theology?" USQR XII, 4 (1957)
29-37, especially p. 35.

[7] For instance, "The Birth of Benjamin," JBL 75 (1956) 194-201;
"The Form and Structure of the Covenantal Formulations," VT 9 (1959)
347-65.

[8] See "The Gains of Form Criticism in Old Testament Studies," ExpT 71;
No. 8 (1960) 229-33, especially p. 231.

[9] See "A Study in Hebrew Rhetoric: Repetition and Style," VTSup I (1953)
97-111; "The Linguistic and Rhetorical Usages of the Particle כי in the Old
Testament," HUCA 32 (1961) 135-60.

Dr. Muilenburg's later years at San Anselmo Theological Seminary brought to fulfillment what was seminally present from the beginning of his career in theological education. In his essay on "Form Criticism and Beyond," he says clearly that he does not intend to repudiate form criticism, any more than he repudiated completely the older method of source criticism. There are some instances in which form criticism works well. But when carried to an extreme, it has certain inherent weaknesses. For one thing, form-critical analysis of a literary genre tends "to lay such stress upon the typical and representative that the individual, personal, and unique features of the particular pericope are all but lost to view." Often, he points out, we do not find a Gattung in pure form but rather imitations of it, detached from its original Sitz im Leben and refashioned with such superb literary artistry that we are enabled "to think the thoughts of the biblical writer after him." A second criticism is that form criticism, when strictly applied, resists all efforts to gain a psychological understanding of an author or to sense the concrete historical situation in which he spoke.[10]

The immediate context of Dr. Muilenburg's sensitivity to the extremes of form criticism was his work on the prophecy of Jeremiah, which has been one of his major interests throughout his career. At San Anselmo he was engaged in writing a commentary on Jeremiah, using the method of rhetorical criticism. The unfinished manuscript, which I have been privileged to read, seeks to demonstrate that the literature, although making use of traditional literary genres,provides access to the mind of the prophet and the concrete situations in which his words were spoken. "The call of Jeremiah," he observes in his presidential address, "is something more than the recitation of a conventional and inherited liturgy within the precincts of the temple [contra H. G. Reventlow, Liturgie und prophetisches Ich bei Jeremia], and the so-called confessions of the prophet are more than the repetition and re-production of fixed stereotypes, despite all the parallels that one may adduce from the Old Testament and the Near Eastern texts for such a po-sition."[11] What the critic finds in the case of Jeremiah is also evident elsewhere in the Old Testament. Very often, he emphasizes, the literary genres do not appear in pure form but are imitated, that is, they are used creatively by a writer who draws them into the context of his own thought. Thus the conventional is stamped with individuality, the old wine is poured into new wineskins. For this reason it behooves the scholar to hold fast to the assured gains of form criticism but to go beyond. The sensitive literary critic, he says, "will not be completely bound by the traditional elements and motifs of literary genre; his task will not be completed until he has taken full account of the features which lie beyond the spectrum of the genre."

In his presidential address Dr. Muilenburg suggested that rhetorical criticism is applicable to all of Israel's scriptures, but he concentra-ted on the poetic, and especially the prophetic, sections of the Old Testament. He did not face directly the implications of rhetorical criti-cism for the Pentateuch which traditionally has been the testing-ground

---

10 "Form Criticism and Beyond," 4-6.

11 Ibid., 6.

12 Ibid., 7.

for critical method. It was in this area, of course, that Gunkel, whom Muilenburg acclaims as "the pioneer and progenitor" of Gattungsforschung, carried out his investigation with fruitful results. It is my conviction that Muilenburg in his own way has raised some important questions concerning "The Composition of the Pentateuch," to hark back to the paper that his students were required to write. The following brief remarks are intended only to indicate the new frontier which demands exploration.

Let us begin with Muilenburg's observation that genres are often transformed when appropriated for new literary contexts. Gunkel, of course, maintained that the proper starting-point in form-critical investigation is the isolation of discrete genres, such as the Sagen of Genesis. Moreover, it was alleged that the genres of oral tradition are usually brief pericopes which can be detached from their present narrative context and studied from within, in their own Sitz im Leben. Indeed, one of the guidelines in traditio-historical investigation of the Pentateuch, as I have formulated it with reference to Martin Noth's work, is: "Earliest traditions are formulated in small units and in concise style in contrast to later material which tends to appear in large units composed in discursive (ausgeführt) style."[13] Now, it is undoubtedly true that the Pentateuchal tradition does contain hints of units that were closely related to folk life, and often the critic can isolate them and study them by themselves (e.g. Gen. 6:1-4; 32:22-32). The problem is that in many cases Gunkel's small unit is beyond recovery and, in any case, is so closely integrated into the narrative complex (Gunkel's Sagenkranz) that its meaning cannot be understood from within. The unit, whatever its original setting, now functions in a new context which has transformed its original meaning.[14]

This hermeneutical problem is illustrated in a perceptive essay on Genesis 22 by George Coats, one of the leading younger form critics.[15] The point of departure for his form-critical study, he states, is "the received text [including the somewhat "anticlimactic" verses 15-18], not a hypothetical reconstruction of earlier levels," and this demands that the passage must be understood in relation to the larger context in which it now functions, that is, "the scope of theology about Abraham and his promise." This is an important statement, one that suggests "form criticism and beyond." No longer does the genre have a vague setting in

---

[13] See the introductory essay to my translation of Martin Noth, A History of Pentateuchal Traditions (Englewood Cliffs, N.J.: Prentice-Hall, 1972), xxiii-xxiv. This essay was presented to, and discussed by, a group of form critics, including James Muilenburg, at the 1968 meeting of the Society of Biblical Literature.

[14] Here I acknowledge my indebtedness to a paper on "Saga" by Robert Neff at a form-critical seminar held during the 1973 meeting of the Society of Biblical Literature.

[15] George W. Coats, "Abraham's Sacrifice of Faith: A Form-Critical Study of Genesis 22," Int 27 (1973) 389-400.

folk life, as Gunkel would have maintained, but has a narrative setting or
Sitz im Text, whether that setting was provided by oral prose composition
or by a literary author/redactor.[16] If this is the case, the situation
in the book of Genesis is analogous to that of the poetry of Second Isaiah
where, as Muilenburg points out, traditional genres like the covenant
lawsuit (rîb) or the Heilsorakel are creatively appropriated by a literary
artist and made to function in a new context.[17]

Let us turn to another matter, which is related to the foregoing
discussion. At the conclusion of his presidential address, Dr. Muilenburg
raises the question of the source of Hebrew rhetoric. "Persistent and
painstaking attention to the modes of Hebrew literary composition," he
states, "will reveal that the pericopes exhibit linguistic patterns, word
formations ordered or arranged in particular ways, verbal sequences which
move in fixed structures from beginning to end." These phenomena, he
insists, "cannot be explained by spontaneity." Even though the writers
creatively produced their own literary style, "it is also apparent that
they have been influenced by conventional rhetorical practices." And on
the heels of this question comes another: "How are we to explain the
numerous and extraordinary literary affinities of the Gattungen or genres
and other stylistic formulations of Israel's literature with the literatures
of the other people of the Near East?"[18]

These questions are particularly puzzling when we turn to the literature
of the Pentateuch, whose history moves from oral composition to written
fixation. In contrast to Wellhausen, who placed excessive emphasis upon
the "sources" of the Pentateuch which were dated in the period of the
monarchy, Gunkel maintained that the oral (pre-state) period was the creative time, when the experiences of the people found expression in genres
related to folk life. Undoubtedly Gunkel was inspired by a sound insight.
For the prose narratives of the Pentateuch not only rest upon ancient oral
tradition, as form critics emphasize, but bear "the formal and rhetorical
stigmata" of oral composition.

As Dr. Muilenburg admits, here we are moving into a misty area in
which it is difficult to find our way. Since we have no immediate access
to the prehistory of the Pentateuchal narratives, the problem is to find
some analogy in a preliterate society, still open to investigation, which
may help us to understand the rhetoric of oral composition. This problem
becomes peculiarly difficult when we contemplate the possibility that no
analogy can do full justice to ancient Israelite society which may have
been unique in its understanding of the spoken and written word. Perhaps
some light may be cast on the problem by Albert Lord's reconsideration of

---

[16] Coats seems to abandon the search for a Sitz im Leben in Gunkel's
sense. In his brief section on "Setting" (p. 199), he states that the
legend "reflects a folk tradition, a style of storytelling that cannot
easily be tied to one particular institution," and that the story in its
present form has been consciously adapted to fit it into a "literary
construct."

[17] See the Princeton Theological Seminary doctoral dissertation by
Edgar W. Conrad, Patriarchal Traditions in Second Isaiah (1974), where the
implications of Muilenburg's approach are further, and fruitfully, explored.

[18] "Form Criticism and Beyond," 18.

Homeric literature in his work, The Singer of Tales, even though it must
be admitted that no exact parallel can be drawn between non-literate folk
communities of Yugoslavia and ancient societies, especially Israel. He
challenges the notion that poets "did something to a fixed text or fixed
group of texts"[19] and maintains that stylistic features, which seem to
suggest a writer "with pen in hand," actually arose in oral narration in
which the singer creatively utilized formulaic patterns and various stereotyped devices in his improvisations.[20] This study, it seems to me, may have
a heuristic value in that it helps us to perceive aspects of Israelite
composition and particularly to consider the relation between the spoken
and the written word. Dr. Muilenburg has observed that "the difficulty
with historical criticism," meaning the kind of criticism practiced pre-
eminently by the Wellhausen school, "is that it always tended to view the
literary material too much as written products;" and he sides with Gunkel
who "sought to liberate the literary forms from the written page and to
place them. . . into the immediacy and concreteness of speaking."[21] It
should be added, however, that even when the narratives of Genesis were
written, say, by the Yahwist, they were intended for oral reading--not
for silent reading in some library! This was also true of the oracles
of the prophets, at least in the first stage: when they were dictated to
a disciple, as in the case of Jeremiah's scroll, they were intended to
be read publicly or perhaps they were preserved for reading in years to
come when the people might listen and understand. It is very likely that
when the Old Epic tradition of the Pentateuch was reduced to writing, it
reflected the rhetoric of oral performance, so that even today we are able
to listen to "the speaking of Israel," as Muilenburg used to tell his students.

In any event, we now have the traditions in written form and it is with
the final text that the literary critic must deal. Albert Lord stresses
that a decisive act occurred when the Singer of Tales allowed his oral
composition to be written down finally and to become, as it were, a canonical text. Something similar must have occurred when the Old Epic tradition
was written down and, above all, when it was incorporated into the Priestly
Writing. For the Pentateuchal materials to which scholars have assigned
the siglum P does not represent the work of a mere editor who harmonized
the Old Epic (JE) tradition with an independent priestly "source;" rather,
as Frank Cross has rightly observed, P was an author (or "tradent") who
creatively "shaped and supplemented the received Epic tradition of Israel"[22]
and, in so doing, gave the tradition a definitive and final written form.

---

[19] Albert B. Lord, The Singer of Tales (Harvard University Press, 1960),
11.

[20] Ibid., 57.

[21] "The Gains of Form Criticism. . . ." 231.

[22] Frank Moore Cross, Canaanite Myth and Hebrew Epic: Essays in the
History of the Religion of Israel (Harvard University Press, 1973),
chap. 11, "The Priestly Work," especially 301-21.

Rhetorical criticism is a new impulse which may well shift the emphasis in Pentateuchal studies. Under the influence of Gunkel, the investigation of the literary "sources" of the Pentateuch ceased to have ascendency and scholars turned their attention to the preliterary period, the stage of oral transmission. This is supremely evident in the monumental commentary on Genesis by Claus Westermann, who in his own way is profoundly indebted to Gunkel.[23] The question that many are raising these days, however, is: What is the <u>relative</u> value of going behind the final text into previous levels of tradition that can be reconstructed only hypothetically? How much light does the prehistory of the text throw upon the final text-- the one that has functioned in Judaism and Christianity and the one that we read today?[24]

This kind of question has been raised by literary critics in other fields. Roland Frye, for instance, has pointed out that in the field of the humanities literary critics have found explorations behind the text to be unfruitful, and he has issued a challenge to biblical critics to show "a primary exegetical respect for the final literary work itself."[25] Speaking of the Gospels, he writes: "To dissect them, put each segment under a microscope, and then reassemble the parts in some hypothetical form hopefully representing an earlier form of the tradition can be a fascinating endeavor, but again it will divert our attention and energies from a more productive kind of study. To attempt to dissect the Gospels as historical dramas and force the fragments back into earlier forms and stages is like putting Ariel back in the pine cleft."[26] Frye's remarks about the Gospels as dramatic history could apply <u>mutatis mutandis</u> to the Pentateuchal story. This kind of literary criticism, however, could lead to the dubious conclusion that all attempts to go behind the text and inquire into authorship, provenance, life situation, are in vain and have no bearing upon exegesis. I am sure that Dr. Muilenburg, who has a profound appreciation of both English literature and biblical literature, would be the first to rise to his feet and protest the extremes of the new literary criticism. Nevertheless, in a period when the scholarly habit has been to engage in excursions behind the text, there is much to be said in favor of "a primary exegetical respect for the final literary work itself"--its rhetorical features and its dramatic quality. For the final text is not just the result of adding together various units of tradition, each of which can be studied by itself and whose meaning is contained within itself, but is a whole which is more than the sum of its parts. What Nahum Sarna says about documentary analysis is eminently true: "things in combination possess properties and produce

---

23 See Claus Westermann, <u>Ertra̋ge der Forschung: Genesis 1-11</u> (Darmstadt: Wissenschaftliche Buchgesellschaft, 1972) 1-2. This little book summarizes the history of research presupposed in his <u>Genesiskommentar</u>.

24 See my review of the first five fascicles of Westermann's commentary on Genesis, <u>JBL</u> 91 (1972) 243-245.

25 Roland M. Frye, "A Literary Perspective for the Criticism of the Gospels," <u>Jesus and Man's Hope</u> (eds. Donald G. Miller and Dikran Y. Hadidian, Vol II; Pittsburgh Theological Seminary, 1971) 193-221; quotation from p. 215.

26 Ibid, 212.

qualities neither carried by, nor inherent in, any of the components in isolation."[27]

In his presidential address Dr. Muilenburg makes it clear that he does not intend for a moment to forfeit the substantial accomplishments of the scholarly tradition in which he stands. He has been a debtor to Wellhausen, despite reservations about his historical criticism, and to Gunkel, from whom he learned most. This is especially clear to me as I consider his thesis "form criticism and beyond" in the context of his whole career. His essay opens up a new frontier for exploration, not least of all in the field of Pentateuchal studies. He concludes the essay by saying: "We affirm the necessity of form criticism"-- and that demands appropriate exploration of the prehistory of the text; "but we also lay claim to the legitimacy of what we have called rhetorical criticism"-- and that requires attention to the text itself: its own integrity, its dramatic structure, and its stylistic features.

[27] Nahum M. Sarna, Understanding Genesis (New York: McGraw-Hill, 1966 xxv.

RHETORICAL CRITICISM OF GENESIS 7

Martin Kessler

State University of New York at Albany

There are basically two possible approaches to the biblical text; the genetic[1] approach deals with the historical question as to how the text got into its present form.[2] On the other hand the teleological approach studies the meaning of the text as it stands; its analytical concerns propel it into dealing with structural and morphological characteristics.[3]

The two approaches are not, or should not be, mutually contradictory, but capable of cross-fertilization. Indeed, both the historical and analytical approaches contribute to an informed interpretation of the biblical text. However, particularly in the Pentateuch, scholars have been excessively preoccupied with genetic criticism.[4] In their concern for source analysis,[5] critics spend insufficient time on the analysis of the text. Accordingly, most critical commentaries first isolate the sources and then proceed to comment on them separately, without considering the final stage of the preliterary history, when the alleged sources or strata or traditions were joined together to form the present text.[6]

---

1. The terms are Northrop Frye's.

2. Diachronic criticism.

3. Synchronic criticism.

4. Hermann Gunkel wrote concerning Gen 6-9: "Die Quellenscheidung zwischen J und P ist ein Meisterstück der modernen Kritik." (Genesis übersetzt und erklärt [6. Auflage; Göttingen: Vandenhoeck & Ruprecht, 1964] 137).

5. A familiar and extreme example remains C. A. Simpson, The Book of Genesis (IB, 1; Nashville: Abingdon, 1952).

6. To mention but a few examples, in the commentaries on Genesis by Skinner (ICC), Gunkel, and von Rad, the flood story is discussed separately according to component sources. Speiser (AB) marks the sources but comments on the narrative as a whole.

The present study of necessity must take into account source critical conclusions but it is not concerned with anything approaching a full scale evaluation of the merits and demerits of the documentary hypothesis because its focus is synchronic. Rather, it hopes to contribute to the ongoing dialog between methods, in the realization that the crucial problem is not which (single) method deserves to stand alone, all others having fallen before it, or even how various methods may be mutually reconciled, but instead to show how one method may furnish a fresh vision of the literature.

Professor Muilenburg's preoccupation with the prophetic literature and the Psalms has demonstrated, in classroom and publications, the unusual sensitivity of his perception of the formal character of biblical texts together with his keen sense of literary artistry, both contributing to penetrating interpretation. It is a pleasure to honor a gratefully remembered teacher with this analytical and rhetorical study of Genesis 7.

I

It might be argued that Genesis 7 does not possess independent literary status and that it therefore ought not to be treated separately from its context within the literary cycle called the flood story (Gen 6-9). There is some merit in this argument; however as this study intends to show, the concentration on such a limited unit as this in itself is entirely justified.[7]

Since Wellhausen, the flood story has been viewed as a combination of two roughly parallel[8] accounts:

---

7. It is increasingly recognized that the delimiting of pericopes, once considered a prime methodological requirement for form criticism (cf. H. Gressmann, "Die literarische Analyse bei Deuterojesaja", ZAW 34 [1914] 259, and O. Eissfeldt, "Die kleinste literarische Einheit in den Erzählungsbüchern des alten Testaments", Kleine Schriften, I [Tübingen: J.C.B. Mohr, 1962] 143-149),is only valuable to a degree, as the setting of "units" within larger structures is discerned. For a study of the interpretation of the flood tradition see Jack P. Lewis, The Interpretation of Noah and the Flood in Jewish and Christian Literature (Leiden: E.J. Brill, 1968).

8. Both 6:14-22 and 7:1-5 deal with the ark; rather than being parallel, they are consecutive however: the former relates YHWH's command to build the ark (the execution of which is stated by means of the obedience formula, 22), the latter states the command to Noah to enter the ark. Therefore the criterion of "doublets" does not apply here.

	J	P
Concerning the Ark	7:1-5	6:14-22
Advent of the Flood	7:7,8,10,12,16b	7:6,9,11,13-16a
The Flood	7:17,22,23	7:18-21,24[9]

Gen 7, an episode in the larger unit comprising the flood story, may be outlined as follows:

1-4   Divine command with motivation (kî, 4)

5-9   Execution of divine command, preceded by the obedience formula[10] and a time-clause

10-12   The flood: mê hammabbûl (10), haggešem (12)

13-16   Execution restated, ending with: wayyisgōr yhwh ba‘adô, 16

17-20   The flood: the waters prevail

21-23   Description of resulting universal death

24   The flood: waters prevailing

---

9. N. Habel, Literary Criticism of the OT, (Philadelphia; Fortress) 32.

10. This formula, which usually serves as a shorthand device for restating the execution of a command in the same language as the command (as occurs repeatedly in the Ugaritic corpus for example), contains the following elements:

     1) the verb ‘ŚH, usually in the narrative form: wayya‘aś
     2) predicate, with the subject YHWH and the verb ṢWH: kekōl 'ašer ṣiwwā yhwh.

In this case, the use of the obedience formula does not prevent the writer from describing the execution of the command in a more elaborate form than in the command. Cf. W. Baumgartner, "Ein Kapitel vom hebräischen Erzählungsstil", EUCHARISTERION Gunkel (FRLANT 19; Göttingen: Vandenhoeck & Ruprecht, 1923) 141-151. The obedience formula also occurs in 6:22 (referring to the command to build the ark), in lieu of a description of the execution, contrary to ch. 7 where the execution is rather fully described not once but twice, each ending with abbreviated obedience formula's:

   9   ka'ašer ṣiwwā 'elōhîm 'et-nōaḥ

  16   ka'ašer ṣiwwā 'ōtô 'elōhîm ...

The obvious duplications, viz. the execution of the divine command (7-9; 13-16) and the description of the flood (17-20; 24) may be suggestive of the narrator's "framing"[11] method:

7-16   Execution - FLOOD - Execution

17-24   Waters prevailing - DEATH - Waters prevailing.

Thus, in 5-16, the execution of the divine command is the all-important feature of the story (restated for emphasis), which, for Noah and his companions (YHWH's $š^e$'ẽrît, cf. 23) counteracts the deadly power of the flood. On the other hand, the prevailing waters, (heavily stressed for emphasis) bring death to those outside the ark (17-24). This pivot between the "saved" and the "lost", between those chosen to survive and those assigned to drowning, is indicated by the verbal clause which divides this unit into two parts: wayyisgōr yhwh ba^{ca}dô, 16b.

The first part, 1-16a deals with the divine favor toward Noah (6:8), the saddîq,[12] together with his family and the chosen animals who enter the ark: imperative bō', 1, on the compliance of which hinges the survival of mankind. The entry of humans and animals is recorded separately in both accounts of the execution, as follows:

         7 humans   8f. animals

       13 humans   14ff. animals,

both enumerations ending with an abbreviated obedience formula (9,16) which serve as a kind of counterweight to the longer formula in 5, so that the following scheme is obtained:

Command,	)		)	Abbreviated formula, 9b
	)	Obedience formula,	)	
	)		)	
1-3	)	5	)	Abbreviated formula, 16a.

Cf. Gerhard Liedke, _Gestalt und Bezeichnung alttestamentlicher Rechtssätze_ (WMANT 39; Neukirchen: Neukirchener Verlag, 1971) 192.

11. S.E. McEvenue, _The Narrative Style of the Priestly Writer_ (Rome: Biblical Institute, 1971) passim.

12. Note the two kî-clauses: kî-'ōt^{e}kā rā'îtî saddîq... and kî l^{e}yāmîm ^{c}ôd šib^{ec}ā... which both serve as motivation for YHWH's gracious dealings. See J. Muilenburg, "The Linguistic and Rhetorical Usages of the Particle כִּי in the Old Testament", _HUCA_ 32 (1961) 135-160.

The destination is the ark; hence, the key phrase (Leitmotiv!)
'el-hattēbā[13] (in 1 [command], 7, 13 [execution: humans], 9, 15
[execution: animals]).

The second part, 17-24, describes the flood and its lethal effects
on those lacking the ark's protection. The increasing narrative
pace is indicated by the multiple yiqtol-x forms:[14]

Part One (7:1-16) -- 7 times (in 16 verses)

Part Two (7: 17-24 -- 14 times (in 8 verses), as follows:

17	4	
18	3	Prevailing of the waters
19	1	
20	1	
21	1	Death of earthly life
23	3	
24	1	Prevailing of the waters

---

13. The word tēbā only occurs in two contexts in the Hebrew Bible. In
addition to the flood story, it refers to the basket in which Moses was
placed among the reeds of the Nile. Whereas in the flood story the
tēbā was used to save a remnant of the doomed world, so in Exodus it
is used to save Moses from drowning in the Nile -- the fate of other
Hebrew children. Noah is the ṣaddîq, Moses the sent one, the prophet;
both represent, however, the nucleus of a delivered remnant: the
former, as progenitor of the whole world (represented by their ancestors
Shem, Ham, and Japheth), the latter as the spiritual leader of a chosen
people.

14. See W. Richter, Traditionsgeschichtliche Untersuchungen zum
Richterbuch (BBB 18; Bonn: Hanstein, 1963) 354ff. This form is also
called "imperfect with waw consecutive" (GKC 111); Joüon calls it
"futur inverti" (Grammaire de l'Hébreu Biblique [Rome: Institut
Biblique, 1923] 47.

Source critics have labelled the narration of the first part
(1-16) J with the following qualifications:

1. Vss. 6 and 11, being chronological notations, are P.
2. The second account of the execution, 13-16 is P.
3. The first account, 7-9, is J, though Pfeiffer and Habel ascribe 9 to P.

Disregarding the chronological material momentarily, the question
is how the two execution accounts are mutually related.[15] As the
divine command simply orders Noah and his fellow-travelers into the
ark, so the execution lists all humans and animals which are going
aboard. The parallelism of the two accounts of the execution seems
obvious:

7:7	7:13
	$b^e {}^c e \c sem \ hayy\hat om \ hazze$
wayyābō' nōaḥ	bā' nōaḥ
ûbānāyw w^e'iŝtô	w^{e}ŝem-w^{e}ḥam w^{e}yepet b^{e}nê-nōaḥ
	w^e'ēŝet nōaḥ
ûn^{e}ŝê-bānāyw 'itto	ûŝ^{e}lōŝet n^{e}ŝê-bānāyw 'ittām
'el-hattēbā	'el-hattēbā

In both verses the entry of Noah with his family[16] into the ark is
recorded (Noah and his sons / his wife and their wives) with the
following differences:

---

15. The question as to the ultimate origin of the two accounts is left
open, because the present concern is whether the present form of the
text can be explained by the narration technique. In a sense, this
investigation deals with the evaluation of the work of the final editor,
redactor, R -- or whatever label one may prefer to use. Gunkel, falling
short of praising his work, has written that the study of the redactor's
work in the flood story is "besonders instruktiv." (Genesis, 139).

16. "Segen und Heil können ... von einem frommen Vater auch ohne dessen
Zutun auf Frau und Kinder ausströmen." (Josef Scharbert, Solidarität in
Segen und Fluch im alten Testament und in seiner Umwelt (BBB 14;
Bonn: Peter Hanstein, 1958) 256.

1. In 7:13 the names of Noah's sons are given, which the source
    critic describes to P's propensity for enumeration.

2. 7:13 is preceded by a time-clause indicating the day when the
    flood started, 7:11, linking the first-execution account with
    the account of the commencement of the flood preceding it.

    The comparison of the lists of animals entering the ark (the
first has been labeled J, the second P) is somewhat more complex.

7:8, 9	7:14-16
	(14) hemmā
(8) min-habbᵉhēmā haṭṭᵉhōrā	wᵉkol-haḥayyā lᵉmînāh
ûmin-habbᵉhēmā 'aᵛšer	wᵉkol-habbᵉhēmā lᵉmînāh
'ênenna ṭᵉhōrā	wᵉkol-haremeś hārōmēś ᶜal-
ûmin-hāᶜôp	hā'āreṣ lᵉmînēhû
wᵉkōl 'aᵛšer-rōmēś ᶜal-	wᵉkol-hāᶜôp lᵉmînēhû
hā'ᵃdāmā.	kol ṣippôr kol-kānāp.
(9) šᵉnayim šᵉnayim	(15) wayyābō'û 'el-nōaḥ 'el-hattēbā
bā'û 'el-nōaḥ 'el-hattēbā	šᵉnayim šᵉnayim mikkol-habbāśār
	'aᵛšer-bô rûaḥ ḥayyim.
zākār ûnᵉqēbā	(16) wᵉhabbā'îm zākār ûnᵉqēbā
	mikkol bāśār
ka'aᵛšer ṣiwwā 'ᵉlōhîm	bā'û ka'aᵛšer ṣiwwā 'ōtô 'ᵉlōhîm..
'et nōaḥ	

Though the form varies, the two accounts are quite similar
materially:[17]

---

17. Cf. W. M. Clark, "The Animal Series in the Primeval History,"
VT 18 (1968) 433-449.

1. Each list has four categories of animals; both mention birds and creeping things; 7:8 subdivides the $b^eh\bar{e}m\bar{a}$ into clean and unclean[18] while 7:14 distinguishes between ḥayyā (wild animals) and $b^eh\bar{e}m\bar{a}$ (domesticated animals).

2. While the divine command has the compound adjective mikkol and the preposition min (2), the first execution account uses the preposition min three times (8), suggesting the process of selection, while the second has kol six times, thus expressing the completeness of the representation, which is finally summed up by the phrase mikkol-(hab)bāśār, 15f.: the divine command has been executed to perfection! The second version employs the root BW' three times; Noah, a second Adam, is the destination (cf. Gen 2:19). Just as (the first) Adam had named the animals and sent them away, so Noah (as another Adam) selects pairs of all animals to preserve their kind (mîn). Man's lordship over creation (Gen 1:28) remains (cf. Gen 9:2).

3. The phrase "clean and unclean" is repeated from the command; "male and female," recognized as a typical P-phrase, is used in both execution accounts though not in the command.

4. The question of seven versus two pairs of animals, which has been the subject of much discussion among source critics, is treated elsewhere by the present writer. However, the expression "clean and unclean" suggests a reference to the command which calls for seven pairs of clean animals.

5. Both accounts relate that the animals "came to Noah, to the ark" and end with the (shortened) obedience formula: ka'^{a}šer ṣiwwā '^{e}lōhîm ('et-nōaḥ).

6. The second account is somewhat more fully developed. It uses four categories, each ending with l^emînāh or l^emînēhû. The formal scheme of enumeration seems to suggest the same:

(1) (7:8) min...ûmin...ûmin...w^ekōl (summarizing)

(2) (7:14) l^emînāh...l^emînāh...l^emînēhû...l^emînēhû: the list is not halted by a summarizing clause, but the monotony is sustained to suggest cumulation and careful enumeration. Yet, the second list also summarizes, viz. toward the end of its description; the first list has no phrase corresponding to: $š^e$nayim $š^e$nayim mikkol-habbāśār '^{a}šer-bô rûaḥ ḥayyim... zākār ûn^{e}qēbā mikkol-bāśār (15f.)

7. Both accounts borrow liberally from what has been considered typical P-vocabulary as in Gen 1: 'adāmā (1:25), $b^eh\bar{e}m\bar{a}$ (1:24), zākār ûn^{e}qēbā (P), mîn (1:12), the root RMŚ (1:24) and the obedience formula.

8. The style of both is enumerative. The ark enables God's original creation to survive and to make a new beginning.

---

18. Though the source critics assign this vs. to J, Gunkel remarks that 7:7-10 is "stark glossiert." (Genesis, 62).

In sum, convincing evidence is lacking that the two accounts are contradictory in any way. Assuming that the writer wished to provide a duplicate account, he could either create two verbally identical accounts (which biblical writers [19] generally avoid), or he could create "variation by design," in other words, write an alternate, duplicating materially synonymous account, in the spirit of parallelismus membrorum. The latter seems to be essentially the case here.

Wedged between the two execution accounts is a brief mention of the beginning of the flood and the chronicler's spirit is once again in evidence : each of the three verses (10-12) has a temporal clause or a date, all in connection with the beginning stages of the flood, which is referred to by the phrases mê hammabbûl (10) and haggešem (12). Introduced by the resumptive clause bayyôm hazze, the cosmic phenomena causing the flood are described in chiastic form (11).

                              III

Though not until part two (7:17-24) the flood with its furious destruction moves to the foreground, in the preceding it is a crucial factor as well. A number of expressions, roughly synonymous or at least moving in more or less the same Wortfeld, must be considered; first, the word mabbûl:[20] .

6:17   (P)   YHWH is about to bring hammabbûl mayim on the earth --
             the first announcement, made in connection with the command
             to build the ark.

7:6   (P)   Noah was 600 years old w[e] hammabbûl hāyā mayim [c]al-hā'āreṣ.
             This statement is closely related to:

7:7   (J)   Noah and his family entered the ark mipp[e]nê mê hammabbûl.
             In the context of the first account of the execution, these
             two clauses sketch the background of the actions.

----

19. In contrast to e.g. the Ugaritic literature.

20. Originally, this seems to have been a terminus technicus signifying the heavenly ocean or cosmic waters. Taken with 7:11 one is tempted to conclude that the "flood" is understood as a cosmic catastrophe. On the other hand, the terms MṬR (hiphil, 7:14, J) and gešem (7:12, J) seem to suggest a localized referent. See J. Begrich, "Mabbul, eine exegetisch-lexekalische Studie," Zeitschrift für Semitistik 6 (1928) 135-153.

7:10 (J) After the announced seven days (4,J), ûmê hammabbûl hāyû
ᶜal-hā'āreṣ. 7:10-12 are sandwiched between the two execution
accounts to emphasize the background, viz. the flood. Noah's
execution of the divine command and the coming of the mabbûl
are portrayed as taking place simultaneously.

7:17 (J) wayᵉhî hammabbûl 'arbaᶜîm yôm ᶜal-hā'āreṣ: This is an opening
statement of part two which deals with the flood in detail.

Though the use of the word mabbûl is virtually limited to the flood
story (it also occurs in Ps 29:10), its exact meaning must be derived
from the context: in apposition with mayim[21] (except in 7:17a, but from
17b to 24 the word mayim occurs six times). The fact that it is mentioned
five times in the narrative, at significant collocations, demonstrates
intended emphasis.

In addition to mabbûl there are other expressions for and statements
about the flood:

7:4 (J) YHWH says: 'ānōkî mamṭîr ᶜal-hā'āreṣ - in seven days, for a
period of forty days, to destroy all life.

7:11 (P) After a noun clause giving Noah's precise age, a closer
description of the flood is given: "All the foundations of the
great deep burst forth and the sluices in the sky broke open."
(Speiser, Genesis 48).

7:12 (J) Though the word mabbûl, associated with mayim, has been generally
used heretofore, presently another word is introduced: wayᵉhî
haggešem ᶜal-hā'āreṣ, forty days and forty nights. Speiser (48)
and NAB render: "heavy rain."

Source criticism has assigned the references to a forty-day "rain"
to J: hiphil of MTR (7:4), haggešem (7:12) and somewhat surprisingly the
"fountains and sluices" reference to P (11b). That leaves three
occurrences of mabbûl to J and two to P in the section 6:17 - 7:24.

Actually, MTR (hiphil), haggešem and hammabbûl are all used interchangeably in connection with the 40-day flood:

7:4 'ānōkî mamṭîr ᶜal-hā'āreṣ - forty days and forty nights

7:12 wayᵉhî haggešem ᶜal-hā'āreṣ - forty days and forty nights

7:17 wayᵉhî hammabbûl ᶜal-hā'āreṣ - forty days

---

21. See R.J. Williams, Hebrew Syntax, par 68: apposition of material
and P.P. Joüon, Grammaire, 131d. McEvenue translates 6:17 "the Mabbul
as water upon the earth." (Narrative Style, 45).

Commentators have pointed out that the "fountains and sluices" passage suggests the reversal of God's original creative activity;[22] after this, haggešem may seem rather pallid. The consideration that gešem is at least a heavy rain, "a downpour", sometimes with destructive effect, may be helpful; thus, in Ezek 13:11, 13, a gešem šōṭēp (overflowing rain?) parallels "great hailstones" and a "stormy wind" as YHWH's agents of destruction. The solution may lie in the proposal that the term mabbûl, though originally a terminus technicus for cosmic flood, has been used with sufficient flexibility to include the entire semantic range between "heavy rain" and "cosmic flood." The narrative's slow motion and love of synonyms and repetition may warrant this conclusion.

Part Two (7:17-24), detailing the ascendancy of the flood on the earth, is dominated by the motifs of the water (mayim) prevailing, or being strong[23] (GBR, 18,19,20,24) and increasing (RBH, 17,18), causing progressively:

1. the ark to be lifted (NŚH, 17), rising above the land (RWM, 17), and floating (HLK, 18)

2. the highest mountains to be covered (KSH, 19,20)

3. all living creatures to die (MWT, 22), expire (GWH, 21), to be blotted out (MḤH, 23bis: the implied subject is God) -- only Noah and those with him in the ark to remain alive (Š'R, 23).

The divergent fate of the inhabitants of the ark and those remaining outside is contrasted in 17, 18:

EARTH (Doomed)		ARK (Saved)	
mabbûl ʿal-hā'āreṣ	(17a)	mayim raise ark mēʿal-hā'āreṣ	(17b)
mayim prevail and increase ʿal-hā'āreṣ	(18a)[24]	tēbā floats ʿal-peʿnê hammayim	(18b)

22. Cf. G. von Rad, Genesis (Philadelphia: Westminster, 1961) 124; N.M. Sarna, Understanding Genesis (New York: Schocken, 1970) 55.

23. Skinner felicitously refers to a "contest between the water and the dry land" (Genesis, 165). The repeated use of the roots GBR suggest the image of a hostile, irresistable force embattled against God's created order.

24. Note that the expression hammabbûl mayim or mê hammabbûl is here broken up. See E.Z. Melamed, "Break-up of stereotype phrases as an artistc device in biblical poetry," Scripta Hierosolymitana 8 (1961) 115-153, S. Talmon, "Synonymous Readings in the Textual Traditions of the Old Testament," Scripta Hierosolymitana 8 (1961) 335-383, and G. Braulik, "Aufbrechen von geprägten Wortverbindungen und Zusammenfassen von stereotypen Ausdrücken in der alttestamentlichen Kunstprosa," Semitics 1 (1970) 7-11.

17a and 18a describe the earth as dominated by the mabbul / mayim, while 17b and 18b relate the fate of the ark -- for the time being associated with the waters:

$$\text{me}^{\text{c}}\text{al hā'āreṣ...}^{\text{c}}\text{al-p}^{\text{e}}\text{nê hammayim.}$$

This may be schematized as follows:

17 hammabbûl...hā'āreṣ / hammayim...hattēbā (a b/a'c)

18 hammayim...hā'āreṣ / hattēbā...hammayim (a b/c a).

The fate of all mankind impinges on the dominance of water (expressed emphatically by the recurrent roots GBR and RBH) but that is where the similarity of fates ends; the same (divinely ordained) waters not only engulf the doomed remaining on earth but also buoy up the ark; in other words, the water (mabbûl / mayim) serves at once as instrument of destruction and of salvation. Thus, a kind of three-storied world emerges:

> tēbā (afloat, preserving, alive)
>
> mayim / hammabbûl
>
> 'ereṣ (life destroyed).

With 19, the ark is temporarily left out of sight; the change of syntax (x-qatal form), signals a focus on the effects of the flood on earth;[25] 19a virtually copies 18a:

18a wayyigb^{e}rû hammayim wayyirbû m^{e}'ōd ^{c}al-hā'āreṣ

19a w^{e}hammayim gāb^{e}rû m^{e}'ōd m^{e}'ōd ^{c}al-hā'āreṣ.

On the other hand, 19 and 20 are linked by the repeated verbs GBR and KSH (object: the mountains); together they form the background of 21f. The narration technique of interweaving finds an excellent example in 18-20, where 20:

1) summarizes 19 (20a / 19a, and 20b / 19b) and

2) adds a clause concerning the crest of the waters.

Once more, this time in sweeping summary form, a listing of animals appears; placed between two "inclusion" formulas "kol-bāśār hārōmēś ^{c}al-hā'āreṣ" and "ûb^{e}kol-haśśereṣ haśśōrēṣ ^{c}al-hā'āreṣ", the listing used in 14 recurs: ^{c}ôp, b^{e}hēmā, ḥayyā, as in 14. The listing is climaxed by the brief but painful: w^{e}kol hā'ādam. A restatement

---

25. McEvenue writes: "Certainly the inversion 7, 19a... (does) not make climaxes." (Narrative Style, 35). This may be true; here it suggests a change of focus, which is certainly a story-teller's technique.

follows in 22 ending with the word mētû, an obvious parallel to the first word of 21: wayyiqwa^c. The same theme is stated for the third time in 23, using the verb MḤH (an "echo" form 7:4 and 6:7). For the last time, the earth's destroyed creatures are mentioned in summarizing fashion, by means of an expression reminiscent of merismus:

mē'ādām ^{c}ad-b^{e}hēmā ^{c}ad-remeś w^{ec}ad-^{c}ôp haśśāmayim.

The exception to this picture of universal destruction is Noah and the other inhabitants of the ark; significantly, the root Š'R appears; in the familiar form š^e'ērît it occurs in the prophetic literature.

7:21-23 may be diagrammed as follows:

ALL LIVING CREATURES ON EARTH			NOAH AND HIS ARK
21	(P)	GWH	
22	(J)	MWT	
23	(J)	MḤH$^{(bis)}$	Š'R.

Thus, in 23 the fate of the two categories of creatures is once more juxtaposed; wayyimmāḥû...wayyiśśā'ēr. In both cases, man is passive, God being the actor.

The final verse of ch. 7 functions as a kind of ironic "tranquil conclusion." Obviously it clamors for a sequel and is therefore not a genuine conclusion but only a convenient temporary halt in the narration which is resumed in 8:1 where attention is once more directed to the fate of the ark with its inhabitants.

IV

The narrative quality of this literature is paradoxical. On the one hand its style is annalistic, chronological, enumerative, as well as repetitive;[26] the story often moves slowly and its pace (as may be gauged by the frequency of yiqtol-x forms) seems sluggish. On the other hand, having recognized that this is not poetry with its particular demands for a certain quality of artistry, but theological narrative,[27] one has to conclude that this pericope displays considerable

---

26. Cf. Gunkel, Genesis, 138.

27. The great majority of biblical narrative is of course theologically oriented. In the flood story, Noah hardly comes alive as a flesh and blood person (like Jacob, David or Jeremiah), so that Gunkel's comment is justified: "Der Noah des P ist keine lebendige Gestalt, sondern nur noch der blasse Typus des Frommen." (Genesis, 138).

artistic sophistication in which every single detail seems not only
to serve its purpose formally and materially, but also to express
the concerns of the narrative.

The various narrative techniques employed by the writer, far from
being futile artistry, are actually studied means to specific ends.
Notable in this pericope are the means by which emphasis is achieved:

1. Repetition of certain roots, particularly in part two where the
   narrative picks up speed. Further, several key phrases occur at
   significant collocations (e.g. 'el-hattēbā). The repetition of
   certain features within enumerations is noteworthy: min...ûmin...
   (in 8) and lᵉmînāh etc. (14). In 14 and 15 kol bāśār serves as
   a summarizing phrase.

2. From the standpoint of the history of biblical criticism, material
   duplication is even more significant; source critics have often
   utilized this feature for their distinction between J and P; they
   have not done so consistently, however; as argued above, though
   mabbûl, mayim, and gešem are more or less synonymous, they are
   distributed between the two sources. More significantly, though
   this pericope is indisputably prose, formulaic word pairs, often
   disregarding sources, are in evidence throughout:[28]

   > yôm / layᵉlā   (Gen 1:5)
   >
   > 'ereṣ / mayim   (Exod 20:5)
   >
   > zākār / nᵉqēbā   (Deut 4:16)
   >
   > maᶜyᵉnōt / 'ᵃrubbōt   (Gen 8:2)
   >
   > ṣippôr / kānāp   (Ezek 17:23)
   >
   > bᵉhēmā / ᶜôp / ḥayyā   (Lev 11:46)
   >
   > RMŚ / ŠRṢ   (Lev 11:46)
   >
   > RWM / NŚ'   (Isa 33:10)
   >
   > GWᶜ / MWT   (Gen 25:8)
   >
   > MṬR / gešem   (Ezek 38:22).[29]

Such usage is undoubtedly related to the repetitive nature of the
narrative as a whole, which is not so much telling a story as
intoning a sermon. On the other hand, the occurrence of word pairs

---

28. A rapidly increasing bibliography is emerging on this subject.
For a recent provocative treatment see P.B. Yoder "A-B pairs and oral
composition in Hebrew poetry," VT 21 (1971) 470-489.

29. Surprisingly tᵉhôrā is not balanced by ṭumᵉ'ā; the writer seems
to have wanted to avoid the negative connotation of that word.

should not surprise us, as much of what is called "prose" in the Hebrew Bible is actually some intermediate form between prose and poetry; in such literature formulaic word pairs may be expected.[30]

3. Viewing the framing technique superficially, a reader might conclude that the narrator is guilty now and again of mindless repetition.[31] However, beyond simply repeating e.g. the execution account, they have been so placed as to provide a kind of frame for the brief description of the flood (10:12) as if to say: provisions are being made to except some from the imminent catastrophe. On the other hand, the notice of the flood lends color and urgency to the execution accounts. The simultaneity of the beginning of the flood and the entry into the ark by Noah and his company is expressed by the resumptive clause b^{e}c$e\underline{s}$em hayyôm hazze, 13, as well as by the two time-clauses about Noah's age in vss. 6 and 11.

4. Another technique which the author has used to stress the divine gracious purpose as executed by Noah the ṣaddîq is the close correspondence between the command and the remainder of the chapter. "Enter (the ark)!" sounds the imperative: the keynote of part one.[32] The chart below shows where this and additional elements in the command are taken up in the remainder of the chapter. It illustrates eloquently the coherence of the narrative as a whole.

Command	Execution #1	Flood Notice	Execution #2	Part Two
Enter ! (1)	7, 9		12, 15, 16	
You and your house (1)	7		13	
Into the ark! (1)	7, 9		13, 15	
Choose animals (2,3)	8, 9		14-16	
Rain in 7 days (4)		10		
Rain for 40 days (4)		12		
MḤH (4)				23 bis

---

30. The comments in this paragraph have been inspired by Prof. Shemaryahu Talmon, in a course on Hebrew Narrative at Brandeis University.

31. "There is such a care to repeat and balance materials in interlocking symmetries that the effect is closer to a minuet than to a free run." (McEvenue, Narrative Style, 28). Cf. J. Muilenburg, "Hebrew Rhetoric: Repetition and Style," Congress Volume Copenhagen 1953 (SVT 1; Leiden: E.J. Brill, 1953) 97-11, which deals with the repetition of single words and brief phrases in poetic literature. His comments on the "iterative propensity" of Israelite literature (100) and on "repetition as a creative literary device" (103) may be extended to prose narrative.

32. When this has been executed, YHWH himself closes the ark; this notice signals the end of part one.

5. Inversion (from yiqtol-x to x-qatal in the case of verbal clauses) is another means by which attention is called to what follows. An effective example is 19 which is preceded by a series of seven yiqtol-x forms in 17 and 18; by breaking this sequence the reader's attention is directed to the subject: <u>hammayim</u>. Other examples are 9a, 16a$^{\alpha}$, 22.

V

Bypassing the usual source division, this study has taken the literature as it appears in the MT and subjected it to rhetorical criticism. The rationale for such a procedure should not be difficult to find; in spite of voluminous studies on Genesis and the flood story, biblical criticism has been virtually dominated by source criticism, presently linked to the more recent methods of form criticism and traditio-historical criticism.

Rhetorical criticism is of course only one exegetical method among many. Both methodological and material limitation of this paper preclude any sort of sweeping generalizations. Nevertheless, a few comments may be offered here.

1. The criteria whereby sources are isolated are at least problematic in Gen 7. As to the criterion of the divine names, YHWH occurs thrice and Elohim[33] twice. In 7:1 YHWH issues the command, 5 has the obedience formula with YHWH, but both execution accounts use Elohim (9,16); finally, in 16 YHWH closes the ark. It is difficult to see how this could possibly tie in with the criterion of duplication as e.g. in the two execution accounts.

Likewise, repetition is not simply due to the literary conservatism of R, or the result of some kind of mindless heaping up of literary baggage, but a deliberate device to emphasize certain features of the story. Thus, the same God who decreed the universally destructive flood also issued the orders leading to deliverance of a chosen remnant: he is at once savior and destroyer. The double execution account stresses that the world was to have a future thanks to the divine gracious purpose which made use of the obedience of Noah, the ṣaddîq.

Much has been made in source criticism of what Gunkel terms "Widersprüche und Unebenheiten." If they are relevant in Gen 7 at all they seem to disappear when a deliberate attempt is made to fathom the narrative technique. That unevenness is widely attested

---

33. One might perhaps expect that one account would have YHWH and the other Elohim.

in biblical literature is of course indisputable, but not in Gen 7.
There are no "seams" in Gen 7; the garment is of one piece and if
materials should be of different provenance, their joining has been
executed with such artistry that they have been dissolved in the
whole. This is not to deny the validity or the necessity of genetic
or historical criticism, but rather to point out that the Graf-Well-
hausen model fails to do justice to the quality of the literature,
which it has vastly underrated. Genetic criticism will have to find
other ways and design different criteria from those set forth in the
19th century by the creators of the documentary hypothesis.

2. There is a pressing need to develop and refine rhetorical methods
of literary criticism along the lines of modern language criticism.
Biblical scholars are beginning to pursue such promising lines of
inquiry as motif analysis,[34] archetypal criticism,[35] in addition to
rhetorical criticism which has already scored some notable results.
Developments in contiguous disciplines, above all modern literary
criticism should be taken seriously. Surely, our Wissenschaft can
stand on its own feet, it is claimed; has it not taken tremendous
strides in the last two decades? This does not excuse us, however,
from the perpetual task of challenging all sorts of long-standing
assumptions. Because they support the entire building, the foundations stand in constant need of re-examination.[36]

------

34. For a fine example of this see S Talmon, "The 'Desert Motif'
in the Bible and in Qumran Literature," Biblical Motifs A. Altmann,
ed. (Studies and Texts, III; Cambridge: Harvard University, 1966)
31-63. See E. Frenzel, Stoff-, Motiv- und Symbolforschung (3. Auflage; Stuttgart: J.B. Metzler, 1970).

35. Particularly Northrop Frye. See his Anatomy of Criticism
(Princeton: Princeton University, 1957).

36. Cf. F.V. Winnett, "Re-examining the foundations," JBL 84 (1965)
1-19.

THE SHAPE OF GENESIS 11:1-9*

Isaac M. Kikawada

University of California

Berkeley, California

This paper is gratefully dedicated to my beloved teacher, Professor James Muilenburg, through whose teaching I gained a methodology for Old Testament study.

The purpose of this paper is to recover the underlying schemes or any unifying principles of organization that have fashioned the story of "The Generation of Division" or "The Tower of Babel" into a particular shape; in order to do this, we must observe certain rhetorical features and structural devices. The paper also examines the ways in which these schemes influence our understanding and appreciation of the story.

In order to facilitate our description of various levels and subunits of the story we have employed the following terms hierarchically:[1]

Story: unit designating the whole of Gen 11:1-9

Episode (Ep): composed of one or more paragraphs

Paragraph (A, B, C...): composed of one or more verses

Verse (v): equivalent to the traditional verse

Line (ln): refers to line presented in illustrations in this paper

The full text and a literal translation of the story is presented on the following page to show the positional relationship of the rhetorical features and of the hierarchical building blocks:

---

* This study is based on the paper, "An Hourglass Shaped Story: Genesis 11:1-9," presented at the 1968 SBL meeting in Berkeley, California. My hearty thanks are due to the Rev. Dr. Ivan J. Ball and Prof. Bruce W. Jones for their kind advice and assistance.

1. I am indebted to Prof. Francis I. Andersen for his suggestions on the organization of descriptive terminology.

	1 Once upon a time, the whole earth,	ויהי כל הארץ	1
	The language was one,	שפה אחת	
	The vocabulary was one.	ודברים אחדים	
A			
	2 At that time in their march from the East,	ויהי בנסעם מקדם	2
	They found a plain in the land of Shinar,	וימצאו בקעה בארץ שנער	
	And they were living there.	וישבו שם	
Ep 1	3 And they said, each to his friend:	ויאמרו איש אל רעהו	3
	"Habah, let us brick bricks,	הבה נלבנה לבנים	
	Let us burn them burningly."	ונשרפה לשרפה	
	So they had brick for stone,	ותהי להם הלבנה לאבן	
	Bitumen had they for mortar.	והחמר היה להם לחמר	
B			
	4 And they said:	ויאמרו	4
	"Habah, let us build us a city and tower,	הבה נבנה לנו עיר ומגדל	
	Whose top is in the sky,	וראשו בשמים	
	Let us make us a name,	ונעשה לנו שם	
	Lest we be scattered	פן נפוץ על פני כל הארץ	
	Upon the face of the whole earth."		
	5 Then YHWH came down to see	וירד יהוה לראת	5
Ep 2 = C	The city and the tower,	את העיר ואת המגדל	
	That the children of man were building.	אשר בנו בני האדם	
	6 And YHWH said:	ויאמר יהוה	6
	"Behold, the people is one,	הן עם אחד	
	The language is one for all.	ושפה אחת לכלם	
	This is the beginning of their doing;	וזה החלם לעשות	
	Now, it will not be withheld from them,	ועתה לא יבצר מהם	
	All that they scheme of doing.	כל אשר יזמו לעשות	
B'			
	7 "Habah, let us go down,	הבה נרדה	7
	Let us confuse their language there,	ונבלה שם שפתם	
	So that they will not hear,	אשר לא ישמעו	
	Each his friend's language."	איש שפת רעהו	
Ep 3			
	8 And YHWH scattered them from there	ויפץ יהוה אתם משם	8
	Upon the face of the whole earth.	על פני כל הארץ	
	And they stopped building the city.	ויחדלו לבנת העיר	
A'			
	9 Because of this, one calls its name Babel,	על כן קרא שמה בבל	9
	For there YHWH confused	כי שם בלל יהוה	
	The language of the whole earth.	שפת כל הארץ	
	And from there YHWH scattered them	ומשם הפיצם יהוה	
	Upon the face of the whole earth.	על פני כל הארץ	

The following sections under the headings I through VII contain descriptions of the principles of organization that we wish to advance here.

I Quantitative Balance

The story is composed of three episodes (Ep 1, Ep 2, and Ep 3). The first and the last episodes are made up of two paragraphs each (A B and B' A'), and each of the four paragraphs includes two verses of various numbers of lines. But Ep 2 consists of only one paragraph which is only one verse in length. This means that v 5 functions not only as a paragraph but also as an episode, giving an overall symmetry, articulated as:

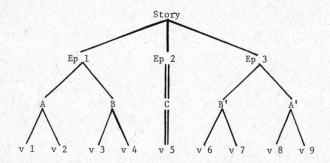

Furthermore, if we note such grammatical categories as indirect and direct discourse, we discover an identical distribution of quantitative balance with respect to narrative character. The indirect discourse of vss 1-2 corresponds to that of vss 8-9; thus, A corresponds to A', the former an introductory and the latter a concluding paragraph. B and B', on the other hand, are predominantly direct discourse, and are separated by the narrator's indirect discourse, C, which in turn marks the midpoint of the story. Thus, the overall narrative pattern emerges as A B C B' A'.

Similarly, quantitative balance is observed on smaller scales when we note the rhythmical or "poetic" quality of the narrative. A consists of two verses which are very much like two sets of tricola. Exactly the same word opens both lines 1 and 4, both of which lines introduce the two lines that follow, both exhibiting parallelism. The first is the well-formed bicolon describing the oneness of the language and the second is the double-line expression of specific locality.

In B one also encounters unmistakable parallels and doublets. Exactly as in A, each of vss 3 and 4 begins with the same expression

introducing the first person direct discourse. The initial word
of the men's speech is הבה in each case.[2] The first הבה (v 3)
is follwed by a set of four lines composed of two synonymous
bicola. In the former bicolon each line consists of a verb in the
cohortative with its cognate object. In the latter the first two
elements of the first line are in reverse order in the parallel
line forming a pattern a b c // b' a' c', as follows:

<pre>
        c   b   a
   נתהי להם הלבנה לאבן

   והחמר היה להם לחמר
     c'   a'   b'
</pre>

The second הבה also begins a set of four lines:

הבה נבנה לנו עיר ומגדל

וראשו בשמים

ונעשה לנו שם

פן נפוץ על פני כל הארץ

In this case, however, the cohortatives are in the first and
third lines. The alternate lines, 2 and 4, complete the thought
of the foregoing. Quantitatively, lines 1 and 4 balance each other,
likewise lines 2 and 3 which also rhyme. These four lines of v 4
quantitatively balance those of v 3.

B' presents many features that are found in B; as in B, both
sets of direct discourse begin with interjectory words, "Behold"
in v 6, and another repetition of "Habah" in v 7. Each of these
introduces a well-formed bicolon. The remainder of each contains
explanatory material of 3 and 2 lines respectively.

The two verses of A' are not as well balanced quantitatively
as in A, since v 9 is composed of almost twice as many words as
v 8. All eight lines of A', however, should be taken together as
a unit. Lines 1 and 2 are repeated in lines 7 and 8 with the two

---

2. Outside of Gen 11:1-9, הבה immediately preceding a cohortative
   appears only once in Exod 1:10, and it is an interjection in this
   configuration. We did not translate it in order to preserve
   the euphonic expression.

elements in ln 1 being reversed in ln 7, thus forming an inclusio
for this paragraph:

b   a

וי<u>פץ יהוה אתם משם</u>

<u>על פני כל הארץ</u>

c

a'   b

<u>ומשם הפיצם יהוה</u>

<u>על פני כל הארץ</u>

c

All eight lines are bound together by an interlocking pattern
of threefold repetitions of words and phrases.

2   1

וי<u>פץ יהוה אתם משם</u>

4   3

<u>על פני כל הארץ</u>

ויחדלו לבנת העיר

3

<u>על</u> כן קרא שמה בבל

1   2

כי <u>שם</u> בלל <u>יהוה</u>

4

שפת <u>כל הארץ</u>

1   2

<u>ומשם הפיצם יהוה</u>

4   3

<u>על פני כל הארץ</u>

Four words (1, 2, 3, 4) are repeated three times each; in each case
a word appears twice in identical phrases and once with a slight
variation.

Word 1. The Divine Name occurs three times; twice following
the root פוץ (lines 1 and 7) and once more following a different verb
(ln 5).

Word 2. שֵׁם occurs twice in the phrase מִשָּׁם (lines 1 and 7)
plus one more time without the preposition (ln 5). We may note both
of the above examples are found only in odd numbered lines; the
unique form in each case happens to be in ln 5.

Word 3. The preposition על appears twice in the phrase על פני (lines 2 and 8) and once in the phrase על כן (ln 4).

Words 4. The expression כל הארץ occurs twice in the phrase פני כל הארץ (lines 2 and 8), and one more time in construct with the word שפה (ln 6). Note, too, that the above two examples are found in even numbered lines.

In this regard ln 3 is unique since it does not contain any repeated expression.

II Chiasmus and Introversion

Perhaps the term chiasmus should be reserved for the particular relationship of four elements in A B B A arrangement, whereas such relationship of five or more elements in A B C B A or A B C C B A would properly be called "introversion."[3] Therefore, the reversal of the elements which we have seen in the latter part of v 3 and in the inclusio of A', vss 8-9, is a chiasmus.

It is an introversion of paragraphs, A B C B' A', that solidifies the overall structure of the story as indicated in the previous section.[4] What has not yet been discussed, however, is the structure and the function of the central v 5 that acts as paragraph C as well as Ep 2.

We have construed this verse in three lines of nearly equal size. The first line includes a unique word in the story, לראת, and introduces the new subject YHWH. The second line consists of the familiar pair of direct objects which may in this position be seen as quasi-double-duty[5] objects, while the third line is a dependent clause that modifies the second. The third line also includes a unique word, האדם, which is placed in a position that creates a sharp contrast with the key word of the first line, YHWH.

On the episode level, C is, we would suggest, the crossover point, as its structure demonstrates very well:

Ep 1 - Human deeds

וירד יהוה לראת

את העיר ואת המגדל

אשר בנו בני האדם

Divine deeds - Ep 3

---

3. I am grateful to Prof. F. I. Andersen for making this suggestion.

4. Cf. Y. Raddai, בית מקרא 20-21 (1964), 48-72, esp. 68. I thank Mr. Ziony Zevit for this reference.

5. Cf. Mitchell Dahood, *CBQ* 29 (1967), 574-79

The first line points down to Ep 3; the verb וירד terminates
in v 7, הבה נרדה, the sensory verb לראת finds its destination
in another sensory verb ישמעו, and the Divine Name YHWH
initiated here and repeated four times becomes the decisive subject
throughout Ep 3. The latter two lines point back to Ep 1 as can
be seen by the configuration of the three key terms, עיר , בנה
and מגדל which are also found in v 4 above. The unique האדם
reflects the significance of the human actors in Ep 1. For these
reasons we call C the interlocking crossover point of this introversion.

Another example of the same phenomenon is found in Gen 2:8.
The initial word of the verse points down to the following verse,
especially to the first word, while the last word points back to the
preceding verse, especially to the first word.[6]

III Inclusio

The very beginning and the very end of the story are clearly
marked by the repetition of the phrase כל הארץ . The key word
שפה is also found in both vss 1 and 9. It is noteworthy in this
regard that the geographic designation שנער of v 3 is resolved in
בבל of v 9 as well.

כל הארץ also delimits the extent of the first episode,
as the last line of B concludes with פן נפוץ על פני כל הארץ
constituting another inclusio with the beginning of the story.
Likewise, the first line of B and the last line of B', both of
which include the words איש and רעהו, constitute still another
inclusio. This inclusio sets off the beginning and the end of
the direct speech portions.

On the paragraph level we have already noted the inclusio in A'.

---

6. Detailed discussion including the treatment of it in a larger
   context will be published elsewhere.

IV Linear Progression

There are two types of linear progression. One is a phenomenon similar to that of *Leitmotif* in music and drama, which provides a continuing thread to integrate a work. Such terms as ארץ and שָׁם, that are connected with land, and such as בנה and לבן, that have to do with building, are repeated strategically all through the story, intertwined with other similar sounding words and expressions to create puns along the way.[7]

The repetition of כל הארץ resulting in a double inclusio has already been noted above. Alongside this there is a wordplay between שָׁם and שֵׁם. It begins faintly in vss 2 and 4, as the people find a place to live and settle "there," שָׁם, and Babel is their city "name," שֵׁם, because YHWH confused their language "there," שָׁם. In the same manner, note also the paronomasia of שֵׁם and שמים bringing the third and the fourth lines of v 4 into association.

Similarly, many words, that include ב, נ and/or ל carry the story phonetically. These words play important roles in v 3, a goldmine of sonority. הבה נלבנה לבנים[8] (ln 2) has its companion in הלבנה לאבן (ln 3). In v 4 it is also subtly reiterated as הבה נבנה לנו. At the midpoint of the story YHWH comes down to see the city and the tower אשר בנו בני האדם. As a result, הבה נרדה ונבלה (v 7), transforming נלבנה of v 3 into נבלה here! These sounds recur in לבנת in v 8 and terminate in the climactic בלל-בבל pun of v 9.

Another type of linear progression is synthetic,[9] i.e., the key words, which are used separately at various points in the story, are collected together at one point, often giving rise to a new significance. The concluding paragraph, A', is largely composed of words that have already functioned significantly in the earlier part of the story. In other words, A' is the destination for the linear progression of many of the key terms.

In v 8 all except אתם and ויחדלו have been used previously. ויפץ and על פני כל הארץ refer back to the premonition expressed in v 4, "Lest we be *scattered upon the face of the whole earth*." YHWH is the key personality introduced in v 5. As discussed earlier, שֵׁם is a key word used in v 2 and elsewhere which now underlines the heightened theme of the land. לבנת העיר refers to the activity in B, which is here overturned and put to an end, ויחדלו.

---

7. For detailed treatment, cf. U. Cassuto, *Genesis II* (1964), 232-34.

8. E. A. Speiser, *Orientalia* 25 (1956), 317-23.

9. Cf. Cassuto, *Genesis I* (1961), 70.

Likewise in v 9, כי, קרא, על כן and בבל are the only
words which have not been used previously; but, as already seen,
Babel is synonymous with Shinar in this story.

Both types of linear progression climactically point to A'.

V Sequential Repetition

Sequential Repetition is a construction in which the same
order of elements is repeated in two or more subunits of a piece.
This is best illustrated in the following:

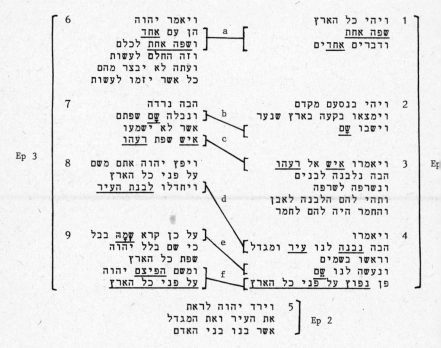

Ep 1 (vss 1-4) is reproduced side by side with Ep 3 (vss 6-9),
while Ep 2 is set apart at the bottom. There is remarkable verbal
correspondence between these two columns of material; not only are
certain key terms and the formulaic combination of words repeated
in both, but also they occur in the same sequence. To be sure, they
are not always exact repetitions but are echoes by which particular
themes of the earlier part of the narrative are replayed in the
latter part with varying intensity and transformed import.

The words depicting the oneness of the language are placed at
the beginning of Episodes 1 and 3, as designated by a. In the
latter case the significance of the oneness is transferred from
that of the language to that of the people, although the same
three key terms are maintained.

Though שָׁם of b may be just an euphonic repetition, the curious
fact remains that the word is repeated at the same relative position.

אִישׁ and רֵעֵהוּ, which have been seen to form an inclusio as
pointed out above, are set in parallel collocation here. During
the interval between the repetition, the story has developed so as
to give an opposite meaning to the same expression when it appears
for the second time. Earlier it depicted those who could communicate
with one another but who now are no longer able to do so. Rather,
the people of YHWH, who do not understand the Babylonian language,
are also included. Every hearer, every reader of the story now
becomes ironically involved in it.

The repetitions of d and e deal with the pride of the Babylonians,
which twice meets an ironic reversal of fortune; first, the proud
"city building" is stopped, and second, their "name" becomes a joke.

In all of the above repetitions, the second occurrence takes on
a transformed meaning which is often the reverse of the original
(cf. b, c, d, e). Ironically, only the dreaded premonition, f, of
v 4 is realized in Ep 3!

We may further note that the chiasms observed in v 3 and in vss 8-9
happen to be in the lower parts of the two episodes.

VI   Broken Symmetry

The basic shape of this story is that of an hourglass.[10] Episodes 1
and 3 form the two glass bulbs which are connected by the narrow passage,
Ep 2. However, this basic symmetry is not perfect on several counts.
First, Ep 3 is longer than Ep 1, although B is longer than B', the reason
being that A' is much wordier than A. The special weight given to A'
was also seen in the discussion on linear progression.

The symmetry of B and B' is broken in that the *formula citandi*
appears at vss 3, 4 and 6. If the material were strictly symmetrical,
we would expect another in v 7, even though that verse grammatically
does not require one since it is the continuation of YHWH's speech.
V 4, on the other hand, needs one, since, strictly speaking, the last
two lines of v 3 are "editorial remarks" though structurally they
are an integral part of the "speech."

---

10. Cf. footnote * at the beginning of this paper.

Note also the great variance in sizes of the formula. The
artistry of this narrative, however, places איש and רעהו in the
last line of the speech itself, v 7, echoing the first *formula citandi*
of v 3, the very beginning of the speech portion of the story
(cf. III Inclusio). This kind of balance cannot be attained by
mere symmetry, but it is only possible as the result of a masterful
composition such as we have in Gen 11:1-9.

The threefold repetition of the formula, הבה plus 2 cohortatives,
also appears asymmetrically in vss 3, 4 and 7, bypassing v 6. The
anticipated symmetry is broken in v 6; instead of הבה we find another
interjectory word הן, and instead of the pair of cohortatives we have
here a bicolon. This bicolon recalls the impressive beginning of A.

No sooner does v 6 break one pattern than it makes another; it
initiates the chain of sequential repetition. It cannot be emphasized
enough that we are confronted with the Hebrew literary genius more
often in the manner in which he breaks the familiar patterns than in
the way in which he follows them.

Moreover, broken symmetry can be seen in the smaller units as
well as in the overall structure. For example, as we have seen in
regard to the quantitative balance of A', only ln 3 does not contain
any of the threefold repetitions. This is the only line which does
not conform to the overriding pattern of A', causing this line to stand
out for extraordinary emphasis. Thus, the pro-"nomadic,"[11] anti-urban
bias of the narrator is given great prominence.

VII Irony System

Irony is also an organizing principle for this story, for it too
brings various elements together into a unified whole. It does still
more than that, because irony not only integrates the story into its
immediate context, namely, the primaeval history, but also into the
whole book of Genesis, or even into a broader context.

Edwin M. Good offers three fluid categories of irony in
narrative:[12]

> It may be a *punctual* irony, the use of words and
> expressions of ironic intention at particular,
> more or less isolated, "points." It may be *episodic*

---

11. The term nomadic is used here in a nontechnical sense; it refers to
    a kind of life style H. Gunkel (*Genesis* [1901]) imagined as the
    background for certain stories of the book of Genesis.

12. *Irony in the Old Testament* (1965), 81f. The writer has also,
    parenthetically, written on the subject of "Irony and Amos"
    [unpublished, May 1964, Kenyon College]; in that paper, the
    three similar categories were described as Aristotelian,
    Sophoclean and Socratic.

irony, the perception of an entire episode with an
ironic aim or content. It may be *thematic* irony,
the conjunction of a number of episodes all of which
point to an ironic theme or motif. These three types
of narrative irony may be interrelated. An episode
may, for example, take its ironic flavor from a
number of ironic expressions and words in it, and
punctual irony may therefore establish episodic
irony...

Punctual irony of a humorous nature at v 5 is reported by
Cassuto, [13] who sees irony in that YHWH *has to come down* to look at
the tower since it is not high enough to be noticed. To this we
may add the ironic reversal of fortune in the city building and
name making of the Babylonians (cf. d and e of sequential repetition).
The ironic inclusiveness brought about by איש and רעהו
discussed in Section V with respect to the c of sequential repetition
is similar to what Good calls episodic irony.

What this ironic inclusiveness brings into focus is the question
of the "original" audience. Most interpretations appear to assume
the audience to be the arrogant people in the story who are destined
to be dispersed. Thus, the major intent of the story has been
understood as that of punishment.[14] But we must remember that the
audience was composed of the Hebrews, and our interpretation must
be based on that fact.

The story begins on the universal note that the entire world
once spoke the same language; then, the scene is quickly localized
to the land of Shinar. The story implies that it is Babylonians who
speak hopefully to one another of their plans for building the towered
city and making a name for themselves. But this eagerness is soon
shaded with an uneasiness, for they may be scattered all over the
world. The last element of their speech, "lest we be scattered upon
the face of the whole earth," brings Ep 1 to a suspenseful close.

Ep 3 unfolds the episodic and tragic irony, in which the protagonists',
i.e. the Babylonians', wishes are entirely disappointed, and further
punishment is inflicted upon them. The story is not explicit as to
exactly why YHWH is displeased with the people, but perhaps one might
suggest hubris or growing power of the single nation as vss 4 and 7 may
indicate. In any case, the story relates that the ambitious urban
project of the Babylonians suddenly comes to a halt (v 8), and that
their fame is turned into a shame (v 9). In addition, there are two
other punishments; one is the confusion of the language[15] and the other
the dispersion. Both of them are disastrous, for the former eliminates
easy communication while the latter disperses a formerly urban people,
perhaps forcing them into a nomadic life, one to which the Hebrew audience
is accustomed.

---

13. *Genesis II*, 224.

14. Typically, G.von Rad, *Genesis* (1961) 23.

15. For Sumerian parallels to this motif, cf. S. N. Kramer, *JAOS* 88 (1968),
    108-111; also, J. van Dijk, *Orientalia* 39 (1970) 302-310.

Secondly, this irony takes on the characteristics of larger or thematic irony, if we take into account the reaction of the Hebrew audience. The disappointment for the Babylonians that is caused by YHWH, the God of the audience, adds much to the cynical joy and mocking humor in the story. What is punishment for the urban Babylonians (and the story is clearly anti-urban and anti-Babylonian) is salvation to the "nomadic" audience; the very scattering that is devastating for the Babylonians is a blessing for the "nomadic" or more properly semi-nomadic[16] Hebrews.

Thirdly, one may speculate that the confusion of tongues creates still a larger, double-edged irony that is addressed to the hearer, or the reader of the story. It first appears to be directed against the Babylonians, thus, for the audience it is salvation. But as the audience realizes that the communication breakdown is really between itself and the Babylonians in the "present" (cf. inclusiveness of v 7, discussed above), then the ironic reversal takes another turn, because the audience, too, must suffer YHWH's punishment for the foreigners. If this interpretation is correct, then we may see "Socratic" irony, didactic irony on the universal level, through which the story makes the theological point that all people are integrally related and YHWH is in control of all.

Concluding Remarks

It is difficult to evaluate how efficiently such an intricate and artistic structure can convey an equally complex message.[17] One of the chief reasons for this difficulty is that all the unifying principles examined above as well as those which this study has failed to note are operating simultaneously, each interacting with the other. We can give only a few examples in this brief study.

Great suspense is generated at the close of Ep 1 by the functioning of several principles. First, the clause, "lest we be scattered upon the face of the whole earth," introduces a curious notion of dispersion, but there is no indication as yet of how it might be accomplished. Second, the notion of scattering, נפוץ, is reinforced by the wordplay, the auditory recollection of its consonants in the phrase, פני כל הארץ further noting the fact that the whole clause is a sound-play of פ, נ and צ. Third, the suspense is brought about by the narrative's pace. Even though the problem of scattering is not resolved, Ep 1 is concluded with an echo[18] of the very beginning in an inclusio.

The unique fifth verse marks the crossover point of the narrative, summarizing what has gone before and forecasting what is yet to come. It is this verse that determines the basic hourglass shape of the story, because this is the dividing point of the sequential repetition and at the same time it is the pivot of the introversion and the decisive funnelling point in the linear progression. This is also the place

---

16. Cf. Norman K. Gottwald's contribution to this book.

17. Cf. Roman Jacobson, "On the Verbal Art of William Blake and Other Poet-Painters," *Linguistic Inquiry* I (1970), 3-23.

18. כל הארץ of v 1 is restated in פני כל הארץ of v 3.

where ironic reversal begins with the introduction of the new subject, YHWH.

Similar interaction of various organizing schemes could be detected and described at many different points in the story. The literary and artistic effect created in the mind of a given audience, however, is not merely the sum total of these schemes and principles but rather is a unified reality transcending the component parts.

Our understanding of the meaning of the story is supported further when we view it in its larger context. Within the primaeval history of Genesis 1-11, our story unit as described above may be argued to form the conclusion, constituting an inclusio with the beginning, Genesis 1. The thematic irony involving the land motif has been already pointed out by Good.[19] Furthermore, Ivan J. Ball has called attention to the significant verbal linear progression and inclusio established by the phrase על פני כל הארץ which is found in the following collocation interlocked with the parallel expression, פני האדמה:[20]

על פני כל הארץ	Gen 1:29	- P creation
כל פני האדמה	2:6	- J creation
מעל פני האדמה	4:14	- Cain
על פני האדמה	6:1	- Daughters of men
מעל פני האדמה	6:7	- Flood
על פני כל הארץ	7:3	- Flood
מעל פני האדמה	7:4	- Flood
על פני האדמה	7:23	- Flood
מעל פני האדמה	8:8	- Flood
על פני כל הארץ	8:9	- Flood
פני האדמה	8:13	- Flood
על פני כל הארץ	11:4	- Babel
על פני כל הארץ	11:8	- Babel
על פני כל הארץ	11:9	- Babel

Other elements of the verbal inclusio are the words, אדם (in the sense of "mankind" rather than the man Adam), and שמים, found both in Genesis 1 and 11:1-9. Besides, two peculiar rhetorical features concerning Divine speech are found in both; one is the Divine direct discourse, and the other is the plural verb form referring to the singular Divine subject, "let us make man..." in 1:26 and "Habah, let us go down, let us confuse..." in 11:6.[21]

---

19. *Op. cit.*, 82 and 84-90.

20. *A Rhetorical Study of Zephaniah*, Dissertation, The Graduate Theological Union, 1972, 46.

21. Other striking parallels will be dealt with elsewhere.

This motif of scattering in our story would then fulfil the blessing given in Genesis 1, since the third element of that blessing is, "Be fruitful and multiply and *fill the earth*," (1:28). Dispersion may be the means of accomplishing this blessing.[22] Moreover, it directly gives rise to the election of Abram. Therefore, this scattering, a gracious act of YHWH, makes a fitting transition between the primaeval history and the patriarchal history. In this sense it can also be seen as a crossover point or a funnel in a larger hourglass, the whole book of Genesis.[23]

---

22. This point can be more forcefully argued if we take into account the overall structural parallel between Genesis 1-11 and the Old Babylonian version of Atra-ḫasīs (Lambert-Millard, [1969]), especially in the light of Prof. Anne D. Kilmer's article, "The Mesopotamian Concept of Overpopulation and Its Solution as Reflected in the Mythology," *Orientalia* 41 (1972), 160-177. As I have indicated in *JBL* 91 (1972), p. 33, "Atra-ḫasīs and Genesis 1-11 are parallel in literary structure and in many motifs, and yet they express completely opposite views on the main ideological issues." In particular, the Hebraic view on "overpopulation" as a blessing is a complete contrast to that of Atra-ḫasīs. This point thus lends support to our interpretation of Genesis 11:1-9 as a blessing, and not a punishment. The writer is in the process of preparing a comprehensive study of biblical parallels with the Atra-ḫasīs Epic.

23. I thank Mrs. Karla S. Lapsley for typing the final copy of this manuscript.

THE LIBERATOR'S ORDEAL[1]

A Study of Exodus 4:1-9

E. John Hamlin

Thailand Theological Seminary

Moses' role as liberator, lawgiver, and leader of his people in the wilderness is well known. His confrontation with God on the mountain in which he is informed of his mission, and of the divine name have been extensively treated. One section, however, has not been given the place it deserves. This is the passage telling of the three signs by which Moses is to authenticate his commission from God. The similarity of the first (rod-turned-to-serpent) and the third (Nile-water-turned-to-blood) with events at Pharaoh's court (Exod 7:8-13, 14-24) have caused many commentators to look on these signs as mere previews of what is to follow, or misplaced elements of tradition, hence lacking any significance in themselves. The fact that they are apparently duplicated by the magicians of Egypt through their own magic arts seems to put Moses in a weak position, and to call into question the purpose of the signs which was to convince his people that the God of their fathers had really appeared to Moses (4:1, 5, 8, 9). It is reported in 4:31 that the people did believe when Aaron, (rather than Moses) "performed the signs." Yet according to 6:9 "The people did not listen to Moses because of their broken spirit and cruel bondage." The second sign (the leprous hand) has been passed over in silence since no clue is apparent in the rest of the Exodus narrative. Despite these confusions it must be assumed that this part of the narrative has intrinsic value of its own, rather than simply a derived or accidental meaning.

Tools for Interpretation

Three tools may be suggested as aids in uncovering the meaning of this passage. First, biblical research; second, comparative religion; and third, contemporary analysis of man and society.

From biblical research the information comes that this passage is part of the script for an annual dramatic recreation of the Exodus. The setting in a cultic drama brings the dimension of art into the focus of the interpreter.

----

[1] An earlier form of this paper appeared in The South East Asia Journal of Theology, 11 (1969) 64-71.

The text is thus not mere reporting, but the reliving of the history of the Great Act of Salvation. The question must then be asked as to the role of the passage in the dramatic setting. Furthermore, the interpreter must inquire into the meaning of the symbols employed in the narrative. A symbol, "addresses itself . . . to the entire human psyche . . . a miracle . . . is a sign-event in which a properly attuned religious consciousness can recognize, so to speak, the handwriting of God."[2]

Comparative religion as a tool of research helps the interpreter enrich his understanding from the universal context of human experience and thought. Symbols are drawn from the deep underground streams of the human psyche, which feeds all religions and cultures. Both analogy and contrast are afforded from this field of research. For example, an analogy to the particular incident before us is found in the initiatory rites of shamans, or of young men entering adult membership of the tribe, or of men entering secret societies. Such ordeals typically include the following:

1. a period of seclusion in the bush (symbol of the beyond) and a larval existence like that of the dead.
2. daubing the face and body with ashes or certain calcareous substances, to obtain the pallid hue of ghosts. Sometimes funerary masks may be used to symbolize an existence like that of the dead.
3. symbolic burial in a temple or a fetish house.
4. symbolic descent into the underworld.
5. hypnotic sleep.
6. tests of endurance, such as beatings, holding the feet near the fire, suspensions in the air, amputation of fingers, and various other cruelties.[3]

These ordeals constitute the commissioning service for the shaman who thereby becomes a technician of the sacred.

While Moses cannot be considered as a technician of the sacred (the Egyptian magicians are certainly that), two key points in the analogy are helpful. The first is Moses' special relationship with divine power through a commissioning ordeal. The second is the function of the ordeal in authenticating him before his people.

The third tool is analysis of the contemporary condition of man and society. This brings new perspective of meaning to familiar passages. For example, Arnold Toynbee, using insights from Marxian thought, has taught us to look for an external or an internal proletariat emerging within an old civilization. The slaves who took

---

[2] Avery Dulles, "Symbol, Myth, and the Biblical Revelation," (New Theology No. 4, eds. M. Marty and D. Peerman; New York: Macmillan, 1967) 39-68, 42.

[3] M. Eliade, Shamanism (London: Routledge, Kegan, & Paul, 1964) 33, 64.

part in the Exodus would thus be classified as an external proletariat. Moses, born a member of this group, had his education within
the dominant civilization. Later he returned to identify himself
with his own people and lead them to victory.

Contemporary experience teaches us to think of the Exodus
as a movement of liberation within a given society rather than an
escape from one society to another across geographical lines. With
this consideration in mind we look for oppressive forces which bind,
warp, alienate, enslave, or dehumanize man. We see the victims of these
forces needing liberation. We look for the liberators who are born
among the victims, educated among the oppressive powers, and return
to liberate the victims. The oppressive forces may be customs, conven-
tions, taboos, religious forces of reaction in traditional society;
they may be spirits and demons along with the attitude of resignation
and irresponsibility that goes with belief in them; they may be a
power elite ruling for the benefit of a few; they may be a dominant
culture and government in relation to ethnic minorities; perhaps the
very structure of society has become oppressive and is in need of
radical reform.

Thus the interpreter must attempt to locate the particular
oppressing forces in his own situation as a means of finding the
thrust of God's word in the contemporary world.

Let us think then of a dance drama portraying the commissioning ordeal of Moses, the liberator. The imagination may add light,
sound, and movement to catch the message of symbol and the thrust of
the divine word in the affairs of men. What follows may be considered
as a preparatory note for the choreographer.

The First Ordeal: Power

Exod 4:2-4.

An examination of the whole passage (vss. 1-9) will show the
key importance of the word "hand" which occurs eight times to which
a ninth, the word "palm (of the hand)" may be added. According to
Hebrew dynamic psychology, the hand is a symbol of the person-in-
action. Action by the person through his hand may include conquest
and plunder (Isa 10:10, 13, 14), killing or crippling (Exod 21:20),
oppression (Exod 18:10), rescue and protection (Exod 13:9, 14, 16;
Isa 11:11; 2 Kgs 14:27).

Three "hands" are prominent in the Exodus narrative. There
is first, the oppressing hand of Pharaoh-in-action or Egypt-in-action
(3:8; 5:21; 14:30; 18:9-10). Over against this there is the mighty
hand of God-in-action to rescue his people from the hand of Pharaoh-
in-action.

I know that the king of Egypt will not let you go,
unless compelled by a mighty hand. So I will
stretch out my hand and smite Egypt (3:19-20).

By the strength of hand, Yahweh brought you out
of this place (14:31).

The hand of Moses-in-action (or of Aaron, which is essentially the same in meaning) is always placed in conjunction with
God's command or power. God puts the power to work miracles into
the hand of Moses-in-action (4:21), commands Aaron to stretch out his
hand (Aaron-in-action) over the waters of Egypt (7:19; 8:1), commands
Moses to stretch out his hand (Moses-in-action) toward heaven and
bring hail (9:22) or locusts (10:12) or darkness (10:21-22) or to
divide the sea (14:16,21,26,27). The hand of Moses-in-action was to
be the embodiment of God-in-action in the struggle of liberation.
The rod, which is an extension of the power of the hand,
also is an important part of the Exodus narrative. It is never described as Moses' rod, but rather "this rod" (4:17) or "the rod which
is in my hand" (7:17) or "the rod with which you struck the Nile"
(17:5). It is, in fact, the "rod of God" (4:20; 17:9). In a later
reference to this rod, God himself lifts it up "as he did in Egypt"
(Isa 10:26).
The first ordeal is meant to mean the transfer of power from
God to the hand of Moses-in-action. It is this supernatural power
at work in Moses which causes the Israelite to "fear Yahweh and believe his servant Moses" (Exod 14:31).
As the ordeal begins, Moses' rod is in his hand. The hand-
holding-the-rod is a symbol of Moses at work keeping sheep for his
father-in-law, reluctant to take up the task which has been given to
him. His divine challenger commands him to throw the rod to the
ground. The rod then becomes a serpent from which Moses naturally
draws back in terror.
The serpent in this passage is more than an ordinary snake.
The word nāḥaš used here is parallel to the word tannîn in Exod 7:
9-12,15. In Isa 27:1 the two terms are in synonymous parallelism
and are mytho-poetic symbols of the power of chaos which will be
finally defeated in the day of God's action. The original act of
creation-salvation is described in Ps 74:12-13
Yet God my king is from of old,
working salvation in the midst of the earth.
Thou didst divide the sea by thy might
thou didst break the heads of the dragons
(tannînim) on the waters.
The symbol of the serpent also refers to Egypt, as seen from Ezek 29:
3 and 32:2 where she is called "the dragon (tannîm) that lies in the
midst of his stream." This double meaning of the serpent (cf. Isa 51:
9-11) makes the Exodus a new creation in which a new act of salvation

is wrought by the defeat of Egypt and the liberation of the slaves.[4]

It will be clear that the text here is much more than a "garbled account of an Egyptian snake charmer's trick."[5] To the sensitive religious consciousness of the Hebrews who witnessed and participated in the dramatic reliving of the Exodus, the rod-become-serpent would carry deep levels of meaning doubtless forgotten or suppressed in the lore of the magicians. It would represent the powers of chaos which have invaded the earth and become focused now in the oppressing power of Egypt. Moses' fear is then the deep anxiety of those who face the demonic power of chaos which destroys and enslaves and dehumanizes. The ordeal gives him a terrible vision of what he must face in the task of liberation.

A second command from the divine challenger instructs the terrified man to put forth his hand (symbol of Moses-in-action) and grasp the serpent by the tail. (The symbolic nature of the narrative is seen in this rather unlikely place to grasp the serpent). By a tremendous effort of the will, he obeys. Suddenly the snake becomes rigid in the palm of his hand (the word kap - palm - emphasizes complete control). The serpent-becomes-rod is in his power, and is indeed a part of his own action.

The meaning of this ordeal may be summarized. By the power of God, Moses will be able to gain victory over the destructive forces of alienation, enslavement, and death. They themselves will be used to thrust forward the victorious purpose of God to liberate the slaves. The hand (man-in-action) limited to pastoral occupation has been forced out of its passivity and slothfulness[6] to a direct confrontation with these powers. From now on, the man-in-action will be participating in the new act of creation-salvation.

-----

[4] cf. G. A. F. Knight, A Christian Theology of the Old Testament (Richmond, Va.: John Knox, 1959) 45, 116, 162-3.

[5] J. C. Rylaarsdam, "Exodus, Introduction and Exegesis," IB I, 877-78.

[6] The importance of "slothfulness of being" in the Marxian analysis of sin has been pointed out by Robert Raines in his article "Sin as Pride and Sin as Sloth," Christianity and Crisis 29 (Feb. 3, 1969) 4-8. Man "does not stand his ground and assert himself over against the given realities but drifts into an opiate, dream-like self-surrendering to the world," 6. Although Marx saw this as a particular characteristic of the disinherited, Raines points out that it is today a sin of the affluent bourgeoisie who are "seduced into a passive, self-forgetful relationship to their existence," 7.

The Second Ordeal: Death

Exod 4:6-7.

The second ordeal begins with the mysterious command
"Put your hand in your bosom," meaning into the fold of the
garment across the chest. From a parallel use of this expression in Ps 74:11 we learn that this action means a voluntary
renunciation of power. The hand (man-in-action) is withdrawn
from action. To Moses' horror, when his hand is taken from the
fold of his cloak it is "leprous, white as snow."

"Leprosy" is the name of a skin disease common in the
ancient Near East, usually not to be identified with Hansen's
Disease known today as Leprosy.[7] In the OT it is looked on as
an act of God which requires a miracle of divine grace for healing. A particularly interesting example is the case of Miriam
(Num 12:1-15) who was stricken with this disease (in this case
probably psoriasis) as a punishment for her prideful and selfish
opposition to Moses. Aaron's entreaty expresses the relationship
of this whitening of the skin to death: "Let her not be as one
dead" (vs. 12). The initiation rite of the shaman immediately
comes to mind. White ashes rubbed on the skin symbolize an
inner death by simulating its color. Further, Miriam was required to spend seven days outside the camp before her return
and restoration. On comparison to the initiation rite mentioned
above, the suggestion is obvious that the seven days of Miriam
represent a sojourn in the land of the dead.

Seen in its dramatic setting, the leprosy of Moses' hand
was a symbolic death of the man-in-action. It is analogous to the
experience of Isaiah whose cry "Woe is me" indicates a death, to be
followed by a resurrection given by the words of the seraph "your
guilt is removed." The death of Moses-in-action is the death of
pride and personal ambition. Moses was warned against acting
like the Assyrian king who boasted "By the strength of my hand
have I done this!" (Isa 10:13). In his hand, symbol of power,
he would carry the memory of death, so that God's living power
might be manifested through him (cf. 2 Cor 4:7-11).

The marks of the death of pride are seen in Moses' life
as leader of his people. His suffering is a prominent part of
the Exodus narratives. He suffers with his people (16:3; 17:2),
is threatened with violence (17:4; Num 14:10), and faces their
rebellion (Num 14:2). He is attacked by Miriam and Aaron (Num
12:1-2). He complains bitterly to God, desiring death in preference to this kind of mission (Num 11:11-15). Nevertheless,
he is meek throughout: humble in acceptance of suffering

---

[7]R. K. Harrison, "Leprosy," IDB, K-L, 111-113.

but firm in his mission of liberation. This meekness was the sign
to the people that he had renounced his own power in favor of God's
power.

Death is followed by resurrection. Moses' hand is restored
to life and action and power. The hand which could seize the
dragon in the name of God becomes the hand which carries the people
in his bosom as a nurse carries a child (Num 11:12) or as a man
carries a lamb (2 Sam 12:3; cf. Isa 40:11). In renouncing his
personal power and submitting to death, he was raised from death
to become God's servant "meeker than all men who were on the face
of the earth" (Num 12:3).

In the first ordeal, Moses was endowed with power and
forced out of his passivity and slothfulness. In the second ordeal, he submitted to death and was warned of the dangers of
power.[8]

The Third Ordeal: Blood on the Land

Exod 4:8-9.

The third command now is given. Moses stoops to gather
water from the Nile into a bowl. Despite the location of the incident at Mount Sinai, the Nile is "present" in dramatic symbolism.
He rises slowly, lifting it over his head, and with a quick turn of
his hand, he dashes the water to the ground. A cymbal crash and a
change of light heightens the dramatic effect of the ground
reddened with blood.

The Nile was in fact and symbol the source of life for
Egypt. Its annual inundation brought silt to renew the soil, and
lifegiving water to swell the seedlings, just when the land and
people needed them most. The god Osiris was believed to bring the
"pure water" or "young water" of new beginnings, and to be manifested in it. Thus Osiris was the fertilizing power of the flood,
causing the earth to bring forth fruit. When the water began to
recede, Osiris died by drowning and was buried. His life force

---

[8]Raines, ibid., sees Reinhold Niebuhr and Karl Marx as
representing two sides of a dialectic necessary for modern man.
The problem for Niebuhr is the selfhood of man. The problem
for Marx is the environment of man. On the one side is the
"frantic anxiety" and urgency of the New Left who see "the eclipse
of civilization" under an older affluent but slothful generation.
On the other side is the relativity of human planning, the need
to recognize "'the other' who stands over against us and our plans,"
the need for humility, "surrendering of our will to be absolute,"
so that we can "continue in the unfinished dialectic between man's
selfhood and his environment."

passed to the freshly sown grain which would sprout in the dry-
ing fields.9

The importance of the Nile for the political life of the
nation was symbolized by the identification of the late Pharaoh
with Osiris, while the reigning Pharaoh was identified with Horus,
son of Osiris. The Pharaoh was thus son of the Nile, giving life
and vitality to his people.

The primary meaning of blood in this episode is death.
The sword of warfare may be described as "drunk with blood"
(Isa 34:6; cf. Deut 32:41-42), while a land stricken with war and
disaster is "soaked with blood" (Isa 34:7). In this ordeal, Moses
is given a sign depicting symbolically the events in which he will
have a part. The life force of Egypt which should bring vitality
and fruitfulness to land and nation will be overcome by death.
The "pure water" will become blood on the land. A later poetic
description of disintegration and ruin in Egypt will be helpful
in understanding the meaning of this sign.

> The waters of the Nile will be dried up,
>   and the river will be parched and dry;
> and its canals will become foul,
>   and the branches of Egypt's Nile will diminish
>   and dry up,
>   reeds and rushes will rot away.
> There will be bare places by the Nile,
>   on the brink of the Nile,
> and all that is sown by the Nile will dry up,
>   be driven away, and be no more.
> The fishermen will mourn and lament,
>   all who cast hook in the Nile;
>   and they will languish who spread nets upon the water.
> The workers in combed flax will be in despair,
>   and the weavers of white cotton.
> Those who are the pillars of the land will be crushed,
>   and all who work for hire will be grieved.
>   (Isa 19:5-10)

The plagues on Egypt are pictured in the Exodus narrative
as a curse on the land, bringing death and disintegration. A re-
view of the account brings this out quite clearly:
The fish in the Nile died (7:21)
The water became foul (7:21)
The land was ruined because of the flies (8:20)
All the cattle died (9:6)
Boils were upon the magicians and on all the Egyptians
                                        (9:11)

9H. Frankfort, Kingship and the Gods (Chicago: University
of Chicago, 1948) 190-193.

Hail struck down everything that was in the field,
>   man and beast, plant and tree (9:25)
Not a green thing remained (10:15)
Yahweh smote all the first born of Egypt (12:29)
The Egyptians cried "We are all dead men!" (12:33).

Thus did the water of life, the original vitality of the
civilization, turn to the blood of death on the land. This awesome
power was somehow in the hand of Moses, the liberator. He seems
to stand at a moment of history like that of Isaiah who was commissioned to proclaim the word of God

>   until cities lie waste
>   without inhabitant,
>   and houses without men,
>   and the land is utterly desolate (Isa 6:11)

It is similar to Jeremiah's time when

>   Death has come up into our windows,
>   it has entered our palaces,
>   cutting off children from the streets,
>   and young men from the squares.
>   The dead bodies of men shall fall
>   like dung on the open field,
>   like sheaves after the reaper,
>   and none shall gather them. (Jer 9:22)

Like Jeremiah, it was Moses' task to "pluck up and to
break down, to destroy and to overthrow" (Jer 1:10).

At the same time, blood on the dry ground would evoke
other meanings in the minds of the participants in the passover
drama. Its primary meaning in the OT was as a symbol of the life
of man or animal. Blood-symbolizing-life used in the cult was
effective in restoring the relationship between man and God.

>   For the life of the flesh is in the blood and
>   I have given it to you upon the altar to make
>   atonement for your souls, for it is the blood
>   that makes atonement by reason of the life (Lev 17:11).

When a sacrificial animal was slaughtered, the persons involved
in the sacrifice would place their hands on the head of the victim,[10]
whose blood was poured on the ground at the base of the altar (Exod 29).

Is it too bold to suppose that the blood on the land of Egypt
in the dramatic symbolism of the passover would carry with it the
connotation of sacrifice as well as death and destruction? Pharaoh's
first born was slain because he would not let Yahweh's first born
son, Israel, go free (Exod 4:22-23). The death of one meant life

---

[10]Cf. D. M. G. Stalker, "Exodus," Peake's Commentary on the Bible
(rev. eds. M. Black & H. H. Rowley; London: T. Nelson, 1962) 236. According to J. Pedersen, Israel III-IV (London: Oxford University, 1940) 454,
the laying on of hands signifies a transfer of sin of the Israelites to the
goat.

for the other. The redemption of first born sons of Israel by
the slaughter of a sacrificial animal (Exod 13:13; 34:20) was
associated with blood on Egypt's soil:

> For when Pharaoh stubbornly refused to let us go,
> Yahweh slew all the first born in the land of Egypt,
> both the first born of man and the first born of cattle.
> Therefore I sacrifice to the Lord all males that open
> the womb; but all the first born of my sons I redeem.
> (Exod 13:15).

The same idea was restated by Isaiah of the exile when a new Egypt
(Babylon) was about to be sacrificed for Israel's liberation: "I
give Egypt as your ransom" (Isa 43:3).

This connotation of the meaning of blood on the land in the
Third Ordeal, puts Egypt in an entirely different perspective. Egypt
is, as it were, a ransom for God's first born! It is clear, further,
that a larger purpose was at work than the liberation of Israel. The
purpose of the plagues was that Egypt "may know that there is none
like Yahweh in all the earth"... "so that my name may be declared
throughout all the earth (and) you may know that the earth is Yahweh's"
(Exod 9:14,16,29).

"All the earth" includes Egypt. Egypt also belongs to Yahweh.
Blood on the land of Egypt is thus for the future life of Egypt
as well as the life of the nations of the earth.

The hope implicit in this third ordeal is clarified in the
following passage:

> Yahweh will make himself known to the Egyptians
> and the Egyptians will know Yahweh in that day...
> and Yahweh will smite Egypt, smiting and healing,
> and they will return to Yahweh and he will heed
> their supplications and heal them...In that day
> Israel will be a third with Egypt and Assyria,
> a blessing in the midst of the earth, whom Yahweh
> of hosts has blessed, saying "Blessed be Egypt my
> people, and Assyria the work of my hands, and
> Israel my heritage."   (Isa 19:21-22,24-25)

The meaning of the third ordeal is this: The task of
liberation will involve disintegration and death of the old society
of Egypt in order that the new people of Israel may be born. But
the liberation of Israel through the ransom price of Egypt means
the eventual liberation of Egypt.

THE "PRINCIPLES" OF DIVINE ELECTION

Wisdom in 1 Samuel 16

by

Ashley S. Rose

Elmhurst College

David's achievement lay in his exercise of royal power to a degree unprecedented during Saul's lifetime. In consolidating his political and military hegemony he also redirected the self-understanding and the aspirations of a community, and produced momentous alterations in the structures of its corporate existence. In contrast to the tribal federation, only slightly affected by the relatively few changes imposed upon it by Saul, a new and in many ways very different social reality emerged under David's influence. But how could the "Israel" of an earlier day be related to a national state that eventually became a full-scale empire? What considerations could be adduced to answer the question of the legitimacy of David's place and function in the ongoing life of God's people? Was the relationship between YHWH and David to be understood on the same grounds as that of his predecessor?

In order to provide answers to questions concerning the relation between the old and the new orders, as well as to explicate the meaning and the promise of the newly founded Davidic monarchy, an extensive literary work was composed which described David's early career leading to his accession to the throne. 1 Samuel 16 serves as an introduction to this narrative.[1] In this composition the author undertakes an elucidation of David's ineradicable impact upon the people of God. He does this by delineating what may be termed the "principles" of divine election. These serve as the fundamental premises upon which the subsequent literary, thematic, and theological exposition proceeds.

It is our thesis that the chapter is uniquely formulated in categories of thought, and with literary features, similar to those found in the traditionally defined wisdom literature (Job, Proverbs, Qoheleth, Ahiqar, Ben Sira', Pirqe Aboth). If this contention may be demonstrated, it follows that the author of 1 Samuel 16 advances an

---

[1] A. Weiser, "Die Legitimation des Königs David," VT 16 (1966) 325, 330f. For a somewhat different view see J. Grønbaek, Die Geschichte vom Aufstieg Davids (Copenhagen: Prostant, 1971) 16f., 25ff., 37ff.

interpretation of the royal figure and institution in Israel reflecting a basis quite different from those passages where covenant and/
or cultic associations are paramount (e.g. 2 Samuel 7, Psalm 89). In
order to sustain this argument, we shall analyze the rhetorical
structure of the chapter for the purpose of drawing certain conclusions pertaining to the character of the author's thought and intention.

I

1 Samuel 16 consists of two main divisions, the story of David's
anointing (vss. 1-13), and a tradition describing how he first
entered into service at the royal court (vss. 14-23). In all probability these units originally circulated independently. However,
the present form of the text furnishes many indications -- both literary as well as substantive -- that a single author-compiler brought
the narratives together in order to form a unified composition for
reasons which will become clear as we proceed.

When we turn to the first section, it may be observed that the
subject is delineated by means of a compositional pattern characterized by alternation between divine address and human response.
YHWH's introductory speech (vs. 1) uses general terms to announce
the main theme of the narrative, which then is given specific contextual setting by means of Samuel's reply (vs. 2a). Similarly, a
series of three divine utterances (respectively vss. 2b-3, 7, 12b)
are succeeded in turn by notices of Samuel's correlative speech or
action. With ever-increasing precision these alternations lead toward the conclusion (vs. 13) where the purpose advanced indefinitely
at the outset finds concrete fulfillment. A closer scrutiny of the
elements comprising this literary structure will have an important
bearing upon our interpretation of the author's purpose.

The introduction (vs. 1) consists of a rhetorical question (^{c}ad
mātay) which leads directly into the articulation of a command
(malle'). Each of these clauses serves both a literary and a thematic
function. The leading verbs of the former (vs. 1a) express motifs
which are highly reminiscent of the traditions relating the withdrawal
of Saul's right to the kingship (see 15:35, l^{e}hit'abbēl; 15:23, 26,
lim'ôs; cf. 13:14; 15:11, 28). The literary link thus formed with
these narratives assumes added significance when we observe that
preliminary reference to the theme of Saul's rejection constitutes a
necessary premise for the further development of the story. Similarly,
the sentence beginning with the injunction (vs. 1b) reflects, on the
one hand, the theme of anointing[2] as the special act of election in

---

[2]E. Kutsch, Salbung als Rechtsakt (BZAW 87, 1963) 2f., 55; for a
different view see L. Schmidt, Menschlicher Erfolg und Jahwes Initiative (WMANT 38, 1970) 179.

which a king was authorized, honored, and strengthened (see 9:16f.; 10:10, 24; 15:1, 7), while it anticipates, on the other hand, the main subject of the present piece, the consecration of David as Saul's successor (vss. 12b-13).

The introductory divine address consequently establishes the literary and thematic context in which YHWH's selection of David for the royal office must be viewed. But more importantly, the author's use of a special kind of rhetorical question is particularly revealing. He has conjoined an admonishment signalled by the phrase ^{c}ad matay with an imperative sentence specifying a course of action sanctioned by the speaker. This particular collocation of literary elements is especially effective in contexts where an author's central purposes are didactic. The course of our subsequent discussion will serve to clarify this observation.

In what appears to be an impassioned retort, Samuel responds to the divine word by means of a rhetorical question formally echoing the way in which the piece begins ('ēk 'ēlēk..., vs. 2a). This scene is reminiscent of the occasions where such leaders as Moses (Exod 3:11) or Gideon (Judg 6:15) object to a divine commission.[3] However, it is unlikely that there is any connection here with a particular kind of stereotyped literary formulation.[4] This contention may be vindicated in the light of historical probability. We may assume that the tension between Samuel and Saul which is reflected in chs. 13 and 15 resulted in an open break between them to the extent that the prophet may very well have lived a risky existence in proximity to Saul's area of influence. Any behavior which appeared inimical to the king's power or authority might be expected to have elicited his strong opposition, much as the later traditions remembered his resistance to the real or imagined danger presented by David.[5]

The difficulty to which Samuel calls attention accordingly precipitates a divine word which may be characterized as a torah-unit (vss. 2b-3) in agreement with its function in the present context. It may be observed, for example, that YHWH issues here a series of directives which are calculated to avert the specific impediments presented by the historical situation, and to achieve the goal enunciated in Samuel's commission. At the same time, an important motif is added which contrasts with these highly specific instructions because of a singular absence of detailed reference, namely, YHWH's promise to convey further information when the need becomes evident.

---

[3]Schmidt, ibid., 38ff., 49.
[4]H.Reventlow, Liturgie und prophetisches Ich bei Jeremiah (Gütersloh: Gerd Mohn, 1963) 45ff.
[5]J. Bright, A History of Israel, 2nd ed. (Philadelphia: Westminster, 1972) 187.

('ōdî[a]ca_kā..., vs. 3b). The purpose of this teaching is later disclosed through the final clause of the divine utterance (ûmaśaḥtā..., vs. 3b). Here the veiled allusion to the one intended by YHWH functions as a literary anticipation of the occasion where his name will be specifically communicated (vs. 13a). As a consequence of the vocabulary of teaching together with two important pedagogical emphases -- mastery of the contingencies of a circumstance and attainment of a predetermined end -- our classification of the divine address here as a torah-unit would seem to be confirmed.

If the foregoing conclusion may be accepted, a further consequence can be drawn concerning one of the specific uses of divine torah in this context. We refer to the fact that YHWH communicates to Samuel only the information sufficient and necessary to enable the prophet effectively to accomplish the immediate task at hand. All other matters -- including the specific content of his purposes -- YHWH refrains from mentioning. Samuel is not apprised of the identity of the man whom YHWH has chosen. There is perhaps to be noticed here an intentional contrast to an important theme of the Samuel-Saul traditions, where the prophet had assumed much of the initiative in connection with Saul's anointing (see 10:1ff.). Whether or not such an argument can be sustained, it is nevertheless clear that in our context Samuel is relegated to a passive role by virtue of his complete dependence upon YHWH's intentions as expressed through teaching.[6]

Samuel's obedient response to the divine torah (vss. 4-6) proceeds felicitously until a hasty and unheedful gesture results in an infringement of YHWH's earlier directive. For Samuel attempts to arrogate to himself the right of evaluating Eliab's fitness to rule (neged YHWH m[e]śîḥô, vs. 6b). This act once again calls forth a divine word which, after careful investigation, can be shown to assume both a structurally and a thematically determinative role in terms of the author's delineation of the subsequent narrative materials.

The divine utterance in question may be regarded as a second torah-unit (vs. 7). This conclusion is warranted on the grounds of vocabulary and use in a context where we might have expected language expressing cultic matters.[7] Instead of this both the form and the content of the speech reflect characteristic elements of teaching. For YHWH is again required to issue instructions in order that the course of events might proceed according to his purposes. Samuel had failed to heed the promise of instruction YHWH had made at an earlier occasion (vs. 3b). Rather, the prophet himself had rendered a judgment favoring Eliab (vs. 6b), presumably on the basis

---

[6]Cf. M. Kessler, "Narrative Technique in 1 Sm 16, 1-13," *CBQ* 32 (1970) 548.

[7]Contra Grønbaek, *op. cit.* (n. 1) 76.

of criteria that had formerly been regarded as essential attributes
of kingship, namely, impressive physical stature and appearance (see
9:2; 10:23). As a consequence, in order to reinforce his intentions
and to secure at the same time human responses conforming to them,
YHWH admonishes Samuel in a way that carries with it a two-fold
didactic thrust. On the one hand, the warning serves to instruct
Samuel against assuming unwarranted authority over against YHWH's
sole competence to judge matters pertaining to the kingship. On the
other hand, the specific content of the admonition indicates that
the criteria of appearance and stature henceforth shall not become
significant factors in the selection of a new king.

There is yet another indication that the admonition addressed to
Samuel functions as torah. The author's reasons advanced in support
of the injunction are formulated aphoristically, summarizing conclusions deriving from reflection based upon generally available human
experience. Thus, it would appear that the claim which the divine
word lays upon Samuel rests neither upon legal nor religious presuppositions, as we might ordinarily expect. If they did so, self-
evidently they would require submission to the power, authority, and
holiness of the God of Israel. Instead, behavior consonant with the
intention of the admonition will result exclusively from an intellectual assent to its validity, and that of the arguments presented in
its behalf. It is our contention that this is precisely the kind of
speech one finds in certain pedagogical contexts where a teacher will
advance ideas by means of proverbial utterance. The pupil will be
expected to decide for himself whether experience confirms or con-
tradicts the notion thus presented. Accordingly, he utilizes the
criterion of reason in order to arrive at his determinations.[8]

Since the divine speech under consideration gives evidence not
only of promulgating specific instruction, but seems also to reflect
a kind of didactic situation, we may legitimately describe it as a
torah-unit. This contention receives additional support from the
nature of the literary components of the sentence and their relationship to the more extensive narrative to which there is thematic and
structural affinity. The following schema will facilitate illustration of these broader implications of the divine address at this point.

Admonition	'al	tabbēṭ
	'el	mar'ēhû
	wᵉ'el	gᵉbōᵃh qômātô
Explanation	ki	mᵉ'astîhû
	ki	lō' 'ᵃšer yir'eh hā'ādām
	ki	hā'ādām yir'eh laᶜênayim
Climax	wYHWH	yir'eh lallēbāb.

---

[8] H. Hermisson, Studien zur israelitischen Spruchweisheit (WMANT
28, 1968) 63, 80.

The second torah-unit is constructed as a series of interconnected triads. In each instance one may observe a regular pattern of composition uniquely suitable for expression of emphasis, for the beginning line of the triad exhibits a primary accent followed by two secondary stresses in the succeeding lines. The initial unit is comprised of an alliterative alternation between two forms of the homograph 'l. The central element of concern here -- the admonition -- is announced through the negative adverb 'al which is then provided with contextual support by means of two echoing phrases, each of which is signaled by repetition of the preposition 'el. Similarly, the succeeding triad establishes at the outset the fundamental reason accounting for the issuance of the admonition by employing a kî-clause at the very place where a new major accent occurs.[9] This is followed once again by repetitive phrases with kî leading toward the climax of the utterance which occurs in emphatic accentual position in the last line. Additional emphasis upon this latter element is secured through a skillfully executed overlapping of triadic units. Whereas the final line is discontinuous with the preceding triad in terms of accent -- it here assumes primary position -- it is nevertheless continuous with it in terms of content. For it represents the culminating expression of the three-fold repetition of yir'eh[10] toward which both of the conjoined triads have been aiming.

This analysis would appear to be confirmed when we observe that the rhythmical undulations of the triadic series coincide exactly with the expression of certain antitheses forming the substance of this torah-unit. Samuel, to whom the admonition is addressed, stands over against YHWH in terms of the right and the capacity to decide upon Saul's successor. But it is not simply the juxtaposition of the human and divine figures through which contrast is exhibited. This occurs also by means of the associated ideas. Whereas the one cannot avoid decisions based upon superficial considerations, the other penetrates to the profound center of the matter, by implication the only knowledge capable of assuring the election of a qualified king. That meaning and structure coincide here may be noted by the fact that the antitheses to which we have called attention are expressed at places comprising the major accents of the torah-unit. Thus, it may be concluded that the author intended to advance the idea of YHWH's exclusive jurisdiction over the matter of selecting David by expressing this point at the climax of the speech. This also follows from the fact that this utterance contrasts thematically with the actions that had been earlier repudiated at the emphatic beginning and middle of the torah-unit respectively, namely, Samuel's

---

[9] J. Muilenburg, "The Linguistic and Rhetorical Usages of the Particle kî in the OT," HUCA 32 (1961) 147f., 152, 154, 157; cf. W. Richter, Recht und Ethos (München: Kösel, 1966) 39, 175ff.

[10] The LXX inserts yir'eh hā'elōhîm; since a discussion of this textual matter is not germane to our thesis, we shall read with the MT.

judging by appearances and his assumption of the divine prerogative. This contention may claim the support of three additional antitheses. Each of these underscores the same contrast of ideas by citing the disfavored element at an unstressed position while correspondingly emphasizing the acceptable view at the culmination: mar'ēhû/lēbāb, hā'ādām/YHWH, ʿēnayim/lēbāb.

The climax serves as an epitome of the rational justification upon which the admonition is grounded. One of the reasons why it can function in this way is the kind of relationship it bears to the immediately preceding line. Here we have to do with a style of formulation that is especially familiar from collections of didactic sentences as represented, say, in Proverbs 10ff. A concisely worded declarative sentence expresses a thought which is essentially a distillation of experience. To this statement another is correlated -- in this case in synonymous parallelism -- which typically expresses an antithetical idea, as it does in our example. The following schema will support our contention that the final two lines of the torah-unit comprise a proverb that has been either adapted to the present context or coined especially for it:

$$(k\hat{\imath}) \ h\bar{a}\textrm{'}\bar{a}d\bar{a}m \quad yir\textrm{'}eh \quad la^{c\bar{A}}\bar{e}nayim$$
$$w\textrm{Y}HWH \quad yir\textrm{'}eh \quad lall\bar{e}b\bar{a}b.^{11}$$

The occurrence of an admonishment in close association with a proverbial sentence, together with its special construction and vocabulary, permits us to conclude that the second torah-unit (vs. 7) exhibits didactic affinities. The same view ensues from a scrutiny of the special use which the verb r'h receives in this speech. By this means the author apparently seeks an answer to the question, Who may rightly elect the new king?

Without exception the root r'h occurs in ch. 16 in association with acts of selection. The connotation "choosing" belongs to the semantic field defined by the verb through a natural extension of its function, and undoubtedly represents common usage (e.g., Gen 22:8; Deut 12:13; cf. 2 Kgs 10:3; Esth 2:9). It is nevertheless not fortuitous that r'h is used in our context either with the nuance "to choose," or with the basic meaning "to see" connoting at the same time a fundamental means by which selection is accomplished. This contention may be supported when we reflect that other verbs were commonly available to express the same idea, and further that the narrative offers, without precedent, an especially large number of occurrences of the word in connection with the aforementioned motif (vss. 1b, 6a, 7b, 17, 18a). For example, r'h is employed as a specification of the primary theme of the chapter's first narrative

---

[11]For a conceptually similar, but stylistically different, formulation, see Prov 15:11 (cf. Prov 16:2).

section, since it describes an act of YHWH which prefigures at the
same time the outcome of the story (rāʾîtî...lî melek, vs. 1b).
More importantly, however, the root functions as an essential element
of the resolution of a conflict over the important question of the
right of designating the king. The exclusive validity of the divine
choice (rʾh, vs. 1) is established through the repudiation of an
attempt by Samuel to exercise this prerogative. As soon as he had
seen Eliab (wayyarʾ, vs. 6a), Samuel drew an immediate conclusion
about him (vs. 6b). YHWH's admonitory address instructs against
this procedure, supplying the reason through a cognate root (nbṭ,
vs. 7a) which carries with it the implications of external observation (e.g., 1 Kgs 19:6; Isa 18:4; Exod 3:6; 33:8; Num 12:8; 21:9).
This characterizes the way man necessarily reaches his determinations,
inadequate in so weighty a matter as the election of the one to
assume royal responsibility.

It is not without consequence for our interpretation of the
author's purpose here that objective illustration of the aforementioned idea occurs later on in the literary presentation of David's
career. Eliab in fact shows himself to be unfit for the throne by
virtue of his heated and prejudicial response to, and the hasty and
unfounded conclusions he formulated about, David's presence at the
camp (17:28). This man, the one of Samuel's choosing, would hardly
have served Israel well. Accordingly, only YHWH may justifiably act
in a matter of such momentous implications for his people. This conclusion represents the import of the three-fold repitition of yirʾeh
in vs. 7b. The author claims that YHWH alone knows the criteria
enabling the choice of a new king. In contrast to the Samuel-Saul
traditions, no one, not even YHWH's prophet, is permitted to share
in this act of election (cf. 9:17; 10:24).

However, the motif of selection, which the second torah-unit so
carefully associates with the divine prerogative, nevertheless illustrates human actions in the succeeding literary division of the chapter. Two further examples of the root rʾh, with the same connotation as we have already experienced, will provide the evidence for
this contention. The first of these is exhibited when Saul orders
his servants "to find" a skilled musician for him (rᵉʾû, vs. 17b).
The reference at this point to an unspecified "seeking out," "choosing," becomes more closely defined through an anonymous servant's
announcement immediately conjoined with the king's command. Alluding
to David, the lad addresses Saul in the following way: rāʾîtî ben
lᵉyišay bêt hallaḥmî yōdēᵃᶜ naggēn, vs. 18a. This utterance entails
the servant's prior selection of a man possessing the appropriate
qualifications to act for the immediate relief of the king.

It would appear at the same time that the servant's speech represents the author's intentional application of the teaching of vs. 7
to the new literary context reflecting the court of Saul. The torah-
unit, as we have noted, establishes a clear distinction between divine
and human rights, criteria, and methods of making important determinations. God's competence and authority alone can be acknowledged as

self-authenticating. Human choices, however, may function unwittingly
to corroborate the divine intention. The author presents the servant's
recommendation of David here in precisely this frame of reference, for
the address to Saul, a portion of which we have quoted above (vs. 18a),
is virtually identical in thought and language with YHWH's introductory utterance: (...yišay bēt hallaḥmî) kî rā'îtî b^ebānā(y)w lî melek
(vs. 1b). There is little reason to doubt that the literary resem-
blance between the two statements is intentional. What is of significance, however, is the primary difference. Here it is established
that the human coice of David is for an entirely different purpose
(l^enaggēn) than that intended by YHWH (lî melek). In this sense,
then, there can be no question of a finite attempt to displace divine
authority as Samuel did in the earlier story. Commensurate with the
instruction of the torah-unit (vs. 7), divine and human choices con-
verged on David for reasons proper to their respective environments.
At the same time the fact that the conjunction of the two yielded a
concretely beneficial effect, resolution of Saul's difficulties (vs.
23), seems to indicate that the author intended to establish a correlation between the divine and human dimensions in terms of the motif of selection as expressed by the verb r'h.

While man's decisions are based on superficial and therefore incomplete and unreliable grounds, we have argued that his choices may
nevertheless agree with God's purposes whether wittingly or unwittingly. The resulting behavior will in either case be crowned with
success. The reason for this is that in principle the divine will
authenticates and sustains that toward which it aims. Accordingly,
YHWH abets endeavors that either deliberately or accidentally lead
toward the fulfillment of these ends. This would appear to be the
significance of the author's intentional application of the motif of
selection to the context of Saul's court. When certain men in Israel,
including the king, choose David for reasons of their own, without
being aware of it they have chosen the man elected by YHWH. This act
furnishes the initial opportunity through which YHWH exhibits the
character of his intentions with respect to the anointing of a king
for his people. What David is able to do for Saul, having been
selected for a specific task, is in a sense an objective demonstra-
tion of what YHWH in principle intends for Israel through his establishment of the Davidic monarchy. It is consequently no accident
that the denouement of the story is a happy one (vs. 23).

There is a further didactic role served by the torah-unit which
we have been considering (vs. 7), that focuses upon the question of
the identity of the one whom YHWH has chosen. This occurs through
the relationship it establishes with the subsequent report of Samuel's
obedience to the admonition's teaching (vss. 8-11). On the one hand,
the fact that YHWH reserves the selection of the king for himself is
emphasized by means of a three-fold repetition of lō' bāḥar (vss. 8b,
9b, 10b). YHWH demonstrates his right to elect the king by rejecting
through Samuel all of Jesse's sons who are present and "visible" at
the sacrifice. From the human perspective an insurmountable impasse
would apparently have been reached. Nevertheless, the teaching of

the admonition, that there can be no cognizance of superficial human
criteria, is vindicated by YHWH's inscrutible purview in connection
with the shepherd motif (vs. 11a). The very one whom YHWH had already
chosen (see vs. 1b; cf. 13:14b; 15:28) would have been ignored by the
assembled citizens.

On the other hand, there occurs a positive reference to the forthcoming king, based, once again, on a motif expressed definitively in
vs. 7. We refer to the description of the yet anonymous David as he
is brought in from the field (vs. 12a). It is made clear that David
possesses a physical endowment easily the match of Eliab's. Ironically,
the description includes two features closely related to what YHWH had
formerly taught Samuel to avoid, namely, the specification that David
was $y^e p \bar{e} h$ $^c \bar{e} n a y i m$ $w^e \underline{t \hat{o} b}$ $r \bar{o}' \hat{\iota}$ (vs. 12a; cf. mar'ēhû, vs. 7a). It would
appear that the author attributes to David the very qualities that
attract those who make judgments from a superficial perspective. At
the same time, owing to YHWH's torah (vs. 7), it cannot be said that
these unessential attributes were regarded by the author as significant for the question of David's authority. For YHWH's election of
this man rested upon criteria which only he could discern, but his
choice nevertheless recommended itself to Israel.

A third important divine utterance follows the foregoing description. This consists of a command together with a tersely formulated
explanatory clause (kî zeh hû', vs. 12b). We may designate the latter
as a torah-unit because it functions didactically here as in the
earlier two examples of divine address (vss. 2b-3, 7). The utterance
designates specifically whom YHWH has all along intended to succeed
to the throne of Saul. Moreover, it marks the fulfillment of YHWH's
promise of additional teaching earlier delivered to Samuel (vs. 3).
At the same time, the primary literary purpose of this section of the
narrative is brought to its culmination by means of this sentence. A
concluding notice of human response then occurs which we have come to
expect (vs. 13a), where the ritual act itself is reported. In contrast to the Samuel-Saul traditions, the investiture of the spirit is
here directly associated with David's anointing (cf. 10:1, 6). The
conferral of the spirit is the sign of YHWH's authorizing him for
special office. Saul, on the other hand, had shared in the spirit
common to the prophetic guilds (cf. 10:5). By means of the motif of
the spirit, the author has introduced an element at the conclusion of
the introductory narrative which will function thereafter as a unifying theme. For the antithesis between the investiture of David (vs.
13a) and the spirit's departure from Saul (vs. 14a) becomes the fundamental literary premise without which the forthcoming narrative cannot be understood. Then, too, David's possession of YHWH's spirit
has an important bearing upon the final outcome of the story (vs. 23).
Finally, the section is brought to a formal conclusion[12] by means of

---

[12] I. Seeligmann, "Hebräische Erzählung und biblische Geschichts-
schreibung," TZ 18 (1962) 308.

the notice of Samuel's departure (vs. 13b).

The introduction to the second section of the chapter (vs. 14) is an editorial description of the main theme of the story, the withdrawal of the spirit from Saul and his consequent status as God's unwitting enemy. At the same time, the sentence establishes a thematic juncture with the foregoing material because of the explicit association of the investiture of David (vs. 13a) with Saul's experience of the attack of the malevolent spirit. YHWH himself initiates both acts through which he determines the character of his future relationships to Saul and David respectively. Moreover, the juxtaposition of the introductory sentence (vs. 14) with the motif of the spirit already enunciated (vs. 13a) furnishes the literary premise on which are based the irony and pathos which later emerge at the point where the legitimate and rejected kings encounter one another for the first time (vs. 21).

That YHWH had rescinded Saul's right to govern is delineated in a way that bears remarkable affinities to the structure of the foregoing narrative. Following the introduction, two torah utterances alternate with appropriate responses in much the same manner as the formal structure of vss. 1-13, except that the denouement is not consistent with this pattern.

The author seems to regard the onset of the evil spirit as an objective witness to YHWH's rejection of Saul, carrying with it serious consequences both for the king and his people.[13] The royal servants (n^{ec}arîm) are able to perceive a problem connected with Saul's person which they then recognize to be weighty enough to require his attention. Thus, it would appear that a crisis of national importance had been identified. If Saul's difficulty were not of such proportions, there would be no satisfactory explanation of the way in which a possible solution is articulated. This occurs through a scene portrayed as a formal advisory session conducted before the royal court (vss. 15b-16). This contention may be supported by the following analysis of the servants' speech.

With an emphatic summons for a hearing (hinnēh-nā', vs. 15b) the servants describe the nature of the problem by means of a declarative sentence that virtually reiterates the substance of the author's introductory statement (vs. 14b). This would seem to confirm our earlier observation that the editorial introduction was intended to join together the two halves of the present chapter. The servants' speech noting the attack of the evil spirit (vs. 15b) would then belong to the freely circulating tradition. On the other hand, the author himself composed the introduction to serve as a middle term by which this motif could be related to the mention of David's investiture in the preceding, originally independent, narrative (vs. 13a).

---

[13]J. Pedersen, Israel III-IV (London: Oxford, 1940) 76ff.

Without attempting to specify details concerning the implications of Saul's difficulty, the servants initially request a royal edict authorizing the action which they have determined to be appropriate in relation to the circumstances (yō'mar-nā' 'ᵃḏōnēnû -- note the jussive formation -- vs. 16a). Since his sanction is necessary in order that the forthcoming advice might become effective, the main point of the address which follows -- the proposal for a solution to the problem -- also calls for Saul's explicit decision through the use of a second verb with jussive meaning (yᵉḇaqšû, vs. 16a).

The recommendation is constructed according to a tripartite schema that evinces a well-reasoned plan for dealing with problematic situations. There is little cause to doubt that the formal structure of the advice here possesses a universal applicability which, if consistently and prudentially employed, could contribute to the alleviation of virtually any human difficulty. The servants are evidently experts at formulating counsel, as the following will demonstrate.

First, the servants advance a suggestion which describes the appropriate means for reaching a solution, taking into consideration both the unique character of the context and its particular requirements. Here, the proposal concerns the services of a specially qualified individual ('îš yōdēᵃᶜ mᵉnaggēn bakkinnôr, vs. 16a).[14] Following this the servants then proceed to specify the concrete circumstance which requires the application of the means they have recommended (wᵉhāyāh bihyôt ᶜale(y)kā... rûᵃḥ...rāᶜāh, vs. 16b). Thereupon, they describe the particular method which, they claim, will be effective in such a situation (wᵉniggēn bᵉyāḏô). Finally, the servants bring their counsel to a climax by stating the goal which the previous suggestions are designed to realize (wᵉṭôb lāk, vs. 16b). These remarks may justly be characterized as systematic guidance through the complexities of a situation to an end that effectively surmounts all of the intervening conflicts. In this sense the speech serves a didactic purpose and may be compared to the torah-units which we have earlier examined. In effect, then, the servants are presented as royal counselors engaged in the promulgation of policy relating to affairs of state.[15]

The servants' counsel precipitates a response from Saul. His role, like Samuel's in the foregoing story, is essentially passive, as can be determined by the fact that his command issues in language nearly identical with the servants' formulation (vs. 17b). In the present context Saul can do nothing except react to the circumstance in which he finds himself -- he is incapable of directing matters to his own benefit.

As a reply to the permission granted by Saul, an anonymous member of

---

[14]"Expert player on the lyre" -- probably hendiadys and not a double reading, contra H. Hertzberg, I and II Samuel (Philadelphia: Westminster, 1964) 140 n. "b."

[15]W. McKane, Prophets and Wise Men (SBT 44, 1965) 55ff.; P. de Boer, "The Counsellor," VTSup 3 (1955) 56f.

his entourage offers counsel which serves as a nearer specification of
the more general proposal formerly submitted by the counselors as a group
(vs. 18). Commencing his speech, as they had done, with a summons for a
hearing (hinnēh, vs. 18a; cf. 15b), the counselor here recommends a certain individual who is, in his opinion, qualified to serve as the means
for resolving the difficulty in question (rā'îtî bēn l^{e}yišay ... yōdē$^{-ac}$
naggēn, vs. 18a). It is significant that the advice here concerns only
the first element of the counselors' tripartite suggestion earlier advanced, namely, the means by which the solution is to be attained. This
would permit the inference that the servant's emphasis here lay upon the
anticipated efficacy of the man whom he is proposing. The remainder of
the address clearly bears out this interpretation. For the counselor pro-
duces further considerations which reinforce his recommendation by flesh-
ing out the picture of the man's capacities and achievements (w^{e}gibbōr
ḥayil ... wYHWH ^{c}immô, vs. 18). The other two elements of the counsel
omitted by the servant -- the method relative to circumstance and the
desired result -- occur at the climax of the present narrative (vs. 23).
There the author describes the satisfactory resolution of the problem.
By this means he exhibits the fact that the counselor's expectations concerning the abilities of the man he had recommended were fully and
finally realized.

According to a pattern consistently practiced in the present context,
a speech that functions didactically meets with a response by the person
addressed, indicating that the teaching has been accepted. Saul's reaction to the second utterance of counsel is no exception. He evidences
his approval of the suggestion when he undertakes its implementation (vs.
19a). Thus, it is the king himself who first enunciates the name of
Jesse's son about whom the counselor had only alluded (vs. 19b). As a
consequence, the command functions as a recognition of the validity of
the counselor's previous recommendation, and furthermore demonstrates
that Saul himself had specifically chosen David for the relief of his own
problem. The author has undoubtedly intended this passage ironically, in
that the very one later to become David's chief adversary is nevertheless
the one who initially introduces him to the royal court (thus publically
to Israel) and attests his remarkable abilities.

Saul's designation of David by name is a response to the particulariz-
ing counsel offered by the anonymous servant, while the foregoing indefi-
nite proposal by the assembled entourage (vss. 15b-16) had been answered
similarly, through a general expression of Saul's permission (r^e'û -nā' lî
'îš, vs. 17b). Moreover, the latter is thematically related to YHWH's
choice of David announced in the introduction to the first narrative section, as we have earlier observed (rā'îtî ... lî melek, vs. 1b). Additional
evidence of a deliberate correlation of the two stories on the basis of
the theme of David's selection is provided by the associated motif of his
occupation as a shepherd. Before bringing him to Samuel, Jesse accounts
for his absence from the ceremonies by informing the prophet of his where-
abouts (baṣṣō'n, vs. 11a). Correspondingly, Saul indicates to Jesse the
identity of the son whose services he seeks by using exactly the same term
(vs. 19b). These structural and thematic correspondences would appear to
indicate that the author intended to juxtapose two dimensions of the motif

of selection through the combination of traditions here. On the one hand, YHWH had elected David to exercise the special office of kingship in Israel, granting him authority and inspiration. On the other hand, even before he was able to accede to temporal power, Saul had not only recognized David's singular capabilities, but had acted to secure his services for his own and the nation's benefit. It therefore does not appear to be accidental that the narrative of David's introduction into the national life included the warrants of both the divine and the royal authorities.

The foregoing conclusion may be corroborated when we turn to the denouement of the chapter (vss. 20-23). Here, the formal correspondences between the two major traditions, as well as the two dimensions of the choice of David -- the divine and the human -- converge thematically.

After noting Jesse's obedient response to Saul's command (vs. 20; cf. 12a), David's arrival at court is described with what is perhaps a deliberately ambiguous phrase (wayya^{ca}mōd l^{e}pānā(y)w, vs. 21a). On the one hand, the well-attested meaning "to serve" seems to be intended, indicating the final result of the actions precipitated by Saul's summons. On the other hand, there is a sense in which the literal meaning of the root may be understood here as well. For it occurs in the description of the scene where Saul and David encounter one another for the first time. Just as Samuel had earlier pronounced a favorable though hasty judgment upon Eliab after his first experience of the young man (vs. 6), so here Saul responds to the presence of David with a gesture of royal favor (wayye'^{e}habēhû m^e'ōd, vs. 21b). In any case, the motif of selection finds its culmination here through the notice that Saul appoints David as his armor-bearer (nōśē' kēlîm, vs. 21b). Despite the connotation of its official designation, this office undoubtedly entailed honor and responsibility, not merely the duties of a battlefield lackey.[16] If this conclusion may be accepted, it would sustain our previous observation of the correspondence between the divine and human selection of David. Saul elevated David to a high position among the people of God, just as YHWH had done.

A final structural comparison may be made here with the introductory narrative (vss. 1-13). Saul's message to Jesse serves essentially as a public confirmation of David's acceptance at court (kî māṣā' ḥēn b^{ec}ênay, vs. 22b). Although very different materially, this notice would seem to perform a function identical with that of YHWH's third torah utterance earlier addressed to Samuel (vs. 12b). There YHWH publically designates David as his chosen one. The rite of anointing succeeded by investiture with the spirit (vs. 13) indicate his permanent position in YHWH's service. Consequently, the combined narratives show that David is chosen both by God as well as by Israel's temporal ruler in order to perform functions appropriate to their respective requirements.

The conclusion of the narrative juxtaposes these two kinds of service

---

[16]Cf. McKane, I and II Samuel (London: SCM, 1963) 107; J. Mauchline, 1 and 2 Samuel (London: Oliphants, 1971) 131.

which David has been outfitted to perform. For on the one hand, whenever the evil spirit beset Saul, David's expertise with the lyre permits him to assuage the king's torment (vs. 23a). As a result the previously submitted counsel is vindicated by David's effectiveness conforming to the details of the advisors' suggestions. Accordingly, David proves himself able to function successfully on the human level. On the other hand, there is every reason to believe that the author's language describing the results of David's efforts (vs. 23b) is a deliberate reminiscence of the motif of the spirit upon which the second narrative section of the chapter commences. This, as we have seen, presupposes the notice concerning David's permanent possession of the divine spirit that accompanied his anointing (vs. 13a). David therefore effects Saul's healing, not principally by means of his own skill (vs. 23b), but on the basis of the divine gift which thus had equipped him to exercise control over the supernatural evil spirit. In the service of YHWH, David is enabled to bring about a state of šālôm for Saul which he could not secure for himself. Accordingly, expectation of what David might one day accomplish for Israel appeared at the outset of his career to be particularly bright.

II

The foregoing analysis has disclosed that the author constructed both sections of 1 Samuel 16 as a series of didactic utterances followed by notices of responses corresponding to the content of the teaching. When we consider the affinities of the author's stylistic techniques, this literary propensity can be explained as the precipitate of a milieu in which intellectual matters were of principal concern.

The admonition comprising the second divine torah-unit (vs. 7) is a kind of formulation especially at home in didactic contexts, as recent studies have succeeded in demonstrating. W. Richter, for example, has advanced the thesis that the admonition -- or more precisely, the vetitive -- was a form of expression frequently employed by teachers associated with schools where young men were trained for public careers.[17] The form is used characteristically as an expression of both a wish and an expectation that a particular act should not occur.[18] This was conveyed by a regular use of 'al with jussive, succeeded by a ki-clause functioning as an explanation.[19] In general, the form expressed punctiliar rather than timeless associations, concrete rather than abstract circumstances.[20] Accordingly, it was particularly well suited for the instruction of pupils in the specific kinds of behavior unacceptable to the community into which they would one day enter. Concomitantly it recommended to them those actions that ought rather to be undertaken. This indicates that the admonition generally presupposed an ethical standard pertinent to the social class to which the speaker belonged.[21] Emphasis on a didactic rather than a moralizing or legal use of the form, however, can be determined by the fact that

---

[17]W. Richter, op. cit. (n. 9) 71 (see also 71 n. 34), 182.
[18]Ibid., 71; [19]ibid., 39; [20]ibid., 71; [21]ibid., 145, 183ff.

the alternation between proscribed and commended action required the pupil
rationally to evaluate the relation of the acts to the implied standard.
The speaker did not inculpate the pupil on the basis of a violation of an
explicit obligation, as in other contexts, nor did he attempt to achieve
the desired end through the imposition of other forms of coercion except
that of reason alone. The employment of the admonition (vetitive) in contexts which are unambiguously didactic would confirm the foregoing argument.[22]

A quite different view has been promulgated by E. Gerstenberger in connection with his investigation of the origin of the legal prohibitive. He
contends that the admonition arose in the context of the extended family
(Sippe), antedating any institutionalized wisdom such as the school. The
function of this form of speech, like the prohibitive, is thus best understood as a device by which a father could teach his son (or elders the
younger generation) how to contribute to the well-being of the group, both
by avoiding deleterious behavior and by undertaking instead actions which
were positively evaluated by the community.[23] Later, when developing
social conditions brought a wider application of the form, it found frequent use in wisdom circles as a means of character-building as well as
teaching the pupil how to avoid social faux pas.[24]

Despite profound differences in their positions concerning the origin
of the form in question, both scholars nevertheless agree on its didactic
use. This conclusion would appear to confirm our earlier discovery that
YHWH's admonishment of Samuel (vs. 7) served not merely to redirect his
behavior, but also to instruct him with respect to the fundamental premise
underlying the divine right of selecting the king.

That the author's employment of an admonition for didactic purposes
is not an isolated phenomenon in 1 Samuel 16 may be confirmed by scrutiny
of the formulation with which the piece begins. Here an admonition is expressed through a rhetorical question introduced by the expostulatory ad-
verbial phrase ꜥad mātay (vs. la). Formally, statements prefaced in this
way censure particular acts or situations, whereas alternatives leading to
approved results are presented in a second clause constructed either as an
imperative or hypothetical sentence. Except for two occasions where this
form is used exclusively to convey a reprimand (1 Sam 1:14; Exod 10:3), the
remaining occurrences would seem to disclose a clear "didactic intent."[25]
The Pharaoh's advisers, for example, use a variation of the admonitory
rhetorical question to instruct him concerning the adverse effects of his
policy of resistance to Moses' demand (Exod 10:7). Wisdom herself (ḥokmôt,
Prov 1:22f.) censures the simpleton (pᵉtî) because her attributes are not

---

[22]Prov 1:8f.; 3:1f., 11f., 25f. (cf. 27-30), 31f.; 4:21f.; 6:25f.;
23:6f. (cf. 3-5), 20f. (cf. 31f.); 24:1f. (cf. 15, 17f.), 19f. (cf. 28f.);
25:6f. (cf. 8); 27:1 (cf. 10).

[23]E. Gerstenberger, Wesen und Herkunft des "Apodiktischen Rechts"
(WMANT 20, 1965) 130; [24]ibid., 128.

[25]H. Wolff, Amos' Geistige Heimat (WMANT 18, 1964) 8.

the object of his desires. At the same time, she offers for his serious reflection the hypothesis that by submitting to her discipline, the fool would not only acquire for himself her characteristic perspicacity (rûªḥ) and substance (dābār), he would also avoid destruction (Prov 1:32b).

In both of the foregoing examples the result of the articulation of this special form of admonition is to require the one addressed to make a determination of its validity by means of a rational evaluation of conduct undertaken in accordance with its recommendation. Since one of the primary aims of teaching is to effect this kind of intellectual response, we may conclude that the form in question can be used for specifically didactic purposes. YHWH's introductory address (vs. 1) appears to function similarly. By means of an admonishment and a command YHWH's speech introduces the theme of David's eventual supersedure of the old Saulide order. The necessity to act upon the divine injunction challenges Samuel first to resolve a conflict over the claim of divine authority with regard to a future event and the present fact of Saul's temporal power. We have seen how the prophet's initial response in effect challenged the validity of YHWH's admonitory address and thus his control of history (vs. 2a). It would appear that the information that YHWH had intended to communicate to Samuel had been rejected out of hand by the prophet on the basis of his own rational evaluation of the circumstance. As a consequence, Samuel's response precipitates the ensuing torah-units. If these considerations are valid, the didactic affinities of the admonitory formulation of the rhetorical question under consideration may be regarded as a secure conclusion.

When we turn to the proverb expressed in the second torah-unit (vs. 7b), no discussion is necessary in order to affirm its relationship to instructional literature. That it also functions didactically here seems to follow from the fact that it rationally establishes the main point of the admonition (vs. 7a), and furnishes the conceptual background against which the developments in vss. 14-23 are to be understood.

Finally, there occurs an especially revealing collocation of didactic elements in the delineation of what we have called the royal advisory session (vss. 15-19). Because a king's enlightened purposes and programs are the basis for the health and vitality of his people,[26] availability of reliable counsel to facilitate his decisions contributes to his capacity to exercise office effectively. When courtiers defend their analysis of a circumstance in connection with a recommendation for action, thus requiring the king's reasoned adoption or rejection of the proposed policy, the situation becomes in effect a specialized context for teaching. This is precisely the result of the servants' speeches before Saul. It must be observed, however, that whereas their remarks apply exclusively to his particular condition, the format in which the teaching occurs does not appear to be unique. Rather, it may be contended that the royal advisory session

---

[26]Pedersen, op. cit. (n. 13) 81, 86; de Boer, op. cit. (n. 15) 46, 47 n. 2, 50.

(1 Kgs 1:4b). The primary reason for this is the fact that the unsatis-
factory results of this advisory session serve as the literary premise of
the conflict over the royal succession subsequently to be reported
(1 Kgs 1:5ff.).[28]

The undeniable formal congruence of the foregoing examples may be explained as the literary precipitate of the practice of statecraft.[29]
Effective government required that counselors demonstrate expertise in
ascertaining and promulgating sound policies leading toward realistic and
attainable goals for the national welfare. In order to do this it was
necessary that they persuade the king to adopt their particular proposal
as against other possible courses of action. Accordingly, counsel became
partly a matter of instruction in order to teach the king to recognize the
validity of the counselors' insights. It may be argued, then, that the
literary form of the royal advisory session evidences didactic intent.
Accordingly, in connection with David's introduction to the court of Saul,
the form displays the same affinities as the other primary structural
elements of 1 Samuel 16. If this conclusion may be accepted, an important
question nevertheless remains unsettled. To what extent does the author's
employment of literary and conceptual elements appropriate to a teaching
milieu reveal his interpretation of the monarchy when he undertakes this
description of David's emergence into Israel's public life? To a consideration of this issue we now turn.

III

If structurally important literary features may be regarded as providing fundamental assistance in exhibiting the character of an author's
thought, then the use in our context of materials reflecting a didactic
background may be accounted for as follows. First, our earlier structural
analysis disclosed the fact that the author employed a triadic series of
divine toroth in order to reveal the identity of Saul's successor, how he
was chosen, and upon what authority his office rests. In this connection
we also saw that the counsel delivered by influential men of Israel was
intended to recommend David as an instrument for effective action leading
to the king's and the nation's well-being. In both examples it can be said
that the author employed didactic means in order to establish his interpretation of David as the man chosen both by God and the leaders of Israel
for their own respective, yet mutually related, ends.

Secondly, it may be contended that the use of literary features associated with teaching resulted from the author's intention to promulgate a
completely new understanding of the historical role of kingship and the
place it occupied in relation to YHWH. This interpretation is epitomized
by the speech of the anonymous servant when he presents Saul with a list
of recommendations certifying David's usefulness at court (vs. 18). It can

---

[28]Ibid.
[29]McKane, op. cit. (n. 15) 23ff.; see 2 Sam 16:20-22; 17:1-14.

represented a regularly established means to persuade a king to accede to
certain policies. These would be commended to him by his counselors who
would elucidate the results of their investigations into, and reflection
upon, matters of national consequence. This argument may be supported by
the striking parallels to be observed in an account whose function is very
much like the one under review.

The question of David's advancing age (1 Kgs 1:1-4) was one that carried with it serious consequences with respect to the maintenance of national stability, because the king's person was the central factor holding
together a tenuous political compromise. Without adequate preparation for
his senility, disability, or death, the disintegration of David's entire
political achievement would doubtless ensue. Nevertheless, the matter of
co-regency or the specific designation of a successor had not in fact been
officially determined, to judge from information presented in the narrative
as we have it. Preservation of his vitality, as especially demonstrated
through sexual potency,[27] was consequently necessary in order to preserve
order until such time as these other issues could be resolved. The delineation commences with an editorial announcement of the nature of the problem
(1 Kgs 1:1b), just as the problem of Saul's relation to the spirit had been
introduced (1 Sam 16:14). David's courtiers then proceed to advance a
specific proposal for the amelioration of the king's situation (1 Kgs 1:2).
This corresponds formally to Saul's servants' recommendation, except that
here the counselors do not preface it with a statement concerning the
nature of the problem. Just as the advisors had once suggested to Saul the
services of an anonymous individual whose skills would effect his relief
(1 Sam 16:16a; particularized in the servant's address, vs. 18a), so here
the $n^e\bar{c}\bar{a}r\hat{i}m$ forecast a resolution of David's crisis through the special
"qualifications" of a $na^c\bar{a}r\bar{a}h$ (1 Kgs 1:2a; particularized editorially, vs.
3b). Moreover, it is striking that in both narratives, the formal proposal
commences with the jussive of the root $bq\check{s}$ (1 Kgs 1:2a; 1 Sam 16:16a).
This implies that the king's sanction is required -- indicating his acceptance of the proposal -- in order that the counselors' teaching might become the basis of action. Whereas Saul enunciates a command (1 Sam 16:17b),
David here remains entirely passive. Additionally, it may be observed that
the physical appearance of the individual who is recommended to the king
becomes a matter of concern in both contexts ($y\bar{a}p\bar{a}h$, 1 Kgs 1:3a; $\hat{\imath}\check{s}$ $t\bar{o}'ar$,
1 Sam 16:18a). If we may assume that service in the royal court required
not only that the individual possess skills that would serve to the king's
advantage, but also that physical endowments were a matter of no less importance (cf. 1 Sam 9:2b; 10:23b); then these corresponding notices would
serve further to confirm the relationship between the two passages which
we have been considering. Accordingly, the royal advisory session appears
to have constituted a specialized occasion for teaching with its own formal
structure. This conclusion may be maintained even though it can be said
that the results anticipated by Saul's counselors were accomplished whereas
the advice to the aged David did not prove effective after its adoption

---

[27] J. Gray, I and II Kings, 2nd ed. (Philadelphia: Westminster,
1970) 77.

Expertise on the lyre, however, does not in itself substantiate the author's intention with respect to the interpretation of David's role, since it may be argued that anyone -- wise or foolish -- with normal motor reflexes could be taught how to play the instrument. Although this is generally true, it is our contention that the particular detail under review cannot be dissociated from the author's propensity to employ literary forms at home in didactic settings. David's musical skill has to do with effective action, an important consideration in instructional contexts. Moreover, when we evaluate this mention of David's musical dexterity in the light of one of the succeeding predications, the didactic intent of the author here would appear to be assured.

The description of David as n^{e}bôn dabār (vs. 18a) is found elsewhere only in contexts in which didactic concerns are paramount. In such instances the perspicacious and intelligent man (nābôn) is typically contrasted with one or another kind of fool (Prov 10:13; 14:6, 33; 15:14; 17:28; 19:25), although he can be specifically compared to or arrayed along with the wise man (Prov 16:21; 18:15; Qoh 9:11). An especially revealing association occurs in Proverbs 1:5, where the nābôn is said to acquire taḥbulôt, special skills for guiding one's way through the complexities and ambiguities of experience.[34] This is the conceptual aspect of wisdom having to do with shrewd, pragmatic, and decorous behavior in human company. It is the correlative of that dimension of wisdom which otherwise manifests itself on the technical level of experience.

There are occurrences of the term nābôn outside of the compass of proverbial collections which nevertheless demonstrate the same regular association with wisdom. On occasion the reference may be to individuals in authority or classes of men of rank (Deut 1:13; 1 Kgs 3:12; Isa 3:3; 5:21), or to the wise without more particular qualification (Deut 4:6; Isa 29:14; Jer 4:22; Hos 14:10). An especially illuminating association occurs in the scene where Joseph counsels the Pharaoh. Here the terms nābôn and ḥākām are juxtaposed in such a way that the latter becomes a more specific designation of the former. Joseph recommends that a man possessing these traits should be appointed as administrator of the agricultural policy he had formerly delineated (Gen 41:33). The Pharaoh does not hesitate to conclude that Joseph himself is the man with these very qualifications (Gen 41:39). It would appear that the attribute nābôn self-evidently constituted a recommendation of the highest order, especially when it was a question of the undertaking of grave responsibility. If this conclusion may be accepted, there is little reason to doubt that the same conception is reflected in the utterance of Saul's counselor about David, since the larger context also concerns the latter's appointment to high office. Moreover, it can be argued that there is no cause to suspect the servant's speech here of reflecting a background other than a didactic one, since elsewhere the term in question never occurs apart from this association. Accordingly, our claim that the author intended to present David as the wise man qualified to serve as Israel's king by describing him as nābôn seems to be warranted.

---

[34] Ibid., 421.

be observed that nothing in the list but the reference to David's musical ability has a corresponding basis in the narrative, with the possible exception of the predication 'îš tō'ar (cf. vs. 12a). The only unequivocal information pertinent to David's background are two notices concerning his experience as a shepherd (vss. 11a, 19b). These hardly suffice to commend him as a valorous, experienced soldier (gibbôr ḥayil wᵉ'îš milḥamah, vs. 18a). Accordingly, it may be concluded that the other notices have been placed in the counselor's mouth in order to support the author's interpretation of David. Since the advisor's speech at this point serves as a particularization of the counsel proffered to, and accepted by, Saul (vs. 17b), there would have been no need for him to present David in the "most favorable picture possible," in order to secure his acceptance.[30] The king had already shown himself committed in principle to the choice his servants would make for him. Hence, either the succeeding predications of vs. 18 must be considered gratuitous, or it may be contended that the content of the specific counsel here had a wider scope than the immediate context to which it has been applied. It would appear that the latter is the case when we observe that the servant's speech in many ways serves a didactic-thematic function in relation to the subsequent delineation of David's career.[31]

Aside from the obvious foreshadowing of David's military competencies (see 17:39ff.; 18:5, 7b), three of the predications issued by the servant disclose the fact that David is regarded as a divinely endowed wise man. At the same time, his supernatural gifts were construed as being perceptible to those who were wise in Israel, attested initially by Saul's counselor. First, it is suggested that David is the man fit for the task at hand by virtue of his musical accomplishment. There was in all periods[32] an underlying conceptual as well as practical association between "wisdom" (ḥokmāh, ḥakam lēb) and the mastery of some kind of technical skill (cf. Exod 28:3; 36:1f.). The reason for this is the fact that acquired dexterities presupposed discernment of the end for which the technique had been developed and the method of its accomplishment. The connection between wisdom and aptitude lay in the individual's capacity to analyze and then to master what comprised the requirements necessary for the control of the limited range of experiences in question. This consisted in the recognition of certain patterns and sequences, real and merely apparent possibilities, and similar observations. The skillful man was one who had discovered a kind of "order."[33] His capacity actually to subjugate the particular field of experiences served then as verification of his "insights." "Wisdom" thus became the precondition for the occurrence of certain kinds of manual actions. Conversely, execution of certain deeds objectively attested the prior possession of "wisdom."

---

[30]Hertzberg, op. cit. (n. 14) 141.
[31]Cf. Grønbaek, op. cit. (n. 1) 72.
[32]Contra G. von Rad, Weisheit in Israel (Neukirchen-Vluyn: Neukirchener Verlag, 1970) 77.
[33]Idem, Old Testament Theology I (New York and Evanston: Harper and Row, 1962) 421f., 428, 435.

The foregoing contention receives additional support when we observe that the phrase n^{e}bôn dābār reflects an intellectual context in which great importance was attached to the ability to engage in effective speaking. Egyptian texts have furnished evidence that indicates that scribes there considered this capacity to represent one of the chief purposes of their intellectual and vocational training.[35] It was the aspiration of the pupil eventually to attain to a position of influence, prominence, and respect as a functionary in some agency connected with the operation of the royal court. In order to achieve this goal it was necessary for him to master certain fundamental intellectual and practical skills. But more importantly the pupil was aware that success depended heavily upon his ability to acquire a reputation as a man of sound insight and reliable counsel, because it was precisely these capacities that would recommend him to superiors. Although the training itself aided in the development of his natural perspicacity and provided him with a fund of knowledge, success finally was contingent upon the pupil's ability to argue his policies intelligently and persuasively. If action based upon his reasoned advice led superiors consistently to profitable results, the consequent record of proven suggestions would enhance the scribe's reputation, assure the demands for his services, and correspondingly increase his chances for promotion to higher levels of responsibility at court. Hence, to become an eloquent and sagacious speaker was an ideal to which virtually every apprentice of the Egyptian scribal profession aspired.

These remarks appear to explain Joseph's success, as we have earlier observed. As one whom the Pharaoh could identify as a wise man (nābôn w^{e}hākām, Gen 41:33a, 38) through his eloquence and accordingly promote to the highest possible office, it can be said that Joseph epitomized the Egyptian scribal ideal.[36] In this connection, accordingly, it does not appear to be fortuitous that David is described as n^{e}bôn dābār -- "powerful in speech" as von Rad appropriately understands the phrase.[37] Curiously, in our context David says nothing. Nevertheless, as in Joseph's experience, it later becomes evident that David's success is in no small measure dependent upon the same educational and rhetorical skills which -- however the affinities may be explained -- Egyptian scribes valued as essential to the successful counselor. This may be observed on several subsequent occasions where his speeches before Saul are unsurpassed in their well-reasoned outline, clear purpose, and persuasive force (see, e.g., 17:34ff.; 24:10ff.; 26:18ff.). It would appear, then, that the servant's description of David serves as a literary prolepsis of these occasions. At the same time, it functions as a declaration that David possesses the qualifications of the effective wise man, according to the view of a royal counselor who, because of his status, was competent through his training to render a sound judgment on the matter.

---

[35] Ibid., 431; idem, "Josephsgeschichte und ältere Chokma," VTSup 1 (1953) 121f. = Ges. Stud. (München: Kaiser, 1961) 274; idem, "Die ältere Weisheit Israels," KD 2 (1956) 64.

[36] Idem, Genesis (Philadelphia: Westminster, 1961) 371; cf. E. Otto, "Bildung und Ausbildung im alten Aegypten," ZÄS 81 (1956) 46.

[37] Von Rad, op. cit. (n. 33) 430.

If the foregoing conclusion is correct, it may appear odd that an author would represent David as a wise man without crediting him with the kind of formal instruction that attainment of such a status normally requires. However, the conclusion of the servant's address to Saul furnishes evidence that the author conceived of David's endowments in this connection as the result of the gift of YHWH. Just as the spirit had been granted to David simply as a consequence of the divine election (vs. 13a), so here the servant offers no further corroboration of David's attributes and accomplishments save the declaration, YHWH ^cimmô (vs. 18b). That this must be regarded as more than a pious commendation can be supported by the following considerations.

Use of the phrase "Nn (nomen dei) is with ... " in extra-biblical royal inscriptions (appropriately adjusted to context) suggests that it had a long history as a means of attesting to divine grace. It most often occurs in connection with a regent's claim to have been installed in, and authorized to execute, the office of kingship by one or more deities.[38] Their "being with" the king accordingly was viewed as providing the security of the throne against all opposition.[39] Moreover, the gods' unfailing presence was understood to sustain and bless the king's efforts to realize the purposes with which they had graciously entrusted him.[40]

The phrase YHWH ^cimmô as applied to David in the present context seems to express the idea "successful issue." In light of the aforementioned royal inscriptions, notice of the accompanying presence of YHWH here will hardly occasion the expectation of David's failure. Nor does the ensuing denouement of the narrative furnish any reason to suspect the accuracy of this connotation of the phrase in question. On the other hand, further evidence of the nuance "successful issue" occurs elsewhere in a somewhat different manner. At various intervals in the narrative of David's career, the phrase is enunciated by individuals who -- probably uttering the author's sentiments -- by this means attest to David's steady progress in his attainment of the throne (17:37; 18:12, 14 cf. 28; 20:13; 2 Sam 5:10).[41]

Thirdly, YHWH ^cimmô serves as an affirmation concerning the special character of God's historical activity. In a recent study, H. Preuss has discovered that the formula originally had to do with God's promise to accompany, protect, and lead individual patriarchs in their wanderings.[42] The experience of YHWH's guidance and protection along the way prevented these journeys from becoming merely aimless pursuits. Instead, they represented stages leading toward ends which YHWH had already established. One of the ways in which these purposes in history were realized occurred

---

[38] zkr 202 A 3, apud H. Donner und W. Röllig, Kanaanäische und aramäische Inschriften I (Wiesbaden: Harrassowitz, 1962) 37; pnmw 214/2, ibid., 38.
[39] zkr 202 A 14, ibid., 37; pnmw 214/3, ibid., 38; see ibid. II (1964) 217.
[40] pnmw 214/3f., cf. 8, ibid. I 38.
[41] With appropriate contextual adjustment; cf. Grønbaek, op. cit. (n. 1) 79.
[42] H. Preuss, "'...ich will mit dir sein!" ZAW 80 (1968) 152f.

through the direction and support which YHWH provided for particular men, matched by their faithful response.[43]   Consequently, to say "YHWH is with" someone is to assert that the individual in question is engaged in executing God's historical designs.[44]   This is precisely what the author asserts about David through the mouth of the servant. For this introductory predication accurately describes what David subsequently accomplishes. When he arrives at Saul's court he exercises control over those forces adversely affecting the king and thereby brings about a state of šalôm which Saul is unable to achieve for himself. If it is the author's intention to exhibit David as the divinely outfitted wise man, as we have argued, a more fitting illustration could not have been chosen. For the wise man, through discernment and expertise, must above all be effective. He must be able to make an objective difference wherever resolution of an ostensibly intractable conflict is required. David's wisdom is equal to the task. Moreover, since David has received these qualities as a divine gift to further the divine purpose, the character of his first public act augurs well for the success which is later shown to accompany all of his undertakings.

IV

The author has depended heavily upon conceptual and literary elements of his intellectual background in order to formulate an introduction to the narrative of David's early years. In the presentation he has articulated three expository "principles" through which the new experience of Israel under the Davidic monarchy may be interpreted. Their delineation is essential for a satisfactory clarification of certain ambiguous ideological considerations.

The first of these is that David's election and authorization are founded upon the promulgation of YHWH's torah. David's exercise of office depends upon the explicit will of the God of Israel, and not, in the first instance, upon his own self-interest or the sanction of men. Secondly, however, the author advances the "principle" that this divine torah concerning David can be objectively verified. The man of YHWH's choosing possesses at the same time qualifications for service distinguishable by those who are capable of making the appropriate evaluations, namely, Israel's scribes or wise men. Accordingly, the author -- probably himself a member of this class -- utilized literary forms and themes associated with a didactic milieu in order to convey this idea. In this way he also bestows the highest tribute upon David. Because he is portrayed not merely as a wise man, but one who exhibits divine endowments at the same time, David embodies in his own person the verification of the formerly proclaimed torah. Thirdly, as the reason for this, the author establishes what may be termed the "principle" of successful issue. David cannot be censured for ruling on the basis of manipulation of unauthorized temporal power. Rather, YHWH guides history according to his purposes and David simply works to realize these ends

---

[43]Ibid., 154 157.   [44]Ibid., 156, 158.

through faithful response. David's successes -- his creating a new life and a new future for Israel and all that these entail -- attest historically what YHWH has all along purposed for the blessing and fulfillment of his people.

RHETORICAL CRITICISM AND THE SONG OF HANNAH

A. David Ritterspach

Elizabethtown College

For nearly two decades, Professor Muilenburg has concerned himself with what is being called with increasing
frequency "rhetorical criticism,"[1] a special type of form
criticism which is interested primarily ". . .in exhibiting
the structural patterns that are employed for the fashioning
of a literary unit, whether in poetry or in prose, and in
discerning the many and various devices by which the predications are formulated and ordered into a unified whole."[2]
The Song of Hannah in I Sam 2:1-10 yields considerable meaning when subjected to such an analysis utilizing the principles which Muilenburg has made clear in articles and in
the classroom.

Text and Context

As is the case with many passages in I Samuel, the text
of the pericope before us is problematical in a number of
instances. The translation presented below incorporates the
following emendations:

vs. 3a. Delete the second gbhh which is unnecessary for the
meaning of the line since it is a repeated word. In 4QSam[a]
from Qumran the line appears without the second gbhh.

vs. 3b. Here the present wl' ntknw 'llwt makes very little
sense as it stands. The reading of the LXX (kai theos etoi-
mazōn epitēdeumata autou) suggests emendation as follows:
w'l tkn 'llwt ("a God who discerns deeds").

vs. 5a. The last two words of the line (ḥdlw 'd) could be
amended to ḥdlw 'bd ("they shall cease to work"). However,
the passage is clear if 'd is read with the next line: "even
the barren one gives birth to seven."

---

[1] James Muilenburg, "Form Criticism and Beyond," JBL
LXXXVIII (1969) 1-18; "The Linguistic and Rhetorical Usages
of the Particle in the Old Testament," HUCA 32 (1961) 135-60;
"A Study in Hebrew Rhetoric: Repetition and Style," Vetus
Testamentum Supplement I (1953) 97-111; "The Terminology of
Adversity in Jeremiah," Translating and Understanding the Old
Testament (Nashville, 1970), chapter 2.

[2] Muilenburg, "Form Criticism and Beyond," 8.

vs. 10a. mryrw should be amended to the plural form as suggested in Qere. Yahweh is the subject of the line, and yhtw
should be amended to the singular, yht. The second colon of
this line, 'lw bšmym yr'm, is difficult to translate without
amending 'lw. Various emendations are possible such as 'lywn
("the most high")[3] or 'lh ("he ascends"),[4] which would then
allow one to translate, "Yahweh it is who. . .ascends into heaven
and thunders." However, in the Psalms 'ly is translated as a
divine name, on the basis of Ugaritic parallels, by Dahood.
Hence, in Ps 7:9 we read šptny yhwh kṣdqy wktmy 'alay. The
final word, which is difficult to render, is re-vocalized as
'elî - an identical form to that in Ugaritic where both 'ly
and 'l appear as divine name or theophoric element. Ps 7:9
then reads admirably: "Judge me, O Yahweh, according to my
righteousness, according to my integrity, O God."[5] With that
in mind, 'lw in the passage before us can be most simply explained as a corruption of 'ly (vocalized 'elî), and the bicola would read, "Yahweh shatters his enemies, God thunders
against them in the heavens."

The extent of the passage is readily seen since it is a
poetic unit in the midst of a prose passage, which describes
Hannah's fervent petition to the priest at Shiloh that she
might bear a child. Her prayer is granted, and in response
she offers her thanksgiving and praise to God in a "song."
The relationship of this Song to its present context is, however, tenuous. Scholars have noted with good reason that the
Song was probably added to the original account by a second
had. In the LXX the verse immediately following the song
(I Sam 2:11a) reads, "She left him there in the presence of
the Lord and returned to Ramah. . ." This verse combines 1:28b
and 2:11a of the MT in such a way as to suggest that the Song,
which separates 1:28 and 2:11 in the MT is not original. The
two verses, read in succession, follow one another quite
naturally. Furthermore, the content of the Song, although
appropriate enough to Hannah, nevertheless goes considerably
beyond her situation in its references to a king (vs. 10).
The Song was undoubtedly originally used in a quite different
context but seemed appropriate in the Hannah-Samuel narrative because of the reference to a barren woman (vs. 5).

---

[3]Karl Budde, The Books of Samuel (Leipzig, 1894), 53.

[4]D. August Klostermann, Die Bücher Samuelis und der
Könige (Nördlingen, 1897), 5.

[5]Mitchell Dahood, Psalms I (The Anchor Bible; Garden City,
New York, 1966), 45.

The Song of Hannah

1. Hannah prayed, saying,
   "My heart exalts in Yahweh; my horn is lifted up before Yahweh.
   My mouth cries out against my enemies, for I rejoice in thy salvation.
2. There is no one holy as Yahweh, for there is none beside thee, and no rock like our God.
3. Do not go on arrogantly; may not arrogance come forth from your mouth,
   For Yahweh is a God of knowledge, a God who discerns deeds.

4. The bows of the mighty are smashed, but those who stumble have gathered strength.
5. Those who are filled shall hire themselves out,
   but those who hungered have ceased.
   Even the barren one gives birth to seven,
   and she who bore many is without.
6. Yahweh kills and brings to life, he brings down to Sheol, and he raises up.
7. Yahweh dispossesses and makes rich; he brings down, yea, he exalts.
8. He raises up the poor from the dust, and the needy he raises from the dung heap,
   to place them with the nobles, and to take possession of the throne of the mighty,
   For to Yahweh belong the corners of the earth, and he places the world upon them.

9. The feet of his faithful he protects, and the wicked he casts into darkness,
   For not by strength does man prevail.
10. Yahweh shatters those who contend with him; God in the heavens thunders against them.
    Yahweh judges the ends of the earth. He gives strength to his king.
    And he exalts the horn of his anointed."

Strophic Divisions

The division of the Song into strophes is essential if one is to comprehend the development of meaning through the passage. Strophic divisions are usually to be identified with new themes or ideas set forth by the poet.[6] Thus, vs. 4 begins with contrasting statements concerning the fate of the rich and the mighty on the one hand and those without any means on the other. Again in vs. 9 a new departure is taken as the poet concludes his poem on the theme of Yahweh's judgment and the deliverance of the faithful. On thematic considerations alone the Song divides into three strophes: vss. 1-3, "Salvation of the Faithful"; vss. 4-8, "Yahweh's Actions";

---

[6]Muilenburg, "Form Criticism and Beyond," 13.

vss. 9-10, "Yahweh's Judgment." The first and third strophes
are of equal length, being five lines each.

Not surprisingly the strophic division is marked by the
use of key words in strategic positions. The last line of
strophes one and two is an exclamation of the sovereignty of
Yahweh who knows all deeds (vs. 3b) and who founded the earth
(vs. 8b). Each of these two lines is introduced by the climactic and exhortative ki, an entirely fitting conclusion to
each of the two strophes because the ki clause provides the
reason or the basis for the claim that is made in each strophe.

Among the strophes the second one (vss. 4-8) is unique
and forms a convincing unit, although it is admittedly rather
long. The strophe is almost entirely given over to antitheses,
in which the fate of those who have succeeded and those who
have failed in life is contrasted: "The bows of the mighty"
versus "those who stumble"; "the barren" versus "she who
bore many children"; and "the needy" versus "the mighty." In
each case Yahweh has reversed the fortunes of the two groups,
as indeed he changed Hannah's fortunes from barrenness to
child-bearing.

As is typical of Hebrew poetry, the first and last strophes are very similar although not identical. The conclusion
repeats the beginning of the hymn by speaking once again of
the blessing that falls upon the faithful one. In the concluding strophe this person is the king, Yahweh's "anointed"
(vs. 10c) whereas when the poem opens the faithful one is the
speaker, or Hannah. It is difficult to resolve such a difference, and we have here evidence that the hymn originated
in a very different (and royal) context. In both the first
and third strophes, the nature of Yahweh is stressed, yet
with certain differences in each case. In the first strophe,
the statements are general and God is defined in negative
terms: "there is none holy as Thee, for there is none beside
Thee and no rock like our God" (vs. 2). By contrast in the
final and climactic strophe the verbs are in the active mood
and certain specific actions are very forcefully stated to
define the divine being: "Yahweh shatters. . .thunders. . .
judges. . ." In both strophes it is God's nature - his holiness and justice - that provides the basis for the speaker's
confidence that Yahweh will sustain the faithful and visit
his judgment upon those who contend with him.

All three strophes are remarkably similar in structure.
In each case the strophe begins by focusing on man's situation but then turns to a promise of God. Hence, the motifs
of thanksgiving for the blessings of salvation on the one hand
and praise of God on the other are intimately connected. In
strophe one, the speaker exults in the blessing accorded her
(vs. 1) and then turns to a praise of God (vs. 2) followed
by a warning against arrogance which is also predicated on an
exclamation of Yahweh's greatness. Strophe two begins (vss.
4-5) with contrasting statements on man's fate followed by
unequivocal claims of God's sovereignty over all events, for

"to Yahweh belong the corners of the earth and the world. . .
upon them" (vss. 6-8). A similar statement about man's condition and praise of God occurs in strophe three where the
faithful (ḥsydw) and the evil ones (rs'ym) are assigned their
respective fates, followed by a tribute to Yahweh, who judges
all and exalts his "messiah" (vss. 9-10).

The overall form which the present song takes is difficult to define in any final way because the Song seems to lie
somewhere between a hymn and a song of thanksgiving. That it
may partake of both is not surprising; Westermann has pointed
out[7] that psalms often combine a report of God's deeds (as
in songs of thanksgiving) with description of his greatness
and glory (the hymns). Such a phenomenon is to be found in
the passage before us. Like the typical hymn, the Song of
Hannah has three sections: the introduction, body, and conclusion. Typically the introduction is a call to praise of
God, but here joy of the worshipper is expressed instead.
The body of the hymn most often states the reason for praise,
as is done in vss. 4-8 of the present work. The conclusion
repeats the summons to praise in most hymns, whereas the
focus in the last strophe of this Song is a climactic prayer
that Yahweh may bless his anointed one. The hymn expresses
thanksgiving to Yahweh as one would expect in a song of thanksgiving but the references remain surprisingly general. Typically one difference between a song of thanksgiving and a
hymn is that the former cites specific items for which one is
thankful. The present hymn does not do this but also spends much
time in describing the nature of God. Yet, of course, its
overall mood is that of thankfulness.

The closest parallel to the Song of Hannah is Ps 75 which
has elements of the song of thanksgiving in it but is most
appropriately viewed as a cult liturgy.[8] The psalm begins
with reference to prior testimony in the cult concerning the
history of God's deeds among them. Then the psalmist proceeds
to contrast the sorry fate of those who would oppose God (vss.
2-8) with the blessings visited upon the faithful. This motif of contrast is but one of the clear parallels between
Ps 75 and the Song of Hannah. Another motif in common is that
of warning. The psalmist warns against arrogance (vs. 4) as
does the author of I Sam 2. Much of the imagery is identical:
God makes firm the pillars of the earth (vs. 3b; cf. I Sam
2:8c); he breaks off the horns of the wicked, but exalts the
horns of the faithful (vs. 10; cf. I Sam 2:1, 10c).

Key Words

As already noted the word ki is used to climax both the

---

[7]Claus Westermann, The Praise of God in the Psalms (Richmond, 1965), 18.

[8]Arthur Weiser, The Psalms (The Old Testament Library;
Philadelphia, 1962), 521.

first and second strophes. It appears two other times in the
initial strophe (1c, 2b) so that the use of ki in this strophe
has a cumulative effect: In the first instance the ki clause
speaks of Hannah; in the second instance the ki clause defines
God but in a negative way. Finally, as the climax of the
strophe the ki clause speaks of Yahweh in the most inclusive
terms as a "God of knowledge" who knows all of man's deeds.
Another important term in the Song is qrn ("horn"), which
stands at the beginning and ending and ties together very
effectively the initial praise to God with the final note of
his blessing upon the "anointed one." An even more crucial
word is rwm ("to exalt") which is used four times in the Song.
It appears with qrn in the first and last strophe as part of
the emphasis on God's salvation for his faithful servant. As
part of the increasing intensity of mood in the Song, the subject for the verb changes from that which is exalted, i.e.
the speaker, to "Yahweh" as the subject followed by the Hiphil
of the verb (v. 10c). Meanwhile in the second strophe this
verb occurs twice (vss. 7-8) in reference to Yahweh's exhal-
tation of the down-trodden and the oppressed. The use of this
verb repeatedly in the Song highlights the basic theme of
God's acts that reverse the normal processes and establish
those whom he favors.

The verb htt ("shatter") is one of the most powerful in
the Song. It appears twice in similar contexts. The first
instance is vs. 4 where the weapons of the mighty "are shattered" by Yahweh; similarly in vs. 10 God shatters or destroys those who contend against him. The use of the same verb
in both strophes (also true of rwm and of gbr, of 'rs, and
yhwh) serves to connect the two strophes intimately and remind
us of deliberate progression of thought. The second strophe
makes clear Yahweh's deeds. The God of history stands behind
all events; he shatters some, sustains others. He deprives
and makes rich. He elevates the poor and brings low those
who "are at ease in Zion." Yet this could be seen as quite
arbitrary and indiscriminate, for no particular rationale is
given. When we move then into strophe three the rationale
becomes explicit. It is the faithful who are blessed. They
are the poor and the needy who now are sustained by God. And
it is the mighty and the rich whom God has judged and found
wanting (vs. 10). Therefore, they are shattered and deposed,
as stated in both strophes.

The second strophe only points to God's jurisdiction over
the entire world in the very last line: "for to Yahweh belong
the foundations of the earth; he places the world upon them."
This theme is given special prominence, however, in the last
strophe, which builds on the closing note of the previous one.
The key word 'rs in this instance is first used in vs. 8c and
then is repeated in vs. 10b as the climax of the Song is reached.
A blessing upon the speaker among the Israelites, with which
the Song began, culminates in a much larger vision - that of
God's judgment on the entire world and the establishment of
his messiah to whom all should turn.

Conclusion

Consideration of the form, internal structure, and key words of the Song of Hannah makes clear its place among the psalms of the Bible as a powerful and passionate statement of God's sustaining power. The Song unfolds its praise of Yahweh in proclamations that move from general statements of his nature through claims that his hand lies behind all events, to thanksgiving for his blessings extended to those who are faithful to him. The majesty and power of Yahweh is never expressed in bland philosophical statements but instead is conveyed in the most forceful verbs: God exalts; he shatters; he brings down and raises up; he thunders.

And yet the Lord of the universe is also the gentle One who cares for the least powerful of his creation. He feeds the hungry, nourishes the poor, reverses the fortunes of the barren one, and exalts those who are without station and power in life. Yahweh's intervention to lift the curse of barrenness is a recurring theme in the Bible (Gen 18:14, 25:20-21; 29:32; Luke 1:36), and thus it is not surprising that the editor of the Samuel narrative would find available a psalm containing that theme for use in his account of the birth of Samuel. Hence, the birth itself of Israel's great leader is put in the theological context of God's acts which alter the course of history and - what is equally important - the course of individual lives. With the exception of the last verse the Song is entirely believable as the kind of thanksgiving that Hannah, grateful for the gift of a son, would have uttered. The Song reaches the level of the most significant kind of scripture: that which is a profound theological statement and at the same time intensely personal and human. Those who know him cannot help but be reminded that this is also the way in which James Muilenburg touches our lives. He presents a profound understanding of the subject matter of the Bible combined with great sensitivity for the stirrings of the soul. Rarely have the scholar and the pastor been so intimately combined as in his person.

THE RAPE OF TAMAR

A Rhetorical Analysis of 2 Sam 13:1 - 22

George Ridout
109 Bolinas Avenue
San Anselmo, California 94960

Among the literary phenomena which the rhetorical critic of the
Bible scrutinizes in carrying out his task, probably foremost is the
phenomenon of repetition. The study of repetitive styles has always been
a concern of James Muilenburg, and he outlined for us some twenty years
ago[1] the various functions of repetition in the Old Testament.

The passage which we will look at illustrates well the importance of
an analysis of instances of repetition by anyone who wishes to understand
the craft of the Hebrew story teller. We will begin with the relatively
simple task of identifying repeated words and phrases. But then we must
move on to the more subjective and central assignment, that of understanding and describing the patterns which we assert our author has consciously
utilized in shaping his narrative. This latter task must remain somewhat
tentative, for only after numerous pericopes such as ours have been inves-
tigated may the students of rhetorical criticism venture to specify the
rules governing Hebrew literary composition.

The brief account of the rape of Tamar contains no less than 11
repetitions of the word "brother" ('aḥ) and eight of the cognate word
"sister" ('aḥôt). A few of the occurrences of these words are quite
conventional. For example, there is nothing unusual in that Tamar and
Amnon address each other as "my brother" and "my sister" (vss. 11-12),[2]
and similarly Absalom could quite naturally address Tamar as "my sister"
(vs. 20). Nor may we assign any importance to the presence of the words

---

1. James Muilenburg, "A Study in Hebrew Rhetoric: Repetition and Style,"
VTS 1 (1955) 97-111. Sensitivity to the elaborate possibilities of Hebrew
repetitive patterns has been characteristic of Muilenburg's exegetical
studies. See especially "Introduction and Exegesis to Isaiah, Chapters
40-66," IB V; "The Intercession of the Covenant Mediator," Words and
Meaning, eds. P.R. Ackroyd and B. Lindars (Cambridge: Cambridge University,
1968) 159-81; "A Liturgy on the Triumphs of Yahweh," Studia Biblica et
Semitica. Theodoro Christiano Vriezen Dedicata (Wageningen: H. Veenman en
Zonen, 1966) 233-51.

2. Absalom and Tamar were full brother and sister, while Amnon was their
half brother. Cf. 2 Sam 3:2-3.

"brother" and "sister" at the onset of the story (vss. 1-2), as here they are necessary to explain the familial relationship of the <u>dramatis personae</u>.

But even excepting all these instances of the words 'aḥ and 'aḥôt, there are still many occurrences of the terms, and these we find to be of rhetorical importance for the passage. In this regard, consider particularly the following:

I love Tamar, the <u>sister</u> of Absalom, my <u>brother</u> (vs. 4)

Go to the house of your <u>brother</u> Amnon (vs. 7)

And Tamar went to the house of Amnon, her <u>brother</u> (vs. 8)

And she brought them to Amnon, her <u>brother</u>, in the chamber (vs. 10)

Absalom hated Amnon for having raped Tamar, his <u>sister</u> (vs. 22)

With all of these examples the Hebrew word 'aḥ or 'aḥôt follows a proper name, be it Tamar, Amnon or Absalom, and therefore is redundant for purposes of character identification.

In the same manner, notice the accumulation of these sibling terms at the point at which Absalom confronts his violated sister:

And Absalom, her <u>brother</u>, said to her, "Has Amnon, your <u>brother</u>, been with you? Now keep this to yourself, my <u>sister</u>; he is your <u>brother</u>; do not take this to heart". So Tamar remained, desolate, in the house of Absalom, her <u>brother</u>. (vs. 20)

We must ask then if perhaps the repeated use of the words 'ah and 'ahot is a deliberate device of the narrator, a stylistic method for conveying his point of view of the events he is describing for us. Looking at the opening verses of the story, we note that all of the persons involved in this sordid tale are within David's immediate family, and that this <u>datum</u> is carefully and emphatically impressed upon us in the introduction:

Now Absalom, the <u>son</u> <u>of</u> <u>David</u>, had a beautiful <u>sister</u>... and Amnon, the <u>son</u> <u>of</u> <u>David</u>, loved her... But Amnon had a friend named Jonadab, the <u>son</u> <u>of</u> <u>David's</u> <u>brother</u> Shimeah; and Jonadab was a very crafty man. And he said to him, "Why are you so haggard looking day after day, O son of the king?" (vss. 1-4)

With his initial stress on the kinship of all the characters, followed by frequent use of the key words "brother" and "sister" as the plot unfolds, our narrator stresses most effectively upon his listener that this is a story of David's family, and how it came about that this royal family started on a tragic course of self-destruction. Amnon's lust for his half sister eventuates in her loss of virginity and thereby any possibility of hope for the future, even though she is the king's beautiful daughter.

Amnon's deed severs his kinship relation to Tamar, as is skillfully noted by our narrator. Before the rape, he has Amnon address Tamar as "my sister" ($^{a}\underline{h}\hat{o}t\hat{\imath}$ -vs. 11), but afterward has him refer to her impersonally as "this thing" ($\underline{'et}$-$z\bar{o}'t$ -vs. 17). Absalom hates his brother for what he has done, and eventually will kill him. And that act in turn leads to a break between Absalom and his father, culminating in still further tragedy.

Finally we notice David's role in the story. Throughout the Succession Narrative,[3] David is portrayed as a father who is unable to control his own sons. So too in our passage (reading with the fuller text of verse 21 as it is preserved in the LXX):[4]

When King David heard of all these events, he became very angry. But he did not trouble his son Amnon because he was his first-born and he loved him.

Is not this weakness displayed by the father ultimately responsible for the disasters which come to the royal family here and throughout the Succession Narrative? Indeed, does not our narrator portray David as the unwitting accomplice of both Amnon's and later Absalom's purposes, so that the sons are shown as repeating the father's original acts of lust and murder (2 Sam 11-12)?[5] It is David who sends Tamar to Amnon (vs. 7). And later David acquiesces, with reluctance, to Absalom's insistent demand that Amnon come to the sheepshearing festival at which Absalom plans to have him killed (2 Sam 13:24-27). Even after the murder of Amnon, David continues to be ineffective as a father, as his son later foments rebellion and threatens even to take David's crown.

The kinship relation of the characters involved in this appalling story is impressed upon the audience in the repetitions of the words "brother" and "sister". By means of this simple compositional device our author communicates to us in a convincing and poignant manner the

---

3. 2 Sam 7, 9-20; 1 Kgs 1-2, the corpus established by Leonhard Rost, Die Ueberlieferung von der Thronnachfolge Davids (Stuttgart: W. Kohlhammer, 1926).

4. A scribe could have overlooked the missing portion of MT by allowing his eye to skip to the second wl'.

5. Cf. Walter Brueggemann, "Life and Death in Tenth Century Israel," JAAR 90 (1972) 105.

rending apart of the royal house.[6]

Let us look briefly at another repeated word, this time the hithpael of the verb ḤLH, "to be sick", occurring three times in our passage (vss. 2, 5 and 6). Careful scrutiny of the manner in which this word is employed gives us further insight into the narrator's attitude toward his subject matter. In vs. 5 Jonadab suggests that Amnon lie on his bed and <u>pretend</u> to be ill.[7] He is then to use this illness as an excuse for requesting Tamar at his bedside. But the same verb has already been used with reference to Amnon's condition at the very beginning of the story (vs. 2) and at that point there was no pretense involved. There Amnon is said to be literally sick of desire for Tamar.[8] The two nuances of the verb, that of feigned illness and that of actual sickness, convey the irony which our author has seen in the situation. It is Amnon's manifest ill appearance which leads Jonadab to ask of Amnon, "Why are you so haggard looking day after day, O son of the king?" (vs. 5). With what ironic ease Amnon is then able to carry out Jonadab's instructions!

And so Amnon lay down and pretended to be ill. And the king came to him and he said, "Let Tamar my sister come to me..." (vs. 6)

Climactically here, the verb functions to describe both the false and the true sickness. Amnon's physical appearance is both feigned illness, intended to deceive his father and sister, and yet it is also his true love sickness of desire for Tamar.

Repetition is also utilized in our story as a technique to retard the progress of the narrative and thereby heighten suspense for the audience. Our author informs us with his first words of Amnon's great affection for his half sister (vss. 1-2) and of Jonadab's plan for getting Tamar to Amnon's side (vs. 5). The narrative could proceed quite rapidly

---

6. One should compare the use of the key word 'aḫ with very similar effect in the story of Cain and Abel. Perhaps the best statement of the function of a key word in a passage is that offered by Martin Buber, "Leitwortstil in der Erzählung des Pentateuchs," <u>Werke</u> II (Munich: Kösel, 1964) 1131:

> Unter Leitwort ist ein Wort oder eines Wortstamm zu verstehen, der sich innerhalb eines Textes, einer Textfolge, eines Textzusammenhangs sinnreich wiederholt: wer diesen Wiederholungen folgt, dem erschliesst oder verdeutlicht sich ein Sinn des Textes oder wird auch nur eindringlicher offenbar.

Similarly for Muilenburg, "A Study in Hebrew Rhetoric," 99. Cf. also Charles Lohr, "Oral Techniques in the Gospel of Matthew," <u>CBQ</u> 23 (1961) 422-24.

7. On this sense of the hithpael, cf. <u>GKC</u>, para. 54e.

8. Note the felicitous rendering of Roland de Vaux, <u>Les livres de Samuel</u>. <u>La Sainte Bible</u> (Paris: Editions du Cerf, 1961): "Amnon était tourmenté au point de se rendre malade à cause de sa soeur Tamar."

from this opening to a description of the actual encounter of Tamar and
her brother, and that would be fully in keeping with Hebrew narrative
style. But in the interest of dramatic effect, our author delays his
arrival at the climactic point of the story. The technique used to
achieve this retardation is a series of requests followed by detailed
descriptions of the execution of those requests.[9] This pattern of
request and report of its accomplishment is really a sophisticated form
of repetition. Each use of the pattern allows the author to linger over
his story and increase the suspense. First Jonadab describes his
proposal to Amnon:

> Lie on your couch and pretend to be ill, and when your father comes
> to you, say to him, "Let Tamar my sister come and give me bread to
> eat, and prepare food before me, that I may see and eat from her
> hand." (vs. 5)

The suggestion is carried out, and reported in full detail:

> And Amnon lay down and pretended to be ill. And the king came to
> see him and Amnon said to the king, "Let Tamar my sister come and
> bake two cakes before me, that I may eat from her hand." (vs. 6)

David in turn commands Tamar:

> Go to the house of Amnon your brother, and prepare food for him. (vs. 7)

Tamar heeds her father's command, goes to Amnon's house, and prepares
food. At this point the narrative becomes even more expansive, introducing
details of no particular importance to the basic plot, but of great
rhetorical effect in serving to increase the suspense:

> So Tamar went to the house of her brother Amnon, where he was lying
> down. And she took the dough and kneaded it and she prepared the cakes
> before him and baked them. She took the pan and turned them out before
> him. But he refused to eat. (vss. 8-9)

Now come further repetitions:

> And Amnon said, "Send everyone outside." And everyone went outside.
> (vs. 9)

---

9. Within the Succession Narrative, the same technique is employed in
1 Kgs 1:5-31, based there on the rhetorical question, "Who will sit on
the throne of David after him?" A discussion of the passage is included
in this writer's 1971 Graduate Theological Union dissertation, "Prose
Compositional Techniques in the Succession Narrative."

And still another command and report of its accomplishment:

> And Amnon said to Tamar, "Bring the food into the inner room and I
> will eat from your hand." Tamar took the cakes which she had made
> and brought them to Amnon her brother in the inner room. (vs. 10)

Yet a sixth request:

> But when she brought them near him to eat, he seized her and said,
> "Come, lie with me, my sister." (vs. 11)

But at this the turning point of the story the chain of command and
ready agreement, adhered to until this moment, is broken. Tamar refuses
this last request and pleads with Amnon, but he forces her.

A further repetitive pattern in our passage is structural, and
elegantly organizes the entire story in a chiastic form. We need to
consider the parts of this structure in detail.[10]

In element A (vss. 1-4) the three major participants in the drama,
Absalom, Amnon, and Tamar, are all introduced:

> Now Absalom, the son of David, had a beautiful sister, and her name
> was Tamar. And Amnon, the son of David, was in love with her. (vs. 1)

Then the motivation for the action to follow is suggested:

> And Amnon was tormented to the point of illness over Tamar his sister,
> for she was a virgin and it seemed impossible to Amnon to do anything
> to her. (vs. 2)

The conclusion of the story, element A' in our scheme (vss. 20-22), neatly
complements its beginning. As at the opening of the pericope, descriptive
narrative rather than dialogue predominates. There is no action or movement at either place. It is as though our author wishes us to step back
both before and after the action to take notice of the characters and
their emotional feelings toward each other. In closing the account, the
status of the major characters is described. Now the obsessive _love_ (vss.
1-2) of Amnon for his sister is gone, but in its place there is now
Absalom's intense _hatred_ of his brother (vs. 22). Tamar, utterly shattered,
lives in Absalom's house. Amnon's father is _angry_ with him but does
nothing because of his _love_ for his first-born son (vs. 21). Absalom will
not even speak to his brother, so abhorrent is he to him.

---

10. The apparent functions of chiastic arrangement are to stabilize the
material enclosed, to enable a story to better resist changes in the course
of transmission, and to provide a pattern which makes more likely the
recall of elements of the whole. Within the Succession Narrative, other
chiastic units are present in 2 Sam 11:20-21, 15:30, and 16:5-14.

CHIASTIC STRUCTURE

A. Amnon is in love with Tamar (vss. 1-4)

   B. Tamar comes to Amnon's house and bakes
      bread for him (vss. 5-9a)

      C. Amnon orders his servants out, that
         he might be alone with Tamar (vss. 9b-10)

         D. Amnon commands Tamar to come lie with
            him; she pleads with him but to no
            avail (vss. 11-14a)

            E. Amnon rapes Tamar, and his love
               for her turns to hate (vss. 14b-15a)

         D'. Amnon commands Tamar to get out;
            she pleads with him but to no avail
            (vss. 15b-16)

      C'. Amnon calls a servant back and orders
         him to lock Tamar out (vs. 17)

   B'. Tamar leaves Amnon's house, mourning her
      fate (vss. 18-19)

A'. Absalom hates Amnon for having raped Tamar
     (vss. 20-22)

If elements A and A' describe emotions of the characters, elements B and B' share in common an ambulatory motif. Element B (vss. 5-9a) of the chiasm relates how Tamar comes to Amnon, while element B' (vss. 18-19) tells of her departure from his house. In contrast to the rather concise statements with which the story opens and closes, at these two points of the structure the narrative slackens its momentum. We have already discussed the expansive style of writing which greatly delays the moment of Tamar's encounter with her brother. Her departure from him following her rape balances that earlier scene relating her arrival. Again the narrator lingers over the scene by specifying details, and the pace slows considerably. Tamar's dress is described and then she rends it in her grief; the once beautiful woman places ashes on her head and wails aloud.

Progressing further toward the center of the chiasm, we meet balanced scenes involving Amnon's servants. When Tamar arrives at Amnon's side, the presence of his servants is the one remaining obstacle to his plan. Their removal from the room precipitates the deed which follows almost immediately (C - vs. 9b). Similarly, following the rape Amnon would attempt to restore his normal circumstances. This he accomplishes by summoning a servant back and commanding him to cast the object of his contempt from the room (C' - vs. 17). In both places Amnon issues orders, fully in control of the situation.

On either side of the apex of the chiastic structure are identically constructed scenes (D - vss. 11-14a and D' - vss. 15b-16). The pattern followed in both is as follows: 1) Amnon orders Tamar to do something 2) she refuses, replying with great eloquence 3) he ignores her plea. In the first scene Amnon commands her, "Come, lie with me, my sister," while in the second scene he coldly tells her to "Get out." In both scenes Tamar begins her plea with the words "No, my brother"[11] and then continues with her reasons, introduced both times with ki. In neither episode does Amnon reply to her pleading. We simply have the narrator's comment that "he would not listen to her." We display now the common elements of these scenes:[12]

---

11. We read 'al-'aḥî kî at verse 16 with Lucian's recension of the LXX. MT is untranslatable. For the less crucial variations in the rest of verse 16 between Lucian and Vaticanus, see S.R. Driver, Notes on the Hebrew Text and Topography of the Books of Samuel (2nd. rev. ed.; Oxford: Clarendon, 1913) 299. The Lucianic recension frequently provides a superior reading to MT of the Succession Narrative. Cf. Driver's comments, xlviii-li.

12. As documented in my dissertation, the author of the Succession Narrative characteristically varies repeated phrases by introducing synonyms, omitting and adding words, or altering the word order. The slight variations in matching parts of these two scenes illustrate this principle nicely.

D - verses 11-14a   D' - verses 15b-16

wayyō'mer lāh   wayyō'mer-lāh 'amnôn

  bô'î šikbî ʿimmî 'ᵃhôtî   qûmî lēkî

wattō'mer lô   wattō'mer lô

  'al-āḫî 'al-tᵉʿannēnî kî---   'al 'aḫî kî

wᵉlō' 'āḇā lišmōᶜa bᵉqôlāh   wᵉlō' 'āḇā lišmōᶜa lāh

The rape takes place at the very center of the chiastic structure
(E - vss. 14b-15a). The whole story builds to and falls away from this
act, but it is only briefly noted, as our narrator is more interested in
the psychological and dramatic aspects of the event. Immediately following
the deed the author interjects a comment on the reversal of Amnon's
attraction to Tamar; his obsession with her, finally satisfied, has now
turned to revulsion:

And Amnon hated her with a very great hatred; the hatred with which
he hated her was greater than the love with which he loved her. (vs. 15)

The inversion of emotions reported here highlights the series of
contrasts upon which the entire chiastic structure has been built. The
beautiful Tamar comes innocently to her brother (B), but leaves with
her life ruined (B'). Amnon pushes his servants out **th**at he might be
alone with Tamar (C), but then calls one back to dispose of her (C').
Amnon's coaxing his sister into a private room with him (D) contrasts
diametrically with the curt manner in which he dispatches her after
satisfying his lust (D').

The major contrast is of course that of love ('HB) and hate (ŚNH).
This theme appears strikingly at the extremes (A and A') and the center
(E) of the chiasm. The narrative pivots about the comment by the author
in verse 15a, which itself begins with a chiastic word order:

wayyiśnā'eh**ā** 'amnôn śin'ā gᵉdôlā mᵉ'ōd kî gᵉdôlā haśśin'ā 'ᵃšer śᵉnē'āh

   a   b   c   c'   b'   a'

mē'ahᵃbā 'ᵃšer 'ᵃhēḇāh.

On the basis of our passage, certainly it can be said that rhetorical
criticism of the Old Testament can yield us much in the way of insight
into Hebrew mentality. The task lies largely before us, but the goal, in

Muilenburg's words, is significant:

> a responsible and proper articulation of the words in their
> linguistic patterns and in their precise formulations will
> reveal to us the texture and fabric of the writer's thought,
> not only what it is that he thinks, but as he thinks it.[13]

---

13. Muilenburg, "Form Criticism and Beyond," *JBL* 88 (1969), 7.

STYLE IN ISAIAH 28 AND A DRINKING BOUT OF THE GODS (RS 24.258)

Jared Judd Jackson

Pittsburgh Theological Seminary

The scholar and teacher whom we honor with these papers has long been interested in the aesthetic appreciation of literary style in the OT,[1] and in the question of the appropriate use of possible parallels to biblical passages.[2] His concern for these matters continues,[3] and his most recent contributions to the understanding of Israel's prophets incorporate his deep insights into the problems which continue to puzzle us.[4] Encouraged by Professor Muilenburg's example, I offer this brief study of Isa 28.

Attempts to explain the form and structure of Isa 28 usually involve assumptions as to the literary history of the chapter and the compilation of the entire book. Since Bernhard Duhm's monumental commentary,[5] it has been customary to set aside vs. 5-6 as a later promise, and to view the farmer's parable in vs. 23-29[6] as distinct from the main body of the chapter.[7] I take it that the major problems presented by the chapter remain:
  a) the relation of vs. 1-4(5-6) to the rest of the chapter;
  b) the relation of vs. 7-13 to vs. 14-22;
  c) the integrity of vs. 16, 17, and 18; and

---

[1] J. Muilenburg, "The Literary Approach - The Old Testament as Hebrew Literature," _Journal of the National Association of Biblical Instructors_ 1 (1933) 14-22.

[2] "The Gains of Form Criticism in Old Testament Studies," _ET_ 71 (1959/60) 229-233.

[3] Introduction to the translation of Gunkel's _The Psalms_ (Philadelphia: Fortress, 1967) v; "Form Criticism and Beyond," _JBL_ 88 (1969) 1-18, esp. p. 9.

[4] "The Terminology of Adversity in Jeremiah," _Translating and Understanding the Old Testament_ (eds. H. T. Frank & W. L. Reed; Nashville: Abingdon, 1970) 42-63; "Baruch the Scribe," _Proclamation and Presence_ (eds. J. I. Durham & J. R. Porter; Richmond: J. Knox, 1970) 215-238.

[5] _Das Buch Jesaia_ (HKAT III/1; 5th ed.; Göttingen: Vandenhoeck & Ruprecht, 1968) 196.

[6] C. Westermann, _Basic Forms of Prophetic Speech_ (Philadelphia: Westminster, 1967) 201 calls it a disputation (Streitgespräch); R. B. Y. Scott, _IB V_, 321, says "it more closely resembles the 'riddles' or proverbial 'dark sayings' of the sages..."

[7] J. Muilenburg, "Isaiah, Book of," Hasting's _Dictionary of the Bible_ (rev. eds. F. C. Grant & H. H. Rowley; New York: Scribners, 1963) 427.

d) the meaning of the "covenant with Death" in vs. 15, 18.[8] Another attempt to break through the impasse posed by these questions can be justified by 1) pursuit of a novel or neglected methodology, in this case the study of Hebrew style[9] as advocated in Dr. Muilenburg's Presidential Address to the Society of Biblical Literature,[10] and by 2) adduction of a pertinent extra-biblical parallel.[11]

I

A most neglected aspect of the study of the Hebrew prophets has been the appreciation of their poetic diction, however this last be understood. Quite apart from the vexed question of Hebrew metrics, which seems no closer to solution than ever,[12] or from the observance of "fixed pairs"[13] and the

---

[8] The solution to the problem of the origin of saw lāsāw etc. in vs. 10 and 13 has been given to my satisfaction by W. W. Hallo, "Isaiah 28, 9-13 and the Ugaritic Abecedaries," JBL 77 (1958) 324-338. It has been recently proposed by G. Pfeifer ("Entwöhnung und Entwöhnungsfest im Alten Testament: der Schlüssel zu Jesaja 28:7-13?" ZAW 84 [1972] 341-347) that in the shocked silence which greeted Isaiah's outburst (vs. 7-8), one could hear the teacher reciting and his pupils repeating the sounds of the letters of the alphabet in the nearby school for sons of priests, who after being weaned (v. 9) would begin their vocational training (cf. 1 Sam 1-2). Whereupon the priests and cult-prophets gave Isaiah to understand that his message was as primitive as the occupation of the schoolmaster, who stood behind his beginners, correcting their initial writing efforts with "here a little (longer on the vertical stroke), there a little (more on the hook)," v. 10.

[9] See especially L. Alonso Schökel, "Die Stilistische Analyse bei den Propheten," VTSup 7 (1959) 154-164; Estudios de Poética Hebrea (Barcelona: Juan Flors, 1963).

[10] "Form Criticism and Beyond."

[11] "After the establishment of the Gattung, with a determination of the formal laws governing its composition, and the Sitz im Leben, with the discovery of the concrete situation in which the words were spoken, Gunkel adduced parallels from other parts of the Old Testament and the Near Eastern literatures. It is significant in the light of later study to observe how much he was aware of the influences from Canaan as well as of Egypt and Mesopotamia," J. Muilenburg, "The Gains of Form Criticism," 229.

[12] S. Segert, "Vorarbeiten zur hebräischen Metrik I & II," ArOr 21 (1953) 481-542, 25 (1957) 190-200.

[13] S. Gevirtz, Patterns in the Early Poetry of Israel (Chicago: University of Chicago, 1963). But see P. C. Craigie, "A Note on 'Fixed Pairs' in Ugaritic and Early Hebrew Poetry," JTS 22 (1971) 140-143, answered by W. G. G. Watson, "Fixed Pairs in Ugaritic and Isaiah," VT 22 (1972) 460-468, who lists 46 sets of words common to Ugaritic literature and Isa, of which only nine are in reverse sequence (466). Yayin // šēkār Isa 5:22; 24:9; 28:7; 29:9; 56:12 are among the latter, while Isa 5:11-12 shares the order škr // yn given in UT 601:3-4, 16; 2 Aqht:I:31-32; and 2 Aqht:II:19-20.

significance this phenomenon may have for our understanding of oral composition,[14] too little attention has been paid to the prophets as masters of the techniques of poetry.[15] Alonso Schökel's work[16] stands almost alone in modern study of the prophets. König's and Gábor's[17] earlier contributions, though still valuable, are more of a rebuke to us than a present help. We need to learn from the intensive study of the poetry of modern languages, and the advances which have been made in literary criticism in recent decades.[18] Especially, we need to observe the felicitous use of the sounds of Hebrew consonants, and where possible, of the syllables, by the prophets.[19] Isaiah's celebrated poetic excellence owes a great deal to his mastery of assonance,[20] alliteration and repetition,[21] as may be shown from almost any passage.[22] Chapter 28, with the famous saw lāsāw, qaw lāqāw, offers an excellent sample of his style.

To begin with, we may agree that the major sense units within the chapter are vs. 1-6,[23] 7-13, 14-22, and 23-29.[24] It is clear from even a casual glance,

---

[14]R. C. Culley, Oral Formulaic Language in the Biblical Psalms (Toronto: University of Toronto, 1967).

[15]J. Muilenburg, "Poetry," Hasting's Dictionary, 778-780.

[16]See note 9; and J. Blenkinsopp, "Stylistics of Old Testament Poetry," Bib 44 (1963) 352-358.

[17]E. König, Stilistik, Rhetorik, Poetik (Leipzig: T. Weicher, 1900); I. Gábor, Der hebräische Urrhythmus (BZAW 52; Giessen: Töpelmann, 1929).

[18]R. Wellek & A. Warren, Theory of Literature (3d ed.; New York: Harcourt, Brace & World, 1963) is still a good introduction to the whole field.

[19]J. Muilenburg, "Old Testament Prophecy," Peake's Commentary on the Bible (rev. eds. M. Black & H. H. Rowley; London: T. Nelson, 1962) 475-483. See also the brief section on Technique in N. K. Gottwald, "Poetry, Hebrew," IDB K-Q, 835.

[20]P. P. Saydon, "Assonance in Hebrew as a Means of Expressing Emphasis," Bib 36 (1955) 36-50. Gottwald, "Poetry," mentions Isa 1:18-20 as an outstanding example of alliteration.

[21]J. Muilenburg, "A Study in Hebrew Rhetoric: Repetition and Style," VTSup 1 (1953) 97-111.

[22]E. g., Isa 25:6. Here is alliteration in the strict sense, as well as deliberate repetition and alteration of [s̆] and [m] sounds. The effect is unmistakable.

[23]On any theory of "composition," vs. 5-6 belong with vs. 1-4, rather than to what follows.

[24]The "farmer's parable" is left out of account here; it is not part of the basic structure of this chapter. See now J. W. Whedbee, Isaiah and Wisdom (Nashville: Abingdon, 1971) 51-68.

however, that the chapter is held together not only by the flow of its subject matter or content but also by the repetition of key words in prominent positions and by the phenomenon of inclusion.[25] The first sense-unit is connected with the second by yayin v. 1 and v. 7 (bis), šikkōrê vs. 1, 3 and šēkār v. 7 (tris), yiblāᶜennāh v. 4 and niblᵉᶜû v. 7 and by hinnīᵃh v. 2 and hānīhû v. 12. The second and third units are connected by hāᶜām hazzeh v. 11 and v. 14, and by yābîn šᵉmûᶜāh v. 9 and hābîn šᵉmûᶜāh v. 19.[26] The first and third are joined by bārād vs. 2 and 17, by sōtᵉpîm v. 2 and sōt sōtēp vs. 15 and 18, and yištōpû v. 17.[27] Inclusion is represented by hāzāq v. 2 and yehzᵉqû v. 22, and by 'anšê lāsôn v. 14 and 'al titlôsāsû v. 22.

Within each sense unit there is far greater use of the poetic devices of rhyme,[28] assonance and alliteration. In the first section, the hôi[29] is clearly to be taken as anacrusis.[30] This leaves a tricolon of 6+4+4 in v. 1.[31] Note the deliberate sounds of final taw (cᵃteret gē'ût), the rhyming of 'eprayim and hᵃlûmê yāyin,[32] the alliteration and assonance of sîs and sᵉbî, the similarity

---

[25] M. Dahood, "Ugaritic-Hebrew Syntax and Style," UF 1 (1969) 15-36.

[26] Possibly also by wᵉgam 'ēlleh v. 7 and zō't....wᵉzō't v. 12.

[27] Perhaps also by tērāmasnāh v. 3 and lᵉmirmās v. 18.

[28] G. Fohrer, Introduction to the Old Testament (Nashville: Abingdon, 1968) 49 cites Isa 7:11 and 31:9.

[29] Most recently, J. G. Williams, "The Alas-Oracles of the Eighth Century Prophets," HUCA 38 (1967) 75-91; W. Janzen, 'Ašre and Hôi in the Old Testament, Harvard Ph.D. dissertation, 1970.

[30] T. H. Robinson, "Anacrusis in Hebrew Poetry," Werden und Wesen (BZAW 66; Berlin: Töpelmann, 1936) 37-40.

[31] Moving hᵃlûmê yāyin to follow 'eprayim, with E. J. Kissane, The Book of Isaiah (Dublin: Browne & Nolan, 1941) I, 313f.; R. B. Y. Scott, IB V, 314. The words are parallel to "drunkards of Ephraim," but make no sense in their present position, where they cannot follow gē' šᵉmānîm, which are not in construct relation with them. This remedy is better than dropping the words as a gloss (most recently, P. R. Ackroyd, Interpreter's One Volume Commentary (ed. C. M. Laymon; Nashville: Abingdon, 1971) 348); or moving them to v. 2 (H. Donner, Israel unter den Völkern, VTSup 11 (Leiden: Brill, 1964) 75-76; or inserting kaᶜᵃteret (O. Procksch, Jesaia I (KAT IX; Leipzig: Deichert, 1930) 347); or dropping gê' šᵉmānîm (R. Kittel, Biblia Hebraica, editio altera (Leipzig: J. C. Hinrichs, 1909) II, 585.

[32] See previous note.

of the roots of 'eprayim and tip'artô, and the repetition of ' and š in 'ašer ᶜal rō's gê' sᵉmānîm.[33] Verses 2 (4+4+3) and 3 (3+4) alternate long, slow cola with short, quick ones. The [m] sounds in 2bα (kᵉzerem mayim kabbîrîm sōṭᵉpîm) form a striking contrast with the harsh, sharp effect of 2bβ (hinnîᵃh lāʾāreṣ bᵉyād);[34] likewise the energic tᵉrāmᵉsannāh[35] and its introductory prepositional phrase bᵉraglayim in 3a make a chiastic balance with 2bβ as the balance point of this first section, so that 3b and 4a, which repeat 1 in large measure, may lead into the climactic simile of the early fig (4b). The latter is distinguished by assonance and alliteration in the phrase 'ašer yeʾᵉreh[36] hārōʾeh 'ōtāhh and by the repetition of mappîq,[37] kᵉbikkûrāhh...'ōtāhh bᵉᶜôdāhh... yibbōl ᶜᵉnāhh.[38]

Verses five and six are carefully joined to the preceding by means of a new use of the words ᶜaṭeret, ṣᵉbî and tip'ārāh (cf. Jer 48:17), together with sᵉpîrāh "chaplet, wreath, crown,"[39] so as to adapt the metaphor concerning doomed Samaria to YHWH's promised protection for his remnant.

---

[33] I cannot agree with Sir Godfrey Driver's revival of the suggestion to read gᵉ'ê sᵉmānîm. G. R. Driver, "'Another Little Drink' - Isaiah 28:1-22," Words and Meanings (eds. P. R. Ackroyd & B. Lindars; London: Cambridge University, 1968) 47-67, 48-50; cf. NEB. The suggestion obliterates the reference to the walls of Samaria, which will collapse as swiftly as a reveler's garland fades. Nor is the semantic transition of √g'h 'surging, proud; muddy' to 'streaming' made clear in Professor Driver's stimulating article.

[34] Cf. Amos 5:7; for the force of bᵉyād, see 2 Sam 23:6; Ezek 12:7.

[35] Liber Jesaiae (ed. D. W. Thomas; BHS 7; Stuttgart: Württembergische Bibelanstalt, 1968) 40.

[36] Driver, "'Another Little Drink'," 50, accepts Houbigant's emendation of yir'eh, to obtain "he who sees it plucks it." The suggestion is in line with the principle of the textual critic, lectio difficilior praestat, yet it restores meaning to the passage.

[37] As in Isa 5:14.

[38] BHS, and Driver, "Drink," 50. This slight change restores the inclusion with v. 1, permits a legitimate translation of bᵉᶜôdāhh ("as soon as" RSV is hardly right), and continues the mappîq series and the long ō sounds. We should understand ᶜayin as "appearance, color," as in Lev 13:55, and translate "its appearance withers." This seems more likely than the meaning "bloom, bud" proposed by Driver, 51, on the basis of Syriac and Greek.

[39] This rare word is rendered by LXX as stephanos, but at Ezek 7:4 (=MT 7:7) and 7:10 LXX omits the phrase; Theodotion in both Ezek vs., and Aquila, Codices Alexandrinus & Marchalianus in v. 10 have plokē, "braid(ing)," probably on the basis of the Isa passage. T. Gaster, JBL 60 (1941) 298 explains the word in Ezek as "the cyclic point," comparing klb spr in Krt 123, 127.

The second section, vs. 7-13, is characterized by a deliberate use of
sounds to emphasize the vivid picture of a drunken orgy. In v. 7 there are
six verbs using the ā, û sequence,[40] with niblecû[41] in the center as balance.
The series of prepositional phrases[42] followed by verbs is reversed once the
subject (kōhēn wᵉnābî') is mentioned; the verse is concessive, "even these...;"[43]
wᵉgam 'ēlleh does not refer back[44] to the drunkards of Ephraim, or to any subject
now missing, but forward to the priest and prophet mentioned for the first time.[45]
Verse eight, the climax of the prophet's reproach[46] or development of the
accusation,[47] introduced by asseverative kî[48] "surely, truly, indeed," uses
the words qî' and sō'āh which are then taken up in the famous reply by the
insulted revelers, in the form of the initials s and q.[49] This speech, quoted
without introduction,[50] is a rebuke to the prophet for his unwelcome words.[51]
It employs repetition, a simple end-rhyme,[52] assonance (a and e in the accented

---

[40]pāqû is assimilated to this pattern, GKC #72 l.

[41]√blᶜ III "be confused" in Niphal; cf. Piel Isa 3:12; 19:3; Pual 9:15;
J. Barth, Beiträge zur Erklärung des Jesaia (Karlsruhe & Leipzig: H. Reuther,
1885) 4-5; KB 131; HALAT 129.

[42]pᵉlîlîyāh does not need a preposition, pace BHS footnote; either one is
to be understood on the "double duty" principle, cf. M. Dahood, Psalms III
(AB 17A; Garden City: Doubleday, 1970) 436, or it is omitted in order to avoid
cacophany of bp, GKC #118g.

[43]GKC #160b; R. J. Williams, Hebrew Syntax (Toronto: University of
Toronto, 1967) #382, 529.

[44]The similar passage in Isa 49:15 is an exceptional case.

[45]GKC #136a; Williams, Syntax #113.

[46]R. B. Y. Scott, "The Literary Structure of Isaiah's Oracles," Studies
in Old Testament Prophecy (ed. H. H. Rowley; Edinburgh: Clark, 1957) 175-186,
180.

[47]Westermann, Basic Forms, 170.

[48]Williams, Syntax #449; J. Muilenburg, "The Linguistic and Rhetorical
Usages of the Particle kî in the Old Testament," HUCA 32 (1961) 135-160.

[49]See n. 8 above.

[50]H. W. Wolff, Das Zitat im Prophetenspruch (Beiheft 4 EvT; München:
Chr. Kaiser, 1937) 20, cited hereafter as Gesammelte Studien zum Alten Testament
(Theologische Bücherei 22; München: Kaiser, 1964) 47.

[51]Cf. Amos 2:12; 7:12-13, 16; Hos 9:7; Mic 2:6; Jer 11:19, 21; 18:18; 20:10.
Wolff, Zitat, 48-49.

[52]Wolff, Zitat, 65, mentions Isa 22:13 with its alliteration; also
Jer 8:20.

syllables of the counter-questions, v. 9b) and alliteration (four m sounds in as many words). The quote-within-a-quote, v. 10, is signalled by recitative kî, "For (he says only)...,"[53] and is answered by adversative kî, "Nay, rather..."[54] This chiastic announcement (with alliteration in a and b') that YHWH will henceforth address "this people" with heteroglot[55] oracles[56] leads into an answering quotation, whose features balance the drunkards' speech. Their taunting mockery of Isaiah's teaching is thrown back in their teeth, as in Isa 30:15-16. The final consequences of God's intervention are summed up in v. 13b in a striking series of assonant verbs.[57]

The third and final section with which we shall be concerned, vs. 14-22, opens with a complaint[58] against the scoffers,[59] summoning them to hear YHWH's dābār. The scene has shifted from Samaria to Jerusalem, where the rulers utter parabolic sayings,[60] one of which is then quoted as a development of the accusation against them.[61] This boast, which unites the type we may call "we have taken appropriate precautions" with the type "nothing can hurt us," each of which has a number of parallels in the prophetic books,[62] includes the famous 'covenant with Death,' to which Hos 13:14 seems almost YHWH's reply. The boast begins with chiasmus in the opening statement, and continues in the result clause with assonance (five ō sounds), employs simple end-rhyme (-Cēlnû six times), and closes with alliteration (sibilants in all five of the closing words).

---

[53]Williams, Syntax #452.

[54]GKC #163b; against Duhm, Jesaia, 198 ("elliptic"), followed by Wolff, Zitat, 10, n. 7.

[55]1 Cor 14:21, in S. Paul's quotation of the passage.

[56]Cf. Jer 5:15, to be reversed in Isa 33:19.

[57]Cf. Isa 8:15.

[58]Scott, "Literary Structure," 179.

[59]Cf. Prov 29:8.

[60]Jarchi: "qui dicunt verba irrisionis parabolice," cited by R. Lowth, Isaiah (Boston: W. Hilliard, 1834) 276. Cf. Donner, Israel, 151. But probably the word is to be taken in both senses.

[61]Westermann, Basic Forms, 170-176.

[62]First type: Isa 9:9; Amos 6:13; Hos 12:9; and esp. Isa 30:15-16, where the boast is turned against the boasters, as in 28:13. Second type: Isa 29:15; Amos 9:10; Mic 3:11; Jer 14:13, 15; 23:17. This has become direct defiance of YHWH in Hos 10:3 (where Israel's leaders kārōt berît); Isa 5:19; Jer 5:12-13; 12:4; 17:15; 18:12; compare the boasting of the king of Assyria, Isa 10:8-11, 13-14.

YHWH's response in v. 16, introduced by the usual announcement formula, is a promise of a "sign"[63] rather than the threat we expect. There is no reason to regard the verse as a late insertion, however, since the promise becomes a threat in v. 17 (w^eśamtî mišpāt l^eqāw) which picks up the closing summary of the boast (śamnû kāzāb maḥsēnû) in v. 15b,[64] itself a rejection of the promised sign in v. 12.[65] Note the deliberate repetition in YHWH's promise (v. 16),[66] and how the threat (v. 17a) re-defines the key word laqaw of vs. 10 and 13. The announcement of YHWH's intervention in vs. 17b-19, which refutes the proud boast of v. 15, climaxes in astounding alliteration (v. 19, seven beths in five words) and a case of assonance with end-rhyme z^ewā^cāh, š^emû^cāh.

The unit closes with the quotation of a proverbial saying (v. 20),[67] the citation of YHWH's ancient deeds[68] as earnest of his determination to intervene once more, to carry out his mysterious plan.[69] Finally, the prophet warns the scoffers (v. 22)[70] that their chains (!) could be tightened, for YHWH has revealed to him his determination to destroy the whole land.

It is no accident that sections two and three are as carefully structured as section one. In the second section, vs. 7-13, an opening verse describes the inebriated and ineffectual priests and prophets, while a second verse (8) describes the revolting scene of their orgy. Then they are

---

[63] Cf. v. 12 and 7:1-9, 10-17; Westermann, Basic Forms, 187.

[64] kāzāb as "idol" in Amos 2:4; šeqer as "the Lie" (idol) in Jer 13:25, J. Bright, Jeremiah (AB 21; Garden City: Doubleday, 1965) 95; sēter in a similar context in Deut 13:7; 27:15.

[65] Cf. W. Eichrodt, "Prophet and Covenant: Observations on the Exegesis of Isaiah," Proclamation and Presence (see n. 4 above) 167-188, 180-181.

[66] The literature on this verse is enormous: e.g. T. O. Lambdin, "Egyptian Loan Words in the Old Testament," JAOS 73 (1953) 148; J. Lindblom, "Der Eckstein in Jes. 28:16," Interpretationes ad Vetus Testamentum pertinentes S. Mowinckel septuagenario missae (eds. N. A. Dahl & A. S. Kapelrud; Oslo: Land og Kirke, 1955) 123-132.

[67] Cf. Hos 4:9a, 14b; J. Jackson, "Yahweh v. Cohen et al.," Pittsburgh Perspective 7 (1966) 28-32.

[68] As in Isa 9:3; 10:25-26; Amos 4:11.

[69] Cf. Isa 5:12, where the drunkards ignore YHWH's deeds.

[70] w^e^cattāh introduces a challenge to serve YHWH alone, as in Exod 19:5; Josh 24:14.

quoted (9), and in turn they quote Isaiah (10). But YHWH has already addressed them (vs. 11-12), and their refusal to heed his words leads to a turning back of their quote against them, with a brief line on the final consequences (13). Mirroring this structure is the third section, vs. 14-22, which opens with a call to the scoffers (14), a quotation of their words (15), YHWH's promise (16), which in turn contains a quotation hamma'^amîn lō' yāhîs,

and is followed by YHWH's announcement (vs. 17b-19) which turns back the boasters' words. The proverb (20), historical reminiscence (21) and final warning (22) complete the unit.

CHART

vs.	Section Two			Section Three	vs.
7	description of drunks	a	h'	call to scoffers	14
8	scene of orgy	b	c'	Quote: scoffers	15
9	Quote: drunks	c	f'	Quote: YHWH's promise	16abα
10	Quote w/in quote: Isa	d	d'	Quote w/in quote: YHWH	16bβ
11	threat: foreigners	e	e'	threat: justice	17a
12	Quote: YHWH's promise	f	g'	Quote turned against	17b-
				the speakers	-19
13a	Quote turned against	g		[Proverbial saying	20]
	the speakers		b'	scene of battle	21
13b	final consequences	h	a'	description of YHWH's	22
				intervention	

Thus the poet's careful use of various stylistic devices, and deliberate structuring of his strophes, matches and bodies forth the prophet's oracles, so that Muilenburg's dictum, 'the proper articulation of form and structure leads to a fuller understanding of content,' once again proves its worth.

II

The interpretation of this text remains somewhat obscure. It is still not clear that the bitter satire on the drunkards (vs. 7-13) has much to do with the threat to the scoffers (vs. 14-22) and the consequences. Fortunately, the background of the whole text can now be elucidated by reference to the literature from Ras Shamra, together with the citation of more familiar Israelite literature.

To begin with, it is clear that the theme of drunkenness and senseless debauchery is dominant throughout Isa 28:1-22. The use and abuse of alcohol is not an unusual motif in the OT, but it is handled in different ways. There are many references to the provision of wine as a staple, and especially as a stimulant for those in distress or exhaustion.[71] There are also

---

[71] E.g. Judg 9:13; 2 Sam 16:2; Ps 104:15; Prov 31:6-7; Eccl 2:3; 9:7; Sir 31:28; 40:20.

references to the proper use of wine at festal times and in connection with the cult.[72] But abuse was frequent, and the drunkard who knew not what he did or what was done to him became a repeated motif in Israelite narrative.[73] There are corresponding passages in the prophetic literature which accuse the Israelites of debauchery, either cultic[74] or secular (esp. of the leaders of Israel).[75] The wisdom writers repeatedly warn against the excesses of drink, usually in the brief, pointed style of the proverb.[76] But there are also more extended treatments of the subject, including satire.[77] This latter genre seems to compare closely with Isa 28:7-8, and with the recently published Ugaritic text RS 24.258.

This fascinating but difficult text, which has already attracted a number of studies[78] since its editio princeps,[79] is unclear in a number of details but certainly includes the account of a banquet for the gods at which El drinks to satiety, becomes hopelessly drunk and has to be helped home, where he encounters or envisions (delirium tremens?) a creature with horns and tail, and finally falls in his own excreta. This last vivid detail reminds

---

[72]E.g. Lev 23:13, 37; Deut 14:26; 1 Sam 1:9, 24; 10:3.

[73]Gen 9:20-23; 19:32-38; 1 Sam 25:36; 2 Sam 11:13; 13:28; 1 Kgs 16:9; 20:16; Hos 7:5; Joel 1:5; Esth 1:10; 7:2; Jdt 12:20; 13:2; Sir 31:29; cf. UT 1 Aqht:I:210-224. Note how many of these references involve women who gain the upper hand by getting the man drunk; an ancient theme.

[74]Hos 4:11, 18; Amos 2:8; Mic 2:11.

[75]Isa 5:11-12, 22; Jer 13:13; 23:9; Amos 4:1; 6:6; Hab 2:5.

[76]Prov 20:1; 21:17; 23:19-21; 31:4-5; Eccl 10:16-17.

[77]Prov 23:29-35.

[78]S. E. Loewenstamm, "Eine lehrhafte ugaritische Trinkburleske," UF 1 (1969) 71-77; J. C. de Moor, "Studies in the New Alphabetic Texts from Ras Shamra," ibid. 167-175; H-P. Rüger, "Zu RS 24.258," ibid. 203-206; B. Margulis, "A New Ugaritic Farce (RS 24.258)," UF 2 (1970) 131-138; J. C. de Moor, "B. Margulis on RS 24.258," ibid. 347-350; L. R. Fisher, "New Readings for the Ugaritic Texts in Ugaritica V," UF 3 (1971) 356; Loewenstamm, "msd," ibid. 357-359; F. C. Fensham, "The First Ugaritic Text in Ugaritica V and the Old Testament," VT 22 (1972) 296-303; M. H. Pope, "A Divine Banquet at Ugarit," The Use of the Old Testament in the New and Other Essays (ed. J. M. Efird; Durham, N. C.: Duke University, 1972) 170-203.

[79]Ch. Virolleaud, "Les nouveaux textes mythologiques et liturgiques de Ras Shamra (XXIVe Campagne, 1961)," Ugaritica V (MRS 16; eds. J. Nougayrol, E. Laroche, C. Virolleaud, C. F. A. Schaeffer; Paris: Imprimerie Nationale, 1968) 545-551.

us of Isa 28:8; but more important for our purposes is the mention of the place where or company with which El sat down to drink. The latter is a marziḥ, and there has been a spate of literature concerning this term recently,[80] especially now that a new text has re-opened the discussion.[81] The word may be rendered "club," which in English can refer both to a voluntary association and the building where its members gather.[82] The word appears only twice in the OT, Amos 6:7 and Jer 16:5.[83] In the former, the term comes at the end and climax of a skilfully worded diatribe against the indolent ruling class, who are warned that their noisy banquets are at an end (sār mirzah sᵉrûḥîm). In the latter, Jeremiah is forbidden to marry and beget children, since YHWH will no longer permit decent burial of the dead in the land which his people have defiled. They are not any longer to resort to the "house of mourning," the bêt marzēᵃḥ. It is now clear that the word, whatever its etymological derivation, must refer to a religious society or association, often under the patronage of a deity, whose members gather periodically to remember their dead and so ensure the "immortality" of the departed. Such occasions were distinguished by consumption of much food and more drink, as by this means the comrades sought to outwit or outflank the inevitability and irreversibility of death. RS 24.258 is clearly a reflex onto the divine plane of such human conduct, as the term and its by-form mrzᶜy is found both in the

---

[80] Y. Kutscher, Words and Their Histories (Jerusalem: Kiryath Sepher, 1961) 167-171; O. Eissfeldt, "Etymologische und archäologische Erklärung alttestamentlicher Wörter," OrAnt 5 (1966) 165-176 = Kleine Schriften IV (Tübingen: J. C. B. Mohr, 1968) 285-296; Eissfeldt, "Kultvereine in Ugarit," Ugaritica VI (MRS 17; Paris: Geuthner, 1969) 187-195; Pope, "Divine Banquet," 190-194.

[81] P. D. Miller, "The Mrzh Text," The Claremont Ras Shamra Tablets (AnOr 48; ed. L. R. Fisher; Rome: Biblical Institute, 1971) 37-49 publishes the new text, RS 1957.702, and gives a brief review of the occurence of the term in other texts, as does Pope in the article cited in the previous note. For full discussion, see Eissfeldt's articles in the same note above.

[82] The translation is that of M. Dahood, "Additional Notes on the Mrzh Text," The Claremont Ras Shamra Tablets, 51-54.

[83] LXX renders the Jer passage: mē eiselthēs eis thiason autōn. Thiasos is only elsewhere used in Wis 12:5, where the received text has ek mesou mystas thiasou (cf. J. Ziegler, Sapientia Salomonis (V. T. Graecum Gottingensis 12/1; Göttingen: Vandenhoeck & Ruprecht, 1962) 133 for variant readings), "These initiates from the midst of a heathen cult," RSV. The Greek world was long familiar with confraternities, one of whose major duties was the festal memorialization of departed members. On the law of the thiasoi, see W. S. Ferguson and A. D. Nock, "The Attic Orgeones and the Cult of Heroes," HTR 37 (1944) 61-173; A. Andrewes, "Philochoros on Phratries, 2. Thiasoi," Journal of Hellenic Studies 81 (1961) 9-12.

alphabetic cuneiform texts and in Accadian documents from Ras Shamra, in reference to human cultic associations.[84] It is worth noting that El in text RS 24.258 is not only patron but also participating member of the mrzh, and that his conduct is not mocked here but is exemplary.

There are biblical passages which may aid us in understanding this custom, even though the word mrzh is not mentioned explicitly. In Isa 56:9-57:13 there is a long poem addressed to the Jewish apostates who have abandoned the pure worship of YHWH in favor of various pagan deities,[85] who were served in the usual ways - sexual rites (v. 5a), child sacrifice (v. 5b), drink- and cereal-offerings (v. 6), etc. Muilenburg[86] has noted the centrality of the oft-repeated "bed" (miškāb, vs. 7a, 8b , 8b) in this context, and the possibility that zikrōn in v. 8a may refer to the male (organ?) rather than to a memorial. However, it would seem that the passage may not deal so much with sexual orgies as with drinking bouts, since the "beds" are an essential article of furniture for this form of excess also, as Amos 6:1-7 (haśśōkᵉbîm ᶜal mittōt šēn, v. 4); 3:12; Hos 7:14; Mic 2:1; Ps 36:5; (cf. Ezek 23:40-42) show. The first Amos passage suggests that Isa 57:8[87] also refers to such a mrzh meeting, where behind closed doors a memorial for the absent members is held (wᵉ'ahar haddelet wᵉhammᵉzûzāh śamt zikrōnēk). The apostates are accused of making a bargain (RSV) or a league[88] with the god(s) of the underworld (wattikrāt lāk mēhem, v. 8), even sending emissaries to Sheol (v. 9), with gifts of oil (v. 8), to conclude a favorable pact.

---

[84] See the articles in notes 80 & 81, esp. Eissfeldt's articles, for full discussion of the occurrence of the term at Ras Shamra, Petra, Piraeus, Palmyra and Elephantine. The custom was widespread and long-lasting.

[85] M. Weise, "Jesaja 57:5f.," ZAW 72 (1960) 25-32, has noted that 'ēlîm in Isa 57:5 must be deliberately ambiguous: both "terebinths" and "(pagan) gods" (worshipped "under every green tree"). LXX and Targum Jonathan both understood the term as "idols," Weise, 26 n. 5. See also W. H. Irwin, "'The Smooth Stones of the Wady'?," CBQ 29 (1967) 31-40, who explains hallᵉqê nahal 57:6 on the basis of Ugaritic hlq, "to die, perish," and renders the phrase "with the dead of the wady is your portion." This would strengthen our case.

[86] IB V, 666-667.

[87] The puzzling yād hāzît at the end of 57:8 may be connected with the word hāzût parallel to bᵉrît in 28:18; yād would then not = membrum virile, contra M. Delcor, "Two Special Meanings of the Word YD in Biblical Hebrew," JSS 12 (1967) 230-240, but would be a verb, similar to the term in Ugaritic, cf. A. Fitzgerald, "Hebrew yd = 'Love' and 'Beloved'," CBQ 29 (1967) 368-374. Translate: "You have made a bargain for yourself with them, you have loved their bed (so far RSV), loved the pact."

[88] J. L. McKenzie, Second Isaiah (AB 20; Garden City: Doubleday, 1968) 157.

Similarly, the Wisdom of Solomon seems to refer to such a custom, in a passage which seems almost an exegesis or application to contemporary circumstances of Isa 28. Wis 1:16-2:24 comprises a speech of the godless and the judgment of the wise and righteous over them.[89] Introducing the wicked men's speech is a brief résumé of their thesis, Wis 1:16-2:1a, contrasting their deeds with the life of godfearing men (1:12-15) over whom Death has no dominion (oute hadou basileion epi gēs, 1:14).

> But ungodly men by their words and deeds
> summoned death;
> considering him a friend, they pined away,
> and they made a covenant with him,
> (kai synthēkēn ethento pros auton)
> because they are fit to belong to his party.[90]
> (1:16, RSV)

Their speech which follows seems patterned on the model of Isa 22:13. Notice especially the reference (Wis 2:7-8) to the garlands of fresh roses with which the revelers crown themselves before they wither, as deliberate symbol of the transience of life and the permanence of death ("Yes, our days are the passing of a shadow, from our death there is no turning back, the seal is set: no one returns." Wis 2:5, JB). We are here in the presence of the same type of reasoning as is represented in Isa 57:5-10.

It is now clear that Isa 28:1-12 represents a carefully reasoned and united whole, in which the banquets of the mrzh members, using garlands of flowers (28:1-4), are contrasted with YHWH who alone is a "crown of glory" (vs. 5-6). The orgy and its consequences is vividly mocked (vs. 7-8; cf. RS 24.258), to which the revelers retort (vs. 9-10) that they are the sophisticates who have no need of the prophet's instruction. The prophet replies with YHWH's word (vs. 11-13): the Israelites have rejected the only true source of comfort.

Therefore, they must now discover that their association with Death will be of no avail: their "covenant with Death" and "agreement with Sheol" will be annulled and swept away (vs. 14-22).[91] The "covenant with Death" is thus not a treaty with Egypt or her gods,[92] but an agreement with Mot, the god of the

---

[89]J. Fichtner, Weisheit Salomos (HAT II/6; Tübingen: J. C. B. Mohr, 1938) 15.

[90]hoti axioi eisin tēs ekeinou meridos einai. The word meris usually renders ḥēleq, as at Isa 57:6; one wonders if it is in these two passages a code word or oblique reference to the mrzh, as RSV "party" would suggest.

[91]Similarly, Job discovers that such an association is useless, since Death cannot be bargained with (Job 17:12-16). See also UT 67:I:22-26 = CTCA 5:I:22-26, in which Mot challenges Baᶜal to eat with his brothers and drink with his kinfolk (cf. Job 17:14). Such a union will avail nothing - even Baᶜal must die and descend into Mot's gullet (UT 67:I:7 = CTCA 5:I:7; cf. Isa 5:14; Hab 2:5).

[92]J. Bright, "Isaiah - I," Peake's (cf. n. 19 above), 509. Scott, IB V, 317, and Ackroyd, One Volume (cf. n. 31 above) 348 are not sure which it is.

underworld. The boast of the revelers that they have leagued together with Death is however empty, since YHWH alone is the "sure foundation" (v. 16).[93] He only is Lord of life and death, and adherence to the covenant with YHWH is the only way to victory over death. Desertion of YHWH and his covenant in favor of the mrzh will indeed prove to be a "lie" and a "falsehood" (v.15), which will end in total destruction (v. 22).[94]

[93]H. Gese, "Die strömende Geissel des Hadad und Jesaja 28, 15 und 18," Archäologie und Altes Testament (eds. A. Kuschke & E. Kutsch; Tübingen: J. C. B. Mohr, 1970) 127-134, explains the difficult phrase sôt sôtēp in Isa 28:15, 18 by reference to the scourge or whip wielded by Hadad(-Rimmon, cf. Zech 12:11), rather than as an "overflowing flood," Procksch, Jesaia I, 361. We may accept this religionsgeschichtliche comparison without the political interpretation which Gese gives to the passage.

[94]I very much regret that A. van Selm's article, "Isaiah 28:9-13: An Attempt to Give a New Interpretation," ZAW 85 (1973) 332-39, did not come into my hands in time for consideration here. His interpretation of the famous saw lāsāw etc. as the garbled words of Assyrian captors as they gave terse commands to the prisoners being led away into exile is more plausible than the interpretations mentioned above in footnote 8. The matter would not seem to affect the thesis of this paper directly.

ISAIAH 40:1-11 -- A RHETORICAL-CRITICAL STUDY

Kiyoshi Kinoshita Sacon

Tokyo Union Theological Seminary

The main objective of this paper is to make a stylistic or rhetorical-critical examination of the above-mentioned passage (Isa 40:1-11). This may well reveal some methodological limitations of the form-critical and tradition-historical study, in the present text at least.

In recent years, stylistic study of the Old Testament has been flourishing on the Continent, in Asia, as well as in the United States. This was already pointed out by James Muilenburg in his Presidential Address delivered at the annual meeting of the Society of Biblical Literature on December 18, 1968.[1]

In Europe, stylistic study, using the results of recent linguistic theories and Literaturwissenschaft has been introduced into the Old Testament field by Alonso-Schöckel and others. It can now be considered as having been established by Wolfgang Richter as a definite part of the methodology of biblical exegesis.[2] In Japan, as far back as 1964, the new stylistic method was proposed for the study of the Hebrew Prophet by Masao Sekine, president of the Society of Old Testament Studies, in his article, "Tradition and Individuality in the Hebrew Prophets--From the Stylistic Point of View--,"[3] as a supplement to the form-critical method.

---

[1] "Form Criticism and Beyond," JBL 88 (1969) 7-8.

[2] Exegese als Literaturwissenschaft: Entwurf einer alttestamentlichen Literaturtheorie und Methodologie (Göttingen: Vandenhoeck & Ruprecht, 1971).

[3] Senkyo To Shingaku. Evangelism and Theology: Essays in Honor of Junichi Asano (ed. N. Tajima; Tokyo: Sobunsha, 1964) 69-95. To quote a sentence, for instance,
> "...more correctly speaking, in the Hebrew prophets, because the portions described in the typical (formularized) style are very small, and because those dissociated from it are very extensive, the form-critical study is not so fruitful as it might be. We propose, therefore, that a new stylistic method should be introduced into the study of the prophets." (Translated by the writer, 73).

In the United States, one of the salient features of recent Old Testament study is the response that has appeared to Muilenburg's proposal concerning rhetorical criticism as supplementary to and going beyond form criticism. This proposal reflects upon the keen and conscious re-examination and re-establishment of <u>Formgeschichte</u> by the Claremont Group[4] (Rolf Knierim, Gene M. Tucker, and others) on the one hand, and gives impetus to the production of such noticeable work as that done by Melugin[5], Doty[6], and others.

Against the background of this recent study, we shall attempt to make a rhetorical-critical approach to Isa 40:1-11. This text is chosen, first, because Deutero-Isaiah is the book in which Dr. Muilenburg made a remarkable scholarly achievement in his commentary,[7] and second, because it is in the prophets that he exhibits the excellency of his methodology both in his commentary and in his Presidential Address, 1968. We shall also attempt to enter into dialogue with recent work done by C. Stuhlmueller,[8] K. Elliger,[9] L. Krinetzki,[10] etc.

I. A Textual-Critical Study

1. Textual criticism is basic for any exegetical study of the Old Testament, and must also be done before one makes a stylistic or rhetorical examination of a certain text.

In the case of Isa 40:1-11, attention will be given mainly to IQIs[a] and the Septuagint (LXX) in comparison with the standardized traditional text (MT). Unfortunately, IQIs[b] is fragmentary with only four words left in the text concerned.

---

[4]Cf. "Form Criticism: The Present State of an Exegetical Discipline" (A paper presented to the Form Criticism Seminar--Hebrew Scriptures, at the SBL Annual Meeting, N.Y., Oct. 27, 1970).

[5]"The Typical versus the Unique among the Hebrew Prophets," SBL 1972 <u>Proceedings</u> II (1972) 331-341.

[6]"The Concept of Genre in Literary Analysis," SBL 1972 <u>Proceedings</u> II (1972) 413-448.

[7]<u>IB</u> <u>V</u> (1956) 381-773.

[8]<u>Creative Redemption in Deutero-Isaiah</u>, Analecta Biblica, 43, 1970.

[9]<u>Jesaja II</u>, BKAT, XI, 1, 1970.

[10]"Zur Stilistik von Jes 40, 1-8," <u>BZ</u>, N. F. 16 (1972) 54-69.

2. Results of the comparison of these texts are shown in the following chart (CHART I).

CHART I

Number	Verse	MT	IQIs[a]	LXX	Vul	Targ
1	1	עמי	x	obj	voc	נבייא
2		אלהיכם (✓ΣΘ)	//	ο θεος 2036α ο	//	//
3	2	מלאה f	מלא m	pass	pass	
4		כי(נרצה) (✓ΣΘ)	//	0	0	//
5		כי(לקחה)	//	//	0	//
6		בכל(חטאתיה)	//	0	//	//
7	3	קול קורא	x	φωνη βοωντος εν τη ερημω	?	//
8		ישרו	וישרו	//	//	//
9		בערבה	//	0	//	//
10		מסלה	//	pl	pl	pl
11	4	גיא	גי	x	x	x
12		העקב	//	παντα τα σκολια	parva	כפלא
13		והרכסים לבקעה (✓A,Σ,θ)	והרוכסים	η τραχεια εις οδους λειας	et aspera in vias planas	//
14	5	ונגלה (✓A,Σ,θ)	//	και οφθησεται	//	//
15		יחדו	יחדיו	το σωτηριον του θεου	//	//
16		פי יהוה	//	O κυριος	//	
17	6	וָאֹמַר	ואומרה	και ειπα	et dixi	//
18		וכול חסדיו (✓A,Σ,θ)	וכל חסדו	και παντα δοξα ανθρωπου	omnis gloria eius	
19		נבל ציץ	//	και το ανθος εξεπεσε	et....	
20	7[b]-8[a]	written above the line		0	//	//
21	9	עלי לך	//	αναβηθι 0	——0 (qui)	
22		מבשרת ציון (✓A fem)	x	ο ευαγγελιζομενος Σιων	tu quae gen obj evangelizas Sion(gen obj)	gen obj
23	10	אדני יהוה	//	O κυριος	//	//

Number	Verse	MT	IQIs[a]	LXX	Vul	Targ
24		פֶּחָזָק	בחוזק	μετα ισχυος	in fortitudine	בתקות
25		וזרעו	//	ο βραχιων 0	//	//
26		(θ,Σ,A`//) משלה לו	//	μετα κυριειας	dominabitur 0	
27		ופעלתו	//	και το εργον 0	//	
28	11	טרעה	x	.	.	Relative Sentence
29		ובחיקו ישא עלות ינהל	// עולות	εχουσας παρακαλεσει	//	//

// indicates the same as MT.
x indicates the impossibility of comparison.
0 indicates no equivalence to MT.

3.   In this text, Isa 40:1-11, variants of IQIs[a] from MT occur in 6 out of 25 cases.   Four other variants from ancient versions have been omitted, which, if included, would have given a total of 29 cases, in addition to the frequent occurrence of matres lectiones.   If we count #20 (the case written above the line) as a variant, the total becomes 7 out of 25 cases. If an exclusion is made, however, as for example in the two cases of the orthographical difference of the pronominal suffix (#15 and 18), variants are reduced to 4 or 5 out of 25 cases. Furthermore, if the case of an additional waw (#8) is seen as one of the many instances which frequently occurred in IQIs[a] in order to indicate a comma or a period,[11] only 3 or 4 cases are left for variants. These are #3, 17, 24 and perhaps 20. As is clearly indicated, the cases of #17, 24 (and 20) are commonly seen as textual variants in the LXX and Vul. In this regard, these cases are qualitatively different from #15 and 18, for example.

In the case of #3, MT reads it as Qal perf. 3rd pers. sing. fem., whereas IQIs[a] has Qal perf. 3rd pers. sing. masc. This is one of the cases which has been the center of discussion. Some argue that the subject of מָלְאָה should be feminine ("she"=Jerusalem) and that צָבָאָהּ should be read as an object since צָבָא is a masculine noun which cannot take a feminine verb,[12] while others like Marti[13] propose מִלְּאָה (Pi. 3p. sg. fem.) for מָלְאָה . Ancient versions generally render צָבָאָהּ as subject and the verb as passive as does also IQIs[a].

---

[11]W.H.Brownlee, The Meaning of the Qumrân Scrolls for the Bible (New York: Oxford University, 1964) 180.

[12]E.g. P. Volz, Jesaia II übersetzt und erklärt, KAT, IX, 2 (1932), 1; L.G.Rignell, A Study of Isaiah Ch. 40-55 (Lund: C.W.K.Gleerup, 1956) 10; C.R.North, The Second Isaiah (Oxford: Clarendon, 1964) 70.

[13]K.Marti, Das Buch Jesaja, KHC, 10, 1900, 270.

In considering three other cases, it may be worth-while to keep in mind the difference in number between the variants of IQIs[a] from MT on the one hand and those of IQIs[a] from LXX on the other. The latter amounts to 19 or 17 out of 24 or 23.[14]

In appearance, statistics show that IQIs[a] is similar in nature to MT and so much different from the LXX. But the problem is not so simple as this, since virtually all the variants between IQIs[a] and MT (#17, 20, 24 and perhaps 3) are included in the variant readings of the LXX from MT, and since #17, 24 and perhaps 3 are also included in the variant readings of the Vul. from MT.

4. For an appropriate judgment in regard to this question, it seems useful to take a general look at recent textual-critical comments on the IQIs[a] as a whole. In 1950-54, in the first period of excitement after the discovery of IQIs[a], Orlinsky argued strongly and consistently that it was inferior in quality to the MT. Toward the last part of this period another view appeared, represented by Gottstein,[15] Rabin[16] and then Talmon,[17] paralleled with that of Albright-Cross.[18] This can be summed up in Talmon's declaration that "this 'liberal' attitude towards divergent textual traditions of the Bible was prevalent...in the second and first centuries B.C.E."[19]

It was in the framework of the assumption of the existence of divergent textual traditions that the problem was again reconsidered as to which IQIs[a] was ascribed among the plural text-forms. In regard to this, Skehan proposed that IQIs[a] was "the kind of glossed and reworked manuscript that the LXX prototype must have been."[20] Ziegler also assumed that there must have been a common text-form behind both the LXX and IQIs[a].[21]

---

[14]Variants of IQIs[a] from Vul. are 9 or 7 out of 23 cases.

[15]M.H.Gottstein, "Die Jesaia-Rolle im Lichte von Peschitta und Targum," Bib 35 (1954) 51-71.

[16]C.Rabin, "The Dead Sea Scrolls and the History of the O. T. Text," JTS, N. S. 6 (1955) 174-182.

[17]S.Talmon, "Aspects of the Textual Transmission of the Bible in the Light of Qumran Manuscripts," Textus 4 (1964) 95-132.

[18]W.F.Albright, "New Light on Early Recensions of the Hebrew Bible," BASOR 140 (Dec., 1955) 27-33; F.M.Cross, Jr., "The History of the Biblical Text in the Light of Discoveries in the Judean Desert," HTR 57 (1964) 281-299.

[19]S.Talmon, "Aspects...," 97. Cf. Rabin's reference to the "principle of limited variability" ("The Dead Sea Scrolls...," 181).

[20]P.W.Skehan, "The Qumran Manuscripts and Textual Criticism," Volume du Congrès. Strasbourg 1956 (VTSup 4; Leiden: Brill, 1957), 151.

[21]J.Ziegler, "Die Vorlage der Isaias-Septuaginta (LXX) und die erste Isaias-Rolle von Qumran (IQIs[a])," JBL 78 (1959), 59.

5. If we consider once again the given text (Isa 40:1-11) after having surveyed these general views of the textual nature of IQIs[a], the following points can be made:

(1) The assumption from the simple statistical data is not correct that IQIs[a] may be placed near MT and remote from the LXX, since #17, 24, (20 and 3) are the variant readings appearing throughout some ancient versions. Thus one may not say that IQIs[a] is near in quality of text to the MT.

(2) With regard to #17 and 24 in particular, it may be possible to see interpretative or explanatory readings, and also possible to assume that some smoother readings might have been perpetuated into a text-form. In this case, however, it seems significant to note that the same variant readings are preserved in the Vulgate which maintains the general tendency to make correction towards the MT. It may well indicate that there are not interpretative readings but rather textual variants in #17 and 24.

(3) As regards #20, two possibilities are to be assumed: a) IQIs[a] transcribed from the same shorter text as the LXX <u>Vorlage</u>. Then, at the second stage, it made correction from a longer text and wrote above the line. This resulted in the agreement with the text-form of MT. b) The Qumran scribes possessed the longer text but wrote 7b-8a by the common mistake of homoiotheleuton. Then afterwards they were inserted above the line.[22] At any rate, it seems evident that the longer text has a better reading.

(4) If we assume the existence of at least two text-forms related to the given text based upon the textual variants of #17 and 24, the difference may not be seen at the level of the consonantal text itself but at the tradition of vocalization.

(5) As regards v. 7c, about which it has been questioned whether it is an addition, we do not find any reason to doubt about its existence at the textual critical level.

(6) It is certainly true that the MT is generally the best preserved text in the given passages, as most scholars have pointed out. It is, however, equally true that in individual cases, IQIs[a] preserves better readings than those of the MT and is regarded as more original as a text than the MT, as Talmon and Brownlee have pointed out.[23] Examples of this

---

[22]As for the LXX, two possibilities may be assumed: a. a homoiotheleuton at translation or at the stage of inner Greek copying, or b. a simple copying or transmission of the shorter text, the <u>Vorlage</u> of which was corrupted by homoiotheleuton.

[23]Cf. S. Talmon, "DSIa as a witness to Ancient Exegesis of the Book of Isaiah," <u>ASTI</u> 1 (1962), 64; W. H. Brownlee, "The meaning...," 216ff. and pp. 172-73 and 248 for 40:6.

are seen in the case of #17 and 24.[24]

(7) A Translation of the text, made on the basis of a textual-critical study, follows:

Strophe I (vss. 1-2)

1 " 'Comfort! Comfort my people!' iterates your God.
2   Speak to the heart of Jerusalem,
    Proclaim to her,
      that her sentence is terminated,
      that her penalty is payed off;
    For she has received from the hand of YHWH
        double for all her sins."

Strophe II (vss. 3-5)

3 A voice proclaiming,
    "In the wilderness make ready the way of YHWH,
    Make straight in the desert the highway for our God!
4   Every valley shall be lifted up,
      Every mountain and hill shall be low.
    The rugged land shall turn to level place
    And the hillocks to plain.
5   Then the glory of YHWH shall be revealed,
      And all mankind shall see it together,
        For the mouth of YHWH has spoken."

Strophe III (vss. 6-8)

6 A voice saying, "Proclaim!"
  And I mutter to myself, "What could I proclaim?
    All mankind is but grass,
    And all its strength like the flower of the field.
7   Grass withers,
      Flower fades,
        When the breath of YHWH blows upon it."
      ____Surely the people are grass.____
8 "Grass withers,
  Flower fades,
    But the word of our God holds good forever."

Strophe IV (vss. 9-11)

9 "Go up with you onto a high mountain,
        Zion, herald of glad tidings.
  Lift up your voice with force,
        Jerusalem, herald of glad tidings.
    Lift it up, have no fear!
    Say to the townships of Judah!

---

[24]It is well-known that, in the case of #24, MT reading of b[e]hazaq is understood as beth essentiae, as is seen in Gesenius-Kautzsch-Cowley, Hebrew Grammar, #119i, followed by E. König, Das Buch Jesaja (Gütersloh: C. Bertelsmann, 1926) 355; Volz, Jesaia II, 2; Rignell, Isaiah Ch. 40-55, 14; and others. It should be noted, however, that #24 is text-critically a parallel phenomenon with #17, as is suggested in (1), (2), (4) and (6) above. If IQIs[a] is taken as better in #17, so may it well be the same in #24.

```
                    'Look!  Your God!'
    10              'Look!  The Lord YHWH!'
            With strength He comes,
            His arm rules for Him
                    Look!  His reward is with Him,
                    His recompence before Him.
    11      Like a shepherd He will tend His flock,
            With His arm He will gather up the lambs,
                    And carry them in His bosom,
                    The ewes He will lead."
```

II. A Rhetorical-Critical Study

1. Now we would like to proceed with a rhetorical-critical study of the given text. It may be presumptuous, however, to assume that additional significant contributions to the subject can still be made after the work done by Muilenburg,[25] Alonso-Schöckel,[26] and most recently by Krinetzki.[27] The present writer came to the conclusion that some room could be found for further work. It is our contention that the sentence-unit should be used as the basis for structure analysis in order to arrive at the rhetorical-critical understanding of a certain text. Other factors such as repetition, chiasmus, inclusio, etc., to be classified as structural features on the one hand, and alliteration, rhyme and various assonances to be classified as sound quality on the other, seem to be best arranged and understood on the basis of a sentence-unit. The result is as follows (CHART II):

CHART II

Adj........	Adjective	O..........	Object
Adv........	Adverb	Prep.......	Preposition
C..........	Clause	PronSuf....	Pronominal Suffix
Conj.......	Conjunction	Ptc........	Participle
ConjS......	Conjunctive Sentence	Quot.......	Quotation
Imp........	Imperative	S..........	Subject
Intj.......	Interjection	V..........	Verb
IO.........	Indirect Object	Voc........	Vocative
Itr........	Interrogative	VS.........	Verbal Sentence
MotivC.....	Motivation Clause	w..........	with
N..........	Noun	⟨ ⟩	omitted
N - N......	Nouns in Construct	⋈	Chiasmus
NegImp.....	Negative Imperative	‿	alliteration
NS........	Nominal Sentence		

---

[25] J. Muilenburg, *IB* V, esp. 386-393.

[26] "Die Stilistische Analyse bei den Propheten," *Congress Volume Oxford 1959* (VTSup 7; Leiden: Brill, 1960) 154-164; "Poésie hébraïque" (DBSup 42; Paris: Letouzey & Ané, 1967) 47-90.

[27] See footnote 10.

STROPHE I (vss. 1-2)

Verse	Syllabic Number	Sentence Analysis	Sentence Number
1	8+6	MotivC(w. Quot)(Imp, Imp O, V S)	1
		N-MŪ N-MŪ MM ŌM-R Ō-M	
2	10	ImpC(Imp Prep + N - N)	
		RŪ L L RŪ-L-M	2
	7	ImpC(Imp Prep + PronSuf)	
		RŪ LĒHĀ	
	7	ThatC (Conj V S)	
		KĪ Ā-Ā S-ĀH·	2
		ThatC (Conj V S)	
		KĪ SĀ ĀH·	
	8	MotivC (Conj V Prep + N - N	
		KĪ Ā-HĀ	
		O Prep + Adj + N)	1
		K H-ĒHĀ	

STROPHE II (vss. 3-5)

Verse	Syllabic Number	Sentence Analysis	Sentence Number
3	3	NS (N Ptc) QŌ QŌ	1
	7	ImpC (Prep + N Imp O (N - N)) BMM-B-R P-NNŪ	2
	14	ImpC (Imp Prep + N O (N - Prep + N)) RŪ B-R-B M-LL L-L-NŪ	
4	5	VS (S (Adj + N) V) K-L Ē Ē	2
	9	VS (S (Adj + N N) V) K-L L	
	9	VS (V S Prep + N) ᶜQ-B	2
	9	VS ⟨ V ⟩ S Prep + N) Ā B-Q-ᶜĀ	
5	7	VS (V S (N - N)) K-B-D Y-H-W	2
	8	VS (V S (Adj N) Adv) K B Y-H-D-W	
	6	MotivC (Conj S (N - N) V) Ī PĪ B-B	1

STROPHE III (vss. 6-8)

Verse	Syllabic Number	Sentence Analysis	Sentence Number

6   3+2   <u>NS</u> (w. Quot)(<u>N</u>   Ptc   <u>Imp</u>) ←

QŌ   Ō-M-R   Q-R   2

3+3   <u>VS</u> (w. Quot)(<u>V</u>   Itr   <u>V</u>) ←

Ō-M-R   M   Q-R

6   <u>NS</u> (S[Adj   <u>N</u>)   <u>N</u>)

KOL   HA-Ś-R   HA-S-R   2

9   <u>NS</u> (S[Adj   <u>N</u>)   <u>Prep</u> + <u>N</u> - <u>N</u>)

KOL   HA-S-D   S-S HA-ŚŚ-D

7   4   <u>VS</u> (<u>V</u>   <u>S</u>)

ĀBĒ   SĪ   2

3   <u>VS</u> (<u>V</u>   <u>S</u>)

ĀBĒ   SĪ

9   <u>ConjS</u> (Conj S[<u>N</u> - <u>N</u>]   <u>V</u>   O [<u>Prep+PronSuf</u>])   1

B   B

6   <u>NS</u> (<u>Adv</u>   <u>N</u>   <u>S</u>)   (1)

8   4   <u>VS</u> (<u>V</u>   <u>S</u>)

ĀBĒ   SĪ   2

3   <u>VS</u> (<u>V</u>   <u>S</u>)

ĀBĒ   SĪ

12   <u>VS</u> (<u>Conj</u> + S[<u>N</u> + <u>N</u>]   <u>V</u>   AdvC [<u>Prep+N</u>])   1

M   M

STROPHE IV (vss. 9-11)

Verse	Syllabic Number	Sentence Analysis	Sentence Number

Verse	Syllabic Number	Sentence Analysis	Sentence Number
9	8+6	ImpC (IO [Prep + N Adj] Imp Voc [N N]) ^{c}AL H-R ŌAH ^{c}AL-Ī L-K M-B-ṠṠ-R-T	2
	8+9	ImpC (Imp Adv[Prep + N] O Voc [N N]) H-RĪMĪ OAH L-K M-B-ṠṠ-R-T	
	8	ImpC (Imp NegImp) H-RĪMĪ Ī-Ī	2
	9	ImpC (Imp IO[Prep + N N]) M-RĪ	
10	6	NS (Intj N) HINNĒ	2
	7	NS (Intj N N) HINNĒ	
	5	VS (AdvC [Prep + N] V) Ō Ō	2
	8	VS (S V AdvC [Prep + PronSuf]) Ō Ō Ō	
	7	NS (Intj N AdvC [Prep + PronSuf]) HINNĒ Ō Ō	2
	8	NS (N AdvC [Prep + PronSuf]) Ō	
11	7	VS (AdvC [Prep + N] O V) R-^{c} Ō R-^{c}	2
	10	VS (AdvC [Prep + N] V O) R-^{c}	
	6	VS (AdvC [Prep + N] V) Ō	2
	5	VS (O V) Ō	

2. After the analysis several salient features may be noticed:

(1-a) Units consisting of a pair of qualitatively identical sentences are predominant in Isa 40:1-11 in general. There are seventeen pairs in all.

(1-b) Omitting v. 6ab, the remaining sixteen pairs are classified into eight pairs of verbal sentences (vss. 4, 4, 5, 7, 8, 10, 11, 11), four pairs of imperative sentences (vss. 2, 3, 9, 9), three pairs of nominal sentences (vss. 6, 9e-10a, 10) and one pair of "that"-sentence (v. 2).

As with the case of an apparent imbalance seen in v. 6ab, a solution might be made by taking קול as an exclamation,[28] but it may be also possible to take it as a dissolution of a pair resulting from a sentence-structure correspondent with that of v. 3a. A better reason should, however, be seen in the fact that v. 6a and b form a pair in the sense that each carries a quotation. This pair reveals an intense inner tension imbedded in the imperative and a deeply projected doubt in relation to it in dialogue style. Furthermore, this inner tension exists between vss. 6-7 and v. 8 in general, and more particularly between v. 7c and v. 8c. Both of them are introduced with the particle כי in form and embody a theological tension of destruction vs. creation (judgment vs. salvation) in content. Here is seen a dramatic style as is mentioned by Staiger and others.[29]

(2) Aside from the strophe of vss. 9-11, it can be seen that a set is composed of the addition of a sentence to a pair consisting of two qualitatively identical sentences at the most significant places of the respective strophes of vss. 1-2, 3-5 and 6-8.

A question may be raised against this observation, particularly on v. la. Taking יאמר אלהיכם as an inserted sentence, many scholars have assumed that vss. 1-2 were composed of three imperatives, of three "that"-clauses, and of three addressees ("my people", "Jerusalem" and "her").[30] It has

---

[28]Cf. GKC, #146b. This is followed by K. Marti, Das Buch Jesaja (KHCAT 10; Tübingen: J. C. B. Mohr, 1900) 271; B. Duhm, Das Buch Jesaia (HKAT III/1; 5th ed.; Göttingen: Vandenhoeck & Ruprecht, 1968) 289, 291-292; M. Haller, Das Judentum (SAT II/3; 2d ed.; Göttingen: Vandenhoeck & Ruprecht, 1925) 23-24; G. W. Wade, The Book of the Prophet Isaiah (Westminster Commentaries; 2d ed. rev.; London: Methuen, 1929) 250-251; Volz, Jesaia II, 1; P. A. H. de Boer, Second-Isaiah's Message (OTS 11; Leiden: Brill, 1956) 3; G. Fohrer, Das Buch Jesaja. 3 Band Kapitel 40-66 (Zürcher Bibelkommentare; Zürich: Zwingli, 1964) 17, 19; and others.

[29]E. Staiger, Grundbegriffe der Poetik (7th ed; Zürich: Atlantis, 1966); W. Kayser, Das sprachliche Kunstwerk. Eine Einführung in die Literaturwissenschaft (12th ed; Bern, Müchen: Francke, 1967).

[30]L. Köhler, Deuterojesaja (Jesaja 40-55) stilkritisch untersucht (BZAW 37; Giessen: Töpelmann, 1923) 92; Muilenburg, IB V, 423; North, The Second Isaiah, 72; Krinetzki, "Zur Stilistik," 59.

usually been assumed that the speaker of vss. 1-2 was God,[31] even if
the addressees might have been either prophets[32] or members of the
heavenly council.[33] It has been, however, recently proposed again by
Elliger,[34] following Begrich,[35] and followed by Fohrer,[36] that vss. 1-2
are spoken by a heavenly being to another heavenly being. Elliger points
out parallels in structure in the fact that both vss. 1-2 and 3-5 consist
of imperative (2a // 3) and indicative (2b // 4-5b) and that יאמר אלהיכם
corresponds to v. 5c which functions as authorizing the whole order in
vss. 3-5, although it is placed not at the end but at the beginning.
We think that our structure analysis supports and is supported by
Elliger's view. We take v. 1 as a motivation clause for v. 2.

As for v. 7d, it is our conclusion that it should be regarded stylistically as an insertion, since it is very much out of proportion to the
sentence structure of the text-unit.

(3) While there is a general consensus in regard to the division
of vss. 1-11 into four parts (strophes), there is still a serious question
as to whether the fourth strophe (vss. 9-11) is a part of the literary
unit vss. 1-8, because Elliger[37] has recently pointed out an obvious break
between vss. 1-8 and 9-11. His points of argument are these: (i) as for
the speaker, it is a heavenly being in vss. 1-8, while it is the prophet
to Zion-Jerusalem in vss. 9-11; (ii) as for the subject matter, vss. 1-8,
being a self-contained unit, concludes with a message to the prophet, stating
an experience of the calling of Deutero-Isaiah, whereas vss. 9-11 states
glad tidings. According to Elliger, therefore, the connection between
vss. 1-8 and 9-11 is an editorial composition; (iii) a temporal sequence is
also detected between the two.

These may not, however, offer sufficient ground for making vss. 1-8
and 9-11 separate units. From the stylistic- or rhetorical-critical point
of view, there is a common structural feature between the fourth strophe
(vss. 9-11) and the first (vss. 1-2) in particular: (i) as has already
been said, the composition of a pair of two qualitatively identical sentences

---

[31]Most recently, Stuhlmueller, Creative Redemption, 179.

[32]E.g. Rignell, Study, 9.

[33]F. M. Cross, Jr., "The Council of Yahweh in Second Isaiah," JNES
12 (1953) 274-77; Muilenburg, IB V, 422-23; N. Habel, "The Form and Significance
of the Call Narratives," ZAW 77 (1965) 314-15.

[34]BKAT XI/1, 6.

[35]J. Begrich, Studien zu Deuterojesaja (Theologische Bücherei 20; München:
Chr. Kaiser, 1963) 61.

[36]Das Buch Jesaja. 3 Band, 16.

[37]BKAT XI/1, 34.

is seen throughout vss. 1-11; (ii) four positive commands can be enumerated
in v. 9 as in vss. 1-2, two of which are the repetition of the same word
in imperative form; (iii) there is a structural correspondence between
vss. 9cde, 10a, on the one hand, and v. 2abcd, on the other, in the fact
that both of them are composed of a pair of two imperative sentences and
of a pair of two sentences containing the contents of the command; (iv)
the repetition of an important phrase[38] placed once in each strophe either
in "your God" (אלהיכם   ) or in "our God" (אלהינו   ) is most significant
for the understanding of the delimitation of a literary unit of the text,
since this phrase carries a central theological message and the connotation
of this unit, which is the advent of YHWH, the Sovereign Lord, in the
immediate future. This is far beyond a simple catch word in Mowinckel's
sense.[39] These features can be most easily explained, when vss. 1-11
are understood as belonging to one and the same literary unit.

3. As with the poetical characteristics exhibited in sound quality,
much has already been done by Alonso-Schöckel in general, and by Muilenburg
in particular in regard to Deutero-Isaiah, and most recently by Krinetzke
in detail in vss. 1-8. Little can be added to the work done by these men
and no repetitious words are needed in this area except for a comment that
such devices as alliteration (e.g., vss. 3, 6, 9), rhyme (e.g., v. 2b and
2e), onomatopoeia (e.g., v. 1), and assonance (e.g., $\bar{U}$ and $\bar{O}$ vowels among
the sonore sounds (l, m, n, r) in vss. 1-2b in contrast to $\bar{I}$- and $\bar{A}$-vowels
among cachophony by the spirants (k, s, h) should not be pointed out at
random but may be observed and appreciated most significantly in the framework of a sentence-unit. Results are shown in CHART II in capital letters
under the sentence analysis.

4. It is now obvious that an exceedingly high stylistic structure is
efficiently handled in Isaiah 40:1-11, along with various techniques of
poetical and phonological artistry. This leads us to assume that a particular
personality stands behind it. We do not agree with Merendino in his recent
attempts to suggest that the Trito-Isaiah's hand can be detected even in
part here chiefly through the phraseological and lexical study.[40]

Here in this text-unit we find basically the sentence-unit of "two",
with an occasional "one". Among these additional "one" sentence-units,
2e and 5c declare, the perfect, the termination of the judgment and the
inauguration of the salvation. The announcement of YHWH's judgment in the
perfect in 7c is put in sharp contrast to that of YHWH's creative word
in the imperfect. Corresponding with the latter is also the imperfect
sentence in v. 1, which goes on to an announcement of the advent of YHWH in
10b and of the shepherdship of YHWH in 11abcd.

---

[38]Cf. esp. J. Muilenburg, "A Study in Hebrew Rhetoric: Repetition
and Style," VTSup 1 (1953) 97-111.

[39]S. Mowinckel, "Die Komposition des deuterojesajanischen Buches,"
ZAW 49 (1931) 87-112, 242-60.

[40]P. Merendino, Corso Esegetico-Teologico su Isaia 40, I Parte:
40, 1-11, 1970, 16-21.

III. Some Observations on Form-Critical- and Tradition-Historical Studies

No space is left for a comprehensive survey of the form-critical study of the given text. Rather, our attempt is limited to some comments on recent studies of this text-unit.

With regard to form criticism it seems, first of all, very important for us to find out a Gattung in which all the vss. 1-11 may be comprehended after we have seen a well-defined structure of the literary unit. Otherwise some degree of the dissolution of a Gattung or the secondary stage of the mixture of Formen must be sought out. We cannot be satisfied with such a form-critical position as was originally stated by Gressmann, namely, that vss. 1-2, 3-5, 6-8 are respectively regarded as a separate oracle introduced and/or concluded by the oracular formula or the like.[41]

E. Nielsen has recently regarded Isa 40:1-11 as a Prozessionsliturgie artistically made up of the fragments of Auditionen of 3-5 and 9-11 with an echo of the experience of a prophetic call (vss. 6 and 8) and also with the introductory Beschwörung (vss. 1-2).[42] He assumes that the Deutero-Isaiah must have been strongly influenced by the liturgies of the Jerusalem Temple, instances of which were claimed to be seen in an Eintrittliturgie in 9-11 and in a Beschwörung in 1-2.[43]

However, it would be more natural to look on the form of the double imperative of vss. 1-2 as an example of Zweierreihe adopted by Deutero-Isaiah from normal Hebrew stylistic devices,[44] and to look on vss. 9-11 as an imitation of the genre of an instruction of the message of victory in war.[45]

As is done by Elliger,[46] a form of a series of the issue of commands may be seen in vss. 1-2, 3-5 and 6-8. It has been said that each of these three sets was introduced by what they generally called Botenformel. Among יאמר אלהיכם (v. 1), קול קורא (v. 3) and קול אמר (v. 6), the first one is the nearest to the traditional messenger's formula (כה אמר יהוה). This style of speaking appears in Isa 1:11, 18 and 33:10 in the form of יאמר יהוה , every instance of which is used when quoting YHWH's saying in the prophetic speech. In Deutero-Isaiah, this appears in a more transformed style as יאמר קדוש in 40:25 and as יאמר מלך יעקב in 41:21. All of these cases are used for quoting

---

[41]H. Gressmann, "Die literarische Analyse Deuterojesajas," ZAW 34 (1914) 262; M. Haller, Das Judentum, 22-25. Cf. also Merendino, op. cit.

[42]"Deuterojesaja. Erwägungen zur Formkritik, Traditions- und Redaktionsgeschichte," VT 20 (1970) 203-4.

[43]Ibid., 195 and 203.

[44]L. Köhler, Deuterojesaja, 98-99.

[45]J. Begrich, Studien, 58.

[46]BKAT XI/1, 6-8.

YHWH's saying with no exception and never like the introductory formulas
of kōh 'amar YHWH. No more words are needed for two other cases. This
little examination not only renders support directly for our understanding
of v. l as a quotation but also indicates indirectly that the genre of the
messenger's formula is greatly transformed into a literary artistry [47]
through the intention (function)[48] of the individual personality of Deutero-
Isaiah.

Another attempt worthwhile mentioning here may be that of N. Habel,[49]
who sees in Isa 40:1-11 such thematic sequences as (i) the introductory
word (vss. 1-2), (ii) the commission (vss. 3-5, 6a), (iii) the objection
(vss. 6-7) and (iv) the reassurance (vss. 8-11). These are commonly seen,
according to him, in the Calls of Gideon (Judg 6:11b-17), Moses (Exod 3:1-12),
Jeremiah (Jer 1:4-10), Isaiah (Isa 6:1-13) and Ezekiel (Ezek 1-3), and may be
derived from a Gattung of the call narrative. A criticism of this rather
tradition-historical approach can be seen in W. Richter's recent work,[50]
in which the following two points at least are made clear: (i) Gattung
may not be an appropriate terminology for what Habel deals with, but the
term Schema should be used in place of it; (ii) the formation of this
Schema should be understood sociologically by assuming such a complex
historical contact as the one between the prophetic circles and a certain
deliverer in the earlier period of history of Israel. There may not have
been a linear development of a Gattung of the call narrative from that of
Gideon to that of II Isaiah. Under the Schema of the calling, Richter
classifies these five points: (i) die Andeutung der Not, (ii) der Auftrag,
(iii) der Einwand, (iv) die Zusicherung des Beistandes, and (v) das Zeichen.
We can only discover some suggestions of (iii) Einwand and slight hints of
(i) here in Isa 40:1-11. Of the three others, each of which carries a
particular phraseology or formula, there is no trace in our text.[51] There
is indicated, first of all, the need for reservation in taking our text itself as belonging to a particular Gattung; secondly, the disruption of a
particular literary form, even if it were assumed; and thirdly, a literary
creation produced by an individual using several literary types.

---

[47]L. Köhler (Deuterojesaja, 102-104) has already discussed the matter
persuasively, taking 40:1-2 as an example of the transformation of the
Botenspruch.

[48]G. E. Tucker, Form Criticism of the Old Testament (Philadelphia:
Fortress, 1971) 16-17.

[49]Cf. fn. 32.

[50]W. Richter, Die sogenannten vorprophetischen Berufungsberichte
(FRLANT 101; Göttingen: Vandenhoeck & Ruprecht, 1970) 136-181, esp. 137,
n. 6 and 142, n. 12.

[51]Such as šelah, lēk for (ii), ᶜimmᵉkā for (iv) and 'ōt(ôt) for (v).

Conclusion

At last, we would like to ask regarding the _Sitz im Leben_ of a text which has seen great deterioration from the original typical literary _Gattung_ and which expresses itself in a highly stylized and original formulation. It is our contention, after we have done some rhetorical-critical analysis of the text with some form-critical and tradition-historical observations, that the _Sitz im Leben_ of the text should be sought, not by tracing it back to an original _Sitz im Leben_ of the literary _Gattungen_ from which the present text might be derived, nor by emphasizing a literary setting of the heavenly council with its tradition-historical background, but by squeezing out from the text as much as possible the concrete sociological, historical and, particularly, spiritual-historical situation in which Deutero-Isaiah lived. We assume that it is fairly well indicated in vss. 2 and 6-7, which describes the exiled community which closed its heart stubbornly, refusing all sorts of comfort ("to speak to the heart of Jerusalem" in v. 2) and which describes also the nihilistic and desperate state of mind in which the prophet lived together with his contemporaries.[52] It is against this background that Deutero-Isaiah was called to be a prophet of the advent of the God of the future.

---

[52]Cf. C. Westermann's exegesis on vss. 6-8, _Isaiah 40-66. A Commentary_ (Philadelphia: Westminster, 1969) 40-43.

*THE HERALD OF GOOD NEWS IN SECOND ISAIAH

Robert W. Fisher

Waterloo Lutheran University

The message of Second Isaiah has received considerable attention in recent decades[1], and it has become commonplace to note that the central core of that message is the proclamation of the ultimate good news of exiled Israel's imminent deliverance and the inauguration of the eschatological reign of God. However, little if any notice has been given to the agent of this proclamation who is, in fact, responsible for its actualization - the herald of good news. This figure appears in the following passages:

40:9   על הר-גבה עלי-לך מבשרת ציון

הרימי בכח קולך מבשרת ירושלם הרימי אל-תיראי

אמרי לערי יהודה הנה אלהיכם

Upon a high mountain get you up, herald of good tidings to Zion;
Lift up with strength your voice, herald of good tidings to
    Jerusalem,
Lift it up, fear not;
Say to the cities of Judah, "Behold your God!"

---

*It is highly appropriate that the following study should appear in a Festschrift honouring James Muilenburg, for the original impetus to investigate the topic came to the author long ago in Dr. Muilenburg's class on Second Isaiah at Union Theological Seminary. It was one of those memorable moments when Dr. Muilenburg, having just raised the question of the herald, in his lecture, suddenly turned on an unfortunate student who was sitting on the aisle down which he was striding and said with that inimitable twinkle in his eye, "Young man, I want you to write a forty page paper on this subject by nine o'clock tomorrow morning." The seed had been sown, and, though it is considerably later than nine o'clock the next morning, here are the results, which are gladly and affectionately dedicated to him who inspired them.

The author also wishes to acknowledge the aid of the Canada Council in supporting the research for this article.

[1]Since Prof. Muilenburg's important work in 1956 ["The Book of Isaiah, Chapters 40-66: Introduction and Exegesis," The Interpreter's Bible V, (New York and Nashville: Abingdon, 1956)], some of the more extensive contributions in this field have been: Claus Westermann, Isaiah, 40-66 ("Old Testament Library"; Philadelphia: The Westminster Press, 1969); idem, "Sprache und Struktur der Prophetie Deuterojesajas," Forschung am alten Testament ("Theologische Bücherei," 24; München: Chr. Kaiser, 1964); Carroll Stuhlmueller, Creative Redemption in Deutero-Isaiah ("Analecta Biblica," 43; Rome: Pontifical Biblical Institute, 1970); John L. McKenzie, Second Isaiah ("Anchor Bible," 20: Garden City, N.Y.: Doubleday & Company, Inc., 1968); Georg Fohrer, Das Buch Jesaja 3. Band: Kapitel 40-66 ("Züricher Bibelkommentare"; Zürich/Stuttgart: Zwingli Verlag, 1964); Harry M. Orlinsky and Norman H. Smith, Studies on The Second Part of The Book of Isaiah ("Supplements to Vetus Testamentum," XIV; Leiden: E.J.Brill, 1967); Jean Steinmann, Le livre de la consolation d'Israel (Paris: Editions du Cerf, 1960); James D. Smart, History and Theology in Second Isaiah (Philadelphia: The Westminster Press, 1965); G.A.F. Knight, Deutero-Isaiah: A Theological Commentary On Isaiah 40-55 (New York and Nashville: Abingdon, 1965).

41:27 ראשון לציון הנה הנם ולירושלם מבשר אתן

Zion gets the first report; behold, the news bringer, and to
  Jerusalem I give a herald of good tidings.

52:7   מה־נאוו על־ההרים רגלי מבשר
     משמיע שלום מבשר טוב משמיע ישועה
        אמר לציון מלך אלהיך

How beautiful upon the mountains are the feet of the herald of
  good tidings,
Who publishes peace, who brings exceedingly good tidings,
  who publishes salvation,
Who says to Zion, "Your God reigns!"

These occurrences suggest that the herald of good news indeed plays a crucial
role in the total dramaturgical framework of Isaiah 40-55 and deserves further investigation.

   In Hebrew, the term "herald of good news" is expressed by the word
mᵉbassēr (feminine, mᵉbasseret)*, the piel participle of the root BSR and
the only form in which the latter occurs in Second Isaiah. However, one of
the difficulties in dealing with the herald in Isaiah 40-55 is the fact that
in 40:9 the feminine form of the participle, mebassereth, is used, whereas
in the other two passages the masculine mebasser is found. The usual explanation of this phenomenon has been that the word refers to Zion-Jerusalem[2] and
the five feminine verbs of v.9 have been adduced as evidence in support of
this position. Thus Zion-Jerusalem is the herald(ess) of good news who is told
to ascend a high mountain (the better to be seen and heard by the other cities
of Judah) and to proclaim to them the coming of Yahweh.

   However, the versions present a somewhat different picture of this feminine
participle in v.9. The Septuagint reads the masculine singular εὐαγγελιζομενος
which would suggest that Zion-Jerusalem was its object but Aquila has the feminine singular εὐαγγελιζομενη and Origen in his fifth column notes that other
Greek manuscripts also have the latter reading[3]. The Targum specifically

---

*Henceforth mebasser and mebassereth

[2]E.g., C.C. Torrey, The Second Isaiah (New York: Charles Scribner's Sons, 1928)
306; Paul Volz, Jesaia II ("Kommentar zum Alten Testament," IX; Leipzig: A. Deichert, 1932) 6; Muilenburg, op.cit., 431f.; Westermann, Isaiah 40-66, 43ff.;
Stuhlmueller, op.cit., 181; McKenzie, op.cit., 15-18

[3]Origenis Hexaplorum, ed. F. Field (Hildesheim: Georg Olms, 1964), II, 509. In
Field's edition, only Aquila is given as reading εὐαγγελιζομενη but several
scholars, e.g., Franz Delitzsch, Biblical Commentary on the Prophecies of Isaiah,
trans. J.S. Banks & J. Kennedy (Edinburgh: T. & T. Clark, 1890), II, 139, and
G.W. Wade, The Book of the Prophet Isaiah ("Westminster Commentaries," 2nd edition; London: Methuen & Co. Ltd., 1929) 252, list Symmachus and Theodotion as
also having the feminine reading. What their source was or how accurate it was
is not known.

identifies the word with the prophets who bring good news to Zion-Jerusalem,[4] which perhaps indicates that its translators did, in fact, read the feminine mebassereth in their Hebrew Vorlage and interpreted it as a collective. This construction is quite possible from the point of view of Hebrew grammar and has been adopted by some scholars, even as early as Ibn Ezra.[5] The Vulgate very clearly translates the participles in the masculine singular and takes Zion-Jerusalem as the direct object: tu, qui evangelizas Sion. However Jerome, in his commentary, confesses that the Hebrew actually read the feminine and that perhaps the matter is not so clear after all:

Porro Hebraicium et caeteri interpretes ponunt
genere feminino, ut dicant, quae evangelizas Sion,
et. quae evangelizas Jerusalem, quod verbum juxta
Graecos ambiguum est, ut possimus accipere, vel
eam quae nuntiat, vel eam cui nuntiatur.[6]

Only the Syriac unequivocally opts for the appositional understanding of the feminine participle, and even it tampers with the text to a certain degree; it completely rules out any other interpretation by inverting the order of the words: . . .‎ܠܝܙܡܒ ܐܠܟܙܝܐ‎|... .‎|ܠܝܙܡܣ ܣܡܝܙ‎ ‎ܝ ܘ ܐܙ‎.

Thus one is faced here with a very interesting phenomenon. All of the major versions give indications of having read the feminine participle mebassereth in their original Hebrew manuscripts, but all of them, save one, reveal a tradition of understanding it as a masculine, as evidenced in their translations. This fact is of considerable consequence for the problem at hand. It does not supply the technical details for a solution of the grammatical problem, but it does show that, although one does not know what they were, these early authorities had sufficient grounds, perhaps both grammatical and contextual, to translate the feminine as a masculine. That is to say, they stood in a living tradition of understanding the text in this manner, and such a living tradition, dating from this early period, may be more significant than the uncertain details of Hebrew grammar.

---

[4]Verse 1, "O ye prophets, prophesy, consolations concerning my people, saith your God," (‎נבייא אתנבו על עמי אמר אלהכון‎); Verse 9, "Get ye up on a high mountain, ye prophets that bring good tidings to Zion. ..." (‎על טור רם סקו לכון נבייא דבסרין לציון‎). Cf. J.F. Stenning, The Targum of Isaiah (Oxford: at the Clarendon Press, 1949), 130.

[5]Abraham Ibn Ezra, The Commentary of Ibn Ezra on Isaiah, ed. and trans. M. Friedländer (London: N. Trübner and Co., 1873-77) I, 173: cf. also e.g., John Skinner, The Book of the Prophet, Isaiah, Chapters XL-LXVI ("The Cambridge Bible for Schools and Colleges"; Cambridge: at the University Press, 1954) 6; Wilhelm Gesenius, Der Prophet Jesaia (Leipzig: F.C.W. Vogel, 1821), III, 39.

[6]S. Eusebii Hieronymi, Commentariorum in Isaiam Prophetam ("Patrologiae Latina," vol. 24, ed. J.P. Migne; Paris: by the Editor, 1845), col. 404.

However, even with regard to these "uncertain details of Hebrew grammar" it may be possible to make a few observations which might help to clarify matters a little. First, it should be realized that the gender of Hebrew nouns is often a very thorny problem,[7] involving not a few irregularities. For example, it is well known that feminine forms are sometimes given to masculine subjects; these are usually abstractions of one kind or another, such as collectives or personifications (e.g., יושבת, "that which inhabits," i.e., the population, Is. 12:6, Micah 1:11f; איבת, "that which is hostile," i.e., the enemy, Micah 7:8, 10) and titles or designations of office, the principal example of which is the Hebrew title of the book Ecclesiastes, קהלת, "one who takes part or speaks in a religious assembly" or "one who collects maxims and aphorisms." Both of these usages have been proposed as explanations for the feminine form of the participle mebassereth.[8] However, there is still another explanation which could be offered with regard to this problem. It has been suggested that masculine nouns are sometimes given feminine endings in order to lend them a certain quality of intensiveness. This is a standard grammatical device in Arabic, where one may find beside a simple form such as راوٍ (rāwin), "story teller," an expanded form such as راوية (rāwiyatun), "great story teller."[9] Thus one more possible rationale for the participle in 40:9 is added to those already at hand.

As mentioned above, it has been argued that the five feminine verbs in Is. 40:9 indicate that mebassereth stands in apposition to Zion-Jerusalem,[10] but this is not correct. These verbs do not add any independent witness of their own, since once a grammatically feminine subject has been established the dependent verbs tend to agree with it, regardless of its real meaning.

A striking illustration of the manner in which feminine nouns and verbs are sometimes used in Hebrew without regard for the actual gender of the subject is provided by two passages from Second Isaiah himself. The first is 41:14 where the text reads:

---

[7]"Le genre du nom offre de multiples difficultés." Paul Joüon, Grammaire de l'hebreu biblique (second edition; Rome: Pontifical Biblical Institute, 1947), 409; "A la 3e personne, l'accord du verbe présente très nombreuses anomalies." Ibid. 458.

[8]E.g., Skinner, op.cit., 5 (collective); Johann August Dath, Prophetae Majores (Halle: Orphanotrophei, 1779), 132 (designation of office).

[9]Joüon, op.cit., 212; cf. William Wright, A Grammar of the Arabic Language (third edition; Cambridge: at the University Press, 1896), I, par. 233, Rem. c.

[10]Torrey, op.cit., 306; Muilenburg, op.cit., 432.

אַל־תִּירְאִי תּוֹלַעַת יַעֲקֹב מְתֵי יִשְׂרָאֵל

אֲנִי עֲזַרְתִּיךְ נְאֻם־יְהוָה וְגֹאֲלֵךְ קְדוֹשׁ יִשְׂרָאֵל:

הִנֵּה שַׂמְתִּיךְ לְמוֹרַג חָרוּץ חָדָשׁ בַּעַל פִּיפִיּוֹת

תָּדוּשׁ הָרִים וְתָדֹק וּגְבָעוֹת כַּמֹּץ תָּשִׂים:

תִּזְרֵם וְרוּחַ תִּשָּׂאֵם וּסְעָרָה תָּפִיץ אוֹתָם

וְאַתָּה תָּגִיל בַּיהוָה בִּקְדוֹשׁ יִשְׂרָאֵל תִּתְהַלָּל:

Fear not (fem. sing.), you worm Jacob, you maggot, louse[11]
    Israel!
I, even I, will help you (fem. sing.), oracle of Yahweh;
    Your (fem. sing.) redeemer is the Holy One of Israel.
Behold, I will make you (fem. sing.) a threshing sledge,
    sharp, new, studded with teeth;
You (mas. sing.) shall thresh mountains and crush them,
    and you (mas. sing.) shall make the hills like chaff.
You (mas. sing.) shall winnow them and the wind shall carry
    them away and the tempest will scatter them.
And you (mas. sing.), you shall rejoice in Yahweh, in the
    Holy One of Israel you (mas. sing.) shall glory.

Here a definitely masculine subject, Jacob, is addressed under the figure
of a worm (תּוֹלַעַת), which in Hebrew is feminine, and the verb and suffixes
for the first three lines (14-15b) are all in the feminine. It is true that
in the fourth line (15c-d) the author changes over to the masculine, but
this is very likely because he has just said that Israel will become a
threshing sledge, which is masculine, and the following verbs which describe
Israel's future actions as a threshing sledge would naturally be in the masculine. Thus the gender of the verb concurs with the gender of the figure,
not of the actual subject. This example does not necessarily prove anything,
but it does illustrate in a rather clear and arresting manner the simple fact
that the gender of a verb does not always indicate the real gender of the subject. Thus the significance of the feminine verbs in Is. 40:9 is greatly
reduced.

Another instance of syntactic inconsistency with regard to gender is found
in Is. 51:12-13, which reads as follows:

אָנֹכִי אָנֹכִי הוּא מְנַחֶמְכֶם מִי־אַתְּ וַתִּירְאִי

מֵאֱנוֹשׁ יָמוּת וּמִבֶּן־אָדָם חָצִיר יִנָּתֵן

וַתִּשְׁכַּח יְהוָה עֹשֶׂךָ נוֹטֶה שָׁמַיִם

וְיֹסֵד אָרֶץ וַתְּפַחֵד תָּמִיד כָּל־הַיּוֹם

I, I am he that comforts you (mas. pl.); who are you (fem. sing.)
    that you (fem. sing.) are afraid
of man who dies, and of the son of man who is made like grass,
and you (mas. sing., IQIsa[a] reads fem. sing.) have forgotten
    Yahweh your (mas. sing.) maker, who stretched out the heavens
and laid the foundations of the earth, and you (mas. sing.) fear
    continually all the day. . .?

---

[11]Cf. Heinrich Ewald, Die Propheten des Alten Bundes (second edition;
Göttingen: Vandenhoeck & Ruprecht, 1868), III, 43, and G.R. Driver, "Linguis-
tic and Textual Problems: Isaiah XL-LXVI," JTS, XXXVI (1935), 399. See also
Brian Walton, Biblia Sacra Polyglotta (London: Thomas Roycroft, 1657), III,
Esaias 109, who, in translating the Syriac ܩܠܡܐ by the Latin pedicule, "Louse,"
anticipated Driver by 278 years.

The irregularity of this passage speaks for itself,[12] and points up once more the dubious way in which gender is sometimes used in Hebrew, particularly in highly poetic and allusive materials such as Second Isaiah.

The basic premises of the preceding discussion could be summarized simply as follows: the use of gender in Hebrew can sometimes be a rather uncertain affair; therefore when gender is made the primary consideration upon which an argument is built, its bases are somewhat tenuous at best.

Thus perhaps the usual translation of 40:9, based upon the feminine form of the participle and understanding Zion-Jerusalem as the herald(ess) of good news, is somewhat more open to question than is commonly thought. Indeed, there are serious objections to this interpretation. First, it is completely out of keeping with the picture of the mebasser given in the other two occurrences in Second Isaiah (41:27; 52:7) where he clearly brings the good news to Zion. The evidence of 52:7 is especially telling at this point. There is an almost perfect correspondence between the elements of this passage and those of 40:9: the mountains upon which the mebasser appears or which he ascends; the proclaiming of the message, which in both cases is precisely the same, i.e., the decisive, momentous announcement of God's coming in great power to begin his eschatological reign(מלך אלהיך / הנה אלהיכם). Everything matches;[13] as a matter of fact, 52:7 is actually an exact description of the execution of the commission given in 40:9. Both passages refer to one and the same reality.[14] Under this view of the matter, it is difficult to avoid the conclusion that, in 40:9, the mebasser(eth) is to carry the good news to Zion-Jerusalem also, as is so clearly the case in 52:7 and 41:27. Otherwise one is faced with a rather jarring inconsistency which seems to exceed the bounds of poetic and prophetic license.

In the second place, the view that the herald in 40:9 is Zion-Jerusalem is out of harmony with the latter's role in the rest of Second Isaiah (excluding the Gordian knot of the Servant Songs), a role which is notably passive. Elsewhere in Second Isaiah, salvation and redemption are always vouchsafed to Zion-Jerusalem, whose major function is simply to receive these blessings.[15]

---

[12]Cf. Christopher R. North, The Second Isaiah (Oxford: at the Clarendon Press, 1964) 213-14: ". . .a somewhat scrappy passage. . . [these verses] present a number of difficulties. Compared with the rest of DI they are jumpy and inconsequent." McKenzie's attempt to smooth things out (op.cit., 120), suggested by D.N. Freedman, is not convincing. The emended text is no more satisfactory than the original.

[13]Stuhlmueller, op.cit., 74, fn. 244.

[14]Westermann, Isaiah 40-66, 250: "52.7-10 form a deliberate counterpart to the final section of the prologue, 40.9ff ... 52.7-10 say exactly the same thing...[as 40.9ff]."

[15]This view is something of a commonplace among authorities on Second Isaiah. See, for example, Christopher R. North, The Suffering Servant In Deutero-Isaiah (second edition; London: Oxford University Press, 1956), 182-84, for some rather convincing data and arguments to this effect.

However, the most convincing argument against the interpretation of the herald as Zion-Jerusalem is the one presented by the passage's own context and its relation to certain other prophetic passages of similar character. The findings of Old Testament form criticism become particularly relevant at this point. It is generally agreed today that the setting of the first eleven verses of Isaiah 40 is the heavenly council of Yahweh.[16] God announces to the members of his council the imminent consolation and redemption of Israel, heavenly voices declare the coming of the יהוה כבוד and command that preparations be made for it. At this point, the prophet, who is himself present in the heavenly council witnessing all these things, breaks in to protest the frailty and impermanence of man before the glory of the Lord. It is possible that, in v.8, the address returns once more to the voice of 6a. Then come vss.9-11. According to the usual interpretation, "the scene shifts from heaven to earth, from the celestial council to Jerusalem. Zion-Jerusalem is addressed as a herald, and she is commissioned to proclaim the good news of the Lord's advent."[17] However, this shift seems to involve an unnecessary and unnatural transition. Judging from the form and content of these verses, it seems clear that Is. 40:1-11 is nothing less than the inaugural audition and call of the prophet--and that v.9 is precisely his commission:[18] the herald is Second Isaiah himself![19] (One is sharply reminded at this point of the way in which Muhammed frequently referred to himself in the Qur'an as the "bringer

---

[16]Frank M. Cross, Jr., "The Council of Yahweh in Second Isaiah," JNES, XII (1953), 274-77; Edwin C. Kingsbury, "The Prophets and the Council of Yahweh, JBL, LXXXIII (1964), 279-86; see also Muilenburg, op.cit., 422, and the literature cited there.

[17]Muilenburg, op.cit., 431.

[18]Cf. Norman Habel, "The Form and Significance of the Call Narratives," ZAW, NF XXXVI (1965) 314-316. Several scholars admit that 40:1-8 is the prophet's call, but leave unanswered the questions as to the nature of 40:9-11. Cf. Sigmund Mowinckel, "Die Komposition des deuterojesajanischen Buches," ZAW, NF VIII (1931), 88-89 [Mowinckel calls vv.1-8 a "Berufungsaudition"]; see also North, The Second Isaiah, p.71.

[19]Although not in connection with Is. 40:9, a number of authorities have at one time or another suggested that the prophet and the herald are the same person. Cf. Sigmund Mowinckel, Der Knecht Jahwäs (Giessen: Alfred Töpelmann, 1921) 12, 17; idem, He That Cometh, trans. G.W. Anderson (Oxford: Basil Blackwell, 1956) 218, n.2; Joachim Begrich, Studien zu Deuterojesaja (BWANT, 77; Stuttgart: W. Kohlhammer, 1938) 121, 153; Aage Bentzen, King and Messiah (London: Lutterworth Press, 1955) 102, n.2; Reuben Levy, Deutero-Isaiah (London: Oxford University Press, 1925) 143; Karl Elliger, Deuterojesaja in seinem Verhaltnis zu Tritojesaja (BWANT, 63; Stuttgart: W. Kohlhammer, 1933) 84, 88; Max Haller, Das Judentum (SAT, pt. 2/3; Göttingen: Vandenhoeck & Ruprecht, 1925) 31; Karl Marti, Das Buch Jesaja ("Kurzer Hand-Commentar zum Alten Testament," Vol. X; Tübingen: J.C.B. Mohr, 1900) 284.

of good tidings." بَشِير and مُبَشِّر Cf. the Qur'an, 2:113; 5:22;
7:188; 11:2; 17:106; 25:58; 33:44; 34:27; 35:22; 48:8.) With this understanding of the material, the entire section takes on form and meaning and
becomes an integrated whole, not a headless torso.[20] Thus Yahweh's command
to speak comfortingly to Jerusalem, found in the opening verse, is fulfilled
in these closing lines by the prophet's specific commission as the mebasser
who is to bring this good news to Jerusalem.[21] "The Prophet's thought begins
and ends with the city (vss.1, 9)."[22]

This relationship between the beginning and the ending of the passage is
further illustrated by the fact that the same Gattung seems to be used in
both verses 1 and 9, the Botenspruch or herald's message.[23] In view of Second
Isaiah's literary sensitivity, it is not likely that such correspondence of
introduction and conclusion is fortuitous; rather it indicates that the same
basic idea is being propounded in both: the proclamation to the people (i.e.,
Zion-Jerusalem) of the imminent coming of Yahweh to assume his eschatological
reign. Naturally this proclamation is to be made by someone other than the
people themselves and all indices clearly point to the prophet as the pro-
claimer.[24]

---

[20]On the unity of 40:1-11, see inter alia Stuhlmueller, op.cit., 74, fn. 244;
also Westermann, Isaiah 40-66, 43.

[21]Note once more that the Targum explicitly addresses the imperative in both
v.1 and v.9 to the prophets.

[22]Muilenburg, op.cit., 425. However, in such statements as these, care must
be taken not to overemphasize the literal geographical aspect of Zion-Jerusalem
as a specific location. The Holy City was the symbolic "heart and soul" of the
exiled nation. As she was destroyed, so they in a sense were destroyed. As
she will be restored, so they will be restored. Thus she is one with her children scattered all over the world, and although Second Isaiah's soaring imagery
is set against a Judean landscape, his audience in Babylon knew that he was
speaking directly to them as well. Cf. North, The Second Isaiah, 73f; Muilenburg, loc.cit.; James D. Smart, History and Theology in Second Isaiah (Philadelphia: The Westminster Press, 1965) 53.

[23]Muilenburg, op.cit., 390, 423; cf. Ludwig Köhler, Deuterojesaja (Jesaja 40-55)
stilkritisch untersucht (BZAW, 37; Giessen: Alfred Töpelmann, 1923) 102ff., and
Westermann, Basic Forms of Prophetic Speech (Philadelphia: The Westminster Press,
1967) 98-128.

[24]L.G. Rignell, in A Study of Isaiah Ch. 40-55 (Lund: Hoakan Ohlssons Boktryckeri,
1956), holds that Zion is both the messenger and those to whom the message is
proclaimed, both informer and the informed (13-14), but surely this interpretation is much too unnatural and strained when compared to the one above.

The mention of the Botenspruch, just made above, points to a crucial factor with regard to the problem of the herald of good news. According to Köhler, there are in Second Isaiah no less than sixty-one instances of this form which have been preserved in one way or another and he concludes that this prophet uses the Botenspruch much more freely than his predecessors.[25] The presence and prominence of this literary type in Second Isaiah is strong evidence for the identification of the mebasser with the prophet. Simple logic demands that the Spruch of the Botenspruch be delivered by the Bote and the fact that the prophet chose this form as the vehicle for so many of his oracles militates with telling force for the view that he himself was the messenger. This understanding of the mebasser as Second Isaiah agrees well with the concept of the prophet in general as Yahweh's messenger. This concept has received significant impetus and development in recent years,[26] and it stands as a powerful witness in favor of the proposed identification.

It is very instructive to compare the present passage with the inaugural vision and call of Isaiah of Jerusalem in Is. 6:1-12.[27] The similarity is striking, and when one recalls the continuity of tradition within the Isaianic circles of prophecy, a continuity which has become increasingly recognized of late,[28] this fact assumes even greater significance. Thus in Isaiah 6 there is the setting in the temple, an ambiguous place which partakes both of heaven and earth and corresponds to the celestial council in 40:1-11; there are the antiphonal cries of the heavenly beings (cf. 40:3,6), the prophet's protest of human weakness and unworthiness (cf.40:6b-7), the response of the heavenly being (cf.40:8?), and, climactically, the prophet's commission by Yahweh to "go and say to this people" (לך ואמרת לעם הזה) a message which he then gives him (cf. 40:9). The only features missing in Is. 40:1-11 which are found in Is. 6 are the descriptions of the visionary elements and the references to the details of the prophet's own concrete, personal situation of the moment, precisely those things

---

[25]Kohler, loc.cit., Joachim Begrich, in Studien zu Deuterojesaja (BWANT, vol. 77; Stuttgart: W. Kohlhammer, 1938), denies the existence of Köhler's Boten-spruch as a genuine Gattung (p.61). Actually, the findings of these two scholars are not so much contradictory as they are supplementary, and their proposed analyses are more compatible than Begrich admits.

[26]Cf. James F. Ross, "The Prophet as Yahweh's Messenger," Israel's Prophetic Heritage: Essays in Honor of James Muilenburg (New York: Harper and Row, 1962) 98-107; Westermann, loc. cit.

[27]Cf. Habel, op.cit., 309-316.

[28]Cf. Douglas R. Jones, "Isaiah--II and III," Peake's Commentary on the Bible, ed. Matthew Black and H. H. Rowley (London: Thomas Nelson and Sons Ltd., 1962) 516: "More recent scholarship has rediscovered, without denying the validity of previous analytical work, the significant cohesion of the whole Isaianic corpus of prophecies. The signs of unity are to be explained not by unity of authorship but by the unceasing work of a school of disciples from the time of the 8th-cent. Isaiah of Jerusalem down to the period following the rebuilding of the Temple (520-516). Second Isaiah was the most distinguished representative of this school."

which one would not expect to find in Second Isaiah. These parallels are significant; in fact, it might legitimately be said that Is. 40:1-11 is the call of Isaiah of Jerusalem translated into terms of Second Isaiah's idiom and represents that phenomenon in both the life and the book of the latter.

This pattern of the prophetic call is further exemplified and elucidated by Jer. 1, although the parallels in this case are less precise. Once more there is the dialogical quality of the passage, the protest of the prophet, the response to the protest, this time by Yahweh himself, and again, most significantly, the prophet's commission to prophecy to "all to whom I [Yahweh] shall send you," including Jerusalem and the cities of Judah, together with what is to be the content of his message and the admonition to "fear not" (אל־תירא). Cp. Is. 40:9c.

It will be noticed that in each of these prophetic calls, as well as others like them (cf. Ez. 1-3, Amos 7), one of the most indispensable elements is the commission of the prophet and some indication of the content of his proclamation. If, in fact, Is. 40:1-11 does represent what may be termed the call of Second Isaiah, and all the evidence strongly tends to this conclusion, then v.9 almost certainly constitutes the commission of the prophet. He himself is to be the herald of good news to Jerusalem and all Judah.

The identification of the mebasser as Second Isaiah himself is strongly supported by the use of the participle in Is. 41:27. However, there appears to be a very serious textual problem in this verse which cannot be ignored if a completely satisfactory exegesis is to be achieved. The MT reads as follows:

ראשון לציון הנה הנם ולירושלם מבשר אתן

The literal translation of this passage is usually rendered thusly:

"First to Zion, behold, behold them,
    and to Jerusalem I give a herald of good news."

It has long been felt by most scholars that the first half of this verse was either corrupt beyond recovery or else so cryptic as to be practically unintelligible, and the best they could do with it was to emend הנה הנם to הגדתיה,[29] thus reading "I first have declared it to Zion" (RSV). This reconstruction seemed to represent at least approximately the intended meaning of the first half of the line since it presumably contained a revelatory statement of some kind parallel to the second half of the line. (Even the present הנה הנם suggests this.) Although this proposal may not have been the exact key with which to unlock this mystery, it was at least a move in the right direction. This is shown by recent evidence from the Dead Sea Scrolls which may at last solve the riddle of 41:27. IQIsaᵃ renders the enigmatic הנה הנם as הנה הנומה. Alfred Guillaume has recognized in this reading a root which is not found elsewhere in Hebrew.[30] This root, נמה, would be related to the Arabic root نمى , "to bring news, inform," and the present occurrence would

---

[29] Cf. D.W. Thomas' notes in "Liber Jesaiae," Biblia Hebraica Stuttgartensia, ed. K. Elliger and W. Rudolph (Stuttgart: Würtembergische Bibelanstalt, 1968) in loco; cp. also Marti, op.cit., 284; Muilenburg, op.cit., 463; as well as C.F. Whitley, "A Note on Isa. XLI.27," JSS, II (1957), 327f. A number of other emendations have been proposed, but the one given above seems to be the most important. D.W. Thomas has recently proposed אֲמַנֶּה , "I appoint," or הִמֶּנָה, "is appointed." Cf. "A Note on the Hebrew Text of Isaiah XLI.27," JTS (1967), 127-28.

[30] Alfred Guillaume, "Some Readings in the Dead Sea Scroll of Isaiah," JBL, LXXVI (1957), 40-41.

represent the Qal active participle written plene, נוּמֶה, "news bringer,
informer."[31] This is a very cogent proposal, for it provides good parallelism with mebasser in the second half line, makes sense out of the nonsensical הֵנֵה הֵנֵם without resorting to actual textual emendation, and generally
makes possible a translation which is satisfactory in almost every respect.
The text could then be rendered:

> Zion gets the first report;
>   behold, the news bringer,
>   and to Jerusalem I give a herald of good news.[32]

However, regardless of whether this particular reading is valid or not,
the important point is that, in the second half of the verse, the agent of
this revelation, who can be none other than the prophet himself, is specifically identified as the mebasser. Here they are clearly shown to be the
same person. The entire burden of the Gerichtsrede in 41:21-29 is to show
that Yahweh, and not the heathen idols, is God because he alone knows and
determines the future.[33] In particular, it is Yahweh, and not the dumb and
impotent images, who has raised up Cyrus to liberate his people and who has
given them a mebasser to announce their deliverance to them beforehand.
However, this function of the mebasser is precisely that which is fulfilled
by the activity of Second Isaiah himself. The prophet is the only one who
fits this role here assigned to the mebasser and he fits it perfectly.[34]

---

[31]North has also noted this variant in the Scrolls and supposes it to be the
Qal participle of a Hebrew root נום, although he considers this particular
form to have been constructed by analogy as if it were from the root נמה .
The root נום in post-biblical Hebrew means "to speak" and is presumably
related to the biblical נאם , "utterance, declaration." On this basis,
נוּמֶה would be given some such translation as "speaker" or "spokesman,"
which, in spite of the different roots, is relatively near Guillaume's rendering. However, after saying all this, North expresses serious doubt as to
whether the Scroll reading is valid in the first place. North, The Second
Isaiah, 104. Cf. also Marcus Jastrow, A Dictionary of the Targumim, the Talmud
Babli and Yerushalmi, and the Midrashic Literature (New York, G.P. Putnam's
Sons, 1903), II, 887, where this very participle נוּמֶה "fr. נמה " is listed
under the root נום , "to speak, say."

[32]Cf. also William Hugh Brownlee, The Meaning of the Qumran Scrolls for the
Bible (New York: Oxford University Press, 1964) 224.

[33]Westermann, Isaiah 40-66, p.91; see also p.15f.

[34]In view of the likelihood that Second Isaiah understood himself as the
mebasser, it is interesting to note the proposal that yet another figure may
have influenced the prophet's image of himself and his mission: Moses. [Cf.
Begrich, op.cit., 101, 152. Bentzen (op.cit., 66-67) rather obliquely suggests the same thing in connection with his discussion of the servant of
Yahweh.] Second Isaiah's conceptualization of the release and return of the
Jews from Babylon as a second Exodus is patent throughout his work. [See
Bernhard W. Anderson, "Exodus Typology in Second Isaiah," Israel's Prophetic
Heritage: Essays in Honor of James Muilenburg (New York: Harper & Brothers,
1962), 177-95, and the literature cited there.] In this connection it has
been suggested that the prophet regarded himself as a kind of second Moses
who would lead his people forth in his new and greater exodus. This is to say
that once more he looked upon himself as a crucial figure in Yahweh's redemption
of Israel. Such a self-image, if it is valid, would agree well with his view of
himself as the mebasser.

With this understanding of the figure of the mebasser in Second Isaiah, it is now possible to proceed with a more detailed consideration of the three contexts in which he appears.

In 40:9, the term is used to indicate the prophet's commission as the bringer of good news to Zion-Jerusalem, which is given to him within the context and setting of Yahweh's heavenly council. The prophet is pictured as a messenger who hurries on ahead of the returning army in order to bring the good news of victory to the waiting populace. However, his news is not merely or even primarily of the return of the exiles. The heart of his message is contained in the theophanic formula with which he begins his proclamation: הנה אלהיכם , "Behold your God!" It is Second Isaiah's basic thesis that the overthrow of Babylon and the restoration of the captive Judeans to their homeland will mark the beginning of the new age and with it the eschatological reign of Yahweh. It is this imminent coming of Yahweh in great power which the prophet proclaims. The return of the exiles is only a sign of the greater reality with which he is concerned. God's advent is his ultimate, his only message, and with its proclamation he has delivered himself of his essential burden. Upon this theme he will play numerous variations which will comprise the larger part of his work. It is in this regard that Is. 40: 1-11 has been called the "prologue"[35] or "overture"[36] to Second Isaiah, and rightly so, for in it the prophet announces the major motifs with which he will be concerned throughout the following chapters: the consolation of Jerusalem, the proclamation of her pardon and release, the consummate revelation of Yahweh's glory, and, climactically, the theophany of Yahweh himself as he comes to establish his kingly rule.

The occurrence of mebasser in Isaiah 41:27 has already been touched upon above in connection with the identification of the herald and the prophet; however, much remains to be said with regard to its total significance. Isaiah 41:27 is found in the context of a Gerichtsrede,[37] a literary type patterned after a judicial process. This passage, which includes vv.21-27, appears to continue the line of thought which was begun in 41:1-7, where the nations in general were summoned to trial before the bar of the Lord of History However, in this case, which is unique in Second Isaiah, the heathen gods themselves are addressed. They are arraigned by Yahweh in a court of law and challenged by him to substantiate their claim to existence. The basis upon which the dispute will be adjudicated is the argument from history, for, according to

---

[35]E.g., George Adam Smith, The Book of Isaiah (revised edition; New York: Harper & Brothers, n.d.) II, 71; Muilenburg, op.cit., 422; Skinner, op.cit., 1, Westermann, Isaiah 40-66, 32-33.

[36]E.g., Volz, op.cit., 2; North, The Second Isaiah, 70; Stuhlmueller, op.cit., 182.

[37]Begrich op.cit., 19, cf. also 19-42; Herman Gunkel and Joachim Begrich, Einleitung in den Psalmen ("Göttinger Handkommentar zum Alten Testament"; Göttingen: Vandenhoeck & Ruprecht, 1933) 364-66; Westermann, Basic Forms..., 124-198; H. Eberhard von Waldow, "Der traditionsgeschichtliche Hintergrund der prophetische Gerichtsreden," BZAW, LXXXV (1963); for the Gerichtsrede in Second Isaiah see Westermann, "Sprache und Struktur ...", 134-144, and H. Eberhard von Waldow, "The Message of Deutero-Isaiah," Interpretation, XXII (1968), 270-274.

Second Isaiah, he alone is God who creates and directs history and who can thus tell the meaning of present events and foretell "what is to come here-after." That is to say, the lordship of history is the hallmark of divinity.[38]

The occurrence of mebasser is of crucial significance for this whole argument, for only in the three words, ולירושלם מבשר אתן, of verse 27 is Yahweh clearly shown to be the one who has that control over history which sets him apart from the false deities as the one true God. However, the mebasser is all that is needed. Through the agency of this herald, Yahweh proclaims in advance the spectacular military triumphs of Cyrus "whom victory meets at every step" (41:2) as he tramples "on rulers as on mortar, as the potter treads clay" (41:25), and whose successes will culminate in the fall of Babylon and the release of the exiles.

Two things become apparent from this analysis of 41:27: 1) once again it will be readily seen that the mebasser is none other than the prophet himself. 2) It is also clear that the phenomenon referred to here is the same as that described in 40:9-10: the prophet-mebasser bringing the good news of God's advent which has been signaled by the victory of Cyrus.[39]

As it has already been pointed out, Is. 52:7 depicts the actual performance of the prophet's commission which was given in 40:9. In a scene of breath-taking poetical beauty, the prophet-mebasser is now described as he makes his way toward Jerusalem over the hills which surround the holy city, running on ahead of the main company to bring the good news to Zion that Yahweh is vic-torious (cf. ישועה in vs. 7 and 10) over his enemies and that the "peace" (שלום) attendant upon his triumph is now in effect. All of this and more the prophet proclaims by means of the simple theophanic formula, מלך אלהיך, "your God reigns," which actually contains his entire message in nuce: Yahweh's eschatological kingdom is now a reality. However at this point the marvelous procession of the redeemed exiles, gently led by the Savior himself, comes into sight and the watchmen upon the walls of the city[40] break into ringing shouts of joy, for they themselves behold, directly and without intermediary (עין בעין), Yahweh returning to his holy city (cf. הנה אלהיכם in 40:9). As the good news spreads throughout the city, the very ruins themselves are summoned to celebrate Jerusalem's redemption. By this great victory (ישועה, vs. 7 and 10), Yahweh has revealed his mighty power (זרוע קדש) to all the world.

---

[38]Westermann, Isaiah 40-66, 15-16, 91.

[39]It is strange that some scholars who maintain that Zion-Jerusalem is the mebassereth in 40:9 refer the situation in 41:27 back to that passage although they clearly realize that here the mebasser unquestionably carries the good news to Zion-Jerusalem. Cf. George A. F. Knight, op.cit., 68; G.A. Smith, op. cit., 125-26; Muilenburg, op.cit., 462-63. Equally difficult to understand are those who link 52:7 closely to 40:9, but still identify the mebassereth as Zion-Jerusalem. Cf. Westermann, Isaiah 40-66, 250, quoted in fn. 14 above.

[40]The usual station for watchmen. Cf., e.g., II Sam. 18:24. Whether the walls are pictured as being in ruins or restored is not clear. V.9 speaks of the "waste places of Jerusalem," but in any case poetry of this kind should not be pressed for too great a degree of consistency.

Thus Is. 52:7 represents the culmination of the use of mebasser in Second Isaiah. Although these three occurrences refer to the same event and cannot really be separated from one another, the fact remains that here the picture is no longer that of the herald being commissioned to deliver the good news (40:9); nor is he spoken of in a somewhat vague way as the means whereby Yahweh makes known his foreknowledge and therefore his control of history (41:27). Rather he is concretely described as now in fact delivering the good news and so inaugurating the new age. The process which began with the call of the prophet in the heavenly council is here completed, the commission is here actually and officially fulfilled.

However, it remains to be asked: how, specifically did the prophet actually carry out this commission? What was the real setting in which he delivered his message of good news? This question raises a fundamental problem which can no longer be ignored: the Sitz im Leben of Second Isaiah as a whole. In the past, this issue has received only occasional attention which has not been sufficient to establish any significant consensus. A number of scholars have simply avoided the question entirely. The reason for this neglect is readily to be found in the forbidding complexities presented by the whole problem. Some scholars have held that Second Isaiah wrote, that with him there appeared something new under the sun: prophetische Schriftstellerei (e.g., Hölscher, Duhm, Muilenburg, and recently, G.A.F. Knight), but in this regard, Gressmann's famous dictum is still basically valid, "Ein Prophet der nur schreibt ist ein Widerspruch in sich."[41] Others have contended that the prophet delivered his oracles in oral form, but they have not been able to supply very detailed or convincing information concerning the setting (e.g., Hempel, Volz, D.R. Jones).[42] One writer was so torn between the two possibilities that he chose to equivocate; Westermann said, "I myself am quite sure that the oracles were originally spoken, but the longer poems like 49.14-26 or 51.9-52.3 may have been literary productions from the beginning."[43] However, in his Bonn dissertation of 1953, Hans-Eberhard von Waldow made what may eventually turn out to be a decisive step toward the solution of this enigma.[44] Building carefully upon the previous results achieved

---

[41]Hugo Gressmann, "Die literarische Analyse Deuterojesajas," ZAW, XXXIV (1914), 255f.

[42]For recent support of the oral nature of these materials, see Fohrer, op.cit., 3; and McKenzie, op.cit., XXXIV-XXXV.

[43]Westermann, Isaiah 40-66, 28.

[44]Hans-Eberhard von Waldow, Anlass und Hintergrund der Verkündigung des Deuterojesaja (Bonn: Fried. Wilhelms-Universität, 1953). See also his more recent, much shorter, and more popular discussion, "The Message of Deutero-Isaiah," Interpretation, XXII (1968), 259-287. McKenzie follows von Waldow rather closely, both in arguing of the oral form of the oracles and in positing a cultic setting for them (op.cit., XXXIV-XXXV), although he demurs on the question of the specific liturgical occasion. See fn. 46 below.

in the field of Gattungsforschung by Gressmann, Köhler, and especially
Begrich, von Waldow reasons in the following manner: (1) as Begrich has
shown, the basic Gattung in Second Isaiah is the priestly oracle of salvation, which von Waldow calls a "prophetic cult-oracle" (profphetische Kult-
orakel); this is prima facie a cultic form.[45]   (2) However, these oracles are
not literary imitations, as Begrich holds, but were actually delivered in a
bona fide cultic setting.[46]   (3) Thus, Second Isaiah was in fact a kind of
cultic prophet who functioned in the context of what von Waldow terms a
Volksklagefeier, a ceremony in which the exiles gathered together to lament
the fall of Jerusalem.[47]   (4) From this basic premise, he is able to account
for the origin of the whole collection, even though parts of it stem from
somewhat different occasions. It is not possible to go into all of von
Waldow's arguments, but it must be said that his general thesis is convincing,
whether one agrees with him in detail or not.[48] He has taken the problem of
the Sitz of Second Isaiah with the utmost seriousness, and until he is proven
wrong (or improved upon, for surely the investigation of this field has only
begun), his analysis will remain the major position to be reckoned with.

---

[45]The occurrence of אל־תירא ("fear not") in 40:9 is of particular significance in the connection. The actual Gattung of 40:1-10 has proven to be something of a problem, as a cursory survey of the literature will readily show.
It has been variously and vaguely described as an "introduction," a "prologue,"
an "overture," or some kind of a hymn, while in fact it functions as the "call"
of the prophet. In any case, the presence of אל־תירא here provides a strong
link with the oracle of salvation and its generally accepted cultic setting.
This is not to suggest that 40:1-10 is a bone fide oracle of salvation, but
only that parts of its vocabulary indicate the same liturgical background.
See J. Becker, Gottesfurcht im alten Testament ("Analecta Biblica," 25; Rome:
Pontifical Biblical Institute, 1965), although he draws somewhat different
conclusions from those presented here.

[46]This is a very important point. Numerous scholars, such as Begrich, readily
admit the cultic nature of the Gattungen in Second Isaiah, but contend that
they are not genuine, only literary imitations. By a careful analysis, von
Waldow shows that this is not the case. The Gattungen themselves give every
evidence of stemming from authentic settings. In general, it should be noted
that the tendency to consider any Gattung as a literary imitation is a very
precarious one, contrary to the most basic principles of Gattungsforschung,
which hold that the determination of the literary type of a unit will reveal
something of its "setting in life." To assume, unless it is absolutely necessary, that such settings are imitated is to undermine the entire enterprise.
It must be granted that there are instances in the OT in which certain Gattungen
are imitated in situations other than their original settings. However, such
an interpretation is to be accepted only when the evidence to this effect is
clear and unmistakable, which is hardly the case in Second Isaiah.

[47]Both Westermann and Stuhlmueller acknowledge the strong possibility of a
liturgical setting for Second Isaiah's activity, but do not draw out the full
implications of that setting. Cf. Westermann, Isaiah 40-66, 5-6, 8; and
Stuhlmueller, op.cit., 25.

[48]Grave reservation must be expressed regarding von Waldow's Volksklagefeier
as the specific occasion for the prophet's oracles. Likewise his position with
respect to the secular setting of the Gerichtsrede must be viewed with considerable doubt, although this understanding of the Gattung has been supported by

Thus the prophet, himself the mebasser, brought the good news of Yahweh's coming and Israel's imminent redemption within the cultic context of the worshipping congregation. It will be admitted that this conclusion raises several interesting issues which cry out for further discussion, but these must await a later opportunity.[49] In any case, the significance of the mebasser in Second Isaiah cannot be denied.

As the bearer of the message of salvation, he is in fact the bearer and bringer of the salvation itself. The spoken word, in a sense, has the power to bring into being its content; proclamation effects that which is proclaimed. Thus the word (רבד) and event (רבד) become one in the creative pronouncement of the mebasser. He proclaims God's advent and the beginning of his eschatological reign, and by virtue of this very act they become reality. Thus the mebasser is the inaugurator of the new age, the agent through whom Yahweh brings it into being, and his importance must be gauged accordingly. He is not merely incidental to the message of Second Isaiah, not just a decorative figure in the landscape, but rather he stands precisely in the center of the picture.[50]

Hans Jochen Boecker, "Anklagereden und Verteidigungsreden im Alten Testament," Evangelische Theologie, XX (1960), 398-412. McKenzie rightly observes that "It is not necessary to identify the utterances of Second Isaiah with any particular festivals in order to accept the view that he spoke in the cultic assembly" (op.cit., XXXV).

[49]For example, does not the identification of the prophet with the mebasser along the lines suggested in this study also imply that the prophet may be the servant of Yahweh as well? There were several points in the previous discussion where it would have been pertinent to touch upon it (Cf., e.g., Fn.34). However, it is clearly impossible to enter into this gargantuan problem within the scope of the present investigation. Only let it be noted that perhaps there is more to be said for the so-called autobiographical theory of the servant than has been thought in recent years. Cf. von Waldow, "The Message ...," 285.

[50]Julius Schniewind, Evangelion: Ursprung und erste Gestalt des Begriffs Evangelium ("Beiträge zur Förderung christlicher Theologie," 2nd series, XIII; Gütersloh: C. Bertelsmann, 1927-31) 39.

YAHWEH THE AVENGER

Isaiah 63:1-6

Fredrick Holmgren
North Park Theological Seminary

Most contemporary biblical scholars affirm a multiple
authorship for Isaiah 55-66.[1] To the present writer this view
has seemed to be one that best explains the diverse literature
in these chapters. While he still tends toward such an understanding of the material, it appears to him that some arguments
supporting a varied authorship and dating of these oracles
are unconvincing. A case in point is Isa 63:1-6. Critics
committed to the above view usually judge this pericope to be
an independent oracle and therefore unrelated to the three
chapters which precede it.[2] In the following pages we will
examine this judgment and the evidence for it.

First let us look at the structure and content of the
oracle itself.

I - Isa 63:1-2

(1)   מי–זה

בא מאדום

A   חמוץ בגדים מבצרה

זה הדור בלבושו

צעד ברב כחו

אני מדבר בצדקה

B רב להושיע

(2)   מדוע

אדם

A'   ללבושך

ובגדיך

כדרך בגת

II - Isa 63:3-6

(3)   פורה דרכתי לבדי

ומעמים אין–איש אחי

ואדרכם באפי

ואָרמסם בחמתי   A

ויז נצחם

על–בגדי

וכל–מלבושי

אגאלתי

(4)   כי יום נקם בלבי

                 B

ושנת גאולי באה

(5)   ואביט ואין עזר

ואשתומם ואין סומך

ותושע לי

זרעי

וחמתי   A'

היא סמכתני

(6)   ואבוס עמים באפי

ואשכרם בחמתי

ואוריד לארץ נצחם

---

[1]For a recent survey of criticism see: K. Pauritsch, Die neue Gemeinde: Gott sammelt Ausgestossene und Arme (AnBib 47; Rome: Biblical Institute, 1971) 1-30 and R. D. Wells, Jr., The State-ments of Well-Being in Isaiah 60-62: Implications of Form Criticism and the History of Tradition for the Interpretation of Isaiah 56-66 (Dissertation; Vanderbilt; Ann Arbor, Mich.: University Microfilms, 1968), 2-73.

An analysis of Isa 63:1-6 has convinced us that the form
of this oracle is a double chiastic structure.[4] The following
phenomena appear to confirm our view.

I - Isa 63:1-2

A	A'
מי-זה	מדוע
מאדום	אדם
בגדים	ובגדיך
בלבושו	ללבושך
צעד בא	כדרך

Sections A,A' represent questions directed to an awesome but
unnamed figure whom we assume to be Yahweh. In the central
strophe (B) Yahweh identifies himself and reveals the purpose
of his intervention, namely, the salvation of his people.

---

[2]See e.g., Pauritsch, Die neue Gemeinde, 138 and 144;
C. Westermann, Isaiah 40-66 (Philadelphia: Westminster,
1969), 384.

[3]The MT reads: צעה

[4]Observe the occurrence of chiasmus in A and A' of
section I and in A and A' of section II. The most thorough
investigation of chiasmus in biblical literature is that of
N. W. Lund, Chiasmus in the New Testament (Chapel Hill:
University of North Carolina, 1942).

II - Isa 63:3-6

A	A'
דרכתי ואדרכם ארמסם	ואבוס
לבדי אין-איש אתי	אין עזר אין סומך
ומעמים	עמים
באפי בחמתי	באפי בחמתי חמתי
ויז נצחם	ואוריד ... נצחם

Throughout these verses Yahweh is the speaker. In strophes
A and A' he describes the destruction that accompanies his
wrathful intervention. Compare A and A' in section I. The
reason for his action (i.e., the redemption of Israelites) is
set down in the middle strophe (B). Notice that the strophe
is introduced by כי , which, as Muilenburg has shown, frequently heads a motive cause.[5] The central sections of both
chiastic structures (I and II) focus on Yahweh's determination to save his people.

The terminology which the two chiastic structures share
reinforces the nearly universal view that sections I and II
(i.e., vss. 1-6) constitute a literary unit. Observe the
appearance of the following terms in this oracle.

---

[5]"The Linguistic and Rhetorical Usages of the Particle כי
in the Old Testament," HUCA 32 (1961) 135-60.

I	II
בא	באה
בגדים ובגדים	בגדי
בלבושו ללבושך	מלבושי
להושיע	ותושע
כדרך בגת	פורה דרכתי

The savage imagery of Isa 63:1-6 is noted by all commentators. Yahweh's full wrath is directed against the nations (vss. 3-6).[6] So fierce is Yahweh's action - so wild is the divine slaughter that the prophet can only liken it to the ancient process of making wine. As grapes squirt their juice on the one treading them, so the life-blood of the nations spurts upon Yahweh's garments as he strikes them with his arm and stomps them with his feet. To the prophet the bloody clothes of Yahweh appear "glorious."[7] Why has this terrible violence seized the nations? The central member of each chiastic piece indicates that the bloody destruction of the nations takes place in order to ensure Israel's deliverance.

"It is I, announcing vindication, mighty to save" (vs. 1).

"For the day of vengeance was in my heart, and my year of redemption has come" (vs. 4).[8]

For many interpreters this violent nationalism has been reason enough for denying 63:1-6 to the hand of the author of

---

[6] The number of terms appearing in this unit with first person prefixes or suffixes (22) highlights the personal character of this passage.

[7] Vs. 2 makes it clear that the redness of Yahweh's garments was not their normal color.

[8] The English translation of the Hebrew text is that of the RSV unless otherwise noted.

chs. 60-62. However, such a judgment needs revision because
any serious reading of Isaiah 60-62 uncovers a strong par-
ticularism in the prophet's hope for the future.[9] Although
the nations are recipients of Yahweh's salvation they are not
full members of this community created by Yahweh. For them
salvation means servanthood to the Jews. The subservient
character of the nations may be clearly seen in several of the
oracles in chs. 60-62. A good example is Isa 60:10-16:

10. Foreigners shall build up your walls,
         and their kings shall minister to you;
      for in my wrath I smote you,
         but in my favor I have had mercy on you.
11. Your gates shall be open continually;
         day and night they shall not be shut;
      that men may bring to you the wealth of nations,
         with their kings led in procession.
12. For the nation and kingdom
         that will not serve you shall perish;
         those nations shall be utterly laid waste.
13. The glory of Lebanon shall come to you,
         the cypress, the plane, and the pine,
      to beautify the place of my sanctuary;
         and I will make the place of my feet glorious.
14. The sons of those who oppressed you
         shall come bending low to you;
      and all who despised you
         shall bow down at your feet;
      they shall call you the City of the LORD,
         and Zion of the Holy One of Israel.
15. Whereas you have been forsaken and hated,
         with no one passing through,
      I will make you majestic for ever,
         a joy from age to age.
16. You shall suck the milk of nations,
         you shall suck the breast of kings;
      and you shall know that I, the LORD, am your Savior
         and your Redeemer, the Mighty One of Jacob.
                    (cp. 60:5-7 and 61:5-7)

---

[9]In agreement are J. Skinner, Isaiah (Cambridge: Uni-
versity Press, 1917) 2. 195-96; J. McKenzie, Second Isaiah
(AB 20; Garden City: Doubleday, 1968) 177; Westermann,
Isaiah 40-66, 374 and 384.

Here is the dream of an oppressed people for the reversal
of fortunes. One day "the wealth of the nations" shall belong
to Israel, foreign peoples will build the walls of Jerusalem
and those who once humiliated her shall come and "bow down at
her feet" (cp. 61:5-7). People who once despised Israel shall
become her servants. It will be a glorious new age for the
Jews.

But what will bring about this revolutionary era? Westermann insists that the response of the nations is a voluntary
one. It is not brought about by war or by force of any kind.[10]
This is the view of the majority of scholars.[11] But does an
examination of the text and of the prophet's own situation
support this interpretation?

It is difficult for us to imagine the prophet believing
that these nations would willingly become servants of Israel--
would willingly bring their wealth to the Jewish nation.
There was nothing in his world of experiences that would lead
him to hope for such a response. In fact, the events surrounding his life suggest other dreams. He belonged to a defeated people whose king had been led away in humiliation and
whose wealth had been carried off to the enemy. Given the
suffering he has shared with his countrymen, it would be no
surprise to us if the prophet looked forward to the time when
Yahweh would subject the nations to the same humiliation
endured by Israel. But the question is, did he? For an
answer we must consider in greater detail some of the prophet's
oracles.[12]

A crucial phrase occurs in 60:11, ומלכיהם נהוגים

[10]Westermann, Isaiah 40-66, 356-57, 359.

[11]So: J. Muilenburg, "The Book of Isaiah: Chapters
40-55," IB 5 (New York: Abingdon, 1956) 702-03; S. H. Blank,
Prophetic Faith in Isaiah (New York: Harper, 1958) 145; C. C.
Torrey, The Second Isaiah (New York: Scribners, 1928) 445;
McKenzie, Second Isaiah, 177; Pauritsch, Die neue Gemeinde,
124 et al.

[12]A similar problem exists with the oracles in Isaiah
40-55. Regarding the outlook of these oracles see H. M.
Orlinsky and N. Snaith, Studies on the Second Part of the Book
of Isaiah (VTSup 14; Leiden: Brill, 1967) and F. Holmgren,
With Wings As Eagles. Isaiah 40-55: An Interpretation
(Chappaqua, New York: Biblical Scholars Press, 1973).

("with their kings led in procession"). The RSV translation
renders accurately the MT with which all the Versions agree.
Despite the single witness of the textual tradition, many
scholars have favored reading an active participle (נוֹהֲגִים)
rather than the passive participle of the MT and translating:
"with their kings leading them."[13] This reading of the text,
it is urged, fits the context of 60:1ff. which sketches an
idyllic scene of people voluntarily submitting themselves to
Israel. Most interpreters agree that the MT creates the impression that the kings are being led into captivity. The
term נָהַג (to lead, drive) frequently conveys this meaning.[14]

Arguing for the retention of the MT, which we favor,
is vs. 12:

> For the nation and kingdom
> that will not serve you shall perish;
> those nations shall be utterly laid waste.

Kings who submit will be led into captivity. Those who refuse
to honor Yahweh and serve Israel will be destroyed. This
verse has only limited value in our study however, because
it is a rare interpreter who does not dismiss it as a later
addition. This judgment may be right. But to identify it as
an editorial comment does not automatically mean that it is
an erroneous interpretation. Representing the earliest commentary on the text, vs. 12 could be a correct understanding
of 60:11. To our mind verses 11 and 12 create no problems as
they now stand in ch. 60.

It is only against the background of the threat of
destruction that we are to understand nations giving up their
wealth, kings submitting to capture and foreigners enduring

---

[13]E.g., B. Duhm, Das Buch Jesaia (Coettingen: Vandenhoeck
& Ruprecht, 1892) 421; F. Feldmann, Das Buch Isaias (EHAT 14;
Muenster: Aschendorff, 1926) 236; Muilenburg, "Isaiah 40-66,"
703.

[14]See e.g., 1 Sam 23:5; 30:2; 30:20; Isa 20:4; Deut 4:27;
28:37. Some scholars retain the traditional Hebrew text of
vs. 11 but understand the disputed clause in terms of an
"inner" or "spiritual" captivity. However, this interpretation is alien to the thought of Isaiah 60-62. See our comments above. Representing the former view is E. Kissane, The
Book of Isaiah, 2 (Dublin: Browne and Nolan, 1943) 268 et al.

the humiliation of becoming second-class citizens--the servants of Israelites. As the Gibeonites of old, the nations choose servanthood to Israel rather than death (Josh 9:3ff.). This same type of reasoning is seen in the decision of the King of Hamath to send tribute to Israel when David was threatening the north country (2 Sam 8:9ff.). Israel herself was urged to respond in a similar manner when she was threatened by a power she could not defeat (Jer 27:8-11). It was a common reaction in the face of danger. Living in such a context it is not surprising that the prophet also thinks in these terms when he envisions the Great Reversal. He is convinced that the divine might displayed on behalf of Israel will compel foreign peoples to submit themselves to her and her God.

Is this hope expressed elsewhere in the oracles of chapters 60-62? We think so. In Isa 61:2 there occurs the phrase "the day of vengeance (נקם יום) of our God." The prophet is addressing Israel and assuring her that a time is coming when she shall be healed, released from captivity and comforted (vss. 1-3). Although the reference to "vengeance" must be seen in the positive sense of deliverance for Israel, it should not be overlooked that there is also a negative meaning to this term.[15] It points to the use of force. Vengeance means the defeat of the enemy, its subsequent destruction or its reduction to the status of a vassal. The latter is referred to in Isaiah 61:5-6.[16]

> Aliens shall stand and feed your flocks,
>   foreigners shall be your plowmen and vine-dressers;
> but you shall be called the priests of the LORD,
>   men shall speak of you as the ministers of our God;
> you shall eat the wealth of the nations,
>   and in their riches you shall glory.

The appearance of these verses in a context of deliverance (60:1-2) indicates to us that the prophet was not thinking

---

[15]See G. Mendenhall, "God of Vengeance, Shine Forth!" (The Wittenberg Bulletin, Special Issue, 1948) 38-40 and J. H. Tullock, Blood-Vengeance Among the Israelites in the Light of Its Near Eastern Background (Dissertation, Vanderbilt, 1966) 100-09.

[16]Torrey (The Second Isaiah, 454) speaks of the "narrow spirit" of 61:5 which he designates an interpolation. Cp. P. Volz, Jesaia II (KAT 9; Leipzig: A. Deichert, 1932), 254.

of a voluntary subjection on the part of foreigners. On the
contrary, he believed they would be forced to this state because of the intervention of Yahweh. No details are given here
concerning the character of this "day of vengeance" but can
it be anything else than battle, blood and death? What is
implied in Isa 61:1-2 is depicted in full color in Isa 63:1-6.

Against the background of the above passages one should
also consider 62:8-9:

> The LORD has sworn by his right hand
>   and by his mighty arm:
> "I will not again give your grain
>   to be food for your enemies,
> and foreigners shall not drink your wine
>   for which you have labored;
> but those who garner it shall eat it
>   and praise the LORD,
> and those who gather it shall drink it
>   in the courts of my sanctuary."

The prophet anticipates the salvation community. It is the
right hand and the mighty arm of Yahweh which guarantees the
security of this gathered people. The imagery, which recalls
Yahweh the warrior, implies that Israel's Lord is prepared to
use force to protect them. If the prophet looks to Yahweh's
"military" power to safeguard this community, could it be that
he also relied on this divine warrior to bring about the deliverance of his people and the subsequent establishment of
this new kingdom? Is this how one should understand Isa
62:1-2?

> For Zion's sake I will not keep silent,
>   and for Jerusalem's sake I will not rest,
> until her vindication goes forth as brightness,
>   and her salvation as a burning torch.
> The nations shall see your vindication,
>   and all the kings your glory,
> and you shall be called by a new name
>   which the mouth of the LORD will give.

The ambiguity of the above passage causes one to be
cautious. Nevertheless the similarity existing between Isa
62:1-2 (cp. vs. 11) and 63:1,6 calls for attention. In the
former verses the prophet waits with intense longing for
Jerusalem's צדקה (vindication) and ישׁועה (salvation) which
is certain to come. When it happens it will be a decisive

143

event. No one will question its meaning. Once it appeared
evident that Jerusalem was forsaken by God. However, when the
salvation event takes place it will be a convincing witness
that God now dwells with her. The unexpected deliverance
which results in a complete reversal of fortunes causes the
nations to stand in awe of the once destroyed city. What is
the character of this vindication? How is this salvation to
be accomplished? Is there any kinship to Isa 63:1-6? Notice
that the last sentence of Isa 63:1 also speaks of Israel's
vindication and salvation. Coming from Edom and bloodied by
battle, Yahweh identifies himself in familiar terms (cp.
62:1-2):

אני מדבר בצדקה רב להושיע

"It is I, announcing vindication- mighty to save."
(cp. 63:5)

The deliverance awaited by the prophet in 62:1 is now announced
as having taken place. It is a deliverance that involves terrible slaughter among the nations. It leaves no doubt as to
the victor. After such a display of divine power on behalf of
Israel, any "thinking" nation will surely "see the light"
realizing that it is better to serve than be severed.[17]

In summary, we believe that several oracles in Isa
60-62 refer to a saving deed to be performed by Yahweh for the
deliverance of his people (60:1ff.; 61:2; 62:1). There is in
these chapters however no full account of the character of this
event. A detailed description is left to ch. 63:1-6. This
phenomenon is similar to the situation existing in Isaiah
40-55. In these latter oracles there are many references to
Yahweh's intervention but only a few pictures of his actual
confrontation with the enemy (cp. e.g., 42:13; 47:3; 49:26).
Although the portrayal of Yahweh in Isa 63:1-6 is shocking,
the figure of Yahweh the warrior is not absent in chs. 60-62.

_____

[17]Torrey (The Second Isaiah, 451) has an interesting
comment on Isa 60:11. He observes that the foreigners who come
to serve Israel and Yahweh do so willingly. He then declares:
"All the reluctant have perished in the great catastrophe,
this is a renovated world." Cp. Y. Kaufmann, The Babylonian
Captivity and Deutero-Isaiah (New York: Union of American
Hebrew Congregations, 1970) 191.

A second reason given for separating Isa 63:1-6 from chapters 60-62 is the apocalyptic character of the former passage and its use of myth.[18] That there is an apocalyptic mood to 63:1-6 seems apparent to us. This, however, is not a sufficient reason for setting it apart from 60-62 and assigning it a later date, for an apocalyptic passage also occurs in ch. 60:19-20.

> The sun shall be no more
>   your light by day,
> nor for brightness shall the moon
>   give light to you by night
> but the LORD will be your everlasting light,
>   and your God will be your glory.
> Your sun shall no more go down,
>   nor your moon withdraw itself;
> for the LORD will be your everlasting light,
>   and your days of mourning shall be ended.

Consistent with his view Westermann denies this passage to the author of Isaiah 60-62. He does so on the ground that the description of salvation in vss. 19-20, as opposed to that in the remaining vss. of ch. 60, transcends history. But this is to limit poetic imagination too rigidly. Basically the above verses express the same utopian dream found in vss. 17-18 and 21-22. Yahweh shall bring about a time of perfect righteousness and peace for his people. At the center of this new community is Yahweh who will be its light. As many have noticed, the affirmation in vss. 19-20 balances well the beginning verses of the chapter which declare that, while the nations shall dwell in darkness, Yahweh shall be a light to his own people.

However, it is urged, what really separates Isa 63:1-6 from chs. 60-62 is the employment of myth in the former passage. Thus, for example, Westermann declares:

> We have found that what supremely marks off 63:1-6
> from the rest of the book is the fact that it depicts
> the battle which annihilates the nations as one waged
> by a single person, and that in the course of it he
> is bespattered all over with blood. There can be no
> doubt that this points to the combat between two

---

[18]See Westermann, _Isaiah 40-66_, 384.

parties or combat at hand to hand as found in myth.[19]

One must give consideration to this suggestion for it is certain that Israel's prophets were well acquainted with the ancient myths. Both the emphasis on Yahweh acting alone (vss. 3,5)[20] and the description of the bloody combat may be interpreted within the context of a mythic battle, like that taking place between Marduk and Tiamat. But even if such an interpretation is accepted it does not necessarily follow that this oracle must be removed from the work of the author of chs. 60-62. A mythological motif occurs in Isa 51:9ff. but no one denies the passage to Second Isaiah on this account. However, we do not care to argue this position for we seriously question the mythological understanding of ch. 63:1-6. In our view another interpretation of the text is to be preferred. Although firm evidence is in short supply we believe that several bits of information suggest that in the above passage there is memory of the ancient kinsman who assumed the role of avenger of blood (גאל הדם). Such a portrayal of Yahweh would not be unique in the oracles of the Hebrew prophets. Second Isaiah, whose influence on many oracles in chapters 56-66 is readily recognized (esp. chs. 60-63), often presents Yahweh as Israel's divine kinsman.[21] Several times in these oracles he assumes the identity of the blood avenger.[22]

The initial reason for considering this interpretation of Isa 63:1-6 is the presence of the terms נקם and גאולים in vs. 4.

---

[19]Isaiah 40-66, 384. Cp. 304-05.

[20]This motif is better related to a similar theme in Isaiah 40-55 (esp. 44:24). See W. Zimmerli, "Zur Sprache Tritojesajas," Gottes Offenbarung: Gesammelte Aufsaetze zum Alten Testament (Muenchen: Kaiser, 1963) 232.

[21]See e.g.: J. J. Stamm, Erloesen und Vergeben im Alten Testament (Bern: A. Francke, 1940) 7-46; C. Stuhlmueller, Creative Redemption in Deutero-Isaiah (Rome: Pontifical Biblical Institute, 1970) 99-167; F. Holmgren, With Wings As Eagles, 71-96.

[22]See Isa 47:3-4 (cp. 49:24-26). For a discussion of these passages consult the volumes listed in the above note.

כי יום נקם בלבי ושנת גאולי באה

For the day of vengeance was in my heart,
and my year of redemption has come.

Two factors indicate the importance of this verse: (1) its
introduction by כי ; (2) its appearance at the center of the
chiastic structure. It is not a chance statement. It proclaims the purpose of Yahweh's intervention. The use of נקם
and גאולים in this central position amidst the violent language
of vss. 3-6 encourages the belief that the prophet had in mind
Yahweh as Judah's blood avenger.[23]

Of further interest is the declaration (vs. 3): "their
lifeblood is sprinkled upon my garments, and I have stained
(אגאלתי)[24] all my raiment." The imagery and the use of גאל
(to stain) in connection with גאל (to redeem) suggests an
allusion to the defiling activity of the blood avenger.[25] That
is, in pursuing his role, the avenger was made unclean by the
blood of the victim which splattered upon him. In the same
fashion Yahweh stains his own garments in bringing about the
redemption of Jerusalem.

---

[23]The following view the text in this manner: E. Merz,
Die Blutrache bei den Israeliten (BWAT 20; Leipzig: J. C.
Hinriches'sche Buchhandlung, 1916) 67-68; D. Daube, Studies in
Biblical Law (Cambridge: University Press, 1947) 55; L.
Koehler, "גאולים" ZAW 39 (1919) 316; Duhm, Das Buch Jesaia,
435 et al. Several scholars see reference in the text to the
year of jubilee in which Hebrew slaves were to receive their
freedom. See e.g., F. Buhl (ed.), Handwoerterbuch ueber das
Alten Testament (Berlin: Springer, 1959) 123. However, the
combat imagery of vss. 3-6 does not lend support to this interpretation. It may be, however, that Daube is correct in
declaring (Studies in Biblical Law): "Quite often a passage
alludes to both redemption of slaves and property and redemption of blood at the same time. It must be remembered that
when God takes back captive Israel he does it, in nearly all
prophecies, not in a mild, quiet manner, but at the same time
destroying the cruel oppressors. . . ." Cp. Isa 60:16.

[24]On the basis of similar forms found in the Amarna
letters, C. H. Gordon and E. Young argue for the retention of
this reading. See their note in the Westminster Theol. Jour.
14 (1951) 54.

[25]We are preparing a paper on the relationship existing
between these two terms.

Lending credibility to this understanding of Isa 63:1-6 is the oracle in Isa 59:15b-20. Shared violence and terminology (12 terms in common)[26] witness to a close relationship between these two passages. It may be that they derive from the same author. Appearing together with words which speak of wrath and vengeance in the latter oracle is the participle גאל (vs. 20). The presence of this title in the context of personal vengeance causes one to see in the figure of the divine גאל , the avenger of blood.

However, it is not only the presence of the term גאולי that suggests the portrayal of Yahweh as blood avenger in Isa 63:4. Pointing in the same direction is נקם which occurs in parallelism with the former word. The term appears rather frequently in contexts which seem to speak of Yahweh as the avenger of blood.[27] Most likely this is the significance of the term in Deut 32:39-43, which reflects a mood similar to that of Isa 63:1-6: Yahweh "avenges the blood of his servants" (vs. 43).

> "See now that I, even I, am he,
>   and there is no god beside me;
> I kill and I make alive;
>   I wound and I heal
>   and there is none that can deliver
>   out of my hand.
> For I lift up my hand to heaven,
>   and swear, As I live for ever,
> if I whet my glittering sword,
>   and my hand takes hold on judgment,
> I will take vengeance[28] on my adversaries,
>   and will requite those who hate me.
> I will make my arrows drunk with blood,
>   and my sword shall devour flesh--

---

[26] H. Odeberg (Trito-Isaiah [UUA 1; Uppsala: Lundquist, 1931] 210-15 and 274-76) lists only nine terms shared by the two oracles. He omits the following roots which also appear in both passages: בוא ; צדקה ; בגד .

[27] E.g., Gen 4:15; Ezek 24:8; Ps 79:10; Isa 47:3; Jer 51:36. See Tulloch, Blood-Vengeance, 100-09.

[28] The English words "vengeance" and "avenges" in this text reflect the Hebrew root נקם .

with the blood of the slain and the captives,
    from the long-haired heads of the enemy."
Praise his people, O you nations;
    for he avenges the blood of his servants,
and takes vengeance on his adversaries,
    and makes expiation for the land of his people.

The above observations are not to be considered proofs of our understanding of Isa 63:1-6. They do, however, serve to highlight some phenomena that make such an interpretation a viable alternative to a mythological understanding of this oracle.

In summary we feel that the nationalism of Isa 63:1-6 is shared with chs. 60-62. While the violent action represented in this oracle is nowhere detailed in chs. 60-62, in the latter chapters the defeat of the nations is assumed[29] and the violence involved in such a humiliation is alluded to several times.[30] Also, as we have noted, the apocalyptic mood of Isa 63:1-6 is not completely foreign to chs. 60-62 (cp. 60:19-20). Further, the representation of Yahweh as the blood avenger of the nation adequately explains the personal character of the battle with the nations. We conclude that there is nothing in Isa 63:1-6 that demands separation from chs. 60-62. Both passages (as well as 59:15b-20) may stem from the same author.

* * *

Dr. James Muilenburg stands as a leading figure in the investigation of the literature of the Old Testament. For over three decades he has enjoyed the reputation of being a creative scholar and a remarkable teacher. Seized by the biblical witness himself, he has shared with those who know him the faith that has nourished his own life. The writer readily acknowledges James Muilenburg to be a central influence in his own life and gratefully dedicates this essay to him.

---

[29] E.g., 60:1ff.; 60:11ff.; 61:5ff.

[30] E.g., 60:11; 61:1; 62:8-9; 62:1-2; 60:12(?).

ISRAEL'S SENSE OF PLACE IN JEREMIAH

Walter Brueggemann

Eden Theological Seminary

It is a delight to offer this essay to James Muilenburg, the only one of his kind in our discipline. His delicate balance of rigorous objectivity and passionate subjectivity is a rare model for us. This paper, which seeks to pursue themes and methods important in his own work, is presented with the gratitude only his students can understand.

I

Recent Old Testament study, in addressing the issue of Israel's view of time and space, has tended to celebrate time and minimize space as an important faith motif.[1] This emphasis was shared not only by Bultmannian scholars[2] but also by some of Bultmann's sharpest critics, who stressed the "Mighty Deeds of God in History."[3] Such a focus was an effective one in a time

---

[1] The most comprehensive statement of this stance is that of T. Boman, Hebrew Thought Compared With Greek (London: SCM, 1960), but a number of other scholars, including Orelli, John Marsh, H. W. Robinson, have contributed to the same tendency. Muilenburg himself, "The Biblical View of Time," HTR 54 (1961) 229, could write, "Of the two great peoples who have exerted a major influence upon the mind and soul of Western Man, Hellas and Israel, the one lived and thought primarily in the world of space, the other primarily in the world of time."

[2] This has received its most extreme form in Fuchs and Ebeling, who regard revelation as "saving event" and that as "language event." Cf. James M. Robinson, "Hermeneutic Since Barth," The New Hermeneutic (eds. Robinson and Cobb; New York: Harper and Row, 1964) 57 and passim.

[3] Cf. G. Ernest Wright, The Old Testament and Theology (New York: Harper and Row, 1969), chapter 2, and B. S. Childs, Biblical Theology in Crisis (Philadelphia: Westminster, 1970), chapter 2, for two reviews of that stress. Both Bultmann and the accent on "Mighty Deeds in History," stressed timefulness as the crucial category.

preoccupied with meaninglessness and boredom, as the recent post-war period was perceived to be.

It is clear in more recent time that the issues of theological concern have shifted radically; instead of speaking of meaninglessness, we may better speak of rootlessness, a sense of the loss of meaningful place.[4] This shift provides an opportunity to look again at the time-space problem in Israel's faith. Without denying the importance of the time emphasis recently made, it is possible to restore a more justified balance. Israel was par excellence, a people with a place, a land of promise, and she was intensely concerned with it.[5]

A movement may be discerned in Israel's faith which moves between landless people yearning for land (the fathers, the sojourn, the exile), and landed people preserving and/or perverting their land (monarchy and prophets, the restoration under Ezra and Nehemiah). Land (and therefore space) is an important component in Israel's faith.[6] Her faith revolved around the question of land, either a desperate yearning for it or problematic possession of it.

As Boman has written of "the uselessness of the Western concept of time"[7] for understanding Israel's notion of time, so

---

[4] This emphasis is reflected in Toffler's popular Future Shock, which is concerned with rootlessness.

[5] The concern of this paper only accidentally intersects with the vigorous arguments of James Barr, The Semantics of Biblical Language (Oxford: Oxford University, 1961) and Biblical Words for Time (SBT 33; Naperville: Alec R. Allenson, 1962). Whereas Barr is concerned that certain words have been wrongly or over-interpreted, my point is that we have simply neglected rather obvious concerns of the texts, no doubt because of our hermeneutical frame. At that point I share Barr's conclusions.

[6] On land as a theological theme, see especially H. Wild-berger, "Israel und sein Land," EvT 16 (1956) 404-22; F. Dreyfus, "Le Theme de l'heritage dans l' AT," Revue des Sciences Philosophiques et Théologiques 42 (1958) 3-49; F. Horst, "Zwei Begriffe für Eigentum (Besitz)," Verbannung und Heimkehr (ed. by A. Kuschke; Tübingen: Mohr, 1961) 135-56.

[7] Hebrew Thought, 129.

151

also modern notions of space and land do not discern what Israel
meant by נחלה.[8] Here I shall examine some uses in Jeremiah.
Jeremiah's time, just before and just after 587, was a time when
the land question was acute and urgent for Israel. For then she
had to ask: How can we keep the land? Why are we losing it?
How shall we live without it? How can we regain it?

Behind this exploration lies the suggestion that we cannot
understand the extremity of Israel's crisis of exile (read loss
of place) unless we face the space category in Israel's faith.

II

Jer 2:4-13. This text is easily isolated as a distinct and
separate unit. Its genre is widely accepted as lawsuit.[9] Williams'
observations relating it to Deut 32 both secure its genre and place
it in the context of a very ancient tradition.[10] The issue of this
lawsuit is: who is to blame for loss of land, Yahweh or Israel?[11]

In this pericope, vss. 6-7 specifically concern us:

They did not say:
Where is Yahweh
    who brought us up from the land of Egypt
    who led us in the wilderness
            in a land of deserts and pits
            in a land of drought and deep darkness
            in a land that none passes through
                    where no man dwells.

---

[8] See von Rad's essays, "The Promised Land and Yahweh's Land
in the Hexateuch," The Problem of the Hexateuch and Other Essays
(New York: McGraw-Hill, 1966) 79-93, and "There Remains Still a
Rest for the People of God," ibid., 94-102.

[9] Cf. H. B. Huffmann, "The Covenant Lawsuit in the Prophets,"
JBL 78 (1959) 287-89; and H. Gese, "Bemerkungen zur Sinaitradition,"
ZAW 79 (1967) 151 n. 57. Gese suggests a very close parallel to
Isa 1:2-3.

[10] P. Williams, "The Fatal and Foolish Exchange: Living Water
for 'Nothings,'" Austin Seminary Bulletin 81 (Sept. 1965) 3-59.

[11] It is striking that the use of lament-complaint forms (as
in Job, Jer, Lam) is especially intense when the land is in jeopardy.

Indeed, <u>I brought you</u> to the land of bounty
                          to eat its fruit and its good things
But <u>you came</u> and you defiled my <u>land</u>
     my inheritance you made for an abomination.

Verse 6 describes Yahweh's action governed by two participles
(המעלה, המוליך)[12] which not only express Yahweh's faithfulness
but describe two <u>places</u> of Israel: a) the place of slavery, and
b) the place of precariousness.

In vs. 7 the rhetoric shifts and is sharpened. Verse 7[a] is
a statement of Yahweh's innocence: "I brought you" (אביא). Verse 7[b]
is a statement of Israel's guilt: "But you came" (ותבאו). With
Yahweh's act, the place of slavery and the place of precariousness are
now displaced by the place of well-being. The statements are clearly
parallel and symmetrical, governed by the same verb. Yahweh's action
leaves the land fruitful and good. Israel's action leaves it defiled
and abominable.

It is striking that in this brief passage the term ארץ occurs
six times, four times as negative land:

> land of Egypt
> land of darkness and pits
> land of drought and deep darkness
> land where none passes through

and the contrast, two times as positive land:

> land of abundance
> my land.

The contrast is complete in affirming Yahweh's fidelity. He not
only leads out but also in. But 7[b] moves to a sharp climax by the
use of chiasmus:

> <u>You defiled my land</u>
>
> <u>my inheritance you set to abomination.</u>

it has been "land," then "my land," but now it is named and
identified "my inheritance." The word pair is as striking and
abrasive as can be imagined: inheritance - abomination.

---

[12] Williams, "Fatal and Foolish," 22.

The crisis of the years before and after 587 is placed in the drama of "salvation history" which is here presented, vss. 6-8, as a history of land. Israel's career with Yahweh is from place to place: from land of slavery to land of precariousness to land of well-being and now to abominable land.[13]

In this same pericope we may note the conclusion of vs. 13. As he has made a dramatic contrast in vs. 7, so in vs. 13 the contrast is simple and total:

fountain of living waters/   / cisterns hewn out
                                 for themselves

The fountain of living water, i.e., a source of fertility given and not manufactured,[14] is closely linked to the imagery of Deut 6:11:

houses full of all good things which you did not fill,
cisterns hewn out which you did not hew,
vineyards and olive trees which you did not plant . . .

Thus the contrast:

in the land of abundance: ברת חצובים אשר לא חצבת
(Deut 6:11).

in the land of defilement: לחצב להם בארות
(Jer 2:13)   בארת נשברים אשר לא יכלו המים

While the relation of Jeremiah and Deuteronomy is complex and difficult,[15] clearly the two texts speak of the same reality and they carry the same power as the previous contrast:

---

[13] The return of creation to chaos is more fully stated in 4:23-26, and earlier in the same tradition in Hos 4:3. The chaos-creation theme is important for exile and displacement as I have shown, "Weariness, Exile and Chaos (A Motif in Royal Theology)," CBQ 24 (1972) 19-38.

[14] In an important but neglected article, Wm. Vischer, "Foi et Technique," RHPR 44 (1964) 102-9, comments on Deut 11:10-15, and contrasts the land of Israel which gives, and the land of Egypt which must be worked, a contrast very similar to the one we have suggested.

[15] See the bibliography of J. Bright, Jeremiah (AB 21; Garden City: Doubleday, 1965) lxxi, nn 19-21, and recently E. W. Nicholson, Preaching to the Exiles (New York: Schoken, 1971).

The land of נחלה has cisterns you do not hew out which
yield life, but
the land of טרעבה has broken cisterns you made but they
hold nothing.

Jeremiah has discerned the next relocation of Israel even as her
whole history is one of relocation. This relocation is dislocation.
Israel now faces a future in defiled space.

III

Jer 3:1-5, 19-25; 4:1-4. This extended poem, which now has
prose elements in its midst, revolves around the motif of turn,
turn away, and return, as has often been asserted.[16] Again we are
concerned with the passage only in respect to our theme of land
and landlessness.

The pericope clearly appeals to the older material of Deut 24:
1-4. I have previously argued that the original material about
marriage in Deut 24:1-4 has been extended to concern the land.[17]
Whereas in Deut it is an actual marital relation which defiles the
land, in Jer 3 the relation of land and defilement is now through
the harlotry of the entire people.

The motif occurs several times in the poem:

Would not that land be greatly polluted (חנרף תחנף)

You have played the harlot (זנית) with my lovers . . .

by the wayside you have sat awaiting lovers like
an Arab in the wilderness

You have polluted (תחניפי) the land in your harlotry (זנותיך)

Therefore . . . (vss. 1-3[a]).

The opening statement of vs. 1 simply makes the link to the old
tradition, then the theme of marital faithlessness is not mentioned

---

[16] See Muilenburg's perceptive comments, "Form Criticism and
Beyond," JBL 88 (1969) 9-10.

[17] "A Form-Critical Study of the Cultic Material in Deuteronomy,"
(unpublished Th.D. dissertation, Union Seminary, New York, 1961) 327-28.

until vs. 20. The motifs in vss. 2-4 are very different. They include the double mention of חנף (once with infinitive absolute) and in both cases the three-fold pattern of a) pollute, b) harlot, and c) land. The older link of harlotry and land is exploited to the full,[18] for in vss. 3-5 it is the destruction of the land in drought which is paramount.[19]

A secondary motif is the word play on רע :

You have played the harlot with many lovers (רעים) (vs. 1[b])

You have polluted the land with your harlotry and with
    your evils (רעתך). (vs. 2[e])

    You have done all the evil that you could (הרעות)
    (vs. 5).

Thus the play on lovers and evil is clear. So also the term ארץ stands in vs. 2[c] as expected, but it is also in vs. 1[c], where one expects האשה.[20] The land is the abused land. The marriage imagery is completely transformed to apply to the land. (The use of חנף, here and in vs. 9, is used elsewhere in Jer only in 23:9, where it also refers to land.)

In 3:1-5, the rhetorical question form is noteworthy:

Have you (hā) not just now called to me . . .

---

[18] von Rad, _Deuteronomy_ (Philadelphia: Westminster, 1966) 150, argues that unchastity and defilement of land is a standard connection.

[19] The cluster of notions related to rain, drought, curse, pollution and abundance, bears investigation but lies beyond our theme. These notions have been largely ignored in the frame of Yahweh versus fertility gods. Cf. the titles expressing this stance, G. E. Wright, _The Old Testament Against Its Environment_ (SBT 2; London: SCM, 1950) and Norman Habel, _Yahweh versus Baal_ (New York: Bookman Associates, 1964). More recently Walter Harrelson, _From Fertility Cult to Worship_ (Garden City: Doubleday, 1969) has moved to a better balance as he is able to assert that "Israelite religion was also a religion of fertility."

[20] The LXX has the expected "woman" but that is likely a removal of a dramatic and unexpected "land" as the object of pollution. Cf. the point made by J. D. Martin, "The Forensic Background to Jeremiah III 1," _VT_ 19 (1969) 83, and his entire discussion.

Will he (hā) be angry forever?

Will he ('im) be indignant to the end?

The question pattern is utilized to ask about the father-son
relation and suggests a context of familial relations, perhaps
not unlike those of which Wolff and Gerstenberger have written.[21]
Thus the form functions in a way most convenient to the matter
under discussion, i.e., how is life to be ordered to secure well-
being, when the father gives the inheritance to his son, and the
son betrays the father?

This unit then has a surprising and diverse development:
a) question which appeals to old law (vs. 1[a]); b) chiastic
structure which begins with a question and ends with a corresponding declaration (vss. 1[b]-2); c) statement of consequence resulting
from the actions in vs. 2 (vs. 3); and d) rhetorical question about
father-son relation (vss. 4-5).

In terms of theme: a) 1[a] husband and wife relation; b) 1[b]-3
violation of land; and c) 4-5 father-son relation. The images of
the two relationships (husband-wife, vs. 1[a]; father-son, vss. 4-5),
frame the theme of pollution of land. Clearly the issue is not
simply perverted relation, as is often suggested in the stress on
שוב [22] but is <u>loss of place</u>.

The poem continues in vss. 19-25, by stating Yahweh's
intention:

And I, I said,
     How I will set you among my sons!
     and I will give to you a pleasant <u>land</u>
         a <u>heritage</u> of all nations most bounteous!

And I said,
     My <u>father</u> you will call me and from after me
     you will not turn.

---

[21] H. W. Wolff, <u>Amos' Geistige Heimat</u> (WMANT 18; Neukirchen-
Vluyn: Neukirchen Verlag, 1964) 7-12, E. Gerstenberger, <u>Wesen und
Herkunft des 'Apodiktischen Rechts,'</u> (WMANT 20; Neukirchen-Vluyn:
Neukirchener Verlag, 1965).

[22] Cf. the exposition of Wm. Vischer, "Return, Rebel Sons!,"
<u>Int</u> 8 (1954) 43-47, which completely ignores the power of the land
imagery.

The structure of this verse is controlled by the double, "I said." The first announces Yahweh's intention: Land for Israel. The second announces Yahweh's condition: Call me "my father." The two belong together. Israel will have the land only when the land is perceived as inheritance from the father: i.e., only when Israel knows itself as heir.[23] In these motifs of נחלה and אבי , the balance of a) eventual, relational time (אב), and b) covenantal space (נחלה) is affirmed.[24]

Finally, the poem concludes with an allusion to the land promise. Though only the last blessing to Abraham is mentioned, clearly the land promise is in purview.[25]

The call to turn is closely linked to care for land. In 4:1 the call for repentance is to "remove your abomination" (שקרץ). In 3:1-2 it is called "polluted" (חנף), as in 2:7, "abomination" (תועבה). It is cogent to understand the removal of abomination as a restoration of נחלה . Jeremiah, seeing the Babylonian threat as Yahweh's will for loss of land, in these poems holds out hope that Israel's destiny may still be the "pleasant land, bounteous heritage, plentiful land," but he also faces the prospect that the place for Israel may be one of defiled land, of drought and death. The judgment of Yahweh in the Babylonian invasion is not perversion of a relationship or

---

[23] It is striking how very differently the father-son imagery can be viewed when the balance of space and time is recovered. An alternative reading of the image is that of G. E. Wright, "How did Early Israel Differ from her Neighbors?" BA 6 (1943) 18-19; "The Terminology of Old Testament Religion and Its Significance," JNES 1 (1942) 404 ff., governed as it is by an antithesis of Israel's concern for relation in history, and Canaan's concern for the natural. Now it can be seen that the image is a viable one for Israel in relation to land, without being perverted by Canaanite religion.

[24] Not only is the Father addressed twice (vss. 4, 19), but Israel is twice called "sons" (vss. 14, 22). Thus land and father-son imagery is closely linked. In the same context, note the repeated use of נעורים (vss. 4, 24, 25).

[25] Cf. Wolff, "The Kerygma of the Yahwist," Int 20 (1966) 156. Note also the land imagery of vs. 3. See my discussion Tradition for Crisis (Richmond: John Knox Press, 1968) 80-82, of Hos 10:12, which is closely linked to this verse.

distortion of an event, but perversion of place and therefore
loss of space.[26]

IV

Jer 12:7-13. Whereas 2:4-13 and 3:1-5, 19-25 hoped for
rescue, with profound pathos 12:7-13 sets forth the hopeless-
ness of Israel (and of Yahweh). The land has now been irre-
vocably lost. The passage is easily divided into two parts:

A. 7-9[a] Images of deserted and perverted land:

I have forsaken my house
    I have abandoned my heritage
I have given the beloved of my soul
    into the hands of her enemies.
My heritage has become to me like
    a lion in the forest.
She has lifted up her voice against me;
    therefore I hate her.
Is my heritage to me like a speckled bird of prey?
    Are the birds of prey against her round about?

The key term נחלה occurs three times with remarkably diverse
images: a) given over to enemies, also called "delight of my
life," treasured and now lost (vs. 7); b) become a lion in the
forest, hostile, defiant, destructive, rejecting everything
Yahweh had intended (vs. 8); and c) a peculiar bird, attacked
by other birds (vs. 9). The imagery is abrupt and inconsistent.
In the first usage the heritage is simply lost, but in the
second it is hostile. In the third, the imagery is unclear,
but probably it is closer to the first usage. In any case, the
entire review is governed by the opening verb, "I have forsaken."[27]
All the trouble follows because Yahweh has left the land to its
own resources, which leads to destruction and death. Again, land
without father is not viable.

---

[26] Note that the dependent prose passage of 3:6-10, 15-18,
which promises restoration, also operates with land imagery. On
the relation of the prose and poetry, cf. Nicholson, Preaching,
and J. W. Miller, Das Verhältnis Jeremias und Hesekiels sprach-
lich und theologisch untersucht (Assen: Van Gorcum, 1955) 90-91.

[27] Cf. Muilenburg, "The Terminology of Adversity in Jeremiah,"
Translating and Understanding the Old Testament (ed. by H. T.
Frank and Wm. L. Reed; New York: Abingdon, 1970) 52-54.

The imagery is reinforced by the torrent of first person pronouns: three times "my inheritance," three first person verbs, and a number of pronominal suffixes. The stunning conclusion: "therefore I hate her," is one of Jeremiah's most radical statements of a time to tear down and pluck up.[28] Yahweh has turned against his own inheritance, i.e., rejecting the promises he has made and the election he has affirmed. The language and imagery is consistently about the land, not about people.

B. vss. 9^b-13 The destiny of the land:

Go, assemble all the wild beasts
    bring them to devour
many shepherds have destroyed my vineyard,
    they have trampled down my portion,
they have made my pleasant portion a desolate
    wilderness.

They have made it a desolation:
    desolate it mourns to me.
The whole land is made desolate,
    but no man lays it to heart.
Upon all the bare heights in the desert
    destroyers have come;
for the sword of the Lord devours from one end of the
    land to the other; no flesh has peace.

They have sown wheat and have reaped thorns,
    they have tired themselves out but profit nothing.
They shall be ashamed of their harvests
    because of the fierce anger of the Lord.

This section is linked to the proceeding by the double use of my "portion" (חלק) (vs. 10), which echoes my "heritage." But the major note is the rich vocabulary of destruction: devour, אכל (vss. 9, 12); destroy, שחת (vs. 10); trample, בסס (vs. 10); desolate,

---

[28] The total rejection of what he is expected to value is perhaps illuminated by E. Würthwein, "Amos 5:21-27," TLZ 72 (1947) 144-52 in which the word hate, along with others, is the antithesis of cultic acceptance by Yahweh. Cf. R. Rendtorff, "Priesterliche Kulttheologie und prophetische Kultpolemik," TLZ 81 (1956) 339-42, for a similar point. The use of cultic terminology may suggest why polluted land is abominable, i.e., repugnant to Yahweh's presence. This is supported by the peculiar use of טמא in an earlier passage (2:7). The balance of a) defiled place, and b) absent duty, is of course reflected in Ezek.

שָׁמֵם (vss. 10, 11);[29] mourn, אָבַל (vs. 11); desert, מִדְבָּר (vss. 10, 12); destroyers, שֹׁדֵד (vs. 12); anger, חָרוֹן (v. 13). The land's inescapable destiny, when Yahweh has abandoned it, is death (cf. vs. 13 as failure in harvest). This poem vividly describes death at the hands of invaders. The description is introduced in vs. 9[a] and concluded in vs. 12 with the same word "devour." The first use is with "wild beasts," the final one is "sword," both characteristic curses.[30] Between these two is the powerful imagery of vineyards being trampled and destroyed, the bountiful spot being reduced to a waste, and finally in vs. 13, the land is totally unproductive. The place of life is reduced to a place of death.

The entire poem is Yahweh's lament following Jeremiah's lament (vss. 1-6), though perhaps this connection is not original. Yahweh himself, according to the form, laments. But in vs. 11 it is the land which mourns. Worth noting is the fact that in 12:4 the prophet uses the same language to describe the land as mourning.

Clearly Yahweh's judgment and Israel's hope concern land. The historical upheavals in the midst of Jeremiah's period are understood primarily as loss of land.[31] Thus the movement is clear from 7-9[a], which speaks about the land being deserted and perverted, to 9[b]-13, which describes the reality of death and the subsequent mourning by the land. In contrast to the earlier poems we have considered, here the issue is settled, and the land is gone.[32]

---

[29] Cf. Muilenburg, "Terminology," 50-52.

[30] Cf. D. Hillers, Treaty-Curses and the Old Testament Prophets (BibOr 16; Rome: Pontifical Biblical Institute, 1964) 54-56 and passim, and F. C. Fensham, "Common Trends in Curses of the Near Eastern Treaties and Kudurru-Inscriptions Compared with Maledictions of Amos and Isaiah," ZAW 75 (1963) 160, 166-68 and passim.

[31] This is the key component in the theme of "tragic reversal" described by N. Gottwald, Studies in the Book of Lamentations (SBT 14; Naperville: Alec R. Allenson, 1954), chapter 3.

[32] Again note the derivative prose passage of 12:14-17 which speaks of hope in terms of land. On the passage see Nicholson, Preaching, 84-88, Gottwald, All the Kingdoms of the Earth (New York: Harper and Row, 1964) 294, and S. Herrmann, Die Prophetischen Heilserwartungen im Alten Testament (Stuttgart: Kohlhammer, 1965) 162-65. Space does not permit comment upon 16:18-21, 17:1-4, 22:28-30, all of which bear upon our theme.

161

V

This experience of disinheritance, an obvious but neglected theme, is essential to understanding the proclamation of exilic hope. Only when the enormity of displacement is discerned is the promise of return as gripping as it is intended by the poets to be.

Jeremiah himself in a dramatic act performs a sign which ends this way:

Houses and fields and vineyards
shall again be bought in the land (אֶרֶץ) (32:15).[33]

This promise, which reverses the curse (cf. Deut 28:30, 38-39; Amos 5:11; Zeph 1:13), grows out of a narrative which gives legal force to the conviction of inalienable right of inheritance.[34]

The theme of regained inheritance is more fully presented in Ezek 47:13-23, in which the return from exile is interpreted as an act of land allocation paralleling that of Joshua:

And you shall divide it equally: I swore to give it
to your fathers and this land shall fall to you as
your inheritance (vs. 14).

You shall allot it as an inheritance for yourselves
and for the aliens who reside among you (vs. 22).

This is the land which you shall allot as an inheritance
among the tribes of Israel, and these are their several
portions, says the Lord God (48:29).

It is no accident that the Ezekiel tradition, which utilizes land-division as a motif of restoration, also speaks of resurrection from the dead (cf. 37:1-14), for the land is the essential component in the resurrection of Israel. Thus

---

[33] See G. Fohrer, Die symbolischen Handlungen der Propheten (ATANT 54; 2nd ed.; Zürich: Zwingli Verlag, 1968) 42-44 and passim.

[34] A closely paralleled text, Gen 23, is a crucial text in P for linking that tradition to Land. The structure of Gen 23 moves from landlessness (vss. 1-4) to land (vss. 17-20), a movement structurally important to P. Cf. Brueggemann, "The Kerygma of the Priestly Writers," ZAW 84 (1972) 397-414, on the priestly tradition and land theology.

Macholz[35] writes: "Nur in diesem Land ist die Existenz Israels
für den Verfasser denkbar; auch das neue Israel kann nur
existieren in diesem selben, freilich erneuerten und umgestalteten,
Lande."

All three exilic prophets, Jeremiah, Ezekiel and II Isaiah,
understand the inherited land to be the most visible, most
significant embodiment of deliverance from exile and restoration.
This balance of loss of land and gift of land provides an
important model for exilic faith. Among the themes derived from
and related to this model are:

1. The tradition of Jeremiah as it now stands is dominated
by the motif of "building and planting, plucking up and tearing
down" (1:10; 12:14-17; 18:7-9; 24:6; 31:4-5, 27-28; 32:41; 42:10;
45:4), which may well be an image of loss of land and restoration
of land.

2. A parallel motif is that of scattering-gathering which
has clear and obvious derivation from loss of land and regaining
land (cf. Jer 23:2-3, Ezek 11:17, Isa 54:7). The motif is
frequent, especially in Ezek.

3. Through a careful analysis of vocabulary, Tom Raitt[36] has
been able to show that rejection-election is a theme especially
appropriate to Jeremiah and Ezekiel. The notion of rejection-
election concerns not simply Yahweh-Israel, but Yahweh-over-the-
land and Israel-in-the-land.

4. The use of divorce-remarriage in both Hos 2 and Jer 3,
moves back and forth between covenantal relations and placement
in the land. Thus the vocabularies of abandonment (עזב) and
harlotry which Muilenburg has analyzed,[37] are not simply relational motifs as they have often been presented, but they concern placement in the land as the image of produce and fertility
as Hos 2 clearly indicates. That the Valley of Trouble becomes
the Door of Hope (2:17; Eng 2:15) is imagery of reentry into the
land, for which the type is Josh 7. All these models suggest

---

[35] "Noch Einmal: Planungen für den Wiederaufbau nach der
Katastrophe von 587," VT 19 (1969) 349. Cf. Isa 49:8, for the
same motif handled differently by II Isaiah.

[36] "Function, Setting and Content in Jeremiah's Oracles of
Judgment," SBL Seminar Papers I (1971) 207-28.

[37] "Terminology," 52-54.

that we have read space concerns as relational concerns, and
in the process we have neglected a primary dimension of the
text.

VI

The prominence of land as space is a central motif of
Biblical faith, which has been largely unexplored both by
an existential and by an historical hermeneutic concerned
with covenantal, relational, eventful categories. Biblical
faith in the upheaval of exile returned to the basic land of
promise (cf. Jer 4:1-2,[38] Ezek 20:42, Isa 51:2). In so doing,
it affirmed that Yahweh wills rootage and not rootlessness for
his people (or chaos, cf. Jer 4:22-26, Isa 45:18-19).

The persistent concern of Biblical faith for the poor
and disenfranchised (widows, orphans, lepers, "publicans and
sinners"), is precisely that they have been dis-inherited and
rendered both rootless and powerless--and Yahweh does not will
it so! This central concern of Biblical faith has been lost
and can be rightly appreciated only when land as rootage and
place is understood, when the Biblical gospel is understood
as Yahweh's "territorial imperative."[39]

This motif makes contact between Biblical faith and contemporary social and theological upheavals. The domesticated
quest for "meaning" has been largely replaced by a demand for
place. This is true of the Jews, who must perenially struggle
with the "disenlandisement" and the problem is only more clearly

---

[38] Wolff, "The Kerygma of the Yahwist," 156-57, has shown
how this links to the older tradition.

[39] M. Eliade, in his various writings, has described the
significance and function of sacred space. Cf. Cosmos and
History (New York: Harper, 1954) 12-21, The Sacred and the
Profane (New York: Harcourt, Brace, 1959) chapter 1. Remarkably, even Eliade, Cosmos and History, 102-12, overstates
the case for time in Israel. Again, it is the contrast of
Israel and other peoples which causes one to overlook land as
place, which is so crucial for Israel's self-understanding.
The crisis of exile can hardly be understood apart from this,
nor is the return expressed in a different idiom.

focused by the modern state of Israel.[40] This is true for the Black, who "like the Jew, has always had a land problem."[41] And it is true in a parallel way for every person who in a time of upheaval and future shock experiences rootlessness:[42]

> They will not want to play Russian Roulette with their children's schools, and they will see, one hopes, that a child is better reared in a neighborhood than in a glorified bus terminal . . . Without this early experience of territoriality it is doubtful if anyone can learn to regard the whole earth as his turf.

Our hermeneutical investments influenced by salvation history or existentialist categories have led us to neglect this aspect of Biblical theology. Perhaps these categories have been a reaction against the Fascist tendency to equate religion and land.[43] In any case, a very different situation calls for fresh categories. Thus the point of the Jeremiah exegesis in this paper is to call attention to the blindness created by our recent hermeneutical categories, which has closed off motifs especially significant in a time of rootlessness.

The meaning of the notion of inheritance as space in the New Testament lies beyond the scope of this paper. But attention may

---

[40] This has been given various forms of expression, most passionately in the several writings of Richard Rubenstein. Cf. Isaac H. Jacob, "Israel History and the Church," CCI Notebook (American Jewish Congress; Commission on Community Interrelations), April 1972, Jacob Neusner, American Judaism: Adventure in Modernity (Englewood, New Jersey: Prentice-Hall, Inc., 1972) 105, who uses the infelicitous term, "enlandisement."

[41] Preston N. Williams, "Toward a Sociological Understanding of the Black Religious Community," Soundings 54 (1971) 261. Having said this, Williams quickly subordinates space to time, but his point is made.

[42] J. H. Snow, On Pilgrimage: Marriage in the 70s (New York: Seabury, 1971) 38.

[43] Curiously, Rubenstein uses rhetoric for "religion of the soil," not unlike that of the Hitler movement. Thus, for example, he speaks of "Israel's earth and the lost divinities of that earth," After Auschwitz (Indianapolis: Bobbs-Merrill, 1966) 70.

be called to Paul's use of the motif of inheritance in Rom 8:
16-17 and Gal 4:4-7. It is striking that in both cases the
phrase "Abba, Father" is linked not only with sonship but
with heirdom. The convergence of motifs is the same as in
Jer 3:4, 19; "claiming the inheritance" is related to confessing
the father.[44]

Even more striking is Gal 4:1-7, where the motifs of father
and inheritance are joined with the notion of "fullness of time."
It may be an interesting development of hermeneutical stress on
time to note that the full time is the time when the son receives
inheritance, i.e., it is a time for receiving space in which to
live.

---

[44] J. Jeremias, Abba (Göttingen: Vandenhoeck & Ruprecht,
1966) 64-67, views the matter differently, denying the tradition
connection suggested here.

JEREMIAH'S DELIVERANCE MESSAGE TO JUDAH

Thomas M. Raitt

The College of Wooster

A. The Problem

   With James Muilenburg, as with so many men of faith and theological
insight, some of the richest thoughts have come in his mature years. By
analogy it is unfortunate that so many things conspire to deprive us of
any reasonably assured sense of what the prophet Jeremiah had to say to
Judah in his mature years. The loss is doubled because those years coincide with what all historians of Israelite religion acknowledge to be
the greatest crisis for that people's faith in its classical period: the
Babylonian deportation of Judah's leaders and ruling classes in 597
followed by the destruction of Jerusalem and the exile of its survivors
in 587. Unlike his somewhat younger contemporary, Ezekiel, Jeremiah remained in Jerusalem between 597 and 587; it is even thought that Jeremiah
escaped the second deportation and stayed for several months in the
environs of Jerusalem before taking exile in Egypt. How did Jeremiah
interpret those events? What difference did God's punishment make, in
the form of these catastrophes, for the way Jeremiah was led to interpret
Judah's relation to God? We know that Ezekiel's message went through a
a dramatic shift from words of judgment to promises of salvation once
Jerusalem fell. Is there evidence of a comparable shift in the way that
Jeremiah interpreted God's will?

   The ironic, but self-contradictory, situation which prevails in
Jeremiah scholarship is that nearly everyone is ready to affirm that
Jeremiah did indeed turn toward a message of deliverance for Judah toward
the end of his life. But at the same time it is harder to find solid
footage on passages reflecting the content and tenor of that message,
than it was for Jeremiah to avoid sinking into the mire at the bottom of
a cistern into which a nervous citizenry had thrown him. Jeremiah's last
insightful words seem to have been muddied over by shadowy "deuteronomists"
who added something here and changed something there. Or so we are told.
It is often urged by some scholars (whose source analysis seems hopelessly
confused with aesthetic preconceptions) that Jeremiah would not, or did
not write in the allegedly dull, uniform, deuteronomistic prose of this
era. Baruch is made out to be Jeremiah's only disciple—and a somewhat
more independent, less faithful, disciple than either Isaiah or Ezekiel
attracted to pass down their words. When it comes to the use of prose
and the possibility of a real shift, with dramatically changed historical
circumstances, to a message of deliverance, Jeremiah seems to be ripped
out of his place in time and made the last of the eighth century "doom"
prophets instead of the first of the sixth century prophets. The notion

is found that Jeremiah preached salvation to the Northern State Israel
early in his ministry, but hardly, if at all, to Judah late in his life.
A recurrent assumption is that any oracles of weal which presuppose exile,
or catastrophe on Jerusalem, have to have originated after Jeremiah's
death, even though he had the clear precedent of 722 made real for Judah
by the events of 597 and the increasing inevitability of their recurrence
as 587 drew closer. These assumptions and prejudgments, singly and in
concert, conspire to deny Jeremiah a single authentic promise of deliverance to Judah. Are we thus actually reduced to a situation in which it
can only be affirmed that Jeremiah proclaimed deliverance to the survivors
from Judah toward the end of his life, but are disenabled to say what he
proclaimed?

B.   Some Disclaimers

     The point of this study is not to isolate the very words of Jeremiah
himself: as though that were possible, as though they were sharply discontinuous theologically and aesthetically with the words of his closest
disciples, as though that discovery would bring us closer to The Word of
God. I am, however, concerned to delineate passages that were added to
fit the Jeremianic corpus to a situation of different dimensions than
the prophet together with his first generation of disciples faced. We
want to distinguish and separate pericopes which are not genuinely representative of the distinctive Jeremianic mode of interpreting God's will.
But where the passage is true to Jeremiah's thought and within the horizon
of the situations he felt it was his ministry to interpret--where in fact
the words and ideas have a strong likelihood of originating from Jeremiah,
then it is not the concern of this study to decide whether the words are
recorded just as Jeremiah thought them, or whether his thoughts are faithfully expressed by his first circle of tradents. It will be difficult to
maintain this distinction in the limitation on the results we seek, because many of the source analysts and commentators do not admit that they
are only making informed guesses about the authorship of particular passages.

     All articles have assumptions. One of mine is that the men of biblical
times were not notably more dishonest than men today. Therefore when the
Book of Jeremiah has attracted more than 30 Oracles of Deliverance, I
assume that this is not because editors and third generation disciples
manipulated his message to fit a need and a time wholly unanticipated by
Jeremiah. Rather, I think they probably saw themselves as continuing a
tradition of deliverance preaching firmly rooted in Jeremiah himself. This
leads me to the optimism that the issue is where we shall find Jeremiah's
deliverance message to Judah--not whether we shall find it.

C.   The Booklet of Little Comfort

     It is a commonplace of biblical scholarship that if any genuine
Jeremianic words of salvation are to be found, they will be seen within
the collection of poems in chapters 30 and 31. Close examination of these
chapters leads to disappointment. Even with certain verses excepted, it

hardly presents the unified poem which Volz and Rudolph thought to find here.[1] Without regard to the pericopes (a difficult determination in these chapters), the following verses do not contain a message of deliverance, but one of judgment or admonition: 30:4-7c, 12-15, 23-24; 31:15, 18-19, 21-22, 29-30. Of what remains, many verses are rightly rejected as being composed outside the Jeremianic circle: 30:1-3, 30:8-9, 30:10-11; 31:7-9, 31:10-14, 31:23-25, 31:26-28, 31:35-37, 31:38-40.[2]

It seems gratuitous that these chapters have so frequently been entitled "The Little Book of Comfort." At best they are highly composite and fragmented. It can hardly be assumed that meter is a reliable guide to authenticity here. Of what remains, 30:16-17 comes at the end of a strange pericope where the dominant motif seems to be pity, or mocking admonitions, as God looks at his wounded people (30:12-15). I cannot think of anything like this elsewhere in Jer. The glee at the destruction of Judah's enemies (vs. 16) and the emphasis on Zion (vs. 17) sound more typical of writings later than Jeremiah. 31:15-22 is a mixed genre. It begins with a corporate lament (vs. 15), followed by two verses of a quite generalized promise (vss. 16-17). Verses 18-19 seem to interrupt the flow of thought with something like one of Jeremiah's "private confessions." The rhetorical questions at the beginning of verse 20 are quite exceptional in a promise of deliverance. It ends with a note of admonition (vss. 21-22). This passage does not invite ready comparison with any of the deliverance promises which we will consider below.

Aside from the great prose passage 31:31-34 which will be considered in the following section, the only two significant promises which remain, 30:18-22 and 31:2-6, seem to fit very well into the suggestion from Volz and Rudolph that these promises were directed to the Northern Kingdom.[3] Since their authenticity is almost universally supported, we must at least consider them in relationship to Jeremiah's deliverance preaching. But, we are left with the conclusion that if any solid basis for a deliverance message to Judah is to be found within Jeremianic material dating after 598, that foundation will be discovered outside these chapters.

---

[1]Paul Volz, Der Prophet Jeremia (KAT; Leipzig: Deichert, 1922) 283-285, 296-298. Wilhelm Rudolph, Jeremia (HAT, 2; Tübingen: J.C.B. Mohr, 1958) 172-173, 188-189.

[2]J. Philip Hyatt, "Jeremiah: Introduction and Exegesis" (IB, 5; Nashville: Abingdon, 1956) 1023-1041 rejects all of these verses. Georg Fohrer, Introduction to the Old Testament (Nashville: Abingdon, 1965) 400 agrees in denying the authenticity of most: 30:8-9, 10-11; 31:7-9, 10-14, 23-25, 26-28, 38-40. My own reasons for dropping these 27 verses can only be hinted at here: 30:10-11 and 31:10-14 show the influence of Second Isaiah; 31:35-37 employs an argument from nature to history utterly unlike and contradictory to what Jeremiah says elsewhere, etc.

[3]Volz, Jeremia (KAT) 296-298; Rudolph, Jeremia (HAT) 172-173.

D.   Jeremiah 24:4-7 and Five Related Passages

It is the central claim of this article that Jeremiah's message of
deliverance to Judah has its textual foundation in a series of six prose
passages as follows: 24:4-7; 29:4-7, 10-14; 32:6-15, 42-44; 31:31-34;
32:36-41; and 33:6-9.[4] These are listed in a sequence approximating the
degree of certainty which I think we can have that the words and ideas
are authentically Jeremianic.[5] In a sense the sequence also gives priority to the passages which are most basic for understanding this phase
of Jeremiah's ministry after 598 when he promised salvation to the survivors of Judah. I claim that: 1) these passages, taken together,
represent the mind of Jeremiah as concerns Judah's future after it has
gone into exile; 2) that there is a strong probability that they are
from a single source; 3) that this source is Jeremiah together with his
own first circle of faithful tradents. With the three pivotal passages--
24:4-7; 29:4-7, 10-14; 32:6-15, 42-44--we have the significant advantage
of possessing Jeremiah's word of deliverance in the midst of the narration

---

[4]The position I take is that the theologically more significant
portion of chapter 29, vss. 10-14, belongs together with the almost unquestionably authentic letter to the exiles in 29:4-7 as its interpretation. And 32:42-44 stands in much the same relationship to the undoubtedly
factual symbolic act described in 32:6-15. This position on 29:4-7, 10-14
is supported by Rudolph, Jeremia (HAT) 168-169, Artur Weiser, Das Buch des
Propheten Jeremia (ATD 4; Göttingen: Vandenhoeck und Ruprecht, 1960)
251-255, John Bright, Jeremiah (AB 21; New York: Doubleday, 1965) 210-211
et al. The decision on 32:6-15, 42-44 is supported by Volz, Jeremia (KAT)
302, Rudolph, Jeremia (HAT) 189, Elmer Leslie, Jeremiah (Nashville:
Abingdon, 1954) 240-242, Bright, Jeremiah (AB) 297-298, et al.

[5]Accepting at least a kernel of authenticity in 33:6-9 are Rudolph,
Jeremia (HAT) 198, Weiser, Jeremia (ATD) 303, Bright, Jeremiah (AB) 298,
A. W. Streane, Jeremiah (CBSC; Cambridge: University Press, 1913) 207,
and Leslie, Jeremiah, 243-244. The famous passage 31:31-34 has been abundantly analysed in a series of commentaries, journal articles, disserta-
tions, and monographs. It is beyond the interests and scope of this
article to comment on that literature (my argument actually hinges on
24:4-7; 29:4-7, 10-14; 32:6-15, 42-44). We can say, however, that a clear
majority of scholars attribute the words and/or the thoughts of 31:31-34
to Jeremiah himself. Jer 32:36-41 has drawn less attention that it deserves. One wonders why its strong parallels with 24:4-7 (see Diagram A)
and its freshness of conception have not given it a position of priority
over 31:31-34, which it is often said to imitate. Supporting its authenticity are Bright, Jeremiah (AB) 297-298, R. H. Pfeiffer, Introduction
to the Old Testament (New York: Harper, 1941) 503, and Streane, Jeremiah
(CBSC) 207.

of undoubted episodes in his ministry which provide the context for understanding his promise. This affords us tools for analysis which were not available in the heterogeneous sequence of uprooted speeches in chapters 30-31.

Nine of the most prominent scholars who have written on Jer firmly underline the authenticity of 24:4-7.[6] Hyatt stands alone in denying this passage to Jer.[7] His reasons are obviated among the exegetical observations which follow.

Perhaps the most obvious feature of Jer chapter 24 is the radical distinction made between the deliverance which God promises to bring to the exiles (vss. 5-7) and the severe judgment which he announces he will visit on their brethren who escaped the deportation of 597 (vss. 8-10). The basis for this distinction has not generally been well understood. The injustice which Hyatt thinks he sees in this division is a major consideration in his denying the passage to Jer.[8] But in fact the distinction found here is consistently carried out in the deliverance preaching of Jeremiah and Ezekiel and supplies one of the most fundamental reasons for their shift from a message of judgment to one of deliverance. In chapter 29 Jeremiah sends a letter to the people in exile expressing God's encouragement to them to live (vss. 5-7), and promising God's deliverance to them when the years of the exile are completed (vss. 10-14). When Jeremiah buys a field as an act symbolic of hope, it is clear that the restoration of the people to their land will only come after an intervening period when they are separated from it (32:14-15). The one Oracle of Deliverance assuredly uttered by Ezekiel before 587 (11:15-21) is specifically designated for those already in exile, while the earlier part of the chapter expresses a harsh judgment for the part of Judah yet in Jerusalem (11:1-12). If Rudolph is correct that the only words of salvation spoken by Jeremiah early in his ministry--otherwise marked by a proclamation of judgment on Judah--were directed

---

[6]Sigmund Mowinckel, Zur Komposition Des Buches Jeremia, (Kristiania: Jacob Dybwad, 1914) 21 [his source "A"]; Volz, Jeremia (KAT) 244-247; Rudolph, Jeremia (HAT) 145; Weiser, Jeremia (ATD) 213; Fohrer, Intro. O.T. 398; Otto Eissfeldt, The Old Testament (New York: Harper, 1965) 353; Pfeiffer, Intro. O. T. 503; Leslie, Jeremiah 203; and Bright, Jeremiah (AB) 194.

[7]Hyatt, "Jeremiah: Exegesis" (IB) 996-998; "The Deuteronomic Edition of Jeremiah," R. C. Beatty et. al., Vanderbilt Studies in the Humanities (Nashville: Vanderbilt University Press, 1951) I, 84-85.

[8]As above: "Jeremiah: Exegesis" (IB) 996-998; "Deuteronomic Edition," 84-85.

to the survivors of the Northern State Israel,[9] then this further illustrates the consistency of the principle. Jeremiah and Ezekiel never proclaim deliverance to Judah on her land as a continuation of the theo-political state and the relationship to God traditionally understood. An obvious sequence suggests itself to us here: First, prophetic threats of divine judgment; second, actual historical catastrophe interpreted as God's punishment; third, prophetic promises of God's merciful deliverance. The people's accountability for their sin together with God's attitude and intention toward them are radically shifted when the exile becomes a fact. The punishment itself creates an entirely new situation. If a message of shalom before the exile-punishment was false, then continued predictions of annihilatory judgment to those already in exile would be rigid fanaticism. The deliverance is never spoken at a time, or promised as taking effect at a time, before the threats of judgment would have become a historical fact. I think a huge part of the prevailing misunderstanding of prophetic deliverance proclamations, and estimates of the authenticity of speeches containing this message, result from a failure to come to grips with the points made just above.

Even Rudolph, whose commentary on ch. 24 I find the most insightful,[10] fails to see the distinction grounded in the punishment. Although he begins by saying that "this judgment, good/evil, is not conditional on their characteristics, but concerns itself with their fate,"[11] Rudolph fails to follow through on his own insight, and ends as so many others in attaching a misplaced emphasis on the interior differences between the two groups of people.[12] Actually Jer 24 never says that God is going to treat the Golah with favor because they are good; and it never says that those left are bad. The "good" finds its primary rootage in the intention of God's action: "I will regard as good," "I will set my eyes upon them for good." One should compare this substantive use of טוב with Jer 8:15 ("We looked for peace but no good came, for a time of healing, but behold terror"), Mic 1:12 ("the inhabitants of Maroth wait anxiously for good, because evil has come down from the Lord to the gate of Jerusalem") and Isa 3:10. Amos 9:4 has a phrase identical with Jer 24:6, "I will set my eyes upon them" (שמתי עיני עליהם) the only difference being that the positions of לטובה ("for good") and לרעה ("for evil") are switched. This employment of טוב to designate the content of God's decision as regards an action of deliverance instead of an action of judgment needs to be carefully distinguished from the uses of טוב indicating God's blessing in the deuteronomistic historian as described in a

---

[9]Rudolph, Jeremia (HAT) 172-173.

[10]Ibid. See his explanations on the absence of any alleged conflict between ch. 24 and ch. 29, and in what sense those who fled to Egypt should deserve inclusion in the judgment of vss. 8-10, pp. 145-147.

[11]Ibid., 146.

[12]Ibid., 147.

recent article by Walter Brueggemann.[13] This term is also used to describe God's plan for deliverance in Jer 32:42, 32:39; 33:9 (compare
Jer 15:11; 18:10; 21:10). In these Jeremianic deliverance passages
טוב refers to the quality within an episode of the divine plan and
is a near synonym of שלום . The emphasis in its employment within
chapter 24 is on the divine sovereignty: God's will, his prerogative.
His decision only sounds arbitrary when one ignores what has happened
to the Golah: the punishment making them more aware of their sins, the
punishment helping to preserve the integrity of God's justice. Although
it is not yet said as in Isa 40:2 that "her time of service is ended"
or "her punishment accepted" so that the moment of deliverance is in the
present, a time of salvation for the future is assured.[14] It is a future
characterized by God setting his eyes upon them for good and making them
good as 24:7 shows so clearly. Thus judgment and its requirements are
not glibly forgotten; deliverance is affirmed in tension with judgment.
This makes for an altogether realistic and convincing movement from
judgment toward deliverance on the part of the prophet Jeremiah.

It will be useful for us to compare the basic components in Jeremiah's
promise of weal in 24:4-7 with the other prose salvation passages we have

---

[13]"The Kerygma of the Deuteronomistic Historian," Int 22 (1968) 387-402.
In none of the D or d'istic passages which Brueggemann cites (to show that
promise of the "good" is a favorite theme of these sources) does טוב serve
to characterize the quality involved in a divine plan for salvation instead
of judgment. With Deut 30:5 as in 30:9, on which Brueggemann places central emphasis, it is clear that טוב means that the blessing which God
brought on the fathers will also be brought on the children. Brueggemann
himself sees this as blessing (page 393). What I want to ward off is a
facile comparison of this employment of טוב in d'istic sources with the
use of טוב in the Jeremianic deliverance passages under consideration.
The idea of God as the original giver of the "good" (blessing) before 597
turning to give "good" again (Deut 30:9), is just a promise of blessing projected into the future. But for our purposes we must see that the restoration of fertility is not the equivalent of what the major prophets understand
as the deliverance of a people after judgment.

[14]These are my own translations of phrases at the beginning of Second
Isa which are crucial for understanding the relation between punishment
and deliverance.

already suggested are the primary texts for understanding Jeremiah's deliverance message to Judah (29:4-7, 10-14; 32:6-15, 42-44; 31:31-34; 32:36-41; 33:6-9).[15] As counterchecks we can also compare it with the two poetic oracles thought to have come earlier in Jeremiah's ministry (30:18-22; 31:2-6), and with Ezekiel's only promise of salvation assuredly dated before the fall of Jerusalem (11:16-21).

1. The promise is introduced as an oracle from God: 24:5; 29:4; 29:10; (32:15), 32:42; 31:31; 32:36; 30:18; 31:2; Ezek 11:16.[16]

2. The oracle addresses and has its application for those Judeans who are experiencing exile in Babylon, or for whom it is assumed that such experience is inevitable: 24:5; 29:4, 29:10; (32:5), 32:43-44; 31:31f; 32:36-37; 33:7-9; Ezek 11:15.

3. There is a remembrance of a time of judgment, so that the promised deliverance exists in a residual tension with the judgment without that recognition diminishing or qualifying the dimensions of salvation in the new era: 24:5, 6, 8; 29:10-11; 32:5, 14-15; 32:42; 31:31-33; 32:36-37; 33:7; Ezek 11:16, 21.

4. God gives to the people or creates in them a new capacity to respond to him. . . most often with the image of "heart": 24:7; 29:12-13; 31:33; 32:39-40; Ezek 11:19.

5. There is recited something like a formula for remarriage, or reelection (Smend's "Bundesformel") as one of the goals of God's saving intervention: 24:7; (29:12-14); 31:33; 32:38; (30:22); Ezek 11:20.[17]

6. Knowing God, or obeying God, is specified as another goal of the divine intervention: 24:7; 31:33-34; (32:39-40); Ezek 11:20.

---

[15]This is perhaps a good point at which to make clear what will become more apparent from this point in the article unto the end: the methodology being employed. I am looking at motifs within a speech-form, at a gestalt or characteristic pattern of themes and images within the unit, and at the intention and function of the pericope. This is neither Form Criticism narrowly defined nor primarily Rhetorical Criticism, but it is informed by both those methodologies and obtains results which flow back into them.

[16]The verses are put in parentheses when they manifest a partial or indirect example of the characteristic described.

[17]Rudolf Smend, "Die Bundesformel," Theologische Studien 68 (Zurich: EVZ-Verlag, 1963). This is usually some variation on "they will be my people and I will be their God," thought to be a formula for covenant initiation or reinitiation.

7. God restores their fortunes, or returns them to their land,
   by the imagery of שוב , often doubled: 24:6; 29:10, 14;
   32:44; 32:37; 33:7; 30:18.

8. God will build בנה or plant נטע his people: 24:6; (29:5);
   32:41; 33:7; (30:18); 31:4.

9. The saving act involves repentance and turning toward God not
   as a prerequisite but as a consequence: 24:7; 29:12-13;
   32:40.

10. The proclamation of God's initiative, his "I will," comes
    prior to the mention of any human initiative: 24:5; 29:10;
    32:42; 31:31; 32:37; 33:6; 30:18; 31:4; Ezek 11:17.

11. This "I will" initiative may have a goal or intended result
    (changed conditions, changed relationship, changed people),
    but it does not have an explanation in a "ground," "basis,"
    or "motivation" like the Accusation section of an Oracle
    of Judgment: 24:4f; 29:10f; 32:42f; 31:31f; 32:36f; 30:18f;
    Ezek 11:16f.

12. The "fear not" of Second Isaiah's "priestly oracles of favor-
    able hearing" is missing: true of all eleven passages.[18]

We can summarize some of the main implications of Diagram A as follows. With vss. 4-7 taken in conjunction with vss. 10-14 of chapter 29,
and vss. 6-15 with 42-44 of chapter 32, those compound speech units plus
Jer 31:31-34 and 32:36-41 make the strongest parallels with 24:4-7. Features which I take to be quite generic to the majority of Jeremiah's and
Ezekiel's Oracles of Deliverance are #1, 7, 10, 11, and 12. Distinctive
Jeremianic rhetoric are the two images of #8. Oracles which develop the
idea of physical restoration but do not reflect upon what God's action
means in terms of the relationship with his people will lack #4, 5, 6, 9
(true of the prose of 29:4-7, 32:6-15 and the poetry of 31:2-6--also
30:18-22 if 22 is not a genuine part of that oracle).

_____

[18]Joachim Begrich, "Das Priesterliche Heilsorakel," ZAW 52 (1934)
81-92; Studien zu Deuterojesaja [Theologische Bücherei, 20; München:
Chr. Kaiser Verlag, 1938] see 13-26) so thoroughly identified the speech
form of the prophetic salvation oracle with this "fear not" admonition--
which I consider to be a rhetorical feature and not a structure component
of the speech-form--that we do well to remind ourselves of the absence
of this element in Jeremiah's and Ezekiel's promises of deliverance, even
though the intention of this article is not to describe a speech form.

Diagram A

	Jer 24:4-7	29:4-7	10-14	32:6-15	42-44	31:31-34	32:36-41	33:6-9	30:18-22	31:2-6	Ezek 11: 16-21
1. Oracle from God	X	X	X	(X)	X	X	X		X	X	X
2. To Judeans in exile	X	X	X	(X)	X	X	X	X			X
3. Tension with judgment remembrance	X		X	X	X	X	X	X			X
4. God gives them a new heart	X		X			X	X				X
5. "Bundes-formel"	X		(X)			X	X		(X)		X
6. Know God, obey God	X					X	(X)				X
7. 'Restored', 'returned'	X		X		X		X	X	X	X	
8. God will 'build' or 'plant'	X	(X)					X	X	(X)		
9. Repentance is a consequence	X		X				X				
10. Priority of God's "I will"	X		X	X	X	X	X	X	X		X
11. God's act not "motivated"	X		X	X	X	X	X	X	X		X
12. Priestly "fear not" absent	X	X	X	X	X	X	X	X	X	X	X

The elements which seem most distinctive and characteristic of Jeremiah's deliverance message to survivors of Judah after 597 are #2, 3, 4. Of these I take #3 as the most pivotal quality; and it is lacking in the (early) poetry of 30:18-22, 31:2-6. What gives chapter 24 "tension" is that God's regarding them as "good" is never removed from his regarding them as "evil" far enough for the latter to recede from being a frighteningly close alternative. 24:6b also puts the alternatives together in an explicit way. There is, then, no forgetting here the reality of the judgment, or ignoring that at this singular moment of history there are two tracks in God's plan for his people: evil-judgment/good-deliverance running in parallel. This "tension" is not present in 29:4-7 except in the limited dimensions of the framework proclaimed there. Consequences of the judgment are yet to be worked out (run their course), and these provide limits on the visible manifestations of God's otherwise dramatic shift to a plan of salvation for the Golah. But in 29:11c the shalom/evil juxtaposition is clearly stated, and it is implied in 29:11d (before this they had no future or hope). 32:6f follows hard on a prophecy of doom for Jerusalem (32:3) and her king (32:4). The whole action of 32:6-15 is courageously hopeful, probably intended to give heart to those who otherwise saw cause for nothing but despair. Again in 32:42 the evil/good tension is made explicit. One has the feeling here, as in 32:6-15, that the time of "evil" is not yet over, even though the time of "good" is warmly assured. 31:31-34 focuses on the people's sin and covenant breaking, and it is only implicit in the need for a whole new covenant and a time of unconditional forgiveness that the deliverance follows a time of thoroughgoing judgment. 32:36-41 has stronger accents on divine judgment than 31:31-34 which it is often said to "echo." This comes out in vss. 36, 37ab, 40b ("I will not turn away from doing good to them"). It is on this point of "tension" between a freshly remembered, residually present, or actively concurrent time of judgment, and the promised time of deliverance, that the poetic oracles of 30:18-22 and 31:2-6 most clearly reflect a different aura (and intention) than the prose deliverance passages. In 30:18-22 there is no direct mention of any judgment or previous time of "evil." Of course the "restore" and "rebuild" of vs. 18 assume a destruction, but the impression here is that the judgment is a thing of the past. There being no words on restoration of relationship, it does not seem to have been taken as a judgment with such deep implications; therefore, the deliverance is less dramatic. This is all the more true of 31:2-6 which has an altogether lyrical and optimistic tone. Vss. 2 and 3 could refer to the period of wilderness wanderings after Egypt, or the survival of the Northern State. One should note the verb tenses in 31:2-6 and the stress on continuity. The series of "agains" are only mild remembrances of a time of distress--that is, we are further into a mentality of shalom here, and the future is assured in a far more relaxed way than in chs. 24, 29, 32.

As we see from Diagram A the continuities between: 24:4-7; 29:4-7, 10-14; 32:6-15, 42-44; 31:31-34; 32:36-41 are too strong seriously to doubt that they are all of the same source. We use "source" here in the sense of the goal described on pages 2-3. I would say that these speeches were addressed to the same audience, date their first formulation to within less than a decade of one another, and speak to the same constellation of concerns from the same, basic, but rich, theological perspective.

E.   Promises of Hope in Deuteronomistic Histories

We can best see these six (authentic-early) Jeremianic prose salvation passages in perspective if we compare them with other deliverance type passages which have a commonality of intention, prominent themes, ideological gestalt--and therefore probable common authorship. A good beginning point would be to look at undoubted d'istic promises of hope outside of Jer. If there is any objective basis for saying what a deliverance promise of d'istic authorship would look like (inside Jer or not) then surely such passages provide the foundation.

The d'istic promises of a good future which envision or presuppose a time of exile are very limited in number. The three of them, Deut 4:26-31; 30:1-10 and 1 Kgs 8:46-53, have certain qualities in common: 1) It is clearly said that God is the direct agent of the exile-punishment (Deut 4:27; 30:1, 3; 1 Kgs 8:46). 2) The turning point from the time of judgment to the time of deliverance hangs dramatically on whether or not the people repent (4:29, 30; 30:2, 10; 1 Kgs 8:47, 48). The turning point is not a matter of God's decision. Thus, all these promises are sharply conditional. 3) In every case the restoration is performed with some consideration or respect given to God's prior commitment or promise to "the fathers" of this generation (Deut 4:31 "he will not. . . forget the covenant with your fathers which he swore to them"; Deut 30:5 "the Lord your God will bring you into the land which your fathers possessed, that you may possess it"; see also Deut 30:9; 1 Kgs 8:53 "For thou didst separate them from among all the people of the earth, to be thy heritage as thou didst declare through Moses, my servant, when thou didst bring our fathers out of Egypt"; see also 8:51). 4) It is made explicit that God's response involves not only concrete restorations but also an expression of love: (Deut 4:31 נ ת ת ם 1 Kgs 8:50 , ר ח מ ך Deut 30:3 ;א ל ר ח ו ם י ה ו ח ל ר ח מ י ם) all employing the root רחם .

These three d'istic passages which envision or presuppose an exile, and promise hope in the midst of that situation, have in common with our six (early-authentic) Jeremianic prose promises element #1 as described just above: That God is clearly the agent of this misfortune. But in none of the six (Jer 24:4-7; 29:4-14; 32:6-15, 42-44; 31:31-34; 32:36-41; 33:6-9) is there any reference to repentance as a pre-condition for God's gracious act; quite the reverse, God's gracious initiative is unconditional, is usually stated first, and dominates the tone of the entire promise. A second sharp difference is that there is never any reference to "the fathers" and a promise to them as a consideration in God's act of deliverance in Jer 24:4-7; 29:4-7, 10-14; 32:6-15, 42-44; 31:31-34; 32:36-41; 33:6-9. And in none of these six Jeremianic passages is there any reference to or God's "love" (under any other terminology) as part of the word of hope. Of these considerations, what really sets the 6 Jeremianic passages apart from the 3 d'istic promises is that the d'istic passages operate strictly within the sin-punish/repent-forgive logic of the (Mosaic) covenant. I have demonstrated elsewhere that Jeremiah gave the Old Testament its greatest development in the proclamation of repentance and is probably the source of that teaching in the d'istic historians, since Deut itself ironically lacks any evidence for a call to repentance formulation.[19] But it can also be proved that Jeremiah ultimately gave up on the call to repentance as a failure (see in Jer 5:1-6; 9:4-8; 5:21, 5:23, 5:25; 14:10; 13:23; 6:19; 19:15; 15:6-9; 6:27-30; 7:23-29).[20]

When the six prose salvation passages in Jer are compared with passages containing his calls to repentance (3:12-13, 3:14, 3:22; 4:1-2, 4:3-4, 4:14; 7:3-7; 15:19; 18:11; 22:3-5; 25:5-6; 26:13), it becomes quite clear that Jeremiah can only proclaim deliverance because the terms of repentance, as also the terms of the conditional covenant, have been left behind and transcended in God's manifestation of a new unconditional readiness to deliver his people as the beginning of a new era. The d'istic historians know nothing of this important shift. Their so-called promises of weal are nothing more than summonses to repentance projected into the future.

These three passages, Deut 4:26-31; 30:1-10, and 1 Kgs 8:46-53 supply our best direct evidence for what a d'istic promise of hope would look like were it delivered to a situation of exile. Our conclusion is that the six Jeremianic passages are informed by a different set of theological priorities, a distinctly separate vision of the course of the prophetic vocation, and a different constellation of thematic preferences, than these three d'istic passages.

It would be wrong, however, to conclude that the d'istic historians had a single, coherent conception of the pattern of God's dealing with his people in circumstances like the Babylonian exile. In quite a number of passages God promises that the price of the people's disobedience will be their rejection and annihilation by him: Deut 28:47ff, 58ff; 31:16-18; Josh 23:14-16; 1 Kgs 9:7-9; 2 Kgs 17:20; 21:12-15; 23:26-27. These are counterbalanced by important texts like 1 Sam 12:19-22; 2 Sam 7:8-16; 1 Kgs 11:31-39 which emphasize that any punishment for sin will be limited to a chastisement within the continuity of the covenant, and that God's promises for the election of his people or their representative are valid in perpetuity.[21]

---

[19]Thomas M. Raitt, "The Prophetic Summons to Repentance," ZAW 83 (1971) 30-48.

[20]This episode in the radicalization of Jeremiah's judgment message is developed at length in a chapter of an unpublished manuscript on which I have been working the past several years.

[21]See Dennis McCarthy, "II Samuel 7 and the Structure of the Deuteronomic History," JBL 84 (1965) 131-138 on the importance of 2 Sam 7 as a text representative of d'istic thought.

It seems evident, therefore, that the editing of the so-called deuteronomistic histories has gone through several stages such that even at the last stage not all the inconsistencies were removed. Again here Jeremiah shows independence from the several strands of deuteronomistic thought in that: a) he never considers that Judah's election was made in perpetuity; b) he combines a teaching on rejection (Jer 14:19-15:4; 7:29-34; 12:7) with a reinitiation of the relationship in his promises of deliverance; and c) we have already seen that he combined an unconditional promise of deliverance with a vivid remembrance of judgment in these same six passages. Thus Jeremiah was able to hold the polarities together in a meaningful tension seemingly beyond the comprehension of the various d'istic sources.

F.   Comparisons with Twelve Additional Prose Oracles in Jeremiah

Another set of comparisons will bring the distinctive qualities of Jer 24:4-7; 29:4-7, 10-14; 32:6-16, 42-44; 31:31-34; 32:36-39; 33:6-9 into yet clearer relief. Beyond these six prose passages which I have suggested are authentically Jeremianic, there are twelve additional prose passages in Jer that are generally attributed to later stages in the development of this book: 3:15-18; 16:14-15; 23:3-4, 23:5-6; 30:2-3, 30:8-9; 31:38-40; 33:14-16, 33:17-18, 33:19-22, 33:23-26; and 50:18-20. Certain observations and comparisons can be made with regard to them.
1. There is a more relaxed tone than in the (earlier-authentic) six. The problem here is not the people's sin, or the tension in God's plan between judgment and mercy because of that sin, nor in what has happened to the personal relationship between God and Judah as interior consequence of the judgment-exile. The problem is presented as being simply the fact of the exile. These oracles seem to have been spoken at a time when the Exile as God's justified punishment was forgotten, or so thoroughly accepted as to no longer be an issue. 2. Given this perception of what the people need deliverance from, the solution is not regeneration of their humanity, cleansing, or reinitiating the relationship. The distress is resolved simply with the promised return of the people from exile to Judea and the reestablishment there of the visible signs of the theo-political state (faithful rulers patterned after David; Levitical priests; restoration of Jerusalem; repossession of the land as the people's promised inheritance). 3. It is difficult to see how these oracles could escape the charge of being false prophecy unless they had been delivered well after the fall of Jerusalem was an accomplished fact.[22] Had they been delivered before 587 they would be promising a continuation of all the reassuring tokens of God's favor as manifest in the visible signs of the theo-political state without any regard to the people's sin and without

_____

[22]The problem with the oracles of weal of the false prophets was that they "whitewashed" (overlooked) the sin of the people, proclaimed shalom when the portents of history were full of "evil," and failed to read accurately the connection between the people's guilt and the forthcoming doom as God's conscious, just punishment. In the determination of the false prophetic promise from the true one it is crucial, but difficult, to know when it was spoken, when it was to take effect, and to whom the promise was directed.

realism concerning the impending invasion by Nebuchadnezzar (interpreted as God's judgment). 4. These twelve prose oracles find their
closest correlation with two promises added to the end of Amos, probably after the fall of Samaria in 722 (9:11-12 and 9:13-15) and with
Jer 30:18-22, 31:2-6. Because of the relaxed, lyrically optimistic,
emphasis of those two oracles out of "The Little Book of Comfort" upon
the restoration of visible evidences of the theo-political state, I
am inclined to think that perhaps those are oracles of salvation for
the Northern State Israel written by disciples of Amos, Hosea, Isaiah
and Micah and added editorially to Jer. The alternative, with Volz
and Rudolph, is to assume that somehow Jeremiah was motivated to try
to communicate deliverance to Israel during an early state of his
ministry. In any case Jer 30:18-22; 31:2-6, would have all the shal-
low optimism of false prophecy if those words were spoken to Judah
before 587 and meant to have their application then. The only realistic position, it seems to me, is to affirm that the two Amos passages, the two Jeremianic poetic oracles, and the twelve prose promises
within the book of Jer beyond the six discussed earlier, were addressed
to an audience not in peril of an imminent historical cataclysm, but
were spoken well after such a judgment had taken place. 5. Because
of the dissimilarity between these twelve (late) prose promises in Jer,
and the undoubtedly d'istic promises considered above, I think it must
be suggested that the d'istic editors of Deut--2 Kgs were of a different generation or circle than the authors of the (late) prose
promises in Jer. The salient point of division here is that however
oriented either group is toward promising restoration of the visible
symbols of Judah's election, the passages in Jer promise God's intervention toward these ends unconditionally and without prerequisites,
whereas the promises in Deut 4:26-31; 30:1-10, and 1 Kgs 8:46-50 are
sharply conditional on the people's repentance. The diversity of
material within the editorial contributions to Deut--2 Kgs and its
divergence from the anything but homogeneous prose material seemingly
added after the death of Jeremiah and his first circle of disciples,
underlines the possibility that when we designate a unit of prose
material of uncertain authorship stemming from around the 6th century
as "d'istic," it may well be that all we have done is to organize our
ignorance under a label, or explain a lesser unknown by a greater unknown. Nicholson's uncritical identification of all the prose material
in Jer with the "D circle" suggests that the pendulum has swung to a
point of absurdity. From here on we might do well to make careful
distinctions between the sources of the layers of tradition added to
Jer, and to use the term "d'istic" only when we have specific evidence
to link a passage with the edited strata of Deut--2 Kgs.[23] 6. Compared

---

[23]E. W. Nicholson, _Preaching to the Exiles_ (New York: Schocken,
1970). Nicholson simply explains all Jeremianic prose on the basis of
d'istic prose, ignoring unquestioned poetry from earlier prophets as
sources of possible influence including even the totality of Jeremiah's
own unquestioned poetic oracles. The result is thus firmly predetermined from the outset: all Jeremianic prose will be found to demonstrate
d'istic thought and language and widen the base of evidence for d'istic
work during the exile.

with the twelve (late) prose promises in Jer, the six (earlier-authentic)
Jeremianic oracles promise deliverance in awareness of the exile as
God's judgment, and with a conviction that the people of deliverance
must be transformed from the condition of the people who went into judgment. In these six the relationship between God and Judah is seen to
be a fragile variable, yet it is negotiable. But, there is no sense
that restoration will mean a return to the status quo before the judgment.

G. Comparisons with Ezekiel's Deliverance Promises

If we are to take seriously our suggestion in the opening pages
of this article that Jeremiah is the first of the Sixth Century Prophets,
then it is now time to compare our suggested evidence for his actual deliverance message to Judah with the unquestioned oracles of deliverance
in Ezek. As compared with the six Jer promises of deliverance in prose
which we think to be genuine, the eleven Ezek promises of deliverance
differ in the following ways.[24] Ezekiel's promises have certain trade-
marks. 1) Unlike Jeremiah he shows a repeated concern about the observer nations, and the shame and disgrace which Judah has brought upon
God by what has happened to her (20:40-44; 36:8-15, 36:22-32, 36:33-36;
37:24-28). 2) In conjunction with this it may be stressed that God is
taking the saving initiative "for his name's sake" and not out of consideration for Judah (20:40-44; 36:22-32). 3) True to his priestly
background, Ezekiel's description of the people's wrong gravitates
toward imagery involving some idea of uncleanness, like "abominations"
or "detestable things" (11:16-21; 20:40-44; 36:22-32; 37:19-23).
4) Accordingly, Ezekiel carries the idea of God forgiving through the
imagery of a cleansing action (36:22-32, 36:33-36; 37:19-23). 5) Also
in accord with Ezekiel's background on the election of Zion, the Temple,
and David, he stresses repossession of Jerusalem, resanctification of
the Temple, reinitiation of the Davidic kingship, restoration to the
land seen as originally an inheritance much more than Jeremiah did
(only in 32:36-41 and 33:6-9 in Jer; but in Ezek all of the eleven
except 11:16-21 and 34:11-16).

However, in many important ways Ezekiel's oracles are quite like
the six in Jer, in some cases further developing Jeremiah's tendencies.

---

[24]The determination of authenticity for deliverance passages is
much less difficult in Ezek than in Jer. Of four leading source
critics--Walther Eichrodt, Ezekiel (Philadelphia: Westminster, 1970);
Georg Fohrer, Ezechiel (HAT; Tübingen: J.C.B. Mohr, 1955); Pfeiffer,
Intro. O. T.; and Walther Zimmerli, Ezechiel (BKAT, 1-2; Neukirchener
Verlag, 1969)--all four in most cases, and three in the other instances,
support the genuineness of eleven deliverance promises in Ezek: 11:16-21;
20:40-44; 34:11-16, 34:20-24, 34:25-31; 36:8-15, 36:22-32, 36:33-36;
37:11-14, 37:19-23, 37:24-28.

182

1) All are in prose. 2) There is recurrent use of the "Bundesformel"
(11:16-21; 34:20-24, 34:25-31; 36:22-32; 37:19-23, 37:24-28). 3) God
endows the people with something to make them more able to live in relationship with Him (11:16-21; 36:22-32; 37:11-14). 4) We have some
mention of the covenant being reinitiated (34:25-31; 37:24-28).
5) Most important of all, in every case but 34:11-16 and 36:8-15 there
is some clear remembrance of the judgment and the implication that the
deliverance is in tension with it.

   We hypothesize that only prophets who preached judgment included
within their promises of (unconditional) deliverance the otherwise
anomalous and extraneous element of a vivid remembrance of some component of the judgment message. This element may have come in one of a
variety of forms: 1) the explicit indication that God himself has been
the source of the misfortune; 2) a reference to those being promised
salvation as sinful, disobedient, full of abominations even though that
promise does not put preconditions on these people being qualified to
receive it; 3) the explicit or implicit suggestion that the deliverance
constitutes a new beginning--more than just a restoration of what
existed before 597--even though it is with the same people as received
the judgment; seen in: a) Bundesformel as re-election; b) Forgive-Cleanse;
c) God giving New Heart-Spirit; d) Obedience made internal; e) Resurrection; f) New Covenant.

   It is clear that Ezekiel is further into the mentality of deliverance than Jeremiah and gives relatively more stress to deliverance, as
over against remembrance of judgment themes, than Jeremiah. But even
on this point there is considerable overlap. As we have already seen,
Ezek 11:16-21 balances judgment with deliverance and keeps a very sharp,
explicit tension between them. And of course Jer 31:31-34; 32:36-41;
and 33:6-9 all put quite a strong stress on the deliverance and elaborate its details.

   When all the salvation promises in the prophetic books are added
together, the 17 in Jer and Ezek shown in Diagram B emerge from about
50 prophetic Oracles of Deliverance as singularly preoccupied with how
the word of salvation stands against a vividly remembered background
of doom, so that it is quite intentionally affirmed that the deliverance
is juxtaposed to the judgment. What is very striking in the earliest
authentic deliverance promises to Judah in Jer and Ezek is that God is
explicitly said to be the cause of the evil, or judgment, or catastrophe
(Column #1, Diagram B), but this is also the earliest element to drop
out. The first stage of transition from this is when the judgment-exile
is expressed by the verb in the passive (Ezek 20:41 "where you have been
scattered"; also 34:12). Then, it is merely left implicit that the misfortune of Exile is a fait accompli; but, that is not equated with God's
punishment. As this happens there is a concern to show that those in
exile had sinned (Jer 31:32; 33:8; Ezek 20:43; 36:22; etc.).

   I would suggest that these are primary ways in which the early
deliverance message was brought into a kind of organic connection with

Diagram   B

EVIDENCES OF JUDGMENT IN RESIDUAL TENSION WITH PROMISED DELIVERANCE

	God is source of Judgment	Deliverance recipients remembered as sinful	Bundes-formel	Forgive Cleanse	New Heart & Spirit	Obedience Internalized	New Covenant
Jer 24:4-7	vs 5				7	7	
29:4-7, 10-14	vs 4,7,10		(12)			12, 13	
32:6-15, 42-44	vs 42						
31:31-34		vs 32	33	34		33	31, 33
32:36-41	vs 37		38		39	39	40
33:6-9		vs 8		8			
Ezek 11:16-21	vs 16	18	20		19	20	
20:40-44		vs 43, 44		41			
34:11-16							
34:20-24			vs 24				
34:25-31			vs 30				25
36:8-15							
36:22-32		vs 22, 23, 32	29	25, 29	26	27	
36:33-36		vs 33		33			
37:11-14					vs 14		
37:19-23		vs 23	23	23			
37:24-28			vs 27				26

the judgment message, and it was made clear that the mercy of the deliverance did not ignore the integrity of the judgment. In other
words, this was perhaps the way that early deliverance preaching was
shown to be distinct from false prophecy. As events progressed, and
all the survivors of Judah were in exile, and the misfortune-punishment
of exile was a lived experience, this component dropped out and (as in
Second Isaiah's salvation oracles) the concern shifted toward making
the deliverance convincing. But besides this primary integration of
the judgment and deliverance messages, Jeremiah and Ezekiel were unique
in the emphasis given to a secondary, or indirect recognition of the
judgment and its consequences. It is not least of all at this point
that we find the greatest distinction between the weal oracles added
to Amos and to Jeremiah (the prose twelve) where the promise is one of
simple restoration to the same condition the people were in before the
disruptions of the kingdoms ever began, and Jeremiah and Ezekiel's very
clear recognition that God's chosen have not merely met with a political and historical problem that can be described in physical terms.
The Bundesformel, forgiveness promises, words of new covenant presuppose
that a relationship has been broken; the words about gifts of new heart
and internalization of obedience suggest that God must creatively further perfect his people; and the image of resurrection suggests that
the corporate entity had died.

If the six prose passages in Jer (24:4-7; 29:4-7, 10-14; 32:6-15,
42-44; 31:31-34; 32:36-41; 33:6-9) were added after the time of Jeremiah
by d'istic editors, it then becomes inexplicable why these passages have
this very striking residual judgment component in common with the genuine
deliverance promises in Ezek, while in twelve other prose oracles of
weal in Jer (3:15-18; 16:14-15; 23:3-4, 23:5-6; 30:2-3, 30:8-9; 31:38-40;
33:14-16, 33:17-18, 33:19-22, 33:23-26; 50:18-20), this judgment component is strikingly absent. Nothing outside of Jeremiah and Ezekiel
can attest the remarkable combination of unconditional promises of deliverance together with a vivid awareness of the validity and profoundly
serious implications of the judgment. The evidence from Second Isaiah
shows clearly that it was important to hold these two elements together
only in a limited period of Israel's history. And, interestingly enough,
Second Isaiah documents a remembrance that they were held together.[25]
I suggest that only the major prophets had the authority, influence,
and respect to proclaim an unconditional salvation to Judah....including
not merely restoration of what was lost physically, but reinitiation of
the whole inward, spiritual, covenantal relationship. And only in the
primary strata of tradition stemming from Jeremiah and Ezekiel, and in
a quite modified way also Second Isaiah, do we find an acceptance of
the burden of responsibility to make sense of the movement of God's
initiative toward salvation without ignoring the reality and justice
of the judgment God brought on Judah. The second and third generation

---

[25]Isa 45:7; 49:14-15; 54:4, 54:7-8.

of Jeremiah's tradents and editors, as with Amos', contented themselves merely with attaching promises of a restored theocracy. Thus Jer 24:4-7 marks the beginning of a development of extraordinary significance and theological depth. This promise, so clearly transitional from the proclamation of judgment to the proclamation of deliverance, is integrally related to a pattern also seen in 5 other authentic Jeremianic prose promises and 11 authentic Ezekiel prose promises. In the sum of them we find one of the most interesting developments in the history of Israel's faith.

THE CANONICAL WISDOM PSALMS OF ANCIENT ISRAEL--

THEIR RHETORICAL, THEMATIC, AND FORMAL DIMENSIONS

J. Kenneth Kuntz

The University of Iowa

This essay moves on the assumption that at the minimum, a comprehensive study of the canonical Psalms requires some consideration of Israelite wisdom traditions, and similarly, a comprehensive study of Israelite wisdom traditions requires a consideration of at least some canonical psalms. Thorough Psalms research moves into wisdom; likewise, thorough wisdom research moves into the Psalms. Something akin to the first half of this observation led Hermann Gunkel some forty years ago to give an entire section of his masterful Einleitung in die Psalmen over to the subject of psalmic wisdom poetry,[1] and more recently induced Harvey H. Guthrie, Jr., to devote one of the five chapters of his Psalms study to the theme "God as the Source of Wisdom: Torah and Piety."[2] Moreover, the second half of this observation seemingly influenced Walter Baumgartner to present his own classification of canonical wisdom psalms at the outset of his monograph on wisdom[3] and encouraged R. B. Y. Scott to include a rich paragraph on psalmic wisdom compositions within an informative essay, "The Wisdom Movement and Its Literature," which prefaces his Proverbs-Ecclesiastes commentary.[4]

---

[1]Hermann Gunkel, Einleitung in die Psalmen: Die Gattungen der religiösen Lyrik Israels (Göttingen: Vandenhoeck & Ruprecht, 1933) 381-397.

[2]Harvey H. Guthrie, Jr., Israel's Sacred Songs: A Study of Dominant Themes (New York: Seabury Press, 1966) 171-193.

[3]Walter Baumgartner, Israelitische und altorientalische Weisheit (Sammlung Gemeinverständlicher Vorträge, 166; Tübingen: Mohr, 1933) 1.

[4]R. B. Y. Scott, Proverbs-Ecclesiastes (AB; Garden City, N.Y.: Doubleday, 1965) xxi. See also Scott's The Way of Wisdom in the Old Testament (New York: Macmillan, 1971) 192-201.

To be sure, the late Ivan Engnell once asserted, "The truth of the matter is that the Book of Psalms does not contain any 'wisdom poems,' at all."[5] But Engnell was vigorously reacting to opponents[6] who, first, see too much cult-free "lay piety" floating around in a canonical OT book which for Engnell is exceedingly cultic, and second, are easily prone to draw ill-founded analogies between late canonical wisdom psalms and the didactic poems resident in the Psalms of Solomon and the Book of Ben Sira. Therefore Engnell's remark fails as a disinterested observation which might easily induce assent.

In the present essay which is warmly dedicated to Professor James Muilenburg, we intend to offer a select overview of previous wisdom psalms research, identify rhetorical and thematic elements which typically manifest themselves in psalmic wisdom, acknowledge nine compositions as legitimate wisdom psalms, and wrestle with the problem of wisdom forms (Gattungen) in the Israelite Psalter.

Previous Wisdom Psalms Research

In the publications of such scholars as C. A. Briggs, Hermann Gunkel, Sigmund Mowinckel, P. A. Munch, M. Ludin Jansen, Aage Bentzen, and Roland Murphy we have clear evidence that the wisdom psalms have not been entirely ignored by twentieth century biblical investigation. Back in 1906, when his Psalms commentary in the ICC series first appeared, C. A. Briggs demonstrated at least a modest concern for didactic material within the Psalter. Unfortunately, Briggs did not use the adjective "didactic" with precision,[7] and, being a product of his own time, he showed no great interest in form-critical pursuits. While Briggs' commentary remains useful, Gunkel rightly merits the label "pioneer" in OT Psalms research. Indeed, he characterized wisdom poetry in

---

[5]Ivan Engnell, A Rigid Scrutiny: Critical Essays on the Old Testament (Nashville: Vanderbilt University Press, 1969) 99.

[6]Ibid., where R. H. Pfeiffer is the only opponent explicitly mentioned.

[7]This same imprecision in terminology plagues the notes within The Jerusalem Bible where Psalm 32 is called "a didactic poem," Psalm 34 a "wisdom and 'alphabetical' psalm," Psalm 78 "a didactic meditation," and Psalm 90 "a sage's meditation."

some detail. In his Einleitung in die Psalmen Gunkel was
unwilling to accord Weisheitsdichtung status among the major
Gattungen within the Psalter. He did, however, devote sixteen large pages to describing its forms, contents, ancient
Near Eastern affinities, and Sitz im Leben.[8] Gunkel
regarded Weisheitsdichtung as an entirely comprehensive
literary genre which finds its way into pithy proverbs,
longer poems, and even whole books. The first two may be
readily detected within the Psalter. In Psalms 127 and 133
simple proverbs are linked together, and Psalms 1, 37, 49,
73, 112, and 128 present themselves as more fully developed
wisdom poems.[9] These pages of the Einleitung contain
insights and problems. The manner whereby Gunkel sketches
the development from short and simple wisdom forms to longer
and more complicated specimens seems somewhat arbitrary.
Moreover, he is not completely clear in his listing of the
wisdom psalms, and this imputes an unconvincing tone to the
entire section. Nevertheless, it is still worthy of scholarly perusal, and partly so due to its wealth of germane
scriptural citation.

As a third name we cite Sigmund Mowinckel. Though he
had an aversion for the designation "wisdom psalm,"
Mowinckel did attempt a depiction of "learned psalmography."[10] He detects in most all of the so-called wisdom
poems within the Psalter a troublesome non-cultic aspect.
These learned poems are private compositions which typically (1) praise the deity, and (2) instruct the young.[11]
Whereas these compositions direct a fitting word of thanksgiving to the deity and aim a useful word of admonition to
youth, as literary pieces they leave something to be
desired. In them we discover, claims Mowinckel, stylistic
dissolution and the mixing of motifs. The phrase "didactic

---

[8]Gunkel, Einleitung, 381-397. By comparison, he
devoted 62 pages to the Hymn and 93 to the Individual
Lament.

[9]Ibid., 384-385.

[10]Sigmund Mowinckel, "Psalms and Wisdom," Wisdom in
Israel and in the Ancient Near East (VTSup3; Leiden:
Brill, 1960) 205-224, and The Psalms in Israel's Worship
(Oxford: Basil Blackwell, 1962) vol. 2, 104-125.

[11]Mowinckel, "Psalms and Wisdom," 212.

psalm" is therefore a <u>contradictio in adjecto</u>.[12] He quips
that since the presumed wisdom psalms "had no more connection with the cultic life, the real 'Sitz im Leben' of the
psalm poetry, they have failed to realize what a psalm
really is."[13] But Mowinckel treats these "non-cultic"
psalms with less than complete detachment. If their poetry
is not consistently first-rate, neither is it entirely
abysmal, and this assessment applies to acrostic and nonacrostic wisdom compositions alike.

Some of Mowinckel's efforts have gone into depicting
the way in which learned psalmography was utilized in the
context of school instruction, and here two other Scandi-
navian scholars deserve mention--P. A. Munch[14] and M. Ludin
Jansen.[15] Mowinckel, Munch, and Jansen are agreed that a
hybrid thanksgiving-wisdom psalm was often recited by the
sage in the presence of students who had gathered around
him in his school. Munch contends, to Mowinckel's dissat-
isfaction,[16] that learned psalmography had a <u>dual</u> use in
the school system. <u>Schulandachtspsalmen</u> such as 19B, 25,
and 119 were employed to meet a devotional need, whereas
the <u>Unterrichtspsalmen</u> such as 32 and 34 were solely used
for instructional purposes. If Munch has moved beyond what
the evidence allows, he rightly invites us to ponder the
quite natural role that psalmic wisdom must have played in
the synagogue. Jansen's study is less inclined than Munch's
to delineate in precise terms just how these poems were put
to use. Yet it is more intent to examine the psalmic literature as such. Both Jansen and Munch have highlighted
materials contained in Ben Sira and the Psalms of Solomon,
and have drawn analogies (some dubious) with passages resident in the canonical psalms.

In his <u>Introduction to the Old Testament</u>, Aage Bentzen
demonstrates a greater interest in psalmic wisdom than do

---

[12]Sigmund Mowinckel, "Traditionalism and Personality
in the Psalms," <u>HUCA</u> 23/1 (1950-1951) 226.

[13]<u>Ibid</u>.

[14]P. A. Munch, "Die jüdischen 'Weisheitspsalmen' und
ihr Platz im Leben," <u>AcOr</u> 15 (1937) 112-140.

[15]H. Ludin Jansen, <u>Die spätjüdische Psalmendichtung</u>:
<u>Ihr Entstehungskreis und ihr "Sitz im Leben"</u> (Oslo: Norske
videnskaps-akademi, 1937).

[16]Mowinckel, "Psalms and Wisdom," 212, ftn. 2.

Eissfeldt and Fohrer in their corresponding works of OT
Introduction.[17] Bentzen claims that we are only under
obligation to designate three psalms as wisdom composi-
tions--1, 112, and 127. If he is convincing in his evaluation of Psalm 119 as a sui generis entity which incorporates
a host of poetic Gattungen, his estimation of Psalms 32, 37,
and 49 as poems of thanksgiving may be challenged. He pays
insufficient attention to the entirely strategic initial and
concluding strophes of all three. Bentzen has been too prone
to underscore thanksgiving elements at the expense of eclips-
ing wisdom elements. Even so, his study judiciously reminds
us that a locus of mutuality involving thanksgiving and wisdom clearly exists. Further, Bentzen's assertion that not
every psalm devoted to the problem of retribution is to be
termed "didactic" is well taken,[18] and has apparently
impressed Roland E. Murphy whose work also invites our
inspection.

Murphy's brief essay throws light on how the ancient
psalmists freely incorporated wisdom elements into what
must formally be accepted as nonsapiential poetry.[19] After
enumerating certain stylistic and thematic characteristics
which readily typify Israelite sapiential poetry, Murphy
offers Psalms 1, 32, 34, 37, 49, 112 and 128 as his list
of seven authentic wisdom psalms. While he is unable to
posit precisely their Sitz im Leben, he does speak persuasively for their milieu sapientiel. Murphy maintains that
wisdom expressions often belong to the post-exilic cult,
and that thanksgiving confession and wisdom teaching typically intersect. He claims, "As the testimony took on more
and more a didactic character, the role of wisdom within
the cult would have been secured, and with it the independence of the wisdom psalm form."[20] Despite the obvious
strengths of his analysis, not the least of which is his
cogent isolation of seven compositions which we also accept
as authentic wisdom psalms, Murphy may be faulted for having
excluded Psalms 127 and 133 from his enumeration. If Psalm

---

[17]Aage Bentzen, Introduction to the Old Testament
(Copenhagen: Gad, 1958), vol. 1, 161.

[18]Ibid.

[19]Roland E. Murphy, "A Consideration of the Classification, 'Wisdom Psalms'" (VTSup 9; Leiden: Brill, 1963) 156-
167.

[20]Ibid., 161.

127 does not lend itself to easy classification, its extended and impersonal observation (Spruch) in vss. 1-2 and 3-5, its simile in vs. 4, and its ʾašrê formula in vs. 5, to say nothing of its content in celebrating the safe home and ample family, speak for its legitimacy as a wisdom psalm. Moreover, Psalm 133 with its affirmation of the beauty of fraternal harmony and use of the declarative proverb also commends itself for our consideration. On balance, however, Murphy's essay has significantly extended the frontiers of wisdom psalms research.

Rhetorical Elements in Psalmic Wisdom

Both the above attempt at summarizing representative twentieth century investigations and a direct confrontation with the biblical text convince us that if continuing research into the nature of psalmic wisdom is to be effective, then rhetorical and thematic elements will have to be discerned and analyzed with utmost care. A cogent isolation of wisdom components within basically nonsapiential poems and an incisive isolation of authentic wisdom psalms are undeniably contingent upon such considerations. Hence, we propose to consider seven distinct features of psalmic wisdom which may be classified as being rhetorical in character. These are (1) the "better" saying, (2) the numerical saying, (3) the admonition (Mahnspruch) with and without motive clause, (4) the admonitory address to "sons," (5) the ʾašrê formula, (6) the rhetorical question, and (7) the simile. Not every rhetorical element here enumerated is the sole property of wisdom discourse. Nor is each attested in the Israelite Psalter in equal measure. Indeed, no claimed wisdom psalm contains all seven. Nevertheless, concentration upon such matters should facilitate our attempts at coming to terms with the style, content, and intention of psalmic wisdom.

(1) The "better" saying: Designated by Walther Zimmerli as the ṭôb-Spruch, the "better" saying or comparative proverb is common to OT wisdom literature.[21] Although we find only one such saying in the Book of Job (35:3) and it is by no means typical in its structure, twenty-two

---

[21]Walther Zimmerli, "Zur Struktur der alttestamentlichen Weisheit," ZAW 51 (1933) 192-195. See also Glendon E. Bryce, "'Better'-Proverbs: An Historical and Structural Study," SBL 1972 Proceedings, vol. 2, 343-354. Bryce, however, does not address himself to ṭôb-Sprüche in the Psalter.

"better" sayings appear in Proverbs and eighteen in Ecclesiastes.[22] The six "better" sayings in the Psalter are
located in 37:16; 63:4; 84:11; 118:8, 9; and 119:72. Formally these six read either ṭôb...mî/mē or kî ṭôb...mē.
Our earlier approval of Bentzen's assessment of Psalm 119
as being of sui generis character does not give us license
to ignore vs. 72:

> Better (ṭôb) to me is the law of thy mouth
> than (mē-) thousands of pieces of gold and silver.

Addressed to the deity in the spirit of praise rather than
to mankind in the spirit of instruction, this "better" saying attests to the intersection of postexilic wisdom piety
with Torah observance. The Law is venerated through a
wisdom mode of speaking. Of the five remaining "better"
sayings which appear in the Psalter, only 37:16 stands
within a self-evident wisdom context:

> Better (ṭôb) is a little belonging to the righteous,
> than (mē-) the abundance of many wicked.

This ṭôb-Spruch is then extended by means of a motive clause
(introduced by the deictic kî) in vs. 17 which forecasts
doom for the wicked and felicity for the righteous. Nevertheless, it must be admitted that this manner of discourse
which is pronounced within the sapiential books of Proverbs
and Ecclesiastes is virtually wanting within psalmic wisdom
contexts.

(2) The numerical saying: In his penetrating study of
the numerical saying, W. M. W. Roth alludes to three passages
in the Psalms--1:6; 27:4; 62:12-13a.[23] The first is a wisdom
verse revealing a clear-cut interest in "two-way theology."

---

[22]Such verses as Eccl. 2:24; 3:12, 22, which read,
"nothing is better than" (ʾên ṭôb), are not included in the
count, since on the basis of structure and content they
appear to be of another sort.

[23]W. M. W. Roth, Numerical Sayings in the Old Testament:
A Form-Critical Study (VTSup 13; Leiden: E. J. Brill, 1965)
55-56, 70, 92. In addition, the remarks of J. L. Crenshaw,
"The Influence of the Wise upon Amos," ZAW 79 (1967) 49,
and Samuel L. Terrien, "Amos and Wisdom," Israel's Prophetic
Heritage (eds. Bernhard W. Anderson and Walter Harrelson;
New York: Harper and Row, 1962) 109-110 are useful, even
though they are not dealing with psalmic wisdom.

Even so, the lack of specific numbers fixes 1:6 to the periphery of the present discussion. The numerical saying in 27:4 is peculiar insofar as it focuses upon solely one item:

> One thing have I asked of Yahweh, that will I seek after;
> that I may dwell in the house of Yahweh all the days of
> my life,
> to gaze at the beauty of Yahweh and to delight in his
> temple.

If its intensive concern for the one thing needful manifests a wisdom aura, the verse's immediate context does not promote sapiential interests. The remaining passage, 62:12-13a, is significant, for it provides a good example of the graded numerical saying (x / x + 1):

> Once Elohim has spoken; twice have I heard this,
> that power belongs to Elohim; and to thee, O Lord,
> belongs hesed.

Here the two divine attributes of power and love are dialectically related. Because the numerical saying was not solely in the possession of the sages in ancient Israel, how can we be certain that 62:12-13a embodies a wisdom element? Interestingly enough, Murphy has already rightly identified vss. 9-11 which immediately precede this numerical saying as a wisdom component.[24] Here proverbial sayings and admonitions are integrated into a Song of Trust. The sapiential tone in vss. 9-11 extends into vss. 12-13a. Although Murphy does not include 62:12-13a in his listing of wisdom elements appearing within nonsapiential contexts, we shall accept it as a significant graded numerical wisdom saying. But in so doing, we admit that no other numerical sayings, graded or otherwise, have made their way into psalmic wisdom contexts.

(3) The admonition (Mahnspruch) with and without motive clause: This third element is more widely attested in psalmic wisdom than are the first two elements enumerated. The admonition, of course, takes residence in Deuteronomic, prophetic, and wisdom literature alike. Yet its role in wisdom discourse is appreciable. To be sure, some sapiential literary units within the OT have no use for the admonition. Israel's sages often preferred speaking observations in the indicative to uttering admonitions in the imperative. Ordinarily they expected their audience to draw out the conclusion instead of forcing "truth" upon them in the guise of direct command. Even so, immediate counsel via the admonition is scarcely absent in the rhetoric of the Book of Job.

---

[24]Murphy, "The Classification, 'Wisdom Psalms,'" 165.

It is found within Qoheleth's instructions on religious observance (4:17-5:6), and it is sprinkled throughout the Book of Proverbs where it is often accompanied by a _motive clause_, that is, an appended subordinate clause having as its purpose the authorizing or the explaining (usually the latter) of the admonition to better ensure man's obedience. Frequently headed by the deictic and emphatic particle kî, these motive clauses served the pedagogical interests of the sage.[25] They assist in making the admonitions to which they are linked more reasonable and compelling. Yet with or without the motive clause, the admonition enjoys a personal thrust which the impersonal observation, that is, the genuine _Spruch_, cannot claim. Whether it be positive or negative in its formulation, the admonition offers _directive_ counsel, and it can be strikingly effective in its rhetorical power. Though the admonition is wanting in Psalms 1, 112, 127, 128, and 133, it is present to some extent in Psalms 32 and 49, and takes on a dominant role in Psalms 34 and 37 where motive clauses are also sometimes included (e.g., 34:10; 37:2, 9, 17, 22, all of which are introduced by the kî particle). In sum, wisdom-oriented admonitions are by no means infrequent within the Israelite Psalter, and they should be comprehended as a crucial rhetorical element within wisdom discourse.[26]

(4) The _admonitory_ address _to_ "sons": Ancient Israel's sages were often inclined to address their own pupils as sons. On twenty-three occasions in the Book of Proverbs, we encounter the expression, "My son" (b^enî), and often, although not always, this is followed by a personal word of admonition. What is more characteristic of Proverbs than

---

[25]See James Muilenburg, "The Linguistic and Rhetorical Usages of the Particle kî in the Old Testament," _HUCA_ 32 (1961) 153.

[26]For further discussion on the admonition, its form and function, cf. Erhard Gerstenberger, _Wesen und Herkunft des 'Apodiktischen Rechts'_ (Neukirchen-Vluyn: Neukirchener Verlag, 1965) 117-121; Hans W. Wolff, _Amos' geistige Heimat_ (Neukirchen-Vluyn: Neukirchener Verlag, 1964) 30-36; W. Richter, _Recht und Ethos_ (München: Kösel-Verlag, 1966) 52-54; Roland E. Murphy, "Assumptions and Problems in Old Testament Wisdom Research," _CBQ_ 29 (1967) 408-409; and Crenshaw, "The Influence of the Wise upon Amos," 48-49.

such lines as, "Hear, my son, your father's instruction" (1:8), or "My son, be attentive to my words" (4:20), or "My son, keep my words and store up my commandments with you" (7:1)? If the son was sometimes the literal offspring of the father who addressed him within the family context, frequently it was the case of a master speaking to his pupil, and this long-established practice continued into early Amoraic times.[27] Of the ten instances when the noun "son" is employed in the singular within the Psalter, none appears to have any connection with wisdom. The plural "sons," which is attested over thirty times in the Psalter, is used basically in three ways. It can refer to all mankind ("sons of men," e.g., 12:2), or to the Israelite community ("sons of Jacob," e.g., 77:16), or to males within a particular family (e.g., "your sons" in 147:13, or "my mother's sons" in 69:9). Within the family context it is stated that "sons are a heritage from Yahweh" (127:3). Here we are dealing with a wisdom psalm, though this one phrase does not make it so! The only truly significant instance is the vocative statement in 34:12 which heads a strophe of sapiential admonitions (vss. 12-15):

> Come, O sons (bānîm), listen to me,
> The fear of Yahweh I will teach you!

No verse in Psalm 34 has been more celebrated as a wisdom component than this one with its compelling word of invitation. Exercising a kind of poetic license, the psalmist here elects to present himself as a respected wisdom teacher whose task it is to induce a reverential fear of Yahweh in those young men who have, or will, come to him for instruction. Finally, though sons are not addressed, the sage's call for attention via the double appeal to hear in 49:2 and 78:1 manifests a function which is equivalent to that of 34:12:[28]

> Hear this, all you peoples,
> Give ear, all you dwellers in the world! (49:2)
>
> Give ear, my people, to my teaching,
> Incline your ear to the words of my mouth! (78:1)

---

[27]See Robert Gordis, "The Social Background of Wisdom Literature," HUCA 18 (1943) 84.

[28]For further elucidation of the double appeal to hear as the opener of sapiential poetry, see James Boston, "The Wisdom Influence upon the Song of Moses," JBL 87 (1968) 199-200.

It is clear in all three instances that the satisfactory
promulgation of wisdom heavily depends upon the attentive
presence of willing listeners, that is, sons and others
eager to grasp for the good.

(5) The ʾašrê formula: This formula, which appears in
quite varied contexts within the Hebrew Bible, has been
designated by Augustin George as a beatitude.[29] It is an
exclamatory sentence constructed in the form of a nominal
proposition and made to commence with the plural construct
noun ʾašrê (or wᵉʾašrê). This word is much at home in OT
wisdom discourse and is most frequently attested in the
Psalms.[30] Admitting that the ʾašrê formula "corresponds
to the cultic formula bārûk," Fohrer identifies its use in
Psalms 1, 127, and 128 as "an outgrowth of the approbation
formula of wisdom instruction (e.g., Job 5:17)."[31] Commenting on its employment in Prov. 3:13ff., Zimmerli regards
the ʾašrê formula as an intermediate member (Mittelglied)
which stands halfway between assertion (Aussagewort) and
admonition (Mahnwort). As such, it functions as a summons
without casting itself into the form of direct address.[32]
Zimmerli recognizes the significance of this rhetorical
element when he remarks, "It formulates the great concern
of wisdom--who is fortunate."[33] Whereas Psalms 37, 49, and
133 as wisdom psalm candidates lack the formula, it is found
once each in Psalms 1, 34, 112, 127 and 128, and twice in
Psalm 32.[34] It is further encountered within two wisdom

---

[29]Augustin George, "La 'Forme' des Béatitudes jusqu' à
Jésus," Mélanges Bibliques André Robert (Paris: Blond et
Gay, 1957) 398. Their participial construction is empha-
sized by Erhard Gerstenberger, "The Woe-oracles of the
Prophets," JBL 81 (1962), 260.

[30]Two-thirds of the 36 attestations of ʾašrê and wᵉʾašrê
are contained within the Book of Psalms. Elsewhere the term
is found 5x in Proverbs, 2x each in Isaiah and II Chronicles,
and once each in I Kings, Job, and Daniel.

[31]Georg Fohrer, Introduction to the Old Testament (Nashville: Abingdon, 1968) 314.

[32]Zimmerli, "Zur Struktur der alttestamentlichen
Weisheit," 185.

[33]Ibid., 186.

[34]In Pss. 1:1; 32:1, 2; 34:9; 112:1; 127:5; 128:1.

contexts identified by Murphy, namely, Pss. 40:5-6 and 94: 8-15, and is used twice in the first two verses of the sui generis Psalm 119. The formula comes very close to being an exhortation in behalf of the good life, what Klaus Koch designates a little indiscreetly as "worldly well-being."[35] Uttered from the perspective of the detached observer, the 'ašrê formula instructs the beholder in the way that he should go. Although Psalm 127 pronounces the formula on the man who has many sons, and thereby speaks neither positively nor negatively with respect to the Yahweh-man relation, most 'ašrê formulas in the wisdom psalms address individual man's relation with the deity. Because such passages as 2:12; 33:12; 41:2; and 84:5, among others, offer the 'ašrê formula without a sapiential intent, it is not possible to claim that the reader inevitably steps into the precincts of wisdom whenever he confronts an 'ašrê declaration in the Psalter. Nevertheless, the 'ašrê formula is most vividly and completely attested within the Book of Psalms. Here we meet an undeniably crucial wisdom psalms element.

(6) The rhetorical question: Walter Baumgartner, Samuel L. Terrien, and Hans W. Wolff have all drawn attention to the sage's readiness to engage in rhetorical questions.[36] Affirming Amos' contact with wisdom, Terrien observes that it is through the asking of such "interrogative maxims" that Amos "expects to stimulate audience approval in a matter of logical thinking involving assent to the principle of empirically observed causation."[37] Wolff maintains that the sages showed a preference for three types of rhetorical questions--those incorporating analogies from the world of nature, those involving comparison, and those employing the 'im hᵃ interrogative form.[38] The last-mentioned type is met in Ps. 94:9b which involves the wisdom context of 94:9-11. The first two types in Wolff's list, however, are not illustrated by psalmic wisdom. Moreover, Psalms 1, 32, 37, 112,

---

[35]Klaus Koch, The Growth of the Biblical Tradition: The Form-Critical Method (New York: Scribner's, 1969) 7.

[36]Walter Baumgartner, "The Wisdom Literature," The Old Testament and Modern Study (ed. H. H. Rowley; Oxford: Clarendon, 1951) 211; Terrien, "Amos and Wisdom," 112; Wolff, Amos' geistige Heimat, 6-9.

[37]Terrien, "Amos and Wisdom," 112, where he deals with Amos 3:3-8; 5:25; 6:2, 12; 9:7.

[38]Wolff, Amos' geistige Heimat, 6-9.

127, 128, and 133 embody no rhetorical questions at all.
Yet they are present in Ps. 25:12, within the sapiential
context of 25:8-14, and in 34:13 and 49:6. These last two
instances show a marked similarity. First comes the wisdom
summons (34:12 and 49:2-5), then there follows the rhetorical question (34:13 introduced by the interrogative "who"
[mî] and 49:6 by the interrogative "why" [lāmmāh]), and next
comes the answer (34:14f. with its crisp imperative admonitions and 49:7-10 with its detailed claim of faith that man
cannot manage simply on his own). To be sure, several wisdom psalms do not attest the sage's acceptance of the rhetorical question as a valuable pedagogic device. Moreover, the
sages of ancient Israel were not the only individuals who
resorted to rhetorical questions. For example, prophetic
and priestly use of the rhetorical question are respectively
revealed in Mic. 6:6-7 and Ps. 24:3. The presence of a
rhetorical question within the Psalter does not necessarily
warrant the conclusion that a sage has been at work. Yet
the rhetorical question does sometimes take residence within
wisdom contexts, and we ought not lose sight of that fact.

(7) The simile: The Israelite sage knew that the carefully formulated illustration might serve his pedagogical
purpose exceedingly well. Typically he based such word
pictures upon his own inspection of the natural order within
which he found himself. This enterprise often gave rise to
vivid similes. These consisted of fundamentally simple
comparisons designed to reinforce, although not to labor,
that which the sage foremost wished to communicate. Well
known is the simile in Ps. 1:3 which compares the God-fearing
man with a fruitful tree. That same figure of comparison is
set forth in the wisdom texts of Jer. 17:8 and Job 8:16 as
well as in the Egyptian composition of Amen-em-ope.[39] By
means of an intentionally abrupt shift of imagery in Ps. 1:4,
the wicked are compared with worthless chaff. The alarmingly
brief existence of the impious is likened to the temporarily
green field in 37:2, 20. Similarly, in the poetic refrain
contained in 49:13 (so also vs. 21, its duplicate) the pom-
pous man is compared with the "beasts that perish." The
transitory aspect of worldly splendor is deftly emphasized.
According to the simile of 49:15, the arrogant are appointed
to Sheol as if they were sheep who find in personified death
their shepherd. In 32:9 the sage directly instructs his
listeners to "be not like a horse or a mule" insofar as
these animals may lack understanding. In one and the same

[39]ANET, 422.

verse we confront simile and negative admonition. The simile in 127:4 compares the sons of the young father to "arrows in the hand of a warrior." By the time that old age presses in upon him, his sons will have grown into manhood and will be entirely capable of protecting him. The wife and sons of the God-fearing man are likened respectively to a "fruitful vine" and "olive shoots" in 128:3. The prosperity thereby implied is expected to visit the one who walks in Yahweh's ways. Then through colorful imagery, the fraternal harmony celebrated in Psalm 133 is likened to "precious oil upon the head" (vs. 2) and "the dew of Hermon" (vs. 3). These representative examples collectively reveal that the simile had an understandably leading role to play in the poetic expressions of the wise. As poets, ancient Israel's sages astutely recognized that "central to the poet's communication of his experience is the connotation, the allusion, the analogy, which he does not spell out, but leaves to the reader to grasp, understand, and share."[40] We are therefore claiming that rhetorical analysis of psalmic wisdom should seriously examine those simple yet thoughtful similes which artfully contribute to the sage's total effort in dispensing wisdom. At the same time, we recognize that many similes in the Israelite Psalter (e.g., 17:12; 18:34; 21:10; 42:1; 90:5; 147:16) have no connection with wisdom whatever. If a given simile within the Book of Psalms focuses in some way upon the motif of retribution, it may turn out to be an integral part of a recognized wisdom psalm. Still this is by no means certain, for "preoccupation with the problem of retribution does not define a wisdom psalm."[41] If the simile does not present itself as a decisive criterion for distinguishing wisdom psalms, the simile nevertheless enjoys a significant function within didactic discourse to be encountered in the Psalter.

Rhetorical criticism of psalmic wisdom, however, requires us to pursue another course as well. We must also take account of the specific vocabulary of Israelite wisdom, for this likewise relates directly to our quest for sapiential elements within the Psalter. In his incisive 1968

---

[40]Robert Gordis, The Book of God and Man: A Study of Job (Chicago: University of Chicago, 1965) 198.

[41]Murphy, "The Classification, 'Wisdom Psalms,'" 164. See also James L. Crenshaw, "Method in Determining Wisdom Influence upon 'Historical' Literature," JBL 88 (1969) 138, who maintains that the notion of retribution is not solely a wisdom motif.

presidential address to the Society of Biblical Literature, James Muilenburg underscored the interest of rhetorical criticism in such matters as the emergence of structural patterns, the use of particles, vocatives, and rhetorical questions, and the repetition of key words and lines in "rhetorically significant collocations."[42] His presentation amply testified that in ancient Hebrew poetry, specific words can assume an undeniably crucial function in laying bare the very message resident within the composition in question. Whereas the strategic location and deliberate repetition of a word exert a telling influence upon the total impact of a given pericope, the biblical exegete is in one way or another required to notice which words are employed. R. B. Y. Scott has rightly asserted that the wisdom books of the Old Testament manifest a characteristic vocabulary: "The words of this are rarely peculiar to it, but their proportionate frequency is noticeable."[43]

In that connection, Scott issues a list of 77 words which he believes will prove "useful in assessing wisdom influence in other parts of the Old Testament such as the prophetic writings and the Psalms."[44] While we wish to acknowledge the truth in Murphy's observation that "wisdom language does not constitute wisdom,"[45] and to heed Crenshaw's warning that word tabulation should be undertaken only with the utmost care,[46] we are nevertheless persuaded that a consideration of the characteristic vocabulary of wisdom is not out of place within our total research effort into psalmic wisdom. Actually only 13 of the 77 wisdom words enumerated by Scott fail to appear in the Psalter. The 64 which remain and their frequency tabulations are as follows:

---

[42]James Muilenburg, "Form Criticism and Beyond," JBL 88 (1969) 17.

[43]Scott, The Way of Wisdom, 121.

[44]Ibid.

[45]Murphy, "Assumptions and Problems in OT Wisdom Research," 410.

[46]Crenshaw, "Method in Determining Wisdom Influence upon 'Historical' Literature," 133, where he remarks, "When one recognizes that wisdom is rooted in experience, it should be no surprise to discover a common vocabulary among sage, prophet, and priest."

No.	Word	X in Psalms	Meaning[47]	No.	Word	X in Psalms	Meaning
1	ʾāwen	28	evil, wickedness	35	limmad	23	teach
2	ʾōrāh	15	path	36	lāᶜag	4	mock
3	ʾašrē	25	happy, fortunate	37	lēṣ	1	insolent, scoffing
4	bîn	26	understand	38	mādôn	1	strife
5	bînāh	4	understanding(n.)	39	mûsār	1	training, discipline
6	baᶜar	3	brutish, stupid	40	mᵉzimmāh	5	scheme, scheming
7	daᶜat dēᶜāh	5	knowledge	41	māšāl	4	proverb, wise saying
8	derek	66	way	42	nābāl	5	vulgar fool
9	hebel	9	breath, emptiness	43	nᵉtîbāh	2	path
10	hiqšîb	8	pay attention	44	sôd	6	council; counsel
11	hiwwah	1	inform	45	ᶜawᵉlāh	7	wickedness
12	ḥûš	9	hasten	46	ᶜiwwēt	2	make crooked
13	ḥaṭṭāʾ	6	sinner	47	ᶜāmāl	13	toil, trouble
14	ḥākam	4	be wise	48	ᶜēṣāh	13	advice, counsel
15	ḥākām	2	wise	49	petî	3	simple, uninstructed
16	ḥokmāh	7	wisdom	50	saddîq	50	righteous
17	ḥānēp	1	godless	51	qālôn	1	contempt
18	ḥēpheṣ	4	pleasure; thing, affair	52	rîb	5	contend, dispute (v.)
19	ḥāqar	3	investigate	53	rîb	7	dispute, accusation (n.)
20	ḥēqer	2	investigation	54	rᵉmiyyāh	6	neglect, deceit
21	heḥĕrîš	2	be silent	55	rāṣôn	13	wish, favor (n.)
22	ḥāšab	18	think, devise	56	rāšāᶜ	81	wicked
23	yādaᶜ	92	know	57	śîᵃḥ	14	consider, complain (v.)
24	hôkîᵃḥ	7	decide, reprove	58	śîᵃḥ śîḥāh	7	meditation, complaint
25	yāsar, yissar	9	admonish, discipline	59	taʾᵃwāh	8	desire (n.)
26	yāᶜaṣ	6	give counsel	60	tᵉbûnāh	4	insight
27	yirʾāh	7	fear (of Yahweh)	61	tôkahat	3	rebuke, blame (n.)
28	hôrāh	9	teach, direct	62	tikkēn	1	estimate, measure (v.)
29	yāšār	25	upright, straight	63	tām tāmîm	14	blameless, righteous
30	yōšer	2	uprightness	64	tōm	7	integrity
31	kāzāb	6	lie (n.)				
32	kᵉsîl	3	insolent, stupid				
33	kaᶜas	4	trouble, vexation				
34	lēb lēbāb	133	heart, mind				

---

[47] For convenience we are adhering to Scott's translations.

Twenty-four compositions within the Israelite Psalter fail to employ any of the words listed above, and 21 others mention but one word. Two words are attested in 18 psalms, three in 15 psalms, four in 15 psalms, five in 10 psalms, six in 18 psalms, seven in 11 psalms, eight in three psalms, nine in five psalms (1, 5, 73, 92, 139), 10 in two psalms (10, 107), 11 in three psalms (19, 37, 49), 12 in two psalms (25, 55), 13 in Psalm 32, 15 in Psalm 94, and 28 in Psalm 119.

What are we to make of this kind of evidence? We propose to deal briefly with those 15 psalms which attest nine or more of the conjectured wisdom words. First of all, the quite long and artificially constructed Psalm 119 finds its coherence in its celebration of Yahweh's law. Expressions of thanksgiving, supplication, lamentation, confession, and wisdom coexist in such fashion as to defy form-critical classification. Since matters of form as well as content must be seriously considered in positing which in fact are the wisdom psalms, we cannot comfortably predicate the wisdom psalm label to this purely literary product. Nevertheless, its acrostic format and rich sapiential vocabulary[48] testify that in this quite late composition the interests of legal piety and wisdom have coalesced.

On formal grounds Psalm 94 is to be designated as an individual and congregational lament. Even so, Murphy has convincingly isolated vss. 8-15 as a wisdom element.[49] In vss. 8-11 we confront an admonition to fools which is styled according to the canons of wisdom, and in vss. 12-15 we have an ʾašrê formulation upholding the idea of a sure retribution in behalf of the just and presenting Yahweh's function as teacher. Of the 15 conjectured wisdom words employed in this lament, all but three appear within vss. 8-15.[50] Hence, factors of style, ideology, and vocabulary are all at work in shaping this sustained wisdom component.

---

[48]The wisdom words employed in Psalm 119 may be designated by number as follows: 1, 2, 3, 4, 7, 8, 12, 14, 22, 23, 27, 28, 29, 30, 34, 35, 43, 45, 46, 48, 49, 50, 52, 53, 56, 57, 58, 63. Four of these (4, 8, 34, 35) occur with a frequency of 10 or more.

[49]Murphy, "The Classification, 'Wisdom Psalms,'" 165.

[50]Within vss. 8-15, the following wisdom words appear: 3, 4, 7, 9, 23, 24, 25, 29, 32, 34, 35, 56. Beyond their compass words 1, 47, and 50 also appear in the psalm.

Ranking third in our findings is Psalm 32 with its
attestation of 13 wisdom words.[51] Because the individual
song of thanksgiving addressed to Yahweh (vss. 3-7) is
enveloped by crucial wisdom expressions which contain two
'ašrê formulations (vss. 1-2), the first-person utterance
of the sage who promises to "instruct," "teach," and
"counsel" his listeners (vs. 8), and admonition (Mahnspruch)
with simile (vs. 9), and an impersonal antithetical saying
(Spruch, vs. 10), we conclude with Murphy that the sapiential
elements are the most germane in determining the psalmic
category to which this composition belongs. Moreover, here
we are simply giving requisite attention to how the poem
begins and ends, and are thereby respecting what rhetorical
criticism fittingly designates as "strategic loci."[52] And
if it is correct to say that "the most important formal
feature [of the wisdom psalms] is that...[they] are not
addressed to Yahweh in prayer or praise but to men, and
especially to the less instructed and less devout,"[53] then
here is one more consideration which establishes the poem's
wisdom character. At base this composition reflects one
man's hortatory pronouncements to his fellows. Again, the
factor of wisdom vocabulary buttresses the stylistic and
ideological features of the psalm.

Psalms 25 and 55 each employ 12 words which are thought
to belong to the vocabulary of wisdom.[54] The latter is an
individual lament which reflects the distress which men
sometimes experience when they become the victims of hostility and betrayal. Whatever be the textual and structural difficulties of Psalm 55, its rhetorical and ideological features do not betray the work of a sage. Many of the
so-called wisdom terms attested-- 'āwen, yādac, lēb, sôd,
ṣaddîq, rîb, rāšāc--are found in many different contexts
within the Hebrew Bible. They are not solely the property
of didactic discourse. In this instance, word tabulation
is virtually a fruitless effort, although it does remind us

---

[51]These are 3, 4, 8, 21, 22, 23, 26, 28, 29, 34, 50,
54, 56.

[52]Following Muilenburg, "Form Criticism and Beyond," 9.

[53]Scott, The Way of Wisdom, 197.

[54]These are 2, 8, 13, 23, 28, 29, 35, 44, 30, 34, 47,
64 in Psalm 25 and 1, 10, 12, 23, 34, 44, 47, 50, 53, 56,
57, 58 in Psalm 55. All but the last four words listed for
Psalm 25 appear within vss. 8-10 and 12-14 which present
themselves as wisdom elements.

that Israel's psalmists, prophets, priests, and sages all
drew unknowingly from the entire culture in which they
held membership! By contrast, stylistic and doctrinal
factors reveal that Psalm 25 contains two wisdom elements,
vss. 8-10 and 12-14 which are separated by vs. 11 containing
the lamenting psalmist's supplication for Yahweh's forgiveness.[55] The aphorisms in vss. 8-10, the "who among you"
inquiry in vss. 12-14 (cf. 34:13), the acrostic structure
of the total psalm, and the high frequency of conjectured
wisdom terminologies collectively testify to the authentic
sapiential interests of Psalm 25. Form-critical considerations, however, do not permit us to designate this composition as a wisdom psalm. In the final analysis Psalm 25 is
an individual lament.

In Psalms 19, 37, and 49, eleven so-called wisdom words
are attested.[56] To be sure, Psalms 37 and 49 are widely
celebrated as wisdom psalms. Cast into an acrostic mold,
Psalm 37 sets forth an entire sequence of maxims which reflect
the experienced sage's concern that his student trust Yahweh
fully and not be disheartened by those inequities which presently appear to have the upper hand. Though the psalm lacks
continuity, its belief in the efficacy of retributive justice
is immovable. Within this composition the wicked (rāšāᶜ) are
referred to in 13 instances and the righteous (ṣaddîq) are
mentioned on nine occasions. In five verses both types of
humanity are attested--in vss. 16, 17, and 21 the manner or
condition of the wicked and righteous are contrasted, and
in vss. 12 and 32 the righteous are presented as the sought-
out victims of the insidiously wicked. Finally, the better
saying in vs. 16, which we have already inspected, and the
underlying symbiosis of traditional piety and wisdom throughout constitute two further testimonies of this poem's existence as an authentic wisdom psalm.

Psalm 49 is a self-conscious wisdom composition which
commences with the teacher's admonitory address to "all
peoples" (vs. 2). In the sage's kerygmatic first-person
proclamation he advances his intention to utter wisdom
(ḥokmāh, vs. 4). The proverb (māšāl) and riddle (ḥîdāh)

---

[55]In agreement with Murphy, "The Classification, 'Wisdom
Psalms,'" 165.

[56]These are 4, 14, 27, 29, 34, 49, 55, 63, 2, 7, 11 in
Psalm 19; 4, 8, 16, 23, 29, 34, 40, 45, 50, 56, 63, in Psalm
37; and 4, 5, 6, 8, 15, 16, 29, 32, 34, 41, 60 in Psalm 49.
All but the last three words listed for Psalm 19 appear in
what is commonly designated as Psalm 19B (vss. 8-15).

appear in parallelism in vs. 5 at the end of the opening strophe as objects of prime concern. As the psalm unfolds, the sage meditates upon the fact that powerful and rich men are permitted to intimidate the pious. Nevertheless, the wealth of the arrogant is interpreted as but a temporal reality which is incapable of coping with death. In the concluding strophe of this composition (vss. 14-21) we confront both the sage's admonishment to his audience, "Do not be afraid when a man grows rich" (vs. 17), and an extensive comment on the mortality of the wealthy. The latter achieves its climax in the wisdom refrain of vs. 21 which is itself an intentional repetition of vs. 13:

> Man cannot abide in his pomp,
> He is like the beasts that perish.

In sum, this psalm's very structure, its preoccupation with the idea of retribution, and its forthright employment of wisdom vocabulary jointly defend its merit as a wisdom psalm.

As is commonly acknowledged, Psalm 19 consists of two distinct though related units. Whereas vss. 2-7 (Ps. 19A) exult in the fact that nature reveals the divine glory, vss. 8-15 (Ps. 19B) offer hymic celebration of the law which lays bare the divine will. Psalm 19B resembles Psalm 119 insofar as it employs numerous wisdom terminologies and establishes a firm postexilic link between torah piety and wisdom. Fear of Yahweh (vs. 10) and suitable meditation of the heart (vs. 15) are items of genuine concern to the poet who is drawn toward the concerns of speculative wisdom. Nevertheless, Ps. 19B is as much a prayer addressed to Yahweh as it is a teaching aimed at mankind. The form and content of this poem fail to convince us that this is a wisdom psalm. Even so, its vocabulary along with its respectful and detailed description of the law do attest that this composition has come within the orbit of wisdom influence.

Although Psalms 10 and 107 each attest ten conjectured sapiential words, neither composition can be defended as a wisdom psalm.[57] The former is an individual lament which continues the imperfect acrostic begun in Psalm 9. The remarkably detailed description of the godless man in 10:3-11 may well be the product of empirical observation, but this does not give us due cause to accept it as a wisdom

---

[57]These are 1, 8, 10, 22, 33, 34, 40, 47, 56, 59 in Psalm 10 and 4, 8, 15, 16, 18, 29, 34, 45, 47, 48 in Psalm 107.

component.[58] It is quite suitable to the lament at hand.
While the interests of thanksgiving and wisdom are sometimes honored within the same composition (e.g., Psalms 32
and 34), the lengthy communal thanksgiving offered in
Psalm 107 does not commend itself as a wisdom piece. To
be sure, its final verse consists of a parenthetic wisdom
admonition:

> Whoever is wise, let him heed these things,
> Let him consider the ḥesed of Yahweh.   (vs. 43)

But this does not thereby confer a wisdom status upon the
entire composition. If the results of word tabulation bring
these two poems to our attention as potential wisdom psalm
candidates, the stylistic and ideological peculiarities of
both urge us to think otherwise.

Finally, we shall briefly consider Psalms 1, 5, 73,
92, and 139 which each employ nine words from Scott's listing.[59] Psalm 1 is widely acclaimed as a wisdom psalm. It
opens with the 'ašrê formula, sharply contrasts the fate of
the righteous (saddîq) and wicked (rāšāᶜ) through vivid
similes, and respectfully presents the law as the object of
the pious man's constant meditation. The style, content,
and specific vocabulary of this brief composition all testify
to its legitimacy as a wisdom psalm. Psalm 5, however, is
the fervent prayer on the lips of one who has been falsely
accused. Though it affirms the fear of Yahweh as a necessary and vital ingredient in the God-man relation (vs. 8)
and unreservedly expresses its confidence in the efficacy
of divine retribution (vs. 13), its form and theme both
disclose its status as an individual lament. Indeed, only
one of its 13 verses fails to address the deity in impassioned second-person speech. Any affinities between Psalm
5 and undisputed sapiential contexts in the OT are surely
fortuitous.

---

[58]For an opposing opinion, see Scott, The Way of Wisdom,
201.

[59]These are 3, 8, 13, 18, 23, 37, 48, 50, 56 in Psalm 1;
1, 4, 8, 10, 27, 31, 48, 50, 55 in Psalm 5; 4, 6, 7, 22, 34,
47, 48, 56, 61 in Psalm 73; 1, 4, 6, 23, 32, 56, 29, 45, 50
in Psalm 92; and 2, 4, 7, 8, 19, 23, 34, 40, 56 in Psalm 139.
All but the last three words listed for Psalm 92 appear in
vss. 7-9 which has been accepted as a wisdom element by
Murphy ("The Classification, 'Wisdom Psalms,'" 165).

Many interpreters have claimed that Psalm 73 is a wisdom composition whose sustained treatment of the retribution motif places it in close company with Psalms 37 and 49 which likewise are wisdom pieces given to the same topic. Nevertheless, Bentzen, Mowinckel, and Murphy all aver that a scrutiny of the form and literary style of Psalm 73 shows that here we have a thanksgiving composition.[60] This is especially evident in the strategic opening and closing cola of vss. 1 and 28. When this consideration is wedded with another, namely, that OT reflections on the problem of retribution are not solely limited to wisdom texts, the prospects for defending the wisdom status of Psalm 73 are greatly reduced. The presence of a wisdom vocabulary cannot be expected to turn the tables, though it may suggest that the composition is not entirely void in sapiential nuance.

Nor can Psalm 92 win our assent as a wisdom psalm. Its second-person hymnic introduction (vss. 2-4) and fervent expressions of gratitude for divine deliverance from past affliction (vss. 5, 11-12) reveal that formally it is an individual thanksgiving. Nevertheless, Murphy rightly isolates the impersonal sapiential assertion in vss. 7-9 (where most of the conjectured wisdom vocabulary is to be found) and notes that in a manner that is reminiscent of Psalm 1, the righteous man (saddîq) is likened to a flourishing tree (vss. 13-15).[61] If it is not to be labeled as a wisdom psalm, Psalm 92 does nevertheless contain sapiential material.

Though sustained reflection upon Yahweh's omniscience and omnipresence in Psalm 139 have induced Briggs and Eissfeldt to designate it as a didactic composition,[62] it lacks sufficient stylistic and ideological peculiarities to warrant inclusion in the wisdom psalms category. Its hymnic cola, moving expressions of trust, and fervent words of petition make it a difficult composition to classify. True, the psalm employs wisdom words and seems to represent

---

[60]Bentzen, Introduction to the OT, vol. 1, 161; Mowinckel, "Psalms and Wisdom," 208; Murphy, "The Classification, 'Wisdom Psalms,'" 164.

[61]Murphy, "The Classification, 'Wisdom Psalms,'" 166.

[62]C. A. Briggs, The Psalms (ICC), vol. 2, 491; Otto Eissfeldt, The Old Testament: An Introduction (New York: Harper and Row, 1965) 125.

the psalmist's own observations about his experience with
the deity. But its strikingly personal utterances and sustained second-person address to the deity signal its ineptness
as a wisdom psalm. Moreover, the sage was not the only individual in ancient Israel who was given to thinking about the
omniscience and omnipresence of the deity!

Having inspected those 15 psalms which manifest the
greatest incidence of conjectured wisdom vocabulary, we may
conclude that only four compositions (1, 32, 37, 49) may
legitimately be regarded as wisdom psalms. Four psalms
(25, 92, 94, 107) contain clearly identifiable wisdom elements of varying length, and another four (19B, 73, 119, 139)
reflect some of the concerns and interests of Israelite wisdom. The remaining three psalms (5, 10, 55) simply do not
bear the markings of wisdom influence. If a consideration
of vocabulary frequency is capable of improving our comprehension of Psalms 1, 32, 37, and 49, so be it. Word tabulations, however, cannot be presented as the truly telling
element in our attempt to answer the question, "Which are
the wisdom psalms?"

This becomes all the more evident when we recognize
that five compositions which we are willing to accept on
stylistic and thematic grounds as being wisdom psalms contain remarkably few wisdom words or none at all! Psalm 34
employs six (ʾašrê, yirʾāh, lēb, limmad, saddîq, rāšāᶜ),
Psalm 112 six (ʾašrê, yāšār, lēb, saddîq, rāšāᶜ, taʾᵃwāh),
Psalm 128 two (ʾašrê, derek) and Psalm 127 one (ʾašrê).
Psalm 133 manifests none whatever. To be sure, these poems
are rather short--their average number of verses is 9.4 as
compared with 19.5 in the four wisdom psalms previously
examined. Nevertheless, the rhetorical and ideological
peculiarities must bear nearly all of the burden in selling
Psalms 34, 112, 127, 128, and 133 as wisdom compositions.

While thanksgiving and wisdom elements are both present
in the acrostic Psalm 34, we agree with Murphy that thanksgiving is subordinate to, and stands in the service of,
wisdom.[63] To be sure, in vss. 5 and 7 the poet does allude
to his own deliverance from disaster which was secured
through Yahweh's intervention. He sought Yahweh and not in
vain. Even so, the poet functions primarily as wisdom
teacher. Four sagacious sayings (vss. 8-11) commend the
deity to the audience assembled; terse admonitions (vss.
14-15) affirm the importance of honesty, goodness, and peace;

---

[63]Murphy, "The Classification, 'Wisdom Psalms,'" 163.

and a sequence of seven proverbial sayings (Sprüche, vss. 16-22) either testify to the horrendous end which awaits the wicked or state positively Yahweh's concern for righteous conduct. Throughout the poem the sage draws upon his own experience and education. Moreover, several important wisdom features appear in the middle of the composition. An ʾašrê formula is advanced in vs. 9b and functions there as an implicit admonition: "Happy is the man who finds refuge in him [Yahweh]." In vss. 10 and 12 the fear of Yahweh is upheld as an earmark of piety, vs. 12 contains an admonitory address to sons which we have already inspected, and vs. 13 advances a rhetorical question which deftly advertises the sage's capacity to school his pupils in wisdom. While the so-called wisdom words in Psalm 34 are not numerous, the stylistic and ideological traces of wisdom are many.

Psalm 112 shares with Psalm 1 a concern over the contrasting fates of the righteous and wicked and with Psalm 34 an acrostic form of expression. Also like Psalm 1 it commences with an ʾašrê formula which speaks the language of implied admonition--do this and you will prosper. But unlike Psalm 1 the emphasis now falls upon the praiseworthy behavior as well as sound physical and mental condition of the righteous (vss. 1-9), and little is said about the wretched state of the wicked (vs. 10). If Psalm 112 lacks those rich similes which are vital to the sapiential proclamation of Psalm 1, it is more lucid than is Psalm 1 in its specific definition as to what makes for authentic piety. Delight over the torah and a reverence for its divine giver, fairness in business transactions, and a generous attitude toward the poor are all celebrated as the worthy traits of the righteous man. And once more it is claimed that rewards in this life are in store for those who act righteously as God-fearing individuals. Finally, the presence of some conjectured wisdom vocabulary in seven of the psalm's ten verses reveals that even in this respect the composition does not fare badly.

Since we have briefly stated our reasons for accepting Psalm 127 as a wisdom psalm at an earlier juncture in this essay,[64] little more needs to be said at present. Note, however, that in toto the composition consists of two extended proverbs which may have earlier existed as independent fragments. On the basis of their content, Scott

---

[64]In our résumé of Murphy in the first section of this essay.

associates them with the religious wisdom resident in
Prov. 16:3, 9; 17:6.[65] From beginning to end, this didactic
poem presents itself as an address to man. The climax of
its second proverb is reached through its 'ašrê formula
which strategically brings the psalm to its close. In a
quite deliberate manner, Psalm 128 opens with an 'ašrê
formula which implicitly admonishes men to lead a God-
fearing existence. Though yir'at-YHWH as a terminus
technicus is wanting, the construct form of yārē' is nevertheless present in vss. 1 and 4. The tangible fruits of
such piety are especially well conveyed through two similes
predicated to the godly man's wife and sons (vs. 3) which
we have noted previously. Psalm 133 is a conspicuously
brief wisdom composition which in its entirety consists of
one expanded and picturesque proverb. While it does not
manifest even one conjectured wisdom word, it has been
suggested that its ejaculatory phrase "how good and pleasant"
is in fact a counterpart to the widely attested 'ašrê formula
which plays such a pervasive rôle in psalmic wisdom.[66] Moreover, the presence of the particle hinnēh, which introduces
the poem, emphasizes the importance of the virtue of fraternal harmony that is here celebrated. And like Psalms 127
and 128, the words of this composition are directed earth-
ward as instruction to humanity rather than heavenward as
praise or petition to deity.

To summarize our findings regarding rhetorical elements
in psalmic wisdom: our study has indicated that in ascending
order of significance, the better saying, numerical saying,
admonitory address to "sons," rhetorical question, simile,
admonition with and without motive clause, and 'ašrê formula
exist as identifiable rhetorical features of psalmic wisdom.
In addition, the acrostic arrangement of cola within certain
psalms (e.g., 34, 37, 112) and the second-person discourse
aimed horizontally toward man, rather than vertically toward
deity, may be cited as two further factors which characterize
the style of psalmic wisdom. These factors highlighting the
rhetorical peculiarities of psalmic wisdom, along with the
recurring presence of certain thematic elements, which will
be examined in somewhat more detail in the next section,
encourage us to accept Psalms 1, 32, 34, 37, 49, 112, 127,
128, and 133 as authentic canonical wisdom psalms. An
examination of Psalms 1, 32, 37, and 49 reveals that in
some instances, the wisdom aspect of a given psalmic composition, which is already established by virtue of its

[65]Scott, The Way of Wisdom, 198.

[66]Ibid.

stylistic and ideological peculiarities, may be better
understood when its indigenous wisdom vocabulary is fully
appreciated. Here the position and frequency of conjectured
sapiential words within a given poem are matters of significance. Moreover, our giving attention to wisdom words will
often assist us in positing the degree and kind of wisdom
influence which is manifested within sapiential strophes
that lodge in nonwisdom psalms. Nevertheless, consideration
of vocabulary alone does not prove to be a definitive criterion for identifying wisdom psalms per se. As a supporting consideration, however, its usefulness should not be
overlooked.

Thematic Elements in Psalmic Wisdom

Already we have had occasion to allude to several thematic
elements which inhabit psalmic wisdom. Indeed, considerations
about content inevitably make their way into discussions about
the stylistic peculiarities of a given literary genre. Consequently the present section will confine itself to a few
paragraphs of description and analysis in the hope that even
within this restricted scope, attention might be called to
the leading motifs of psalmic wisdom. Limiting our focus to
those entire psalms and psalm components which we have hitherto
accepted as being unambiguously sapiential in their composition, we acknowledge the following to be the dominant, and
often related, thematic elements within psalmic wisdom: (1)
the fear of Yahweh and veneration of the Torah, (2) the contrasting life styles of the righteous and the wicked, (3) the
reality and inevitability of retribution, and (4) miscellaneous counsels pertaining to everyday conduct. Each of these
will be examined in turn.

(1) The fear of Yahweh and veneration of the Torah:
The sages of ancient Israel often held that wisdom consisted
in fearing Yahweh. This was widely recognized as the
"beginning" (rē'šît) or essence of wisdom. On this consideration John L. McKenzie once remarked, "No one is wise who
does not fear the Lord, and who does not arrange his life
and affairs in the spirit of that fear."[67] Here the sage

---

[67]John L. McKenzie, The Two-Edged Sword: An Interpretation of the Old Testament (Garden City, N.Y.: Doubleday,
1966) 245. Alluding to Prov. 13:14 and 14:27, Walther
Eichrodt, Theology of the Old Testament (Philadelphia: Westminster, 1967), vol. 2, 89, states, "As early as Proverbs
wisdom and the fear of Yahweh are sometimes used as inter-
changeable concepts."

openly manifests his piety. He authenticates such an
observation not so much by making an appeal to commonplace
experience as he does by deferring to Yahweh as the source
of authority.[68] The wise acknowledged the deity to be the
font of wisdom, knowledge, and understanding (Prov. 2:6),
and as such, he and his revealed Torah were to be venerated.
Since Israel's prophets and priests also sought to instill
a reverence for Yahweh in their own following, we obviously
cannot represent this thematic element as being unique to
wisdom circles. Nevertheless, the construct chain,
yir'at-YHWH, may be viewed as a terminus technicus which
was especially, though not exclusively, employed by the
Israelite sages. It is attested thrice in the Psalter
(19:10; 34:12; 111:10) and in each instance it exists within
a didactic context. To be sure, the fear of Yahweh as a
thematic ingredient must also take account of other forms
of the root yr' which within our own designated orbit of
wisdom psalms appear in 34:8, 10 (twice); 112:1; 128:1, 4.
Significantly in 112:1 and 128:1 the fear of Yahweh motif
is established with an 'ašrê formula which heads the composition in question. Moreover, in the wisdom component 25:12-14,
fear of Yahweh and knowledge are firmly equated. To fear
Yahweh is therefore to place oneself in a position to acquire
knowledge. Psalmic wisdom therefore regularly reveals the
sage's predilection to acknowledge Yahweh as the quintessence
of wisdom. In making that confession the sage concomitantly
advances his opinion that man may himself acquire wisdom,
provided that he pursue a reverent course, that he approach
Yahweh in fear. And this, of course, is what the fool is
incapable of doing. Perhaps the truly classical expression
of this point of view is to be found at the heart of Psalm
34 where the sage speaks earnestly in the first person:

> Come, O sons, listen to me,
> The fear of Yahweh I will teach you! (vs. 12)

Clearly, the sage's fear of Yahweh is frequently implied by
expressions which venerate the Torah as that which stands
at the very center of the wise man's pious reflections and
which evokes within him feelings of pleasure. Though Psalm
1 commends itself as the supreme disclosure of this motif,
sapiential utterances within Psalms 19B and 119 likewise
merit consideration. In all instances the sage manifests

---

[68]The remarks offered by William McKane, Proverbs: A
New Approach (Philadelphia: Westminster, 1970) 264, are
helpful at this point.

his willingness to subordinate himself to the divine will.
His task and joy are well defined. His task is to comprehend that will as it is revealed in the written Torah and
his joy is to experience unmitigated delight in his thorough
knowledge of the law. This motif, which we have deliberately
listed first, readily attests to the piety which is indigenous to psalmic wisdom.

(2) The contrasting life styles of the righteous and
the wicked: We have previously observed that in the nouns
saddîq and rāšāᶜ we have terms which achieve a conspicuously
high frequency within the assertions of psalmic wisdom. Our
inspection of Psalm 37 disclosed that the righteous are
regarded as being either the sought-out victims of the aggres-
sively wicked (vss. 12, 32) or the exemplary models of a life
style which is entirely antithetical to that of the wicked
(vss. 16, 17, 21). Moreover, other nouns such as haṭṭā' and
keṣîl, on the one hand, and yāšār and tām/tāmîm, on the other,
further express the sage's understanding that two ways are
available to mankind and that they are, by their very nature,
irreconcilable. Though the existence of the righteous man
is not presented as claiming immunity from the injustices of
the wicked who plot against him, psalmic wisdom does enthusi-
astically endorse the life style, concrete behavior, and end
of the righteous who have obviously acquired wisdom. The
righteous man is portrayed as one who is intimately acquainted
with Yahweh's law and capable of speaking what is wise and
just (37:30-31). He is generous in his dealings with his
fellows (37:21; 112:5) and finds contentment in the little
that he legitimately possesses (37:16). He experiences glad-
ness in his relation with the deity (32:11). He knows first-
hand the efficacy of that divine strength which dramatically
removes him from affliction (34:20; 37:39) and never ceases
to maintain him (37:17, 25, 29). He is the beloved object
of the providential care of a deity who "knows" (1:6) and
sees (34:16) him. In marked contrast, psalmic wisdom deplores
the life style of the wicked. It points up its inherent folly
and confidently anticipates its thorough demise. The wicked
are criticized for their overweening power (37:35), their
dishonesty in financial dealings (37:21), and their aggression
against the poor, needy, and righteous (37:12, 14, 32).
Despite the strength which they appear to possess, their
present existence is scarcely comprehended as enviable, for
they must cope with ill-gotten abundance (37:16), suffer
unfulfilled desires (112:10), and even witness, with envious
eyes, the salutary state of the righteous who are sustained
by divine blessing (112:10). Still worse is their future
existence, for their power will be broken (37:17), their
prosperous condition will abruptly terminate (37:38), and
their progeny will be "cut off" (37:28). Their destruction

is inevitable (37:10, 20, 34; 92:8) and, worst of all, they
will be incapable of enduring Yahweh's penetrating judgment
(1:5-6). Psalmic wisdom therefore distills the reflections
of those Israelite sages who were certain that there was no
middle ground to be affirmed. The world is thought to host
two kinds of men, not three. And in terms of conduct and
consequence alike, the righteous and the wicked are comprehended as utterly antithetical creatures.

(3) The reality and inevitability of retribution: The
third motif understandably presents itself as the logical
extension of the second. The sage who confidently predicted
doom for the wicked and blessing for the righteous was
thereby endorsing the premise that retributions and rewards
for specific human conduct issue according to an underlying
and certain principle of justice. The sapiential piety of
psalmic wisdom affirmed that as the quintessence of wisdom,
Yahweh was unmistakably just. Consequently, hope and dread
might cast their respective shadows over the righteous and
wicked sectors of humankind. We have already admitted that
wisdom compositions which deal with the problem of retribution do not have a corner on the market. Indeed, the
emergence of a moralistic view of salvation is not solely
traceable to the statements of the wise. It is also to be
detected in "the semi-magical nature of the priestly oracular
divination and prophetic symbolism."[69] Nevertheless, the
contrasting fate of the pious and impious is often attested
within those poems which we have accepted as wisdom psalms.[70]
In particular, the two-way theology within Psalms 1 and 112
voices considerable confidence that rewards and punishments
are extended to mankind in just measure. If this strikes us
today as being all too automatic, we can scarcely fail to
recognize in psalmic wisdom the sage's strong confidence in
the deity and the world which he has called into being.
Nor are certain tones of realism wanting in our texts. Certainly the poet in Psalm 49 does not hide his former fears
that injustice is rampant in a world where arrogant and
wealthy men easily intimidate the righteous. His personal
reflections do not betray a frantic grasping for an easy
answer. Rather, they point to the acquiring of a gradual

---

[69]Crenshaw, "The Influence of the Wise upon Amos," 45.

[70]See Pss. 1:6; 32:10-11; 34:16-18, 20-22; 37:12-13,
16-17, 28b-29, 38-40; 112:4-10. Note also that Psalms 127
and 133 are terse compositions which depict the life and
fate of the righteous without entering upon a corresponding
antithetical characterization of the wicked.

and certain trust in the deity which the sage also covets
for his audience. And if the final strophe in Psalm 34
(vss. 16-22) basically reveals an indiscriminately optimistic approach to the idea of retribution, the presence
of vs. 20 ensures that the problem is not handled too
glibly:

> Many may be the hardships of the righteous,
> But from them all Yahweh delivers him.

Whereas the pious may hope to be released from suffering,
he cannot expect to be exempted from its sting.

(4) Miscellaneous counsels pertaining to everyday
conduct: As is manifestly the case in other units of OT
wisdom literature, the wisdom psalms also advance a number
of miscellaneous counsels which instruct the beholder in
quite varied aspects of daily life. Though concrete expectations of piety and ethics ordinarily come to the fore within
such counsels, the interests of pragmatism may also be served.
Hence, psalmic wisdom recommends that man be mindful of the
company that he keeps (1:1) and prudent in his speech (34:14).
He should desist from anger (37:8) and quest for peace (34:15;
37:37), living in true harmony with his brothers (Psalm 133).
In his dealings he is expected to manifest signs of meekness
(37:11; cf. 49:13, 21), generosity (112:5, 9), and integrity
(62:11, 112:5). Moreover, he is admonished to wait upon
Yahweh in a spirit of trust (32:10; 37:3, 5, 7, 34; 62:9)
and confer with the deity in all that he undertakes (127:1-2).
As recompense for his devotion to Yahweh, he may look forward
to a large and prosperous family (128:1-4). Finally, he is
commanded to shun evil and do good (34:15; 37:3, 27). If
such counsels do not lend themselves to facile unification,
they all attempt to advise man in how he should conduct himself in his day to day existence. Such are the leading motifs
of psalmic wisdom. Whereas we dare not accept them as constituting the sole criterion for defining the wisdom psalm,
a thorough familiarity with the topic at hand demands that
we come to terms with them. Indeed, to isolate such thematic
elements is to gain a better understanding of the intention
of psalmic wisdom.

The Problem of Wisdom Gattungen

We understand that in the rhetorical criticism and form
criticism of biblical texts we have scholarly pursuits which
are supplementary in character. To say that the former is
primarily concerned with the very composition of a given

literary unit and to say that the latter is essentially preoccupied with the structure, genre, setting, and intention
of specific texts is to admit that these two modes of biblical criticism intersect. Although this state of affairs
encourages lively possibilities for creative synthesis, confusions can likewise emerge. For example, in our rhetorical
analysis of the wisdom psalms, we had occasion to recognize
the acrostic format of certain poetic compositions as a noteworthy stylistic reality. Presently, however, we shall comprehend the same acrostic format as a structural reality
which determines the shape of one sub-type of wisdom psalm.
In any event, in this final section of admittedly limited
scope, we are in search of answers to these two questions:
(1) What are the basic patterns or structures which the
wisdom psalms project and how may they best be characterized?
(2) What does this biblical material collectively suggest as
to specific sociological contexts which gave birth to and
maintained the communication of psalmic wisdom?

In wisdom psalms research, questions about Gattung and
Sitz im Leben are exceedingly difficult to answer. With
good reason Murphy has asserted that "the Gattung of wisdom
psalms is subject to no clear-cut characterization."[71] The
problem is compounded by the fact that we have only nine
compositions within the Israelite Psalter which legitimately
wear the label, "wisdom psalm," and these poems attest con-
spicuous variation in such matters as length, structure,
acrostic usage, and rhetorical elements employed. Moreover,
the textual material is of such a nature as to discourage
us from confidently positing definitive statements about the
Sitz im Leben of the wisdom psalms. Just as "the setting of
the short proverbial sayings is the broadest one possible,"[72]
the majority of wisdom psalms themselves must be examined
with a similar realization. A careful first-hand reading
of the canonical wisdom psalms gives rise to divergent
impressions. Though Psalm 34 seems to link with the Israelite cult, Psalm 127 appears to relate very naturally to
a family setting, and we may justifiably claim both as wisdom compositions. Typically the rhetorical and thematic
elements of a given wisdom psalm only weakly convey its
Sitz. The instructional intent of the poem may be obvious
enough, but it may not be at all clear just where that
instruction was to have occurred.

---

[71]Murphy, "The Classification, 'Wisdom Psalms,'" 159.

[72]Gene M. Tucker, Form Criticism of the Old Testament
(Philadelphia: Fortress, 1971) 82.

We propose to isolate and describe three sub-types of
wisdom psalms which may be designated as follows: (1) sentence wisdom psalms, (2) acrostic wisdom psalms, and (3)
integrative wisdom psalms. To the first category belong
Psalms 127, 128, 133; to the second Psalms 34, 37, and
112; and to the third Psalms 1, 32, and 49. While these
designations may not prove entirely satisfactory, we have
deliberately kept them simple and have stayed within the
confines of the English language.

(1) <u>Sentence wisdom psalms</u>: Psalms 127, 128, and 133
have several things in common. Each is brief, each employs
the simile as a significant rhetorical expression (127:4;
128:3; 133:2, 3,), each attests an 'ašrê formula or its
equivalent in a structurally significant collocation (cf.
127:5; 128:1; 133:1), and each conveys its truth by way of
the wisdom sentence. Were it not for the expansive quality
of the sentences here communicated, we would be inclined to
designate this group as <u>aphoristic</u> wisdom psalms. But
succinctness is not a feature of the one <u>Spruch</u> which fully
claims Psalm 133 or of the other which involves all of
Psalm 128, apart from its concluding priestly benediction
(vss. 5-6). The two wisdom <u>Sprüche</u> comprising Psalm 127
(vss. 1-2, 3-5) are likewise expansive. Most unique among
the formulations is Ps. 128:1-4 which begins with a third-
person utterance recommending the fear of Yahweh (vs. 1),
shifts to the second person in order to enumerate specific
rewards attached to such conduct (vss. 2-3), and concludes
with an emphatic and reinforcing comment cast once more in
the third person (vs. 4). In all four instances, however,
we confront wisdom sayings which observe <u>what is</u> rather
than admonitions which demand a particular mode of conduct.
To be sure, these <u>Sprüche</u> have a didactic intent insofar
as they seek to influence human behavior along certain
lines. Nevertheless, not one admonition is attested.

The most characteristic feature of Psalms 127, 128, and
133, however, is yet to be mentioned: Apart from the
priestly benediction in 128:5-6, these three compositions
could be transferred into the Book of Proverbs without causing havoc or alarm.[73] Devoted as they are to a description
of the common life, these simple yet picturesque wisdom
sayings manifest only a minimal connection with the Israelite

---

[73]In agreement with Claus Westermann, <u>Der Psalter</u>
(Stuttgart: Calwer Verlag, 1969) 93.

Psalter. Though the brand of piety collectively affirmed is
not out of keeping with psalmic wisdom as the latter is
grasped in its totality, these three poems refrain from
entering into a sharp contrast between the ṣaddîq and the
rāšāᶜ, offer neither positive nor negative admonitions, and
only faintly support a doctrine of retribution. In sum,
these psalms, which stand in close proximity to one another,
are almost entirely devoted to the transmission of a select
number of Weisheitssprüche. While we make no apology in
accepting them as authentic wisdom compositions, they may
be viewed form-critically as constituting a sub-type of wisdom psalm which doubtlessly did not stand at the center of
any discernible psalmic wisdom movement existing within
postexilic Israel.

(2) Acrostic wisdom psalms: Altogether the Psalter
contains eight acrostics: Psalms 9-10, 25, 34, 37, 111, 112,
119, and 145. Only two (9-10, 145) have nothing to do with
wisdom. Clearly, Psalm 119 claims a rich wisdom vocabulary,
Psalm 25 embodies two wisdom elements (vss. 8-10, 12-14), and
the final verse in Psalm 111 declares that "The fear of Yahweh
is the beginning of wisdom." Psalms 34, 37, and 112 are full-
fledged wisdom acrostics.[74] Since six wisdom psalms abstain
from the acrostic principle of arrangement, the Israelite
sage presumably exercised complete freedom in deciding whether
or not he would engage in acrostics. If he thought that this
system might advantageously advertise his gifts of expression,
he might well make the attempt. Of course, if he planned to
compose a short piece (such as Psalms 1, 127, 128, 133), the
acrostic pattern would have been quite out of the question.
Since Psalms 32 and 49, which are nonacrostic, exceed in
length the acrostic Psalm 112, we may infer that their authors
consciously chose not to play according to the alphabetic rules
of composition.

Psalms 34, 37, and 112 do not embody the acrostic principle in identical ways.[75] Continuous thought sequences are

---

[74]The only noteworthy wisdom acrostic which stands outside of the Psalter is Prov. 31:10-31.

[75]The issue, "Why acrostics?" will not be treated in
depth here. We favor, however, Fohrer's statement that
in part they were intended "to demonstrate the skill of
the writer" (Introduction to the OT, 270-271). They may
also have functioned as a mnemonic aid.

lacking in Psalm 37 which contains a lengthy series of maxims on the contrasting life styles and fates of the ṣaddîq and rāšāᶜ along with admonitions to imitate the conduct of the former. Each of the 22 alphabetical entries from 'Aleph to Tāw consists of two poetic lines (ordinarily bicola). Here we are unable to discern any strophic arrangement which honors a meaningful progression of sapiential assertion. In Psalm 112 we have another acrostic which similarly suffers from an atomistic character, yet it distinguishes itself from Psalm 37 in two important ways: (1) each of the 22 cola in this short composition begins with a successive consonant; (2) all but the last three cola depict the praiseworthy conduct and blessed state of the pious man and, in so doing, confer upon this psalm a thematic continuity. Nevertheless, this composition likewise defies attempts at convincing strophic delineation.

Significantly, the cola in Psalm 34 can be grouped into basically coherent strophes. The acrostic form has not frustrated the shaping of discernible thought patterns. It is commonly held that the psalm falls into two halves (vss. 2-11 and 12-22/23), but beyond that we may delineate four separate strophes: hymnic declaration (vss. 2-4), thankful testimony and ensuing instruction (vss. 5-11), instruction via sapiential admonitions (vss. 12-15), and instruction via sapiential sayings (vss. 16-22).[76] The opening strophe (vss. 2-4) functions as an introductory hymnic assertion and call to thanksgiving. As if speaking a vow, the psalmist declares his intention to glorify the deity, and through the imperative which stands at the head of vs. 4, he invites his audience (presumably the assembled worshiping congregation) to do the same. The second strophe (vss. 5-11) offers both a narrative testimony about past deliverance, wherein the poet expresses his feeling of thanksgiving, and four sagacious sayings. The first and fourth (vss. 8, 11) are declarative proverbs, whereas the second and third (vss. 9-10) are imperative admonitions directly calling for obedience. In toto, this strophe moves from confession to exhortation. The third strophe (vss. 12-15) opens with an admonitory summons to listen (vs. 12), procedes to a rhetorical question (vs. 13), and concludes with a series of crisp admonitions (vss. 14-15). The concluding strophe (vss. 16-22) offers seven proverbial sayings (Sprüche) which both positively and negatively affirm the deity's interest in human piety. Notwithstanding the admittedly stringent demands of the acrostic mold, seven different wisdom

---

[76]Ps. 34:23 is an appended element which lies beyond the acrostic framework of the composition.

maxims have been successfully marshalled together so as to persuade the listener into affirming for himself a God-fearing existence. In vs. 12a the sage poet declares, "The fear of Yahweh I will teach you." By the end of the fourth strophe it is quite evident that such teaching has been effectively communicated. In sum, Psalm 34 is the one wisdom acrostic within the Israelite Psalter which successfully takes the divergent demands of internal logic and external alphabetic pattern into account.

(3) Integrative wisdom psalms: This final sub-type of wisdom psalm is admittedly the most difficult to define and defend. At first glance its three examples (Psalms 1, 32, 49) appear to be quite divergent. They vary in length and structure, and employ different formalistic devices. Whereas Psalms 1 and 32 commence with the ʾašrê formula, Psalm 49 lacks this feature and instead opens in a far more elaborate fashion with four bicola of self-conscious intro-duction. By virtue of its introductory position, Psalm 1 fulfills an editorial function with respect to the entire Psalter which is irrelevant to the raison dêtre of Psalms 32 and 49. In its wedding of wisdom and thanksgiving ele-ments, Psalm 32 moves closer to the acrostic Psalm 34 than to Psalms 1 and 49 with which it is here associated. And the studied refrain in Psalm 49 (vss. 13, 21) is unparalleled in Psalms 1 and 32. Nevertheless, these three wisdom psalms exhibit several mutual characteristics: (1) Both the firm-ness of their rootage in the soil of the Israelite Psalter and the general impression which their unfolding declarations make upon the reader argue that they do not belong to the sentence wisdom psalms category. (2) As nonacrostic composi-tions, these psalms obviously cannot be assigned to our second wisdom psalms category. (3) All three psalms appear to be of such intrinsic significance to psalmic wisdom that the implicitly pejorative label "residual wisdom psalms" (an easy out) would be most inappropriate. (4) Although there is no full consensus among scholars as to how it is to be done, these psalms lend themselves to a strophic delinea-tion which reflects an existing continuity of thought.

It is this last characteristic which provides the essential clue, namely, that Psalms 1, 32, and 49 all mani-fest an intrinsic integrative quality. Notwithstanding their respective peculiarities, all three compositions manifest a certain order and wholeness which betray their existence as carefully studied literary units. Each of these psalms offers much more than a random sequence of wisdom sentences. Psalm 1 on the two ways consists of two strophes. Strophe I (vss. 1-3) with its negative and positive components is an extended ʾašrê formula celebrating the righteous man. Strophe II

(vss. 4-6), with its clear-cut beginning (lō'—kēn), focuses
upon the wicked man who is first subjected to a description
of his own and then brought into connection with the
righteous man so that a deliberate contrast may be achieved.
The result is an integrated whole. Psalm 32 on the penitent
and forgiven man contains five relatively short strophes.
The second and third which are devoted to thanksgiving are
enveloped by the first, fourth, and fifth which are didactic
in their intent. In Strophe II (vss. 3-5) the sin is confessed and forgiven and in Strophe III (vss. 6-7) the past
experience of sin and forgiveness becomes the chosen object
of reflective meditation. Artfully surrounding these strophes
addressed to the deity are Strophe I (vss. 1-2) with its two
'ašrê formulas celebrating the forgiven man, Strophe IV (vss.
8-9) with its pious instruction to those who seek wisdom,
and Strophe V (vss. 10-11) with its saddîq/rāšāᶜ contrast
and summons to rejoice in Yahweh which function as an effective component of summation. The poorly preserved Psalm 49,
which meditates upon the sheer vanity of human pretension,
likewise has its integrative aspect. As an element of introduction, Strophe I (vss. 2-5) contains four cola devoted to
the sage's admonitory call for attention. Strophe II (vss.
6-13) speculates upon the temporal triumph of the wicked.
It consists of eight cola with the last functioning as the
crucial māšāl refrain (vs. 13) which is deliberately anticipated by the use of māšāl in vs. 5 toward the end of the
introductory strophe. Then Strophe III (vss. 14-21) treating
the unenviable fate of the wicked and its implication for the
righteous consists of nine cola with the last (vs. 21) reit-
erating the māšāl refrain which earlier brought Strophe II
to its conclusion.[77] To summarize: We believe that despite
their many differences, the sophisticated strophic makeup
and basic integrative capacity of Psalms 1, 32, and 49 may
possibly justify our provisional form-critical attempt to
bring these compositions into juxtaposition.

As a way of concluding our study, what may we posit
about the Sitz im Leben of the canonical wisdom psalms?
Clearly, cultic as well as noncultic contexts must be enter-
tained. For example, Psalm 34 seems to reflect a cultic
Sitz im Leben, although we have almost no clues upon which
to draw. The psalmist does, however, begin with a hymnic

---

[77]Except for our unwillingness to dismiss Ps. 49:16 as a
"pious intrusion," here we are in agreement with Guthrie,
Israel's Sacred Songs, 176-177.

proclamation and later utters numerous sayings and admonitions which he addresses to auditors of some sort, and we have
no good reason for not inferring that this is a congregation
united in an act of worship. Have we here a gathering of the
faithful in cultic meeting, if not in Jerusalem, then somewhere else? Fritzlothar Mand states the case for Psalm 34
quite convincingly: "A teacher has emerged out of the wor-
shiper, a circle of pupils out of the festival congregation,
wisdom out of the witness of tôrāh."[78] It may also be possible to posit a cultic setting for Psalms 32 and 49. Certainly
the former weds public utterances of thanksgiving with didactic
instruction in the hope that the gathered congregation of
righteous individuals will faithfully rejoice in Yahweh. And
while the latter commences with an admonitory summons to "all
peoples," the actual auditors may have been members of the
faithful assembled for purposes of corporate worship. The
use of such compositions in the synagogues where they were
read aloud and expounded would likewise reflect a _Sitz_ involving the gathered community of faith, though admittedly on a
smaller and more intimate level.

Even so, the offering up of instruction in the hope that
it will be carefully appropriated, which is a dominant intention within the wisdom psalms, may occur in many different
places. The home, street, city gate, court, synagogue, and
multi-faceted cult all constitute lively possibilities where
teaching and learning may transpire. Where the element of
divine praise presents itself beside the offering up of instruction as the second and perhaps equally dominant intention of
the wisdom psalm in question, it may be possible for us to
restrict the _Sitz_ to either the cult or synagogue. But even
that cannot be maintained with complete confidence, for on what
grounds can we rule out the home as an equally plausible _Sitz_?
In Israel sapiential instruction and divine praise were offered
within the family context. Granting that the specific situation
varied among families, it is doubtful that at any fixed chronological point within the biblical period such instruction and
praise were lacking in the home. We must therefore approach
the problem of the _Sitz_ _im_ _Leben_ of psalmic wisdom with considerable openness. Though our knowledge of such matters be admittedly incomplete, this need not discourage us in our quest to
grasp psalmic wisdom with appreciative understanding.

---

[78]Fritzlothar Mand, "Die Eigenständigkeit der Danklieder
des Psalters als Bekenntnislieder," _ZAW_ 70 (1958) 212.

WERE THE EARLY ISRAELITES PASTORAL NOMADS?*

Norman K. Gottwald
Graduate Theological Union, Berkeley, California

In a tribute to James Muilenburg, it is appropriate to re-examine the long hypothesized nomadic origins of ancient Israel, inasmuch as it was Muilenburg who first introduced this writer to the so-called "nomadic ideal" in the OT, a theme which he had in turn encountered during his study under one of its earliest proponents, Karl Budde of Marburg. In his "Prolegomenon" to the 1969 reprint of the third edition of William Robertson Smith's Lectures on the Religion of the Semites, Muilenburg aptly summarized the significance of the nomadic ideal in Smith's methodology for reconstructing the prototypical religion of the ancient Semites:

> Originally the Semites represented a clearly defined
> linguistic and ethnic unity, a cultural homogeneity, and
> a geographical region determined by the limits of the
> Arabian Peninsula, which Smith assumed to be the original
> home of all the Semitic peoples. The origins of the
> religions of these peoples he finds in the Arabs. It is
> among them that we encounter the most primitive forms of
> religion; in their records we see a reflection of nomadic
> mentality and the unchanging character of nomadic life.[1]

In his own estimation of the hypothesis of Israel's nomadic origins, Muilenburg is of a divided mind, as expressed by these counter-poised comments on Smith's view: on the one hand, "The whole direction of our approach to the Semitic world has altered radically. For it is not to the desert of Arabia that we now look, but rather to the great Semitic and non-Semitic cultures of the ancient Near East,"[2] but, on the other hand, "...we have often been too exclusive in our stress upon the great Near Eastern cultures in their relation to the Old Testament records. We may be confident that powerful nomadic influences continued to exert themselves upon Israel's religion throughout its history."[3] If Muilenburg fails to reconcile these two accents, he is by no means alone; indeed, his ambivalence reflects the stance of the great majority of OT scholars who have not independently undertaken a thorough sociological

---

* This article will appear as part of Chapter 6 of A Sociology of the Religion of Liberated Israel, 1250-1000 B.C., Orbis Books, Maryknoll: N.Y., 1975.
1 James Muilenburg, "Prolegomenon," William Robertson Smith, Lectures on the Religion of the Semites. The Fundamental Institutions (KTAV reprint of the third edition with introduction and notes by Stanley A. Cook, 1969), 12.
2 James Muilenburg, "Prolegomenon," p. 22.
3 James Muilenburg, "Prolegomenon," p. 23.

and historical critique of the hypothesis of Israel's nomadic
origins. At most a few scholars have challenged or denied any
uniform or dominant "nomadic ideal" as a positive norm in OT
culture and religion, but the basic cultural and historical
critique of Israelite pastoral nomadism remains to be done.

I. The Regnant Theory of Israelite Pastoral Nomadism

If there was a single perspective shared by virtually all
commentators on Israelite origins prior to 1960 it was the
schema of early Israel as a pastoral nomadic people who pene-
trated Canaan from the desert, and who, in the course of
settling down on the land, underwent massive transition to an
agricultural economy and, more slowly and unevenly, through
village organization toward urbanization. Both those who
accepted the conquest model of the settlement and those who
preferred the immigration model of the settlement were alike in
positing for Israel an original socio-economic base of pastoral
nomadism and an original or transitional territorial base in
the desert steppes to the south and east of Canaan. The issues
dividing conquest and immigration theorists had little or
nothing to do with the socio-economic mode or territorial origins of the first Israelites; the disputes rather raged over
the methods and timing of Israel's entrance into and mastery
over Canaan. Did the pastoral nomads who came from the desert
arrive as a unified mass or in various smaller groupings which
only united after entering the land? Did the pastoral nomads
come as military conquerors or did they infiltrate peacefully
and only gradually gain the power to overthrow Canaanite enemies? Naturally, the varying answers to these questions about
the means of Israel's acquisition of the land affected how the
theorists conceived the process of Israelite nomadic accultura-
tion to settled life, but they did not alter the basic presup-
position: Israelites came as pastoral nomads from the desert
steppes. Even those who have more recently sharply challenged
an OT "nomadic ideal" as a positive cultural and religious norm
have generally not doubted that the first Israelites were pastoral nomads; what they have doubted is that later sedentary
Israelites idealized the nomadic way of life practiced by their
ancestors.

The revolt model of the Israelite formation in Canaan
broke flatly with a comprehensive pastoral nomadic explanation
for early Israel.[4] Unfortunately, critics of Mendenhall's
"peasant revolt" model have paid almost no attention to the
historical and cultural foundations of his rejection of early
Israelite nomadism. This neglect followed from the fact that
Mendenhall based his critique on the still unpublished research
into ancient Near Eastern pastoral nomadism at Mari which was

4 George Mendenhall, "The Hebrew Conquest of Palestine," BA
  25 (1962), 67-71 (reprinted in BAR 3, 1970, 101-105).

carried out by one of his students, John T. Luke.[5] The critique of early Israelite nomadism, far from being the idiosyncrasy of one scholar, draws upon a greatly refined understanding of pastoral nomadism achieved in the last several decades in ethnological and ecological studies. Slowly the results have been applied to the demographic, socio-economic and political conditions of the ancient Near East. Bit by bit, but still in a diffuse and indirect manner, word of the altered perception of pastoral nomadism is filtering into OT studies and awakening doubts and second thoughts. Anyone who becomes informed concerning the new data and theories will see at once that it is utterly impossible to retain the hypothesis of original Israelite nomadism in anything like the form it has enjoyed for a century. The notion that replenishment of populations and initiation of cultural and political changes in the historical civilization of the ancient Near East can be accounted for by the Arabian desert as a fertile spawning ground from which pastoral nomads flowed in streams, or flooded in waves, into the settled zone has come under fundamental attack. To employ pastoral nomadism as an explanatory model for early Israel is to go wrong from the start.

In order to understand the critique of pastoral nomadism as an explanatory theory in ancient Near Eastern cultural and historical studies, and especially in the case of Israel, it becomes necessary to grasp pastoral nomadism as a socio-economic type in its relationships to other socio-economic types and to take account of the great variety of ways in which the typical traits of pastoral nomadism have been combined in particular instances. Most biblical scholars lack such a comprehensive analysis of pastoral nomadism, either as a general type or as a particular formation in the ancient Near East, and have thus been at the mercy of the old uncritical constructs of nomadism with their faulty perceptions about the relation between pastoral nomads and settled peoples. For example, it is now widely thought that the hypothesis of early Israelite nomadism can be resuscitated by regarding the Israelites as semi-nomads. The discovery that the camel or horse nomadism so typical of large parts of the Middle East today was not in fact developed until after 1200 B.C. was initially a blow to the nomadic dogma. Advocates of Israelite pastoral nomadism, however, soon adjusted their scheme to speak of ass nomads as "semi-nomads" or "half-nomads." The result was a puzzling and uncritical juxtaposition of empirical observations about "semi-nomads" unrelated to the surviving unrevised structural and developmental assumptions based on the older model of "full nomadism."

5 John T. Luke, Pastoralism and Politics in the Mari Period: a Re-examination of the Character and Political Significance of the Major West Semitic Tribal Groups in the Middle Euphrates (Ann Arbor: University Microfilms, 1965); see also, J. T. Luke, "Observations on ARMT XIII 39," JCS 24 (1971), 20-23.

The matter in dispute is not whether pastoral nomadism existed in the ancient Near East. It is agreed by all parties that it did, although not in the manner popularly imagined. The issues have to do with the forms, functions, locales, incidences, population size, and over-all significance of pastoral nomadism in that time and place, and especially in the formation of early Israel. It is possible to grant that some, even many, early Israelites were pastoral nomads of one sort or another and still conclude that the regnant pastoral nomadic model for early Israel, as well as the sweeping historical and cultural inferences drawn from it, are fundamentally in error.

II. Pastoral Nomadism in the Ancient Near East

What is pastoral nomadism? It is a socio-economic mode of life based on intensive domestication of livestock which requires a regular movement of the animals and their breeders in a seasonal cycle dictated by the need for pasturage and water. World-wide, pastoral nomadism has involved these domesticated stocks: reindeer , sheep, goats, cattle, yaks, horses. asses, and camels. In some cases there is maximum specialization in one animal stock. More often there is a mix of two or more of the animal stocks. When pastoral nomadic communities are studied comparatively, we discover a wide range in the densities of the human and animal populations and an equally wide range in the ratios between human population density and animal population density.[6] Pastoral nomadism develops a close symbiosis between man and animal, so intimate and comprehensive that their respective behaviors and attitudes are changed. I leave aside the modifications in the animals, pointing only to the profound effects upon herdsmen in diet, housing, forms of property, social organization, etc., which result from dependence upon the exploitation of the stock as "living farms, or factories on the hoof."[7]

Because of the specialized ecological niche in which pastoral nomadism is sustained, with attendant rather dramatic effects on the forms of socio-economic life, it is easy to misconstrue the distinctiveness of the pastoral nomadic mode of life as though it were a totally independent self-contained whole, thereby overlooking the many ties by which pastoral nomadism is connected with other socio-economic modes of life. Here we shall restrict our attention to the arid and semi-arid zone of the transcontinental dry belt of central and southwest Asia and north Africa.[8]

6 Lawrence Krader, "Ecology of Central Asian Pastoralism," Southwestern Journal of Anthropology 11 (1955), 301-326.
7 Lawrence Krader, "Pastoralism," International Encyclopaedia of the Social Sciences 11 (1968), 458.
8 E. E. Bacon, "Types of Pastoral Nomadism in Central and Southwest Asia," Southwestern Journal of Anthropology 10 (1954), 44-68; J. I. Clarke, "Studies of Semi-nomadism in North Africa," Economic Geography 35 (1959), 95-108. Note

Given his primary needs for pasturage and water, the pastoral nomad is linked to the settled zone. The prevailing pattern in the Near East is that the winter rains of this region allow the herdsmen to move out into the steppes to graze their flocks and herds, whereas in the summer dry season they must move back into close proximity with the settled zone in order to find pasturage and water. A less frequent pattern consists of upland or mountain grazing in the summer. Nomads must, therefore, reach agreements with the settled peoples as to grazing and water rights. The common practice is for the pastoral nomad to graze his stock in the stubble of harvested fields. The advantage to the agriculturalist is that the animals fertilize his fields for the coming season. Along with this exchange of services there is exchange of pastoral and agricultural products. By some means, the pastoral nomad must acquire agricultural products, which he may do by barter, by exacting tribute, by himself engaging in agriculture, or by raiding.

More must be said about engagement of nomads in agriculture and in raiding as two types of interaction between the settled and nomadic zones. Raiding is actually carried on more frequently among nomadic groups than it is directed against fully settled peoples. Its chief object is to enlarge flocks or herds and to secure the territorial and status "boundaries" of the respective groups. Chronic raiding of the settled zone is not an invariable feature of pastoral nomadism, since, where the pastoral nomads are strong enough, they are likely to establish political dominance and impose tribute on the agricultural settlements. As to engagement in agriculture, some pastoral nomads do not farm at all. They may consider it irreligious or uncouth and thus depend wholly on barter, tribute or raiding.

Many pastoral nomads do engage in agriculture, however, or we may say somewhat more appropriately that pastoral nomadism and agriculture are often carried on within the same human community and frequently are engaged in by the same persons. This is especially true in situations where the animals bred by the pastoralists are no different than those bred by animal husbandry within the farming villages. Such was the setting in the ancient Near East in the period of Israel's emergence. Sheep, goats and asses were peculiar to the pastoral nomads only in numbers bred which necessitated the annual movements

also the interesting attempt to draw together the evidence on pastoral nomadism in these regions and to propose a more refined classificatory typology by D. L. Johnson, The Nature of Nomadism (University of Chicago Press, 1969). Moreover, M. B. Rowton has launched a ten-part study of pastoral nomadism in the ancient Near East, the first two installments of which are "Autonomy and Nomadism in Western Asia," Orientalia 42 (1973), 247-258, and "Urban Autonomy in a Nomadic Environment," JNES 32 (1973), 201-215.

to take advantage of winter steppe pasturage or of summer
upland pasturage. Since it was necessary to return the animals for half the year from the steppe to the settled zone
and to depend upon grazing in field stubble and watering at
springs, wells and perennial streams, it was altogether
natural that many pastoral nomads were also farmers. There
would be an advantage to retaining the ownership of fields
which they could exploit doubly through crops and through
the summer grazing of their animals. The actual forms which
the simultaneous mix of farming and pastoral nomadism have
assumed in one community are numerous. For example, some
pastoral nomads own fields in the arable zone which are farmed
for them. Others plant their fields before departing for the
steppe and harvest them on their return. In some cases,
herding specialists in the farming community take large flocks
and herds out into the steppe, while most of the people remain
sedentary. In still other instances the community is divided
into sedentary farming and nomadic pastoral segments, such as
the modern ᶜAgêdât on the middle Euphrates. In summer the
whole community of the ᶜAgêdât lives in villages and hamlets
along the river in tents, huts and mudhouses. In winter the
pastoral segments take the flocks into the steppes north and
south of the river, returning to join in summer harvest,
chiefly of grain raised by irrigation. The flocks then graze
the field stubble.[9] It is abundantly clear, therefore, that
agriculture and pastoral nomadism are by no means mutually
exclusive but are often combined in the same human community
in manifold forms. The full implications of this undoubted
socio-economic fact will be developed in sections II.C and D
and in the examination of pastoral nomadism in early Israel
in part III.

B. Pastoral Nomadism Distinguished from Migration and from
Other Forms of Nomadism

It is essential to make distinctions between nomadism
proper and migration, on the one hand, and between pastoral
nomadism and other forms of nomadism or itineracy, on the
other hand.

Nomadism is to be understood as regular movement in necessary conjunction with a particular socio-economic mode of
life which is often culturally re-inforced. Migration is to
be understood as any irregular or occasional movement of a
group necessitated by natural or historical factors external
to the intrinsic socio-economic mode of life. Peoples are
nomadic when they move about in the normal and regular exercise of their mode of production, this movement sometimes
being reinforced by a cultural tradition which makes a virtue
of their margination in relation to settled peoples. Peoples
are migratory when wars or political unrest and oppression,
or when change of climate or disease, force them to leave one

9 H. Charles, Tribus moutonnières du Moyen-Euphrate (Documents
de L'Institut Francais de Damas 8, 1939.

region and go to another quite apart from what their mode of
production or cultural traditions may be. As a result of
migratory uprooting, people may make adaptations from a nomadic to a sedentary or from a sedentary to a nomadic socio-
economic and cultural existence. Thus, in spite of superficial
resemblances between nomadism and migration, both in principle
and in practice the distinction between the two is completely
clear.

Moreover, it should be equally obvious that not all
nomadism is pastoral nomadism. Strangely enough, however,
many writers on the subject of nomadism do not acknowledge the
distinction at all or else form judgments in practical ignorance of it. We must therefore underline the point that nomadism is the genus and pastoral nomad is only one of several
nomadic species.

Another species of the nomadic genus is hunting and
gathering nomadism. While this had ceased to be a major, independent socio-economic mode in the ancient Near East, hunting
and gathering as forms of supplementary food-getting did not
cease altogether in historic times. The life of the hunter
or gatherer on the steppes or in the hills is reflected here
and there in ancient Near Eastern literature and in the Bible
itself. Customarily, such allusions to hunting, as in the
cases of Nimrod (Gen 10:8-9), Ishmael (Gen 21:20-21), and Esau
(Gen 25:27-28; 27:1-4), have been naively understood either as
direct references to pastoral nomadism or have been construed
as literary relics of a long defunct hunting-gathering society.
To my knowledge there is no direct attestation in Near Eastern
records of any communities remaining either exclusively or
primarily at a hunting and gathering stage, but it is evident
that hunting and gathering continued to be viable activities
in pastoral and agricultural communities alike, since the
staple products of field and flock could be periodically or
sporadically supplemented by game and wild foods.

Furthermore, it is insufficiently stressed that certain
occupations in the ancient Near East were essentially nomadic
or itinerant, or frequently so, without being necessarily
pastoral. Tinkers travelled in the sale of their wares. At
times metal craftsmen moved camp to secure metal and fuel for
smelting. Some merchants regularly travelled to oversee the
transport of their goods, to sell them in distant locations,
or to arrange business deals. Caravaneers habitually traversed
the trading routes. Given the great distances over which international trade moved in the ancient Near East, the mercantile
forms of nomadism involved sizeable numbers of people for long
periods of time. There is of course the question of whether
tinkers, craftsmen, merchants and caravaneers travelled as
social communities or as family units or whether the practition-
er of the skill or trade journied alone, leaving his settled
community and family for greater or lesser periods of time. I
am not aware that this question has been carefully studied for

the ancient Near East, but evidence from elsewhere suggests
that in some cases the social units involved in craft and trade
nomadism were fairly large living groups which were in fact
complete communities, such as the travelling gypsies. In such
circumstances, the whole family or community was engaged in a
type of economic specialization by which it serviced other
larger communities as travelling "guilds." In such instances,
the primary economic specialization in a skill or trade tends
to be incompatible with the intensive breeding of animals, although craft and caravaneering specializations may at times be
auxiliary activities of small groups within larger pastoral
nomadic communities. It has been proposed with plausibility
that the Kenites/Rechabites within early Israel were a nomadic
community specializing in metal crafts.[10]

Over-all it is perhaps advisable to speak of such travelling occupational specialists as itinerant rather than nomadic,
especially where they do not move as families or communities.
Yet, for our purposes, we bring them into association with
pastoral nomadism because references to these itinerant craft
and trade specialists in ancient Near Eastern texts have often
been uncritically accepted as references to pastoral nomads.

In this connection it is instructive to comment on the
occurrence of the tent as an index of pastoral nomadism.[11] The
mere mention of tents in ancient Near Eastern or biblical texts
is commonly understood as an unambiguous trait of pastoral
nomadism. The contention can easily be demonstrated to be
erroneous. All the nomadic or itinerant crafts and trade specializations named above frequently, although not invariably,
employed tents. For that matter, even pastoral nomads were
not restricted to tents but often lived for varying periods in
grass or wood huts, mudhouses, wind screens or caves. Moreover, there were certain activities of settled communities in
which the tent was often used. For example, armies on expedi-
tion customarily lived in tents, as did royal hunting parties.
Agriculturalists who had considerable wealth in livestock, or
who suffered a shortage of suitable building materials, occasionally lived in tents. It was also not uncommon for cultiva-
tors of the soil, especially where fields were widely spread,
to spend part of the year in huts or tents, particularly during
harvest, in order to hasten the crop-gathering and to keep thieves
and wild animals from stealing or damaging their yield. It is
apparent that the tent can only be taken as an indicator of

10 Frank S. Frick, "The Rechabites Reconsidered," JBL 90
    (1971), 297-87.   For the social location of metallurgists,
    see R. J. Forbes, "The Evolution of the Smith, His Social and
    Sacred Status," Studies in Ancient Technology, (Leiden: Brill)
    Vol. 8, 1964, pp. 52-102.
11 Alfred Haldar, Who Were the Amorites? (Monographs on the
    Ancient Near East 1; Leiden: Brill, 1971), 51-2.

pastoral nomadism when there are other less ambiguous traits
associated with it.

C. Historical and Cultural Implications of the Emergence of
    Pastoral Nomadism out of Agriculture and Animal Husbandry

Recognition of the manifold forms of pastoral nomadism in
relation to farming leads on to the larger issue of the developmental relationship between agriculture and pastoralism as the
context of the specific conditions for the emergence of pastoral nomadism in the ancient Near East. On the basis of 19th
century cultural developmental schemes, it is still widely
taken for granted that domestication of animals preceded the
domestication of plants and that we are to think of early man
in the ancient Near East as having been first a pastoral nomad
and having evolved later into a farmer. Moreover, in a cultural
version of "ontogeny recapitulates phylogeny," it is often
assumed that each historic movement of pastoral nomads into the
settled zone represents "progress" or "advance" toward sedentary
agriculture in recapitulation of the hypothesized original
emergence of agriculture out of pastoralism. Thus, Israel is
pictured as emerging out of its "primitive" nomadic womb in the
desert and reaching its "civilized" agricultural maturity in
Canaan.

It is now overwhelmingly argued by pre-historians and
ethnologists that the underlying developmental conception in
this scheme is grossly mistaken. Neolithic plant domestication and agricultural village life first developed in the grassy
uplands along the foothills rimming the outer edge of the Tigris-
Euphrates basin and then spread into the river valleys as the
complexities of irrigation and transport were mastered.[12] The
neolithic communities moved from general food collecting to
incipient cultivation and domestication of plants to primary
village farming and finally to towns and cities without any
evidence of a transitional pastoral nomadic stage.[13] C. A. Reed
finds that goats were domesticated in the agricultural village
setting before 6000 B.C. and sheep by about 5000 B.C.[14]

12 Robert J. Braidwood, _Prehistoric Men_ (7th ed.; Glenview,
    Ill.: Scott, Foresman, 1967), 81-153.   On the physical
    conditions disposing the neolithic revolution to occur where
    it did in the ancient Near East, consult K. W. Butzer, _The
    Cambridge Ancient History_, 3rd ed., Vol. 1/Part 1, 1970,
    35-62.
13 J. T. Luke, _Pastoralism and Politics in the Mari Period_, 23-
    24, citing Braidwood's studies in Iraqi Kurdistan.
14 C. A. Reed in, _Prehistoric Investigations in Iraqi Kurdistan_,
    eds. R. J. Braidwood and B. Howe (University of Chicago
    Press, 1960), pp. 129-138; for different dates on domestication
    but entire agreement that domestication of animals took place
    in settled communities, see J. Mellaart, _The Cambridge Ancient
    History_, 3rd ed., Vol. 1/Part 1, 1970, pp. 248-254.

The historical and cultural implications of the developmental priority of agriculture over pastoralism in the ancient Near East are far-reaching and pivotal to the critique of the regnant pastoral nomadic model as it has served to explain early Israel's origins. Sabatino Moscati, articulating the long prevailing but not outmoded view of the temporal and cultural priority of pastoral nomadism, summarizes the developmental process in historic times in a manner basically similar to William Robertson Smith's reconstruction more than half a century earlier. Even allowing for a reticence to speak at all about a pre-historic "original home" for Semites and a recognition that it was ass nomadism rather than camel nomadism prior to 12th cent. B. C., Moscati continues to operate with the older assumptions:

> Let us now consider the historical movements of population within the area, and their relations with one another, and ask ourselves whether, in these movements, it is possible to identify a constant direct ion or a predominant law. The answer is immediately evident: there is a direction of movement constantly repeated throughout the centuries, namely, movement from the centre towards the outskirts, from the Arabian desert towards the surrounding regions.[15]

But what was "immediately evident" to Moscati is now seen as the last stand of a rapidly crumbling developmental scheme. J. T. Luke succinctly poses the new understanding in all its diametrical opposition to the preceding view:

> Early Mesopotamian culture evolved _toward_ the steppe and desert, not out of the desert to the sown. As a relatively late rather than an early phase of this process, pastoralism based on sheep and goats--the animals which remain primary for the Near Eastern village today--developed from the agricultural village.[16]

The upshot of this entirely altered developmental perspective on pastoral nomadism in the ancient Near East is that pastoral nomadism must now be seen as a culturally and socio-economically late marginal development. It was a specialized offshoot and adaptation of the agricultural-pastoral village community. The specialization occurred in the form of concentration on stock breeding adapted to the ecological niche of the semi-arid steppe and, to a lesser degree, to the ecological niche of uplands and mountains. This means that pastoral nomadism spread _outward into_ the semi-arid steppe _from_ the settled agricultural zone, and not vice versa. It emphatically did not first arise in the desert and then give birth to agriculture. Furthermore, it is highly

15 Sabatino Moscati, _The Semites in Ancient History: An Inquiry into the Settlement of the Beduin and their Political Establishment_ (Cardiff: Univ. of Wales Press, 1959), 29.
16 J. T. Luke, _Pastoralism and Politics in the Mari Period_, 24.

doubtful that we can characterize any of the later major movements of population in the historic period (e.g., Akkadians, Amorites, Arameans) as mass invasions or incursions of nomads into the settled region. In addition to the already cited searching rebuttal of the Mari nomads as invaders from the desert presented by J. T. Luke, A. Haldar has examined the entire range of evidence on the socio-economic status and origins of the Amorites--including their involvement in metallurgy and merchant caravaneering--and has conclusively demolished the foundations of the hypothesis that the Amorites were pastoral nomads from the desert.[17]

The representation of "land-hungry" nomads lurking in large numbers on the fringes of the sown land, waiting for the chance to break in and dispossess the agriculturalists, is not really a caricature, for a caricature exaggerates a basic feature of some phenomenon; it is rather a parody on a minor motif of nomadism torn out of context and used as a general formula for explaining the origins of historic shifts of power in the ancient Near East. The formula succeeds in reducing cultural and political complexities to an ethnic-cultural formalism on the pattern: desert/nomadism = prior/culturally lower; sown land/agriculture = later/culturally higher. The formula tends to explain cultural and political shifts within the higher formations primarily, if not solely, as the result of eruptions from the lower formations into the higher.

This is not to deny that there were cases of pastoral nomads giving up their way of life and settling down. Nor is it to say that pastoral nomads never fought with sedentary peoples. It is to say rather that the movement flowed in the other direction just as freely, farmers taking up pastoral nomadism, and it is to say that the attacks of pastoral nomads on other pastoral nomads were more frequent than their attacks on settled peoples and that, when pastoral nomads did fight the settled peoples, it was characteristically in resistance to encroachments of the state into the nomadic community. Both what we know of the origins of nomadism and what we know of its operations in historic times, lead us to this conclusion: the movement of pastoral nomads to settled life was more a return than an advance, and the attacks of pastoral nomads on settled peoples were more a matter of internecine strife in an agricultural-pastoral mix, or of a resistance struggle against central authority, than they were attempts at annihilation or conquest by cultural outsiders.

Furthermore, current estimates of the nomadic population of the Near East project approximately 10% of the total population, a figure which seems limited by the inability of the desert steppe to support intensive occupation. No historical factors imply any larger proportion of pastoral nomads in antiquity. It is altogether doubtful that pastoral nomads were numerically capable of the penetrations and conquests of the higher civil-

17   A. Haldar, Who were the Amorites?

izations with which they are credited, especially when their
notorious difficulties in uniting for concerted action are
taken into account. In addition, now that the earlier theory
of a periodic desiccation of the desert as the impulse to
invade the sown land has been effectively eliminated on climatological grounds, no naturally-grounded impulse to move in
a united mass against the settled region can be posited. Also,
the zone in the interior desert of the Near East which could
sustain small cattle nomadism was limited to the area receiving
between 250 and 100 mm. of rainfall per year. Areas receiving
more than 250 mm. became agricultural regions and areas receiving less than 100 mm. did not offer sufficient grazing to
sustain flocks. This meant in effect that the Hamad, or Syrian
Desert, lying in a rough half-circle on the inner flank of the
fertile crescent (to the north of a line extending approximately
from Damascus to Mari) was the only part of the interior desert
available to pastoral nomadism prior to domestication of the
camel, and in fact this semi-arid steppe extended on to the
north and east across the plain between the upper Tigris and
Euphrates Rivers. The drier interior of northern Arabia, the
Nafud, was inhabitable only at oases and crossable only by well-
provisioned and watered caravans keeping to the routes linking
the oases. This area, according to the older nomadic "original
home" thesis, should have constituted the heartland of ancient
Near Eastern nomadism from which the pastoralists flooded into
the fertile crescent, but it was just this region that was
virtually uninhabited before wide use of the camel for transport
and even then could not sustain a sizable population.

Finally, the supposition of sudden massive moves of pastoral
nomads toward settled areas which they eagerly covet depends in
considerable measure on a misreading of the dramatic diminution
of nomadism in the Middle East under the impact of modernization
which has altered aspects of the economic and cultural life of
the steppe irreversibly. At least two things are overlooked
in comparing modern and ancient conditions. One is that the
modern technology and attendant inflation of land values cannot
be credited for ancient times, and the other is that, more often
than not, the pastoral nomad today resists being settled or
re-settled by the central government. In fact, this hostility
of pastoral nomads toward the planned programming of central
authorities gives us a clue to the ancient situation: The
disruption so often read as the offensive penetration of the
pastoral nomad into the settled zone in order to seize land was
in fact more a matter of defensive counter-measures against
governmental authorities who were attempting to encroach upon
farmers and pastoral nomads alike, particularly with the intent
of subjecting them to burdemsome taxation in kind, or to resented
military service or draft labor. The greatly neglected political factor in pastoral nomadism will be developed in Part III of
this study.

D. Transhumance Pastoralism: Winter Steppe and Spring/
    Summer Upland Grazing

Many commentators on ancient Near Eastern or biblical
pastoral nomadism speak of transhumance nomadism. Considerable
unclarity exists concerning transhumance (literally "across
ground") nomadism, since it appears to be used both in a
broader and a narrower sense.

In the broader sense transhumance refers to all pastoral
nomadism in which there is a seasonal movement of livestock to
regions of different climate. As such it tends to be a virtual
tautology for pastoral nomadism per se, at least in those areas,
such as the Near East, where such a movement is inevitable in
the light of the alternating dry and wet seasons. It is in
this sense that transhumance is used by most students of the
ancient Near East and of the Bible, often interchangeably with
the expression "semi-nomadism", where semi-nomadism refers to
sedentation during the summer season and nomadism during the
winter season. The terminological intersection gets extremely
confused at this point, importing all sorts of unexamined
agendas, owing to at least two other senses in which "semi-
nomadism" is used, not always with adequate explanation by the
writer. Semi-nomadism is also used to refer to small-cattle
(sheep/goat) or ass nomadism, as distinguished from full nomadism
or camel nomadism. In this case "semi" is often also taken to
mean "less fully developed" or "less independent of the settled
zone", or both, and "full" is taken to mean "more fully developed"
or "more independent of the settled zone", or both. Yet again
semi-nomadism is employed with the implication that those who
are nomadic during part of the year and sedentary during the
other part of the year are former full nomads in transition
from a continuous nomadic life to complete sedentariness. Those
who use the expression in this way, at least in biblical studies,
very rarely make this one-directional evolutionary understanding
explicit, but its operation force is frequently made clear by
the context in which a mass of roving nomads are presupposed as
falling into greater and greater dependence upon the settled
peoples, more and more attracted by the taste for settled life,
and finally moving in to take over coveted farm lands. Needless
to say, our entire previous discussion calls all of these over-
rinding assumptions into question. Let us see then if we can
bring some understanding to transhumance nomadism which does not
rely upon imported developmental schemes.

There is a narrower sense in which transhumance nomadism
is employed and that is to refer to a form of intensive herd or
flock breeding by communities which are primarily agricultural
and have developed their crop cultivation intensively and may
even be advanced industrial societies. Pastoral role functions
are restricted to a relatively small number of herdsmen-specialists
who accompany the flocks and herds to seasonal pasturage, usually

without their families. This form of transhumance nomadism
has been well known to western observers in the high mountain
regions of southern Europe, notably in Spain and in Switzerland
and Austria, where advantage is taken of the well-watered
summer upland and mountain pasturage. Obviously the predominantly agricultural and industrial mixed economies of these
European countries cannot possible be called "pastoral nomadic."
We speak rather of a limited pastoral nomadic sub-specialization restricted to a small percentage of the populace who are
gone with the stock for a relatively short summer trek. This
form of transhumance pastoralism is not confined, however, to
Europe; it extends through the upland and high mountain region
of the Caucasus and of southwestern and central Asia as far as
Tibet.[18] It occurs in pastoral communities where agriculture
is neither so productive nor technologically developed as in
western Europe and where most of the population is involved in
the summer upland trek, as in central Iran.[19] In other instances,
as among the Masai of East Africa, it is practiced by only a
few of the herdsmen among a people who themselves engage
directly in no cultivation but depend upon tributary peoples
to provide them agricultural products.[20]

It appears that the well-known European form of transhumance
has led to an overly close connection between two traits which
happen to be associated in that environment but are by no means
always found together among other transhumance pastoralists. In
other words, in Europe the hyper-specialization of agriculture
and industry is associated with limited sub-specialization in
summer upland and mountain grazing. When we survey the great
spectrum of pastoral nomadic ecological communities, it becomes
clear that summer upland and mountain grazing is a variable
determined by the specific natural environment, and that its
occurrence does not depend upon intensive agriculture. Moreover,
transhumance pastoralism is not limited to the ecological niche
of summer upland or mountain grazing. Accordingly, we should
view transhumance pastoralism as involving movement of greater
or lesser segments of the community between two or more different
ecological zones which vary in type according to the region.
Sometimes this will entail winter steppe grazing and sometimes
it will entail summer upland grazing, and possibly both occur
together. Sometimes it will involve all or most of the community
and sometimes only a few herder-specialists. Sometimes it will
be associated with intensive agriculture, sometimes with marginal
agriculture, and sometimes with no agriculture at all.

18   L. Krader, "Pastoralism," International Encyclopaedia of the
     Social Sciences, 457.
19   C. Daryll Forde, Habitat, Economy and Society. A Geographical
     Introduction to Ethnology (5th ed.; New York: Dutton, 1963),
     396.
20   C. D. Forde, Habitat, Economy and Society, 287-307.

In the semi-arid region of the Near East in and around
Canaan, the most common form of transhumance pastoralism was
winter steppe grazing. However, where the coastal range extends
down through Syria and Palestine, offering some snowy heights
and well watered ranges facing the sea, the conditions for late
spring and summer upland and mountain grazing are not altogether
absent. In my judgement, although the data are very terse,
some features of biblical accounts of pastoralism may best be
understood in that mode, such as the sons of Jacob taking their
flocks from Hebron to the region of Dothan and Shechem (Gen 37:
12-17), Absalom from Judah shearing sheep in Baal-Hazor of
Ephraim (2 Sam 13:23), and Judah shearing his sheep at Timnah
in the shephelah (Gen 38:12-13). This form of late spring/
summer grazing which moved not toward the desert but toward the
plains, uplands and mountains facing the sea, seems to have
been developed in later Israel as a form of royal or aristocratic
monopoly in herds and flocks which were kept in the most
prosperous regions. Amos remarks that the women of Samaria
are "cows of Bashan," and from other uses of this expression we
gather that the rich grazed their herds on this tableland to
the east of the Sea of Galilee (Amos 4:1; Ps 22:12; Ezek 39:18).
The Chronicler tells of persons appointed as "stewards of King
David's property," which included herds in Sharon, herds in the
valleys, camels, she-asses, and flocks (1 Chr 27:29-31). King
Uzziah is said to have owned herds in the shephelah and in the
plain (2 Chr 26:10), and King Hezekiah is credited with flocks
and sheepfolds and with herds and cattle stalls (2 Chr 32:27-29).
That many of these locations were in the plains or low hills
along the western escarpment of the highlands reflects the fact
that the winter rains seeping into the limestone hillds found
outlet in perennial springs which watered the western plains well
into the summer. Of course in monarchic times the breeding and
grazing of these large herds and flocks was in fact a form of
animal husbandry, "nomadic" only insofar as it involved itineracy
for the herdsmen-specialists. Nevertheless, the monopolization
of summer upland and plains grazing by the urbanized upper classes
and the court appears to rest upon an older form of transhumance
pastoralism which existed side by side with the more frequently
observed winter steppe pastoralism.

The above suggestions about summer upland transhumance
pastoralism in early Israel are very tentative, both because of
the meager biblical evidence and because I am not aware that
the various forms of transhumance pastoralism, other than winter
steppe grazing, have been well studied in the case of the ancient
Near East. The kind of summer upland and plains grazing here
posited for ancient Canaan could easily have been combined with
winter steppe grazing. A key variable in the relation between
summer upland and winter steppe forms of transhumance pastoralism
is certainly the factor of political control. The well-watered
plains, uplands and mountains of Canaan were relatively close to
the major population and governmental centers, at least by

comparison with the semi-arid steppes farther south and east. If we assume that all things being equal the transhumance pastoralist preferred the sea-oriented grazing grounds to the desert-oriented grazing grounds, things generally were not equal politically speaking. The harsh reality of centralized political domination in Canaan would tend to push pastoral nomads toward the steppes, even when they preferred the lusher pasturage scattered through the settled zone. Another variable is the effect of the winter climate in Canaan on the use of the plains and uplands for year round grazing. Winters in Canaan are not so severe as in most of the upland and mountain ranges of the better known transhumance communities. This is the function of lower elevations and of proximity to the sea. Flocks and herds could be left out during much of the winter, except for occasional severe storms. Since deep freezing seldom occurs, pasturage would generally be available year round. This increased the attractiveness of the plains, uplands and mountains as permanent pasturage, which would tend toward monopolization of these regions by the ruling classes, leaving the steppes to be claimed by the more socially and economically marginated peoples. While the subject calls for much further research, it appears to me that summer upland transhumance was one variation of pastoral nomadism which tended to be quickly appropriated by centrally controlled animal husbandry in Canaan, primarily because the best pasturage was within easy reach of city-state control and was dominated by the ruling classes who were already committed to intensive agriculture on feudal-style estates.

III. The Evidence for Early Israelite Pastoral Nomadism

A. Ecological and Political Aspects of Pastoral Nomadism in Pre-Israelite and early Israelite Canaan

We are now in a position to formulate a sketch of the pastoral nomadic parameters in the area of Canaan immediately prior to and coincident with Israel's formation as a people. We may safely exclude camel nomadism from our purview, since the camel-riding Midianites who struck at Israel in the time of Gideon, about a century after Israel's initial formation, appear to have been the first full nomads known to us in the ancient Near Eastern sources (Judg 6:1-6). If the early Israelites were pastoral nomads, their economy was based on sheep, goats and asses, a marginal sub-specialization within the basically well developed animal husbandry practiced by the intensive agriculturalists of the fertile crescent. In the areas of Canaan toward the south and east (i.e., along the margin of the arable land as fixed largely by rainfall patterns), the normal inter-mixture of agricultural and pastoral components in one economy was skewed in the direction of a heavy pastoral component which either made use of the well-watered pasturage in the heavier rainfall zone or turned toward transhumance exploitation of the semi-arid steppes beyond the cultivable boundary. I have argued above that climatological and political

factors tended to close off the year round plains and uplands
pastures to those living a marginated existence, with the
probable result that summer uplands transhumance tended to be
absorbed into a form of ruling class monopolized animal husbandry,
leaving the less hospitable southern and eastern steppes to the
dominated or marginated peoples.

It is completely clear that all of the pastoralists of the
area at this time were fully familiar with agriculture and that
most of them are to be viewed as engaging in some form of
agriculture. Where they did no farming at all, the pastoral
nomads depended on some accommodation with settled communities
for summer pasturage, watering facilities, and for agricultural
products. We are justified, I believe, in regarding pastoral
nomadism in ancient Canaan as a subsidiary offshoot of the
agricultural village, an offshoot marked by its transhumance
specialization in sheep, goat and ass breeding. We may flatly
state that there was no notion of an absolute dichotomy between
cultivating land and breeding flocks and herds requiring transhumance movement. No such notion existed because climate and
terrain and political circumstance combined to make the co-
existence and combination of agricultural and pastoral pursuits,
in varying ways, altoghether viable and frequently necessary for
considerable numbers of people. Given the erratic rainfall
averages over the whole area from year to year and the peculiar
regional variations in rainfall according to altitude and distance
from the sea, combined with the absence of any large-scale
irrigation possibilities, agriculture throughout Canaan was
always precarious--and especially so toward the south and east.
Total dependence on crops could be disastrous. It is true
that lack of water strikes both at crops and at animals. But
with the animals there were certain safety margins not built
into the cultivation of crops. Animals could move about and take
advantage of watering and grazing opportunities over wide areas.
Moreover, the animal products were available to help tide the
famine-stricken farmer over a difficult year. They gave meat
and milk products and some of the necessities of shelter and
clothing. Of course in a prolonged drought the pastoral and
agricultural components of the economy could fail alike. But
the mix of crops and animals provided a better chance for survival
than sole reliance on crops. In fact, the hardiness of sheep,
goats and asses suited them ideally to the steppes which stretch-
ed beyond the agricultural zone, so much so that exploitation of
the otherwise wasted winter growth of the steppes by grazing
animals must have been a very early, completely logical extension
of animal husbandry.

In my view it is impossible to understand pastoral nomadism
in the ancient Near East, and especially in Canaan, without an
appreciation of the political factors at work in its development
and expression. At the time of Israel's appearance, centralized
government had existed in the ancient Near East for at least two
thousand years and probably for a great deal longer. Centralized
authority was more or less solidly based in the most prosperous
regions of the fertile crescent, operating out of urban centers

and extending control into the countryside in the form of
taxation in kind and in forced military service and draft
labor. Often, as in Amarna Canaan, centralized government
was in fact a host of competing jurisdictions in the form
of city-states struggling to extend their control at one
another's expense, over which a single imperial power or
competing imperial powers (Egypt in the case of Amarna Canaan)
sought to impose its superordinate control for the purposes
of raking off the rich economic surpluses and securing
military and mercantile control over the communication routes.

On this way of looking at the political situation in the
ancient Near East, the city stands over against the countryside,
the centralizing and stratified monarchic and aristocratic
classes stand at variance with the peasant and pastoral
populations. Whether the rural population engaged primarily
in farming, or primarily in stock-breeding, or in some combination of the two, all of them shared much more in common than
they did with the urban elites.[21] To be sure the rural populations
might reluctantly concede that obligations to the central
authority were inevitable or even at times worth the gain in
security, if the exactions were held to a tolerable limit or if
the alternative of subjection to a still more onerous power
from without was thereby forestalled. The point is that the
countryside did not accept this domination by the city unquestion-
ingly. Farmers and pastoralists of the underclasses expressed
a general undercurrent of resentment toward the political elites
and practiced a cold calculation of benefits given and benefits
gained, always with a sharp eye to the possibilities for non-
compliance or for open revolt.

As a general rule, it was in the countryside which lay at
the greatest distance from the urban centers and main communication lines, which included the least prosperous and the most
inaccessible regions, where resistance to the central authorities
could be most effectively conducted and where, on occasion,
open revolt could succeed. Pastoral nomadism in such a
political climate of precarious and resisted domination of the
countryside by the city-states must be seen as more than an
economic adaptation to the steppe. It is also viewable in part
as a form of political resistance. The rural segments of the
populace, under pressure from the dominant urban centers, could
relieve that pressure by moving toward pastoral specialization.

21 Gideon Sjoberg, The Preindustrial City, Past and Present
    (New York: The Free Press, 1960), especially ch. 2 on
    "Cities--Their Beginnings," ch. 5 on "Social Class", ch. 7
    on "Economic Structure," and ch. 8 on "Political Structure."
22 M. B. Rowton, "The Topological Factor in the Hapiru Problem,"
    Studies in Honor of Benno Landsberger on his 75th Birthday
    (Assyriological Studies 16, the Oriental Institute of the
    Univ. of Chicago, 1965), 375-87.

Movable flocks and herds were less easily taxed than real
property. The periodic trek over the steppe carried the nomads
beyond the normal reach of the police power of the state, and
made impressment into the army less likely. Nomads who moved
over regions which lay between two conflicting central authorities could parlay advantages by playing one authority against the
other. In short, there were possibilities in pastoral nomadism
for relative political independence vis-à-vis the state in
comparison with the farmer wholly tied to his land.[23]

The political component in pastoral nomadism has been
observed in modern Palestine:

> Occasionally village folk took to Beduin life to evade
> conscription, or to flee from tribute, taxes, blackmail,
> debts or drought. Sometimes too, criminals might turn
> Beduin, having perforce left their villages after comm-
> iting murder or other crimes. Tribal tradition frequ-
> ently has it that a certain tribe or family is of non-
> nomadic origin and at a certain time has gone over to
> the Beduin way of life.[24]

Movement of the pastoral nomads back to a more fully agricultural life may similarly be viewed in a political framework.
As the political pressure from the settled zone declined with
the decay of central authority, some nomadic groups would return
to sedentariness. Thus, in the marginal zone of Canaan (notably
along its eastern and southern flanks), the combination of and
oscillation between agriculture and pastoralism, between sedentariness and nomadism, is to be seen primarily as a unified
development within a single area, unified economically and
ecologically by the close juxtaposition of conditions favorable
to agriculture and to pastoral nomadism and unified politically
by the attempt of the central authorities to dominate the
agricultural-pastoral village and by the resistance of the
village complex which could take the form of pastoral nomadic
"tactical retreat." The pastoral steppe zone on the east and
south of Canaan thus formed both an ecologically specialized
outrunner of the settled zone and a hinterland for political
asylum and re-grouping available to those who found life in
the settled zone no longer tolerable. In all basic respects
the pastoral nomadic ecological zone and its political horizon
were fundamentally bound up with the strains and stresses within
the settled politically-centralized zone.

23 The Mari Iaminites are so interpreted by J. T. Luke,
    Pastoralism and Politics, 84-5.
24 D. H. K. Amiran and Y. Ben-Arieh, "Sedentarization of
    Beduin in Israel," IEJ 13 (1963), 163.

B. Evidence for the Patriarchs as Pastoral Nomads

In estimating the socio-economic status of the persons and groups reflected in Israel's patriarchal traditions (Gen 12-50), it is essential to keep in mind the distinction we have made between nomadism as regular, occupationally conditioned movement, whether pastoral or otherwise, and migration as irregular movement provoked by unsettled political conditions or by disturbances in the natural environment.

The patriachal stories of early Israel tell of many movements of Abraham and Lot, of Isaac, of Jacob and Esau, and of Joseph and his brothers. These movements are pictured as originating in upper Mesopotamia (and perhaps ultimately in lower Mesopotamia), ranging back and forth across Canaan and trans-Jordan, and finally ending in a descent into Egypt. The accounts are edited in such a way as to give the appearance of a continuous line of action involving one group over several generations. As a result of form-critical studies, it has long been recognized that these traditions must be treated individually both in regard to their origins and in regard to their contents. They stem from different traditional circles and, just as it is inadmissible to refer the descriptions in the traditions to a single historical entity, it is inadmissible to assume a homogeneous socio-economic mode for all of the people described therein.

When the editorial schema of one long migration from Mesopotamia through Canaan in Egypt is dissolved, there remain embedded in the several traditions reports of movements which cannot be easily reduced to any single type. Some of the data suggest circumstances typical of transhumance seasonal treks. On the other hand, most of the movements are described with reference to circumstances of famine, inter-marriage, pilgrimage, or inter-group conflict, factors which tend to be better understood as evidence of migration than of nomadism. This may well be due to the dominant conception by which the scattered accounts were absorbed into the central Israelite traditions after the formation of united Israel. The conception is that of migration as preparation for a religious destiny. Israel, in its early patriarchal phase, is viewed as fated to roam over a land which it could not yet possess. Such a tendentious conception, applied ex post facto from a later time when the land was possessed certainly did nothing to encourage a very accurate retention of information concerning the actual socio-economic status of the proto-Israelites who are the subject of the patriarchal stories. It is consequently highly gratuitous to believe that these stories picture the wandering of the patriarchs as functions of their under-development as pastoral nomadic peoples. Only a closer analysis of the modes of production mentioned in the stories may help us to determine the socio-economic realities behind the motif of migration as preparation for a religious destiny.

When we search behind the facade of the anachronistic
patriarchal migratory schema, the socio-economic data generally
taken to indicate pastoral nomadism turn out to be far from
lucid or compelling. There are traits, such as the sizable
flocks and herds, which accord with pastoral nomadism. That
these traits, however, exhibit a form of pastoral nomadism
which set off these proto-Israelites from others living in the
same regions of Canaan at the time is by no means evident. The
basic "at-homeness" of the patriarchal communities in rural
Canaan is emphasized by the prominent agricultural component
in the socio-economic descriptions. Abraham and Lot (Gen 12:16;
13:5; 20:14; 21:27; 24:35), Isaac (Gen 26:14), and Jacob
(32:5, 7, 15) have oxen or cattle, and in the Near East these
bovines were bred only in the settled zone. Abraham buys part
of a field near Hebron to bury his dead (Gen 23). He sacrifices
a heifer, a turtledove, and a pigeon (Gen 15:8), and he offers
his guests bread, cakes made from meal, and a calf (Gen 18:1-8).
Isaac sows and reaps plentifully in the vicinity of Gerar
(Gen 26:12-14), and, as he drinks wine with his meat, Isaac
blesses Jacob with promises of abundant grain and wine (Gen 27:
25-29). Jacob boils pottage of lentils (Gen 26:29-34), and he
gives forty cows and ten bulls to Esau (Gen 32:15). Reuben
gathers mandrakes "in the days of wheat harvest" (Gen 30:14),
Joseph dreams of binding sheaves (Gen 37:5-8), and Jacob sends
balm, honey, gum, myrrh, pistachio nuts, and almonds to Joseph
in Egypt (Gen 43:11).

Now I submit that this is a very considerable body of evidence that the patriarchal communities practiced diversified and
intensive agriculture. I am well aware that some or all of
these features might be dismissed as anachronisms from a later
agricultural stage of Israel's life. However, to strip them
away, would not uncover any undisputed primitive pastoral
nomadic core. As a matter of fact, it would be just as logical,
indeed even more so, to assume that pastoral nomadic traits in
the patriarchal stories are anachronisms to embroider the motif
of migration as a preparation for relgiious destiny. It seems
to me that the anachronizing possibilities cancel one another
out and leave us with no methodological alternative but to
interpret the socio-economic evidence in the several traditions as they stand.

Accordingly, the socio-economic data permit the interpretation that some or all of the patriarchal groups were transhumance
pastoralists. It is clear, however, that they practiced diversified and intensive agriculture and there is no clear indication
that the entire community was engaged in transhumance. In fact,
some of the information (cf. Gen 37:12-17; 38:12-13 cited in II.
D above) suggests that only segments of certain groups were
engaged in transhumance pastoralism. Finally, there is absolutely
nothing in the socio-economic details of the traditions which
argues for the recent intrusion of these patriarchal communities
into Canaan, implying that they are "in transition" to settled
life. The patriarchal communities are not represented as markedly
different in their agricultural-pastoral mix from other peoples
in Canaan and where they are shown in opposition to the native

Canaanites it is not because of friction between farmers and herdsmen in socio-economic competition for the same living space, but due to political conflict as shown by the fact that their opponents are not rural but urban Canaanites. It must be concluded, therefore, that transhumance pastoralism is no necessary correlate of and no sufficient socio-economic explanation for the traditional motif of the patriarchal migrations as preparation for religious destiny.

C. Evidence for the Exodus Proto-Israelites: Biblical Data and the Shosu

Tradition pictures the Israelites as wanderers in the wilderness enroute from Egypt to Canaan. Virtually all scholars have assumed that this is bona fide proof of the pastoral nomadism of early Israel. Unfortunately, the socio-economic data on the Exodus Israelites are as sketchy and uncoordinated as the socio-economic data in the patriarchal accounts. This much is clear: the wandering in the wilderness is not represented as a regular seasonal movement but as a major displacement from one place of settlement to another. It is commonly assumed that only because they were pastoral nomads could the Israelites make their successful trek across the Sinai desert. There is apparently a measure of truth in that claim, but it must be sharply modified and clarified afresh by a closer look at the evidence.

The Exodus Israelites are described as stock-breeders in Goshen, a region of Egypt along the frontier between the Nile Delta and the Sinai peninsula. The legends of Moses' connections with Midian in eastern Sinai and the mention that the God of Israel was to be worshipped at a location three days' journey into Sinai suggest that at least some of the Israelite community regularly moved out into the Sinai steppe in transhumance herding. The reports which detail their domesticated animals are surprisingly meager, and particularly those embedded in the legislation attached to the Sinai events must be treated cautiously since they reflect naive retrojections of later agricultural conditions in Canaan into the archetypally conceived desert period of Israel's origins. Furthermore, while there is a rich Hebrew vocabulary for domesticated animals, some of the generic terms commonly translated "cattle" are used inclusively for sheep and goats, or "small cattle," as well as for bovines. For example, b^ehemah and miqneh are often used in this inclusive sense. In some cases b^ehemah is a class term for all domesticated animals in contrast to hayyah as a class term for all wild animals. The use of miqneh is sometimes extended to all kinds of possessions or acquisitions in wealth. On the other hand, baqar is normally, if not exclusively, restricted to large cattle, i.e., oxen and cows. Even apart from the problematics of biblical terminology for domesticated animals, it has been observed, in connection with the relation

between the Beiruti and zeboid types of cattle in the ancient
Near East, that "the history of cattle in Bible times needs
much intensified study."[25]

If, however, we set aside all references to bovines in the
Sinaitic legislation and in the P materials, there remains a
considerable body of references to oxen or large cattle in JE
narratives, which strongly imply that the Israelites in Egypt
were understood to have been sufficiently tied to the soil to
have bovine herds. Jacob in Egypt has both small cattle and
large cattle (Gen 45:10; 46:32; 47:1), although one passage
implies that at least some of the herds he kept belonged to
pharaoh (Gen. 47:6). If, with Noth, we set aside the Joseph
novella as one of the latest bridging devices in the Pentateuch,
there are still ample references of the same sort in Exodus.
Moses requests that the Israelites be allowed to make a pilgrimage to worship Yahweh accompanied by their small and large
cattle (Exod 10:9,24). At the crossing of the sea, the fleeing
people take their flocks of sheep and goats and their herds of
large cattle (Exod 12:32, 38), which are again alluded to in
the wilderness (Num 11:22; 20:4; 8, 11). Moreover, the com-
plaining Israelites recall a diet in Egypt including fish,
cucumbers, melons, leeks, onions and garlic, which suggests
that they had been fishermen and small gardeners (Num 11:5).
The Israelites also take eagerly to eating the manna which is
described as a bread substitute, "like coriander seed" (Num
11:7-9). Although we should like much fuller information, we
can at least say that the socio-economic data on the Exodus
Israelites are in no way specifically pastoral nomadic and,
in fact, contain items which tell against an exclusively pastoral nomadic reconstruction of the community.

The problems of socio-economic survival for the Israelites
in the Sinai wilderness were assuredly enormous. They were
neither a small, well-provisioned travel party nor were they
camel nomads adapted to fairly rapid movement over inhospitable
and arid regions. We shall not enter into the still vexed
question of the route of the Exodus, although I tend to prefer
the view that they moved eastward along the main coastal route
toward Canaan for some distance before striking out toward
Kadesh in the interior.[26] According to the traditions, although
they were attacked by Amalekites, the major communal obstacles
in the wilderness were environmental. They had to make their

25   F. S. Bodenheimer, "Fauna," IDB, vol. 2, 249. Also see:
     E. Bilik, "Cattle," Encyclopaedia Biblica, Vol. 2, 1954,
     cols. 312-316 (Hebrew), and J. Feliks, "Cattle,"
     Encyclopaedia Judaica, Vol. 5, 1971, cols. 256-257.
26   Yohanan Aharoni, The Land of the Bible. A Historical
     Geography (Philadelphia: Westminster, 1967), 178-84.

way from oasis to oasis (apart from Kadesh none of these locations can be identified with any certainty), while trying to
preserve as many of their animals as possible for a dependable
supply of dairy products and wool for shelter and clothing, as
well as occasional meat and hides. The impression given is of
an eclectic community which as a totality was not familiar with
the wilderness and not accustomed to living there. According
to tradition, the leader Moses had spent long years in Sinai,
living among the Midianites. It is these very people who "serve
as eyes" for Israel, advising them as to "how to encamp in the
wilderness" (Num. 10:31). Even so, the food supply ran danger-
ously low and the people had to learn how to survive on a make-
shift diet, including quail blown in from the sea and a bread
substitute of "manna" (Heb. "what is it?"), possibly an edible
excretion of scale insects deposited on tamarisk bushes.[27] The
implication is that most, if not all, of the animals they started out with from Egypt perished in the wilderness or had to be
eaten for food. Water was a constant deficiency and apparently
only as they found their way to the multiple springs around Kadesh
were they able to establish a viable existence. The tradition
that the whole generation of those who left Egypt died in the
wilderness, except for a favored few leaders, may well reflect
the severe losses from starvation, thirst and exposure which
overtook not only animals but people as well. There are also
highly colored reports of dissension in the decimated ranks and
of contests for leadership so furious that the greatly regarded
Moses was known not to have reached Canaan with his people.
Although the traditions moralize the premature death of Moses
exclusively as a devine rejection, it is probable that they
attest to dissatisfactions with his leadership so great that he
was deposed, banished or killed during the intense intra-
communal struggles for power.

Looking back at the Egyptian matrix of Israelite origins,
there is of course the now-famous report that Israelites were
forced into helping to build Pithom and Raamses, the store
cities which Rameses II erected in the eastern delta to serve
his imperial ambitions in Palestine and Syria (Exod 1:11), and
this is generalized in summary form to state that their lives
were made bitter "with hard service, in mortar and brick, and
in all kinds of work in the field" (Exod 1:13). If one assumes
that the Israelites who left Egypt were a homogeneous group, we
could conceivably hypothesize their condition as follows: they
were a people settled in the irrigated region of Goshen where
they gardened, fished, and grazed flocks and herds, their sheep
and goats being taken into the steppe during the winter rains.
Being under Egyptian tutelage, they were forced into draft labor

27   J. L. Mihelic, "Manna," IDB, vol. 3, 1962, 260. Also see:
      S. E. Loewenstamm, "Man," Encyclopaedia Biblica, Vol. 5,
      1968, cols. 7-10 (Hebrew).

when the pharaoh embarked on large building projects in the area
related to a revived Asiatic imperial policy and, moreover, they
were obliged to work the pharaonic fields.

But the homogeneity of the Israelite community cannot be
taken for granted. It is more probable that the "Israelites"
who left Egypt together were a loose assemblage of people holding in common only the fact that they were lower classes oppressed
by the Egyptian crown who sought relief under opportune leadership
and were only gradually welded together in the cult of Yahweh.
Such an interpretation is hinted at by comments in the traditions
that a "mixed multitude (cēreb rab) also went up with them" (Exod
12:38) when Israel set out from Rameses to Succoth, and that "the
riffraff (ha sphsuph) that was among them" (Num 11:4) agitated
against Moses because of the lack of food. The rare word
asaphsuph suggests a motley assortment of undisciplined camp
followers, an aggregation of persons which has not yet become a
community. Of course the traditions attempt to distinguish
between the main body of Israelites and the mixed followers, but
that is what we should expect from the centralized tradition.
It is rather remarkable that these solid allusions to hetero-
geneity survived as authentic memories of the conglomerate origins of those who banded together in flight from Egypt, not as
a pre-existent community but as those whose intolerable conditions of oppression drove them in the direction of a community
yet-to-be.

Given the probability of heterogeneous origins for the
Exodus Israelites, the various socio-economic data cropping
up here and there in the traditions may in fact belong to
different segments of the proto-Israelites who joined in withdrawal from Egypt. Some may have been fully agricultural and
others transhumance pastoralists, while still others were fishermen. Those impressed into building projects may well have
totally lost contact with their earlier agricultural or pastoral
pursuits, having become wards of the state. The means by which
these groups entered Egypt varied with circumstance. Probably
some had entered the delta region as part of the normal movement
of transhumance pastoralists. Others were probably uprooted
from their former homes by famine and driven into whatever
accommodations they could make in Egypt. Still others were
doubtless captives of war from pharaoh's Asiatic campaigns
who were brought into the region to build the store cities and
to cultivate the crown estates. A large majority of these
peoples would have been militarized, either as capiru troops
taken as captives or as Shosu plunderers seized by the Egyptians. The deepening incursion of pharaonic control into this
region during the 19th Dynasty sparked widespread resistance
among the hitherto separate groups of displaced Asiatics and
set the stage for them to join together in a break for freedom.
What appears to have formed the axis of emerging unity for
these socio-economically diversified peoples was their common
fate of increasing incorporation into the pharaonic state

economy, so that whatever their precise backgrounds and means of production, they were jointly subjected to increasing political control and economic depressment as a reservoir of "coolie" labor on whose bent backs the pharaoh could march to his Asiatic victories.

Of particular pertinence to this assessment of the contention that the early Israelites were pastoral nomads are the Shosu mentioned by the Egyptians as their foes throughout the vast region east of the Delta and extending as far as Edom on the east and northward into Palestine. There has been surprisingly little systematic attention to the Shosu, either in their own right or in their connections with the early Israelites. Since Shosu is normally translated "Bedouin", these people deserve a closer examination.

In a thorough study of the more than fifty Egyptian documentary references to the Shosu, extending from 1500 to 1150 B.C., Raphael Giveon concludes that they were pastoral nomads.[28] The evidence he cites consists of a few texts which show the Shosu bringing their flocks or herds to watering points under Egyptian control (e.g., Papyrus Anastasi VI, ANET, 259), but the observations are so cursory that we do not know either the exact animals bred or in what number and it is not certain whether these are instances of transhumance pastoralism or of extraordinary migrations. That Giveon is somewhat uneasy about the slimness of the data is reflected in his comment that the pharaohs speak so much of pillage of Shosu goods and destruction of the Shosu countryside that it is difficult to regard the land of the Shosu as desert.[29] His misgiving is well advised since the Shosu are found over a vast region ranging from the Sinai and Edom northward into southern Syria. They are often involved in fighting on behalf of cities in Canaan, either as the inhabitants of those cities, as mercenaries in their employ, or as confederates of the urban dwellers. Where places are specifically located in "the land of the Shosu", the heartland appears to have been southern Edom, where an upthrust of mountains makes for a moderately well-watered region suitable for limited agriculture.

When it comes to characterizing the social life of the Shosu, Giveon is again reduced to sparse evidence. He points out that the Shosu are never said to have a "king" but always "a great one" or "chief." He also observes that the Shosu, as well as the Libyans, are said to have the mhwt, a term which denotes a unit of social organization based on kinship. The range of meanings for mhwt, from "near relative" through "family" and

28 Raphael Giveon, Les Bédouins Shosou des Documents Egyptiens (Documenta et Monumenta Orientis Antiqui 18; Leiden: Brill, 1971).
29 R. Giveon, Les Bédouins Shosou, 240-41.

"clan" to "tribe" and even "people," does not permit exactitude in characterizing the social organization of the Shosu.[30] For independent evidence concerning distinctive subdivisions among the Shosu, Giveon can only cite the variations in coiffures in the pictorial representations which he suggests were distinctive marks of particular subdivisions among the Shosu.

As a matter of fact, Giveon has done little more than to show that the Shosu were not organized in a statist form of politics and that a broad "tribal" designation suits them. From this fact he has appeared to find tacit corroboration of their pastoral nomadic condition of life. The anthropological evidence is overwhelmingly clear, however, that tribalism is not restricted to any one socio-economic mode but occurs as a form of social organization throughout a spectrum of socio-economic modes, including pastoral nomadism; hunting , fishing and gathering; equestrian hunting; forest or slash-and-burn agriculture; and intensive agriculture.[31] In fact, where the Shosu appear most vividly in the Egyptian texts, they are marauders and brigands who spring ambuscades on travellers through the pass at Megiddo and in the mountainous regions of southern Lebanon (Papyrus Anastasi I, ANET, 475-79). When Giveon contrasts the Shosu and the Sea Peoples (including Philistines) as confederacies with chiefs, on the one hand, and Hittites and Amorites as monarchies with kings, on the other hand, he inadvertently discloses that the "tribalism" of the Shosu refers to a non-statist social organization and not to any necessary socio-economic mode such as pastoral nomadism. The Philistines were certainly not pastoral nomads. Taking into account that their movement into Palestine was part of an historic migration (as defined above in II.B), we cannot properly call the Philistines nomads at all. In attempting to penetrate Egypt and the Syro-Palestinian coastlands, the Sea Peoples were not engaging in the conduct of their normal occupations, except perhaps to the degree that they had adapted themselves as roving mercenaries. Basically, the Sea Peoples were seeking a new home after having been displaced from their former locales somewhere in the islands of the Aegean or in wester Asia Minor. Finally, Giveon concludes that the etymology of Shosu is not given from an Egyptian word "to roam," as commonly assumed, but from a Semitic root, cognate to Hebrew šāsas=šāsāh, "to plunder."[32]

30   R. Giveon, Les Bedouins Shosou, 255-57.
31   Marshall D. Sahlins, Tribesmen (Foundations of Modern Anthropology Series; Englewood Cliffs, New Jersey: Prentice-hall, 1968), 28-47. For a fuller discussion on the criteria of tribalism and the range of tribal forms, see June Helm, ed., Essays on the Problem of Tribe (Proceedings of the 1967 Annual Spring Meeting of the American Ethnological Society, University of Washington Press, 1968).
32   R. Giveon, Les Bédouins Shosou, 261-64.

The usual English translation of Shosu as "Bedouin" in the
Egyptian texts gives an unjustified socio-economic skewing of
the term, not only because Bedouin is generally reserved for
camel nomads, but because the primary reference of the term is
to "pillagers" or "plunderers" rather than to pastoral nomads
of any sort.

What were the relations among Shosu, ᶜapiru and Exodus
Israelites in the 13th century B.C.? The Egyptian categor-
ization of Shosu refers to people not primarily, and perhaps
even not at all, according to their homogeneous socio-economic
condition but according to their disturbing military-political
effects as plundering and warring elements who upset the imperial
status quo in Syria-Palestine. That certain Shosu are shown in
robber activities analogous to robber activities of ᶜapiru and
of habati, "brigands" (cf. Papyrus Anastasi I, ANET, 475-79
and Amarna letter 318. 12 in J. A. Knudtzon, Die El-Amarna-
Tafeln, 1915, vol. 1, 924-25), whereas ᶜapiru are distinguished
from Shosu (at least in the Booty List of Amenhophis II, ANET,
247), implies that in some circles there were criteria for
representing peoples as Shosu in addition to their plundering.
At the moment we can only speculate about these criteria.
Perhaps one of these criteria was the original cohesion of the
Shosu as a tribally-organized people in southern Edom. As the
term Shosu came to be used, however, it seems to have developed
into a wide-ranging term, a virtual epithet, so that the crude
basis of the distinction between ᶜapiru and Shosu may simply
have been that ᶜapiru were believed to have been groups composed
of outlaw or refugee elements from politically centralized
communities who did not have a native region of their own,
whereas the Shosu were perceived as having a continuous tribal,
i.e., politically de-centralized social organization, with a
known or supposed landed base.[33]

Giveon is impressed by the two-fold geographical and temporal
conjunctions of Shosu and Exodus Israelites: Both were identified with southern Edom (Seir/Paran) and both were in the eastern
Delta region of Egypt during the reigns of Rameses II and
Merneptah. He concludes that the Exodus Israelites may very
well have been Shosu, or that at least some Shosu may have been
included among the proto-Israelites.[34] The first of his
alternatives over-steps the evidence, but the second is attract-
ive as a working explanation for one of the motley components in

33 For another explanation of the differences between ᶜapiru
    and Shosu, based on territoriality, see W. Helck, "Die
    Bedrohung Palaestinas durch einwandernde Gruppen am Ende der
    18. und am Anfang der 19. Dynastie," VT 18 (1968), 472-480.
34 R. Giveon, Les Bédouins Shosou, 267-71.

Israelite origins. Even if all the Exodus Israelites were
Shosu, their pastoral nomadic status is not thereby demonstrated.
Insofar as we allow for others, such as ᶜapiru, in the Israelite
mix, their pastoral nomadic status becomes all the more questionable. It is possible that the Midianite allies of the Exodus
Isrealites were included by the Egyptians under the cover term
Shosu, which invites the hypothesis that the reason the Midianites and Exodus Israelites recognized collaborative interests
was that among the Israelites were Shosu who were originally
from Midian. This may be the socio-political reality presently
masked in the form of legends about Moses' flight to Midian and
his inter-marriage with the Midianites. The extra-biblical data
on the Shosu thus incline us toward the probability that Shosu
were involved in the mixed Israelite origins, but those data do
not speak unambiguously for the Shosu as pastoral nomads. In
this connection it should not be overlooked that there is some
evidence for viewing the Kenite sub-section of the Midianites
as smiths and thus occupational itinerants rather than pastoral
nomads. In my view much the most striking feature of a comprehensive search of the data on the Shosu is their militarization.
Not only the hypothetical ᶜapiru component of Israel but also
the hypothetical Shosu component of Israel emerges as highly
militarized with a long history of plunder and warfare against
the Egyptians. Moreover, neither the militarism of the Shosu
nor the militarism of the ᶜapiru is pictured as a foreign
invasion by cultural outsiders but as elements of strain and
conflict in a chaotic socio-political struggle indigenous to
Syria-Palestine. In this regard, the Exodus Israelites fall
comfortably and logically into the discernible framework of
socio-political conflict at the heart of Syro-Palestinian
society.

      D. Pastoral Nomadism as a Subsidiary Component
          in Israelite Tribalism

     We have concentrated on the biblical traditions about early
Israel prior to the so-called "conquest" of Canaan, for it is
here that the strongest case for the pastoral nomadic origins
of the Israelite people has been thought to rest.[35] In the

35 To my knowledge the fullest and most disciplined attempt
    to examine the evidence for pastoral nomadism in the patri-
    archal, exodus and settlement traditions is in the unpubl-
    ished work of Siegfried Schwertner, "Das Verheissene Land".
    Bedeutung und Verstaendnis des Landes nach den fruehen
    Zeugnissen des Alten Testament (doctoral dissertation,
    University of Heidelberg, 1966) made available to me through
    the courtesy of the author and his mentor Rolf Rendtorff.
    Schwertner finds considerable pastoral nomadism in the
    patriarchal traditions (although possibly among people only
    recently driven from settled life), no pastoral nomadism in
    the exodus traditions, and some pastoral nomadism in

sense that there is evidence that some of the proto-Israelites had large flocks bred under the conditions of transhumance pastoralism, we concur that it is probable that pastoral nomadism was one socio-economic mode of life represented in early Israel. We observed, however, that mixed with the evidence pointing toward two forms of trans-humance pastoralism (winter steppe and summer upland grazing) there is abundant attestation to the fact that these pastoralists lived among the settled peoples of Canaan and Egypt and that they themselves practiced diversified forms of intensive agriculture and raised bovine herds.

What must henceforth be strongly contested are the cultural and historical inferences so widely drawn from the limited evidence for pastoral nomadism in early Israel, inferences either totally unfounded or highly questionable. Neither the movements of "patriarchal" proto-Israelite groups into Canaan and into Egypt, nor the movements of proto-Israelite groups from Egypt into Canaan, may be legitimately understood as military attacks or expropriative infiltrations based on cultural hostility of pastoral nomads for settled peoples or upon covetousness toward their lands. The relationships of the early Israelites with the indigenous peoples run a range from cooperation to open hostility which follow along the lines of social structural tension and conflict within the society. In other words, the relationships between Israelites and other groups are not understandable in terms of Israelite pastoral nomadic status versus Canaanite/Egyptian sedentary agricultural status but rather in terms of Israelite organized opposition to Canaanite/Egyptian centralized political authorities and modes of economic expropriation. This Israelite opposition to statism and economic oppression is an especially sharp and successful instance of the general Near Eastern opposition of tribalism to statism.

There were obviously many distinctive features of Israelite tribalism at the peculiar juncture of forces in 13th-12th century Canaan, but those distinctive elements can only be appreciated and rightly interpreted when we first grant that Israel arose at an intersection or conjunction of social forces which we can clearly identify as widely operative in the ancient Near East. Within that wider social matrix, it can be plainly

the exodus traditions, and some pastoral nomadism in the settlement traditions (mainly among Leah tribes). Schwertner also distinguishes between "transmigration" and "transhumance." There is considerable agreement between our two studies, but Schwertner designates certain biblical data as transhumance (especially in the patriarchal accounts) which I read as transmigration.

seen that the pastoral nomadic Israelites shared with the agricultural Israelites a common resentment toward and a common resistance against the exploitative domination of Canaanite feudalism and Egyptian imperialism at whose hands they suffered alike. A defining feature of the Israelite movement for liberation was that it was not "ghettoized" as a pastoral nomadic movement but represented an effective combination of pastoralists and agriculturalists who managed to subordinate their differences in a unified effort to strike at the source of their common misery. The Israelite movement sought to eliminate the feudal and imperial power organizations from an area in which the communal members could pursue their variegated patterns of farming and herding in autonomous conditions free from crushing taxation and impressment into building projects and wars in which they stood to gain nothing for themselves.

So, while conceding a limited measure of truth to the older hypothesis in the sense that some Israelites were transhumance pastoralists, I offer the following theoretical formulation which sets circumscribed Israelite transhumance pastoralism in its proper context, thereby fundamentally altering and diminishing the cultural and historical significance previously assigned to it:

1) In the total mix of proto-Israelite peoples, as reflected in the patriarchal and Mosaic traditions, transhumance pastoralism was a subsidiary sub-specialization within the dominant socio-economic mode of production, namely, intensive agriculture.

2) The transhumance pastoralism of the patriarchal and Mosaic traditions is best perceived as a sub-specialization altogether indigenous to Syro-Palestine and in no way a culturally foreign intrusion from outside the area. The population movements indirectly represented in the patriarchal travels and in the wandering of the Exodus Israelites are movements within the culture zone or between regions in that zone.

3) The transhumance pastoral element in early Israel did not embody a distinctive monolithic cultural or social organization distinct from the Syro-Palestinian peoples who lived in the countryside, nor did it represent a lower stage of cultural and social evolution than did the Syro-Palestinian peoples in the rural areas. They all belonged loosely to a "tribal zone" of social organization.

4) The transhumance pastoral element in early Israel did not project a unified military attack against settled Syro-Palestinian peoples, nor a more covert infiltration, with the intent of annihilating or displacing the natives so as to take over their agricultural means of production, thereby "advancing" from a lower cultural level of pastoral nomadism to a higher cultural level of intensive agriculture.

    5) <u>Israelite tribalism as a socio-economic, political and religio-cultic form of social organization was in no sense ever a peculiarly pastoral nomadic phenomenon</u>. Israelite tribalism belonged to the sphere of rural resistance to political domination, a sphere which included the agricultural village and the pastoral nomadic sub-specialization within the village or closely related to the village. The transhumance pastoralists of early Israel were aligned with agriculturalists in a common socio-political and ideological perspective which united the resisting countryside (sown land and steppe) in all its converging egalitarian socio-economic dimensions against the walled city with its hierarchic and stratified organization of human social life for the advantages of an elite at the cost of the many.

    I shall now briefly elaborate on the tribal/statist analytic model proposed in the preceding paragraph. In order to clear the air of entrenched misconceptions, it must be flatly stated that the basic division and tension in the ancient Near East at the time of Israel's emergence was not a division and tension between sedentariness and semi-nomadism, between settled zone and desert or steppe. At most, the division between sedentariness and semi-nomadism was secondary, or even tertiary; it was, in fact, not a "division" assuming conflicting interests but a merely relative distinction within a basic continuum. In the main, the relations between the settled areas and the steppe were more socio-economically cooperative than hostile. The zone where agriculture was possible and the adjoining regions where only grazing was possible, and then only during part of the year, were ecologically distinguishable zones to be sure, but they were ultimately integrated within a larger framework of demographic, economic, cultural and political symbiosis.

    The social reality is that the basic division and tension, the crucial conflict of interests, in the ancient Near Eastern society during Israel's appearance was between the city and the countryside. The "city" and the "countryside" as analytic types may be respectively characterized by antithetical traits in the following simplified and schematic manner:

<u>"City"</u>	<u>"Countryside"</u>
urbanism	village life
maximal division of labor	minimal division of labor
social stratification	tendency toward class leveling
imposed quasi-feudal social relations	contractual or kin egalitarian social relations
political hierarchy	diffused and limited self-government

military imperialism	non-cooperation and military self-defense
latifundist agriculture	agriculture by autonomous peasants
commercialism	barter trade
concentration of surplus wealth in a socio-political elite	direct and equal consumption of wealth by the immediate producers of wealth

The analysis indicates that the basic division was not between agriculture and pastoralism but between (1) centralized and elitist controlled latifundist agriculture, animal husbandry and pastoralism subservient to political domination by the city-state, on the one side, and (2) agriculture, animal husbandry and pastoralism by autonomous peasants and herdsmen in a non-statist and egalitarian community, on the other side. For purposes of analysis. the above traits are stated as sharp extremes. The actual historical and social configurations in this generally identifiable conflict naturally varied greatly according to time and place, and in each instance the precise configurations (including the degree to which the above type traits were operative) must be established by careful research. The value of the above analytic model is that it delivers us from an atomistic description of discrete socio-economic modes and sets us on the search for the constellation of social, economic and political forces assembled and interacting in early Israel in conjunction with the corresponding constellations ranged against Israel. In my judgement the key variables in discriminating Israelite from Canaanite/Egyptian society, and in determining their inter-relationships, will prove to be political domination vs. political decentralization and social stratification vs. social egalitarianism, rather than the simplistic and erroneously invoked variables of agriculture vs. pastoralism or sedentariness vs. nomadism.

<u>Lākēn</u>: ITS FUNCTIONS AND MEANINGS
W. Eugene March
The Austin Presbyterian Theological Seminary

        In 1961 Professor James Muilenburg published an extensive
and highly instructive study of the Hebrew particle kî in which he
sought to define not only the lexical but also the rhetorical role of
this often-used term. By way of introduction to his work Professor
Muilenburg commented on the Hebrew particles in general as follows:

> They are the signals and sign-posts of language,
> markers on the way of the sentence or poem or
> narrative, guides to the progress of words, arrows
> directing what is being spoken to its destination.
> They serve to indicate how words are disposed into
> the fabric or texture of speech, how the literary
> types are fashioned into connected wholes. They
> confirm or establish or stress what is being said,
> or underline and give notice to what is about to be
> said, or mark the goal or climax of what has been
> said. They are by no means static linguistic enti-
> ties, morphemes to be scrutinized independently of
> their contexts, but are rather agents of movement.
> The intended meaning becomes alive and dynamic
> in the ways that the particles are employed. Whether
> negations, affirmations, interrogatives, interjections,
> or instruments of connection, they perform their work
> in many different ways and wear many guises. Their
> meaning is often contingent upon the particular func-
> tion they seek to serve so that the same word may
> be rendered quite differently in the same context.
> Without an understanding of their precise function
> not only are the nuances of a text often obscured,
> but the articulation and accents of the thought are
> also lost to view. [1]

In 1968 in his Presidential Address, "Form Criticism and Beyond,"
delivered at the annual meeting of the Society of Biblical Literature,
Professor Muilenburg again reminded us of the crucial function of the

---

[1] James Muilenburg, "The Linguistic and Rhetorical Usages of the
Particle כִּי in the Old Testament," <u>HUCA</u>, 32 (1961), p. 135

Hebrew particles in Hebrew rhetoric and specifically suggested that
studies of these important terms, among which is lākēn, be initiated.[2]
It is with these two comments in mind that this study is presented with
the hope that it may provide more insight into the variety of use and
meaning of Hebrew lākēn and thereby advance our understanding of the
rhetoric and literature of ancient Israel so dear to Professor Muilenburg and us all.

I

Lākēn occurs one hundred ninety-three times in the Hebrew
Bible[3] distributed as follows: one hundred sixty in the prophetic
literature; twenty-one in Genesis-Kings; and twelve in Psalms, Job,
and II Chronicles. The usual translations for lākēn noted in the lexi-
cons are "therefore," "that being so," "surely therefore," and "according to such conditions."[4] These translations certainly reflect the very
early understanding of the term as reflected in the Septuagint, for in the
Greek dia touto[5] and houtō(s)[6] are the most frequent terms employed to
represent lākēn. Further, there are indeed many passages where the

---

[2] James Muilenburg, "Form Criticism and Beyond," JBL, 88 (1969), p. 15.

[3] Solomon Mandelkern, Veteris Testamenti Concordantiae (Tel-Aviv:
Schocken Publishing House Ltd., 1962), pp. 586-587. Mandelkern cites
one hundred ninety-four occurrences of lākēn, but Zech. 11:7 is usually
emended; cf. L. Koehler-W. Baumgartner, Lexicon in Veteris Testamenti
Libros (Leiden: E. J. Brill, 1958) p. 482.

[4] F. Brown, S. R. Driver, C. Briggs, A Hebrew and English Lexicon of
the Old Testament (Oxford: Clarendon Press, 1957), p. 486; Koehler-
Baumgartner, op. cit., p. 482.

[5] E. Hatch and H. Redpath, A Concordance to the Septuagint (Graz-Austria:
Akademische Druck - U. Verlagsanstalt, 1954), p. 297.

[6] Ibid. pp. 1035-1038: Num. 16:11, 25:12; I Sam. 28:2; Is. 61:7;
Ez. 21:9 cf., also footnote 40 below.

English translation "therefore" seems sufficient and appropriate. [7]

But on closer examination numerous texts emerge in which our "therefore" will not do! Pedersen has already noted that rhetorically lākēn does not indicate consequence--the principal function of English "therefore"--but rather signifies connection.

> it [lākēn] consists of two elements: the preposition la, which means connection, continuity, and kēn which, properly speaking, means 'standing place,' but is used as a demonstrative particle, 'that,' 'such circumstances,' the whole word meaning 'connected with these circumstances.' It means that what is now going to be told is connected with the preceding as an indissoluble unity. [8]

The connection may come in the form of what we might term "logical sequence" or at other points as 'moral consequence,'[9] but again, "So far from initiating a logical step forward this word, in accordance with its nature, sometimes rather introduces a contrast."[10] Other studies have recognized the limitations and inappropriateness of "therefore" as the translation of lākēn,[11] but Pedersen points the way to a more useful

---

[7]One thinks of passages such as I Sam. 27:6 or the numerous texts in the prophetic literature where lākēn introduces a divine threat, e.g. Is. 29:14, 30:13, Jer. 9:14.

[8]Johs. Pedersen, Israel: Its Life and Culture (London: Oxford University Press, 1959), v. I-II, p. 116.

[9]Ibid.

[10]Ibid., p. 117

[11]Paul Haupt, "Micah's Capucinade," JBL, 29(1910), pp. 104-105, explains the variety of meaning of the term lākēn on the basis of four different etymologies. This intriguing approach at least serves to underscore the fact that lākēn cannot always be correctly translated by using a single English term. Fredric J. Goldbaum, "Two Hebrew Quasi-adverbs: לכן and אך, "JNES, 23(1964), pp. 132-134, has also argued persuasively against rendering lākēn as "therefore." Goldbaum contends that the term is best understood as introducing a vow and should be rendered "upon my word." There are texts, as we will note below, where this suggestion makes sense, but Goldbaum's thesis that lākēn always carries this connotation is demonstrated from only a limited number of texts (those in Genesis-Kings) and even then does not seem the best explanation in every instance.

understanding of this term by calling attention to its rhetorical role.
Thus, we will begin by considering the various ways this term is used
in certain reoccurring phrases. Next we will examine the use of lākēn
in relation to the particular literary types in which it is employed.
Finally, we will note in a summary fashion the varied meanings this term
conveys.

II

There are eight "phrases" in which lākēn is used which provide
a starting point in our quest to understand the functions and meanings
of this term.

1. One of the most frequent phrases encountered is the familiar:
"lākēn thus says the Lord. "[12] Within the prophetic corpus there are
sixty-one specific occurrences of this term[13] and twenty-seven other
related phrases, thus accounting for more than half the total number of
times the term lākēn is used in prophetic writings. Further, it should
be noted that apart from three occurrences in Amos, four in Isaiah, and
one in Micah, all the others are in materials coming from the late seventh
century and after, particularly Jeremiah and Ezekiel. The following are
typical uses of this phrase:

> a. Amos 3:10-11
>   "They do not know how to do right, " says the Lord,
>   "those who store up violence and robbery in their
>   strongholds. "
>   Lākēn thus says the Lord God:
>   "An adversary shall surround the land,
>   and bring down your defences from you,
>   and your strongholds shall be plundered. "

---

[12]Quotations will be taken from the RSV when citing examples unless
otherwise indicated.

[13]Variation in the particular form of the divine name will not constitute
a significant variant for the purposes of a study of this phrase.

Isaiah 28:15-16

    Because you have said, "We have made a covenant with death,
        and with Sheol we have an agreement;
  when the overwhelming scourge passes through
    it will not come to us;
  for we have made lies our refuge,
    and in falsehood we have taken shelter";
lākēn thus says the Lord God,
"Behold, I am laying in Zion for a foundation
  a stone, a tested stone,
a precious cornerstone, of a sure foundation:
  'He who believes will not be in haste.'

These texts as do others,[14] demonstrate clearly the relational function of lākēn. The term appears, dramatically, immediately preceding the ear-catching "thus says the Lord." Yet, lākēn would be misread if it was interpreted as discontinuous with what precedes! Rather, it connects one kind of language with another. It forbids that hearer or reader stop prematurely or fail to recognize the proper context crucial for understanding. At the same time, lākēn lends emphasis by directing attention to what will follow, prompting the audience to a mood of anticipation. This manner of employing lākēn is by far the most frequent.

    b. Amos 5:16-17

Lākēn thus says the Lord, the God of hosts, the Lord:
"In all the squares there shall be wailing;
  and in all the streets they shall say, 'Alas! Alas!'
They shall call the farmers to mourning
  and to wailing those who are skilled in lamentation,
and in all vineyards there shall be wailing,
  for I will pass through the midst of you,"
                    says the Lord.

    Isaiah 29:22

Lākēn thus says the Lord, who redeemed Abraham, concerning the house of Jacob:
"Jacob shall no more be ashamed,
  no more shall his face grow pale."

---

[14] Amos 7:17; Is. 30:12; Mic. 2:3; Zech. 1:16; Jer. 7:20, 9:6,14, 11:11, 22,et al; Ez. 5:7, 8, 11:7, 13:13, 20, et al; 2 Kings 1:4, 21:12.

In examples such as these[15] lākēn stands as the introductory term of a literary unit. One may interpret this as the result of faulty redaction or transmission of the original material.[16] Or one might contend that in such examples only the distinctive word of judgment has been preserved and should be read against any of numerous statements of accusation found in the surrounding context. But, in either instance, it remains significant that it made sense, by error or design, to recount a word delivered by the prophet with an initial lākēn. To be sure, "thus says the Lord" can stand alone, but it was not considered nonsensical to begin with lākēn!

Perhaps the clue for understanding this phenomenon is to be found in a text like I Kings 22:18-19:

> And the king of Israel said to Jehoshaphat, "Did I not tell you that he would not prophesy good concerning me, but evil?" And Micaiah said, "Lākēn hear the word of the Lord: I saw the Lord sitting on his throne, and all the host of heaven standing beside him on his right hand and on his left.

Or again, Job 20:1-2:

> Then Zophar the Naamathite answered:
> "Lākēn my thoughts answer me,
>   because of my haste within me.

---

[15]Is. 37:33; Jer. 11:21, 18:13, 22:18; Ez. 31:10, 34:20; 2 Kings 19:32.

[16]James Mays, Amos (Philadelphia: The Westminster Press, 1969), pp. 96-97, argues: " 'Therefore' at the beginning of v. 16 points back to an accusation which cannot be found in the exhortation in 14f.; in Amos 'therefore' always binds the two parts of an announcement of judgment together (3.11; 4.12; 5.11; 6.7; 7.17). Taken together vv. 12 and 16f. compose a coherent saying made up of accusation and announcement of punishment." Mays is correct in his basic understanding of the usual function of lākēn, but he does not explain how such an interruption of the normal flow could have been tolerated or promulgated.

Such texts[17] clearly utilize lākēn for emphasis, and further, they disclose a nuance of responsiveness. A speaker can begin appropriately with lākēn as an indication that he is responding to another person or situation. In divine speech frequently lākēn introduces a word spoken in response to some expressed situation or in answer to some implied question or criticism of God by the people. On the other hand, when used in conversation between men, any response might possibly be prefaced with lākēn.[18]

2. There is a second phrase, somewhat like the much more frequent phrase just considered, which occurs twice: "lākēn nᵉ'um YHWH," with the latter two words frequently translated "says the Lord" or "declares the Lord" or "utterance of the Lord."

> Isaiah 1:24
> Lākēn the Lord says, the Lord of hosts, the Mighty One
>   of Israel:
> "Ah, I will vent my wrath on my enemies,
>   and avenge myself on my foes."

> I Samuel 2:30
> Lākēn the Lord the God of Israel declares: 'I promised
> that your house and the house of your father should go
> in and out before me for ever'; but now the Lord declares:
> 'Far be it from me; for those who honor me I will honor,
> and those who despise me shall be lightly esteemed.'

In each of these texts lākēn introduces an emphatic phrase which marks the beginning of another step in the overall argument being presented. Lākēn clearly indicates that other words have preceded while at the same time pointing ahead to what follows. This rhetorical function comes more sharply into focus when the enigmatic nᵉ'um YHWH is left untranslated, for then there is no temptation to hear lākēn as

---

[17] Other examples include: Gen. 30:15; Judg. 8:7, 11:8; I Sam. 28:2.

[18] Martin J. Buss, The Prophetic Word of Hosea: A Morphological Study (Berlin: Alfred Töpelmann, 1969), p. 78, properly emphasizes this function of lākēn.

simply part of the so-called "messenger formula."[19] Lākēn functions to signal an advance in the discussion, to prompt attention to the next important, often crucial, word about to be declared.

    3. In fifteen texts lākēn is used with some form of the verb "to hear" or "to listen." There are slight variations in the person and number of the verb, but in each instance the imperative is employed in an emphatic address to the hearer(s).

      a. Isaiah 28:14
        Lākēn hear the word of the Lord, you scoffers,
          who rule this people in Jerusalem!

      Jeremiah 42:13-15
      But if you say, 'We will not remain in this land,'
      disobeying the voice of the Lord your God and saying,
      'No, we will go to the land of Egypt, where we shall
      not see war, or hear the sound of the trumpet, or be
      hungry for bread, and we will dwell there, 'wᵉ'attāh
      lākēn hear the word of the Lord, O remnant of Judah . . . .[20]

---

[19]For a discussion of the "messenger formula" see: G. von Rad, Old Testament Theology, trans. D. M. G. Stalker, (Edinburgh, London: Oliver and Boyd, 1965), v. II, pp. 36ff. von Rad rightly recognizes that lākēn functions to connect a diatribe and threat into one unit of address (pp. 37-38), but he wrongly leaves the impression that lākēn somehow indicates that the words following are "justified" because of what has preceded. One might argue that "diatribe" justifies "threat," but not from some assumed meaning of lākēn.

[20]It should be noted that the RSV translates the italicized words with the one term "then."

Jeremiah 49:20
Lākēn hear the plan which the Lord has made against
Edom and the purposes which he has formed against
the inhabitants of Teman . . . .[21]

Ezekiel 16:35
Lākēn, O harlot, hear the word of the Lord:

These and similar passages[22] make even clearer the manner in which
lākēn serves as a term appropriate to lend emphasis to a response made
in the heat of discussion and controversy. When the speaker prepares to
deliver the "clincher," lākēn is an effective way to begin.

b. Jeremiah 6:17-18
I set watchmen over you, saying,
    'Give heed to the sound of the trumpet!'
But they said, 'We will not give heed.'
Lākēn hear, O nations,
    and know, O congregation, what will happen to them.

Isaiah 51:21
Lākēn hear this, you who are afflicted,
    who are drunk, but not with wine:

Job 32:9-10
It is not the old that are wise,
    nor the aged that understand what is right.
Lākēn I say, 'Listen to me;
    let me also declare my opinion.'

Job 34:10
"Lākēn, hear me, you men of understanding,
far be it from God that he should do wickedness,
and from the Almighty that he should do wrong.

---

[21] The RSV includes part of MT verse 19 in its verse 20.

[22] Jer. 44:26, 50:45; Ez. 34:7, 9, 36:4; I Kings 22:19; 2 Chron. 18:18.

The use of lākēn in these texts, apart from any direct connection with a phrase like "word of the Lord" or "plan of the Lord,"
confirms the point made above in relation to those texts cited in 3a.
To be sure, in Jeremiah 6 and Isaiah 51 the speaker is the Lord himself and thus his word is at stake in the call to hear. But the two texts
in Job show clearly that lākēn was an "attention getter" to be used as
response was made to explicit or implicit criticism. Lākēn was used
to acknowledge that other points had preceded, but also to declare that
an important response was commencing. In commenting on the climactic
character of Isaiah 51:21-23, Professor Muilenburg writes: "The prophet
employs every device to call attention to the importance of the event he
is about to communicate: first, the climactic position of the strophe;
second, the introductory therefore, so characteristic of the introductory
word of the threat (but instead of threat a glowing promise) . . . ."[23]
Indeed, lākēn functions to emphasize a word complex even as trumpets
announce the arrival of royalty.

4. There are seventeen texts in which lākēn is employed with
one of several verbs meaning "to speak" or "declare." Most frequent
is the verb 'āmar, used two times in the Priestly strata of the Pentateuch[24] and eight times in Ezekiel.[25] In Ezekiel the verb dabbēr occurs
twice with lākēn,[26] and hinnābē'is found five times.[27] Typical of this use of

---

[23] James Muilenburg, "Isaiah, Chapters 40-66," The Interpreter's Bible
(New York, Nashville: Abingdon Press, 1956), v. V, p. 605.

[24] Ex. 6:6; Num. 25:12.

[25] Ez. 11:16, 17, 12:23, 28, 14:6, 20:30, 33:25, 36:22.

[26] Ez. 14:4, 20:27.

[27] Ez. 11:4, 36:3, 6, 37:12, 38:14.

lākēn are the following:

a. Exodus 6:5-6
   Moreover I have heard the groaning of the people of
   Israel whom the Egyptians hold in bondage and I have
   remembered my covenant. Lākēn say to the people of
   Israel, 'I am the Lord, and I will bring you out from
   under the burdens of the Egyptians . . . .'

   Ezekiel 11:16-17
   Lākēn say, 'Thus says the Lord God: Though I removed
   them far off among the nations, and though I scattered
   them among the countries, yet I have been a sanctuary
   to them for a while in the countries where they have
   gone! Lākēn say, "Thus says the Lord: I will gather
   you from the peoples, and assemble you out of the
   countries where you have been scattered, and I will
   give you the land of Israel.'

b. Ezekiel 14:3-4
   "Son of man, these men have taken their idols into
   their hearts, and set the stumbling block of their
   iniquity before their faces; should I let myself be
   inquired of at all by them? Lākēn speak to them,
   and say to them, 'Thus says the Lord God: Any
   man of the house of Israel who takes his idols into
   his heart . . . .'

c. Ezekiel 11:2-4
   And he said to me, "Son of man, these are the men
   who devise iniquity and who give wicked counsel in
   this city; who say, 'the time is not near to build
   houses; this city is the caldron, and we are the
   flesh.' Lākēn prophesy against them, prophesy,
   O son of man."

This particular use of lākēn is limited, as noted above, almost
exclusively to Ezekiel. In each instance the phrase introduces a command by God to his spokesman (Ezekiel or Moses) in which the spokesman is directed to speak on behalf of God. Since all of the texts in
question come from material that is at least exilic in age, it may well
be that the use of lākēn in these texts is heavily influenced by the

practice, well-established by then, of including lākēn in prophetic speech in the significant role already noted above. Indeed, the use made here of lākēn is very much like that most frequent placement before "thus says the Lord." However, the "messenger formula" has been dropped and God directly relates the word that is to be announced.

The function of lākēn again can be seen clearly. It stands as an emphatic acknowledgement of what has preceded in the mind of the speaker and as a call to attention to the response about to be revealed. One cannot stop with lākēn, but must go on to what follows. But beyond knowing that something important is about to be spoken, one cannot be certain what will follow. That tension can be relieved only by proceeding, precisely as intended by the user of lākēn!

5. In twenty-four instances lākēn precedes some form of the emphatic particle hinnēh, behold! There seem to be three basic patterns that emerge.

    a. Isaiah 8:5-7
    The Lord spoke to me again: "Because (ya'an) this people have refused the waters of Shiloah that flow gently, and melt in fear before Rezin and the son of Remaliah; wᵉlākēn, behold (hinnēh), the Lord is bringing up (participle) against them the waters of the River, mighty and many, the king of Assyria and all his glory . . . .

    Isaiah 29:13-14
    And the Lord said:
    "Because (ya'an) this people draw near with their mouth
        and honor me with their lips,
        while their hearts are far from me,
    and their fear of me is a commandment of men learned
        by rote;
    lākēn, behold, I(hinnᵉnî) will again (participle) do
        marvelous things with this people,
        wonderful and marvelous;
    and the wisdom of their wise men shall perish,
        and the discernment of their discerning men shall
        be hid. "

Apart from the use in Isaiah 8 quoted above, where the pronominal

suffix is not attached to hinnēh, the pattern here noted has ya῾an used
to introduce a specific problem or concern. Next follows lākēn and
hinn^{e}nî with a participial form of the verb.[28] The presence of ya῾an
underlines dramatically the function lākēn plays in signaling the immi-
nence of a response. The emphatic character of the particular responses
ascribed to God is heightened by the use of hinnēh and the participle.
In view of what has happened, lākēn, God is about to act.

> b. Hosea 2:16
> "Lākēn, behold (hinnēh) I will allure her (participle),
> > and bring her into the wilderness,
> > and speak tenderly to her.
>
> Jeremiah 23:29-30
> Is not my word like fire, says the Lord, and like a
> hammer which breaks the rock in pieces? Lākēn,
> behold, I (hinn^{e}nî) am against the prophets, says the
> Lord, who steal my words from one another.

The particular feature which connects the above examples and
two other occurrences[29] is the absence of any specific term such as
ya῾an, though lākēn is followed by hinnēh or hinn^{e}nî as in the examples
noted in 5a. In Jeremiah both texts have a specially strong impact
because following the lākēn an especially dramatic conclusion is announced. Likewise in Hosea 2, lākēn, twice in the phrase under consideration here, and one other time as well,[30] is used skillfully to

---

[28] Jer. 23:39; Ez. 16:37, 22:19, 25:4, 9, 28:7; I Kings 14:10. There
are three other texts where the form is altered slightly by the absence
of the participle: Ez. 25:7 (perfect), 29:10 (no verb); 2 Kings 22:20
(imperfect).

[29] Hos. 2:8; Jer. 16:21.

[30] Hos. 2:11

focus attention on the announcement of God's intentions as his response to the rebelliousness of his people is unfolded.[31]

      c. Jeremiah 7:32

         Lākēn, behold (hinnēh), the days are coming, says the Lord, when it will no more be called Topheth, or the valley of the son of Hinnom, but the valley of Slaughter: for they will bury in Topheth, because there is no room elsewhere.

         Jeremiah 48:12

         Lākēn, behold (hinnēh), the days are coming, says the Lord, when I shall send to him tilters who will tilt him, and empty his vessels, and break his jars in pieces.

In these and other examples[32] lākēn is used to introduce the response of God, and coupled as it is with the phrase "the days are coming" lākēn is made even more emphatic. If God's judgments sometimes seem slow, "lākēn, behold, the days are coming . . . ."

      6. In a few texts[33] lākēn is used in close connection with an oath.

---

[31] James Mays, Hosea (Philadelphia: The Westminster Press, 1969) pp. 36-37, 44, recognizes the manner in which lākēn is used to develop the prophet's thought. Mays suggests that three originally distinct oracles may have been worked together into one, but for our purposes it is significant that lākēn could be retained and used pointedly to direct the flow of the piece. Indeed, James Muilenburg, "Isaiah," op. cit., p. 389, points out the importance of repetition in Hebrew poetry, and it may be the case that Hosea 2 represents a well-calculated and well-executed piece of Hebrew rhetoric.

[32] Jer. 16:14, 19:6, 23:7, 49:2, 51:52.

[33] Zeph. 2:9; Ez. 5:11, 35:6, 11; cf. also Ez. 17:19; Jer. 49:20.

For instance:

> Zephaniah 2:8-9
> "I have heard the taunts of Moab and the revilings of
>   the Ammonites,
> how they have taunted my people and made boasts against
>   their territory.
> Lākēn, as I live," says the Lord of hosts, the God of Israel,
> Moab shall become like Sodom, and the Ammonites like
>   Gomorrah . . . .

or again:

> Ezekiel 35:5-6
> Because (yaʻan) you cherished perpetual enmity, and
> gave over the people of Israel to the power of the sword
> at the time of their calamity, at the time of their final
> punishment; lākēn, as I live, says the Lord God, I will
> prepare you for blood, and blood shall pursue you . . . .

Such texts, along with the problem already noted of using English
"therefore" as a translation for lākēn, lend support to Goldbaum's contention that lākēn functions principally to introduce a vow.[34] However,
problems arise which challenge Goldbaum's thesis when these texts
are examined carefully. In Ezekiel 35:6 and 11, for instance, when
the overall context is considered, it is important to recognize that
each clause introduced by lākēn is preceded by a phrase introduced
by yaʻan. This is certainly similar to the pattern noted in 5a above.
It may well be that here, as in many other passages, the pattern of
prime importance is the sequence yaʻan-lākēn rather than the connection of lākēn with the following oath.

Again a text like Ezekiel 5:11 on the surface seems to offer
good support for understanding lākēn as integrally related to the oath,
but when the larger context is viewed, problems arise.

---

[34] Goldbaum, op. cit., p. 133: "לכן performs the function of introducing a vow. The vows may be divided, for our purposes, into two
main categories, 'vows of harm' (punishment, revenge, etc.) and
'vows of benefit' (reward, assurance, etc.) . . . . In addition to
appearing before 'vows of harm' and 'vows of benefit,' occasionally לכן
introduces a kind of adjuration where one imposes a vow on another."

Ezekiel 5:7-11

Lākēn thus says the Lord God: Because (yaᶜan) you
are more turbulent than the nations that are round
about you, and have not walked in my statutes or
kept my ordinances, but have acted according to the
ordinances of the nations that are round about you;
lākēn thus says the Lord God: Behold, I (hinnᵉnî),
even I, am against you; and I will execute judgments
in the midst of you in the sight of the nations. And
because (yaᶜan) of all your abominations I will do
with you what I have never yet done, and the like of
which I will never do again. Lākēn fathers shall eat
their sons in the midst of you, and sons shall eat
their fathers; and I will execute judgments on you, and any
of you who survive I will scatter to all the winds. Lākēn,
as I live, says the Lord God, surely ('im lō') because
(yaᶜan) you have defiled my sanctuary with all your
detestable things and all your abominations, therefore
I will cut you down; my eye will not spare, and I will
have no pity.

In this passage the "yaᶜan--lākēn," the "lākēn--thus says the Lord,"
and the "lākēn--hinnēh" patterns noted above are employed. The
four occurrences of laken in this brief passage punctuate the divine
speech with an ever-increasing mood of expectancy. God is about to
issue a crucial word. In view of what has preceded God is about to
announce a decision. Lākēn, lākēn! And then the climactic word is
heralded: lākēn, and underlined by a divine oath, "as I live." That
lākēn is followed by an oath seems incidental. Its real function is
claiming the attention of the audience for whatever dramatic statement
is about to follow.

A similar reservation must be made with regard to Isaiah 5:8ff
which Goldbaum cites as supporting evidence for his contention concerning the function of lākēn. To be sure, Isaiah 5:8-9 does preserve
a "woe" oracle with the announcement of judgment taking the form of
an oath introduced by "surely" ('im lō'). But it is not so clearly the
case that the following occurrences of lākēn in 5:13, 14, 24, are to be

understood as standing in parallel with 'im lō' as Goldbaum suggests. [35]
In texts like Ezekiel 17:19, 35:6, and Jeremiah 49:20 lākēn is used to
to introduce material that explicitly uses the 'im lō'formula. This
would make it seem unlikely that lākēn would be used as a parallel
term. Rather, without entering into questions concerning the present
arrangement of the material in Isaiah 5, [36] it is more likely that lākēn
is once again used to draw attention to emphatic declarations. In 5:13,
14, clearly, and probably in 5:24 as well, no oath is at stake, but
rather lākēn serves as a verbal asterisk to catch attention and help
focus on the crucial matter. Thus, while lākēn does at times appear
in contexts where vows are made and while lākēn does lend a note of
seriousness and certainty to the material that follows, it is not accurate
simply to identify lākēn with a vow. When this is done, the relational
function which has already become so apparent is likely to go unnoticed,
and the force of lākēn is significantly lessened.

     7. There are three texts where lākēn is immediately followed
by the negative lō'. In Judges 10:13 and Numbers 20:12[37] usage is
quite in keeping with examples noted above. This is also the case with
Micah 2:5, but the Micah passage warrants a closer look in view of the
larger context.

---

[35]Ibid., p. 134.

[36]Otto Kaiser, Isaiah 1-12 (Philadelphia: The Westminster Press, 1972)
pp. 64-65, 68, discusses some of the problems; cf. also, R. B. Y. Scott,
"Isaiah, Chapters 1-39," The Interpreter's Bible (New York, Nashville:
Abingdon Press, 1956), pp. 198-201.

[37]Buss, op. cit., p. 78, has noted that the ya'an --lākēn pattern
found in Num. 20:12 and in numerous other passages noted above is
standard in the deuteronomic history, Ezekiel and P.

Micah 2:1-5

Woe to those who devise wickedness
    and work evil upon their beds!
When the morning dawns, they perform it,
    because it is in the power of their hand.
They covet fields, and seize them;
    and houses, and take them away;
They oppress a man and his house,
    a man and his inheritance.
Lākēn thus says the Lord:
Behold (hinn^{e}nî), against this family I am devising evil,
    from which you cannot remove your necks;
and you shall walk haughtily,
    for it will be an evil time.
In that day they shall take up a taunt song against you,
    and wail with bitter lamentation,
and say, "We are utterly ruined;
    he changes the portion of my people;
how he removes it from me!
    Among our captors he divides our fields."
Lākēn you will have none to cast the line by lot
    in the assembly of the Lord.

It seems apparent in this passage that lākēn first marks the point where the divine reaction to the situation which has prompted the "woe" is to be pronounced. Then, with great emphasis and in direct response to the lament sung by the people, the final judgment is ushered in: "Lākēn you will have none to cast the line by lot in the assembly of the Lord."

8. In both Amos 6:7 and Judges 11:8 the same phraseology is encountered when lākēn is followed directly by 'attāh. It is unlikely that these two instances can be considered as evidence for a well-defined idiom, but for this study both of these texts offer interesting material.

a. Amos 6:4-7

> Woe to those who lie upon beds of ivory,
>> and stretch themselves upon their couches,
> and eat lambs from the flock,
>> and calves from the midst of the stall;
> who sing idle songs to the sound of the harp,
>> and like David invent for themselves instruments of
>>> music;
> who drink wine in bowls,
>> and anoint themselves with the finest oils,
>> but are not grieved over the ruin of Joseph!
> Lākēn they shall now be the first of those to go into exile,
>> and the revelry of those who stretch themselves
>>> shall pass away.

In this passage once again lākēn serves to mark the transition from the accusation expressed so movingly through use of the "woe"[38] to the declaration of God's judgment upon the wayward people. Considering the context and in terms of the way lākēn is used elsewhere in Amos,[39] there is no doubt that what will follow lākēn is the statement of divine judgment. But in a text like this it is possible to read lākēn in a rather wooden manner as a causal connective and miss the dramatic effect produced if lākēn rather is understood as breaking the mood of lamentation by announcing that God's response is at hand: here it comes, get ready!

---

[38]Cf. Mays, Amos, op. cit., pp. 103, 114, for a concise statement concerning the mood provoked by the use of "woe."

[39]In Amos 3:11, 5:16, 7:17 lākēn is used explicitly with "thus says the Lord." In 4:12 and 5:11 the context makes it clear that a divine word is being introduced though no specific formula is used. 5:13 is the only text in Amos, apart from 6:7, where lākēn cannot clearly be shown to introduce a divine word of judgment, and as Mays, Amos, ibid., pp. 96-98, points out, 5:13 may well be a later addition from someone of the Wisdom tradition. In passing it is worth noting with regard to 5:13 that whoever its author lākēn certainly does not lend itself readily to be interpreted as a causal conjunction. Rather it is more appropriately understood as indicating a response evoked by the situation described in the preceding verse(s).

b. Judges 11:6-10
And they said to Jephthah, "Come and be our leader,
that we may fight with the Ammonites." But Jephthah
said to the elders of Gilead, "Did you not hate me,
and drive me out of my father's house? Why have
you come to me now when you are in trouble?" And
the elders of Gilead said to Jephthah, "Lākēn we
have turned to you now, that you may go with us and
fight with the Ammonites, and be our head over all
the inhabitants of Gilead." Jephthah said to the elders
of Gilead, "If you bring me home again to fight with
the Ammonites, and the Lord gives them over to me,
I will be your head." And the elders of Gilead said
to Jephthah, "The Lord will be witness between us;
we will surely ('im lō') do as you say."

The function of lākēn as introducing a response is nowhere
more clear than here. In heated discussion with Jephthah the elders
of Gilead first urge him to come with them, but when reminded that
they have not always been so eager for his leadership, the elders
respond, "Lāken 'attāh," which the RSV renders, "That is why (we
have turned to you) now." This translation is misleading because the
function of lākēn is apparently not recognized. Lākēn joins both the
arguments just presented and what is to follow. "Granted," the elders
say, "but now we are changing our minds!" Lākēn indicates both that
the former statements are recognized and that a response is about to
be made. In this particular passage the climax is reached when the
elders finally swear an oath to show their utmost seriousness in the
matter. Lākēn, which is used to introduce the second response, is
not an oath--the oath is reserved for the final note of emphasis. Lākēn
is used to acknowledge that a discussion is under way and that other
points have already been made while urging the audience to listen to
the next word with the expectancy that something significant, a turning
point, is about to be recorded.

The use of lākēn in Judges 11:8 is not immediately transparent.
Were it not for the numerous other texts already considered, this text
might be particularly bothersome for the translator. Such seems to
have been the case in the LXX where lākēn is rendered ouch houtōs,

which would seem to reflect a MT which read lō' kēn. If Judges 11:8 were the only place where such a problem was found, it would probably be insignificant, but there are at least fifteen other texts where the LXX seems to have interpreted lākēn as lō' kēn. [40] This led Haupt to the conclusion that at points in the MT[41] lākēn should be understood as representing the combination of the negative la with the adverb kēn which would then be properly translated "not so" as in the LXX. [42] It is certainly the case that the term lō' kēn is found in the MT[43] and is often used in situations where one speaker is responding to another, situations not unlike those in which lākēn is often used. [44] Thus, granting that the LXX is correct in translating lākēn at points with ouch houtōs , though there is no agreement on all those occurrences of lākēn where such a translation is appropriate, [45] the question still remains as to why the LXX so translated.

---

[40]Gen. 4:15, 30:15; Jud. 8:7; I Kings 22:19; 2 Kings 1:4, 6, 16, 19:32, 21:12, 22:20; 2 Chr. 18:18; Is. 10:16, 16:7; Jer. 2:33; Job 20:2.

[41]Haupt, op. cit., p. 104, cites Gen. 4:15, Job 20:2, and Jud. 11:8 as examples.

[42]Ibid.

[43]Gen. 48:18; Ex. 10:11; Num. 12:7; Dt. 18:14; 2 Sam. 18:14, 20:21, 23:5; 2 Kings 7:9; Is. 10:7, 16:6; Jer. 48:30; Job 9:35; Ps. 1:4.

[44]Cf. for instance Gen. 48:18; Ex. 10:11; 2 Sam. 18:14, 20:21; 2 Kings 7:9.

[45]Pedersen, op. cit., p. 117, for instance, does not agree with Haupt that Gen. 4:15 or Judg. 11:8 should be translated as does the LXX but would understand the meaning here to be "under these circumstances." Koehler-Baumgartner, op. cit., p. 482, is prepared to emend Gen. 4:15, I Kings 22:19, 2 Chr. 18:18, and Jer. 5:2 to lō' kēn.

Was it because the text was actually different? Or is Haupt's suggestion noted above correct? Or could it be that the LXX preserves a
nuance of lākēn that has been slighted because the causal note has
become so dominant? As may be deduced from what has already
been said in this study, the third alternative is far the best in light
of the evidence. It is quite appropriate to respond lākēn and mean
as in Genesis 4:15 "Yes I hear you, but no, that will not be the case!"
The LXX correctly translates lākēn to convey this function. Or again,
in Genesis 30:15 in response to Leah's accusing question, Rachel can
reply lākēn and indicate that she has heard the criticism but intends to
give answer that will address the situation. It seems better to consider
closely the various ways lākēn was used and to adjust our translations
rather than to jump too quickly to emend the text or to assume several
different terms now hidden beneath the same grammatical form. [46]

III

When we turn our attention to the use of lākēn in various literary
types, we approach our subject from a different angle. While lākēn is
used in a large number of varying materials, there are only a relative
few where it occurs with enough regularity to be considered "typical"
of the genre.

1. The most obvious literary type in which lākēn is to be found
is the judgment speech[47] or prophecy of disaster. [48] The basic form,

---

[46]Haupt, op. cit., pp. 104-105, in dealing with a number of other texts
where the LXX has used the same translation as noted above, e.g. Gen.
30:15; Jud. 8:7; I Kings 22:19; 2 Kings 1:4, 6, argues for another derivation of lākēn which carries the meaning "quite correct" or "all right."
That lākēn may carry such a meaning at times seems quite possible, but
the argument used to substantiate the suggestion is not convincing or consistent.

[47]C. Westermann, Basic Forms of Prophetic Speech, trans. H. White
(Philadelphia: The Westminster Press, 1969), pp. 65ff.

[48]K. Koch, The Growth of the Biblical Tradition: The Form-Critical
Method, trans. S. Cupitt (New York: Charles Scribner's Sons, 1969)
pp. 192ff.

to use Koch's terminology, includes (1) an indication of the situation,
(2) the prediction of disaster, and (3) the concluding characterization.
Preceding (1) there may be a command to the prophet and then an
appeal by the prophet to claim the attention of his audience. The
indication of the situation itself may be initiated with the term ya'an,
by a question, or some other means. Following (1) come both lākēn
and the "messenger formula," "thus says the Lord," followed immediately by (2) the prediction of disaster. The concluding characterization is usually a brief statement introduced by kî which concludes the
oracle. A good example of the basic form is Jeremiah 28:15-16:

> And Jeremiah the prophet said to the prophet Hananiah,
> "Listen, Hananiah, the Lord has not sent you, and you
> have made this people trust in a lie. Lākēn thus says
> the Lord: 'Behold, I will remove you from the face of
> the earth. This very year you shall die, because you
> have uttered rebellion against the Lord.' "

In this passage and in others,[49] where the basic pattern
described above is followed fairly closely, the function of lākēn is
clearly to connect one part of the statement with another. Indeed,
it is easy to understand why the English term "therefore" seems
most appropriate as a linking term, particularly in those many texts[50]
where ya'an, "because," stands as introduction to the indication of
the situation.

However, there are many texts where the material is not
found in exactly the form described above. For instance:

---

[49]2 Kings 1:3-4, 6; Amos 3:9-11, 4:12, 7:16-17; Is. 1:24, 7:14,
28:14-16; Jer. 6:14-15, 8:8-12; cf. also Num. 20:12.

[50]I Kings 14:7-10; 2Kings 1:15-16, 21:11-12; Is. 8:6-7, 29:13-14,
30:12-13; Jer. 19:3-6, 23:37-39, 29:30-32, 35:18-19; Ez. 5:7-11, 13:8-13,
20-23, 16:35-37, 22:19, 23:35, 25:3-4, 6-7, 8-9, 12-13, 15-16, 26:2-3,
28:6-7, 29:6-10, 34:7-9, 36:1-7, 13-14.

Amos 5:10-11
They hate him who reproves in the gate,
   and they abhor him who speaks the truth.
Lākēn because (ya'an) you trample upon the poor
   and take from him exactions of wheat,
You have built houses of hewn stone,
   but you shall not dwell in them . . . .

Jeremiah 5:14
Lākēn thus says the Lord, the God of hosts;
"Because (ya'an) they have spoken this word,
behold, I am making my words in your mouth a fire,
and this people wood, and the fire shall devour them.

Texts like these,[51] particularly when studied against the background
already presented above in this study, unsettle the sure conviction
that the primary role of lākēn is to join "cause" and "effect" and
that "therefore" is finally an adequate translation. For in these texts
the "cause" is presented after lākēn or is presented as part of the
speech lākēn is used to announce.

     Thus, while it is appropriate to say that lākēn is often used in
examples of the prophecy of disaster, it does not always stand in one,
fixed position. Further, the function is not of joining (1) with (2) though (2)
in many instances does respond directly to (1). Lākēn does regularly
precede the divine response to the situation at hand, but not so much
from grammatical necessity as for rhetorical effect.

     2. Another closely related literary type in which lākēn is em-
ployed is the prophecy of salvation.[52] The form is practically identical with the prophecy of disaster except for a prediction of salvation
standing in place of the prediction of disaster. For example:

---

[51]Mic. 3:6, 12; Jer. 25:8, 35:17; Ez. 15:8, 21:29, 31:10, 34:20-21.

[52]Koch, op. cit., pp. 213 ff.

Jeremiah 35:18-19
But to the house of the Rechabites Jeremiah said, "Thus
says the Lord of Hosts, the God of Israel: Because you
have obeyed the command of Jonadab your father, and
kept all his precepts, and done all that he commanded you,
lākēn thus says the Lord of Hosts, the God of Israel:
Jonadab the son of Rechab shall never lack a man to
stand before me. "

Lākēn, in texts like this,[53] is used just as in the prophecy of disaster.

There are two points to notice, however, in connection with
this literary type. First, there are a number of examples[54] where
lākēn is not used at all. Second, in some of the texts where lākēn
is used it is in a very loose relationship with the context. Indeed,
Scott, in commenting on Isaiah 30:18, says, "The break in continuity
at vs. 18 is unusually abrupt . . . . Therefore in vs. 18 does not
establish a logical connection with the preceding oracle; like other
occurrences of 'therefore' in 10:24; 29:22, it seems in later style
to have little more force than 'Behold' when introducing a promise."[55]
These two different sets of data point in the same direction: lākēn
serves principally a rhetorical role of heightening the hearer's
anticipation and thereby giving emphasis to the word thus introduced.
Thus, lākēn is not an essential element in any context, but it is a
term that can be used effectively in a number of different situations.

3. Because lākēn is found in the context of some "Woe oracles, "
some attention should be given this particular genre. The form is
characterized by an introductory hôy followed by a participle or some
substantive descriptive of the subject of the oracle. This in turn is
followed by a participial clause and sometimes other explanatory
sentences using finite verbal forms to specify the offense. There may
even be a series of short "woes" which describe the situation. Finally,

---

[53] Num. 25:12; 2 Kings 19:32, 22:18-20; Is. 51:2, 52:6, 53:12, 61:7;
Zech. 1:16; Mic. 5:2.

[54] I Kings 17:14; 2 Kings 3:16; Jer. 28:2, 32:14-15, 34:4-5.

[55] Scott, "Isaiah, Chapters 1-39, " op. cit. , p. 334.

an announcement of judgment brings the "woe oracle" to its climax. [56]

It is clear that lākēn is not an indispensable element in the form of the "woe oracle" from the fact that there are a number of texts where lākēn is absent. [57] Nevertheless, even in its absence, the climactic response to the situation can be present as in Isaiah 45:9ff:

> "Woe to him who strives with his Maker,
>   an earthen vessel with the potter!
> Does the clay say to him who fashions it, 'What are
>   you making'?
>   or 'Your work has no handles'?
> Woe to him who says to a father, 'What are you begetting?'
>   or to a woman, 'With what are you in travail?' "
> Thus says the Lord, the Holy One of Israel, and his Maker:
> "Will you question me about my children,
>   or command me concerning the work of my hands?

The fact that lākēn is not always used alerts against any rigid or mechanical view of the function or meaning of this term.

Since the genre does not necessitate the presence of this term, what is added to a text where it appears? Let us consider Isaiah 5:8ff once again[58] to catch a sense of the way lākēn can function in such a

---

[56]Cf. E. Gerstenberger, "The Woe-Oracles of the Prophets," JBL 81 (1962), pp. 249-263; J. Williams, "The Alas-Oracles of the Eighth Century Prophets," HUCA 38 (1967), pp. 75-91.

[57]Amos 5:18-20; Is. 1:4, 10:1-3, 5, 17:12, 18:1, 28:1-4, 29:1-4, 15, 30:1-3, 31:1-4, 33:1, 55:1; Hab. 2:6, 9, 12, 15, 19; Nah. 3:1-5; Jer. 22:13, 30:7, 47:6, 48:1, 50:27; Zech. 2:10-11, 11:17.

[58]See above, section II 6.

context. [59] As the text comes to us now, hôy, "woe," occurs six
times (vv. 8, 11, 18, 20, 21, 22) and lākēn three times (vv. 13, 14,
24). It may well be that 5:24 was intended to serve as the judgment
which would fittingly bring to a close this collection of "woe oracles."
If so, the lākēn sets apart the word of judgment and calls special
attention to the dire consequences of rejecting the divine law. In
verses 13 and 14 lākēn also serves to draw attention to the particular word which follows, but in neither instance is a judgment, as
such, announced. Rather, it is as if a parenthesis had been drawn
in the midst of the woes to give the hearer time to reflect on the awful
condition of God's people. The inevitable and terrible picture evoked
by the cry of "woe" is suspended in the midst of its unfolding that the
hearer may consider what is already happening to the people as they
go into exile and as death asserts its awesome power. The pause is
accomplished by the twofold lākēn, but the mood of woe is not diminished in the process. Lākēn . . . lākēn--the flow is temporarily
slowed--but then the unrelenting surge continues with hôy . . . ,
hôy . . . , hôy . . . , hôy, until that final lākēn marks the announcement of that tragic but obvious outcome. Lākēn does not command a
part in the literary form, but by its presence the drama is magnified.

    4. Finally, [60] there are a number of passages which cannot be
grouped by literary type but which nevertheless share the fact that
lākēn is used to introduce a response in answer to one or several
rhetorical questions immediately preceding. One [61] such passage is

---

[59]Cf. also Amos 6:1-7; Micah 2:1-5; Is. 1:24; Zeph. 3:1-8; Jer. 22:18,
23:1-2; Ez. 13:3-8, 18-20, 34:2-7.

[60]In the course of this study, particularly in section II, attention was
given to uses of lākēn which happened to occur in relation to various
literary types. The oath (I Sam. 3:14, 28:2; Jer. 5:2, 14, 49:20;
Ez. 5:11, 17:19, 35:6, 11; Zeph. 2:9), the rîb (Jer. 2:33), the lament
(Mic. 1:14; Is. 16:7, 26:14; Jer. 18:21), and other literary types should
be considered, but in each instance the use of lākēn cannot be said to be
characteristic of the form but rather one of several rhetorical devices
used to heighten the impact of the form employed. Thus, we will not
look in detail at some of these literary types though lākēn is found in
connection with some of the specific examples that have been preserved
in our material.

[61]Other passages that might be mentioned include: Num. 16:11;
Jer. 6:15, 8:10, 12, 23:30, 30:16; Ez. 18:30.

Isaiah 10:15-16:

> Shall the ax vaunt itself over him who hews with it,
>   or the saw magnify itself against him who wields it?
> As if a rod should wield him who lifts it,
>   or as if a staff should lift him who is not wood!
> Lākēn the Lord, the Lord of hosts,
>   will send wasting sickness among his stout warriors,
> and under his glory a burning will be kindled,
>   like the burning of fire.

The function here is emphatically to indicate that answer will be made and soon, and such an example serves only as one last reminder of a pattern already observed repeatedly.

IV

On the basis of the preceding we can summarize the way lākēn is used and designate "meanings" which are appropriate for translation. No one translation can possibly serve for the many different contexts in which we have encountered lākēn, but by differentiating between the several functions of this particle certain suggestions for translation can be made.

First, concerning the usage most widely assumed, lākēn does at times function in a manner very near to "therefore." When a prophet points at the transgressions of his people and then introduces his announcement of God's impending judgment with lākēn, the very certainty of the prophet in such a situation does give to lākēn the sound of a causal conjunction. Because the sin of the people is so manifest and because God will not allow such conditions to go unchallenged, then with great confidence one can expect God's intervention. Any words used to announce such divine decisions, such as lākēn, are colored by the context. Thus, there are occasions when "then," "thus," "so," "therefore" are the best terms to convey the assurance expressed by the speaker in his address. What must be understood, however, is that lākēn does not carry such a meaning by itself in every instance, but takes on this nuance by association with the particular mode of speech. Lākēn serves only to claim the attention of the hearer for what comes next, but in a context like that described above it may be rendered "therefore" because God's response is certain and is provoked by his people's waywardness.

At the other extreme are those texts where lākēn is used to begin a statement that is in no way connected with what has preceded. Here lākēn functions only as an "attention getter," a term utilized to initiate a speech so that no important word is lost because the audience is not yet "tuned in." In contemporary speech there are many such terms: "hey," "boy," "wow," "golly," "now hear this," and so on. Such terms do not communicate much, but rather allow time for the hearer to get ready to concentrate on the important information which will follow. If one walks into a room and says, "Let me tell you!", he is usually not asking permission to speak but is announcing that he is about to speak and thinks he has something to say. In such an instance he could say lākēn and properly declare his intentions.

Lastly, the primary function of lākēn is seen in those numerous contexts in which lākēn serves as "conversation director." That is, lākēn reminds the hearer that a discussion, a dialogue, is in process. The preceding words make what follows necessary or understandable. With an emphatic term which signals, perhaps accompanied by a physical gesture like raising a hand or the voice, the speaker acknowledges what has gone before and makes ready to reveal his next move, his response. Lākēn in such instances functions to heighten expectancy, to move the hearer to the edge of his seat. Contemporary equivalents to lākēn are expressions like "sure I understand, so here's what I'm going to do" or "granted! but now listen to my side" or "yes that's right, and what's more" or "indeed, and further." A one-word translation is difficult because lākēn points both to what has come before and what follows. To choose a translation which neglects this nuance is to do disservice to the original material.

There is no simple formula which will automatically determine which of the above three functions and consequent meanings is operative in a given context. Rather, the interpreter can only be urged to keep the range of function in mind as he seeks to translate for the modern reader. Perhaps this study will help sharpen our sensitivities to one more term much used in Hebrew rhetoric. If so, lākēn, we are one step nearer than when we began!

ADDITIONS TO A BIBLIOGRAPHY OF JAMES MUILENBURG'S WRITINGS

Ivan Jay Ball, Jr.

San Francisco Theological Seminary

Works published prior to 1962 are for the most part given in "A Bibliography of James Muilenburg's Writings" by R. Lansing Hicks in Israel's Prophetic Heritage: Essays in honor of James Muilenburg, Edited by Bernhard W. Anderson and Walter Harrelson, New York: Harper & Brothers, Publishers, 1962, pp. 233-242.

CONTRIBUTIONS TO BOOKS

"The 'Office' of the Prophet in Ancient Israel," in The Bible in Modern Scholarship: Papers read at the 100th meeting of the Society of Biblical Literature, December 28-30, 1964. Edited by J. Philip Hyatt. Nashville: Abingdon, 1965, pp. 74-97.

"A Liturgy on the Triumphs of Yahweh," in Studia Biblica et Semitica: Theodoro Christiano Vriezen Dedicata. Edited by W. C. van Unnik and A. S. van der Woude. Wageningen: H. Veenman en Zonen, 1966, pp.233-251.

The Psalms: A Form-Critical Introduction by Hermann Gunkel with an Introduction by James Muilenburg. Facet Books. Biblical Series--19. Philadelphia: Fortress Press, 1967, pp. iii-ix.

"The Intercession of the Covenant Mediator (Exodus 33:1a, 12-17)," in Words and Meanings: Essays Presented to David Winton Thomas on his retirement from Regius Professorship of Hebrew in the University of Cambridge, 1968. Edited by Peter R. Ackroyd and Barnabas Lindars. Cambridge: At the University Press, 1968, pp. 159-181.

Lectures on the Religion of the Semites: The Fundamental Institutions[3] by W. Robertson Smith with an Introduction and Additional Notes by S. A. Cook [ed. 1927], Prolegomenon by James Muilenburg [pp. 1-27]. Library of Biblical Studies. New York: Ktav, 1969.

"The Terminology of Adversity in Jeremiah," in Translating & Understanding the Old Testament: Essays in Honor of Herbert Gordon May. Edited by Harry Thomas Frank and William L. Reed. Nashville: Abingdon, 1970, pp. 42-63.

"Baruch the Scribe," in Proclamation and Presence: Old Testament Essays in Honour of Gwynne Henton Davies. Edited by John I. Durham and J. R. Porter. Richmond: John Knox Press, 1970, pp. 215-238.

CONTRIBUTIONS TO COMMENTARIES, DICTIONARIES AND ENCYCLOPEDIAS

"Old Testament Prophecy" and "Ezechiel," in Peake's Commentary on the Bible, Edited by Matthew Black & H. H. Rowley. New York: Thomas Nelson and Sons, Ltd., 1962, pp. 475-83, 568-90.

Consultant and Contributor to The Interpreter's Dictionary of the Bible. An Illustrated Encyclopedia in four volumes. New York: Abingdon, 1962. Vol. A-D, "Ataroth" p. 305; "Ataroth-Addar" pp. 305-06. Vol. E-J, "Gilgal" pp. 398-99; "Holiness" pp. 616-25; "Jeremiah the Prophet" pp. 823-35. Vol. K-Q, "Magor-Missabib" p. 226; "Merathaim" p. 351; "Mizpah" pp. 407-09; "Nehelam" pp. 532-33; "Obadiah, Book of" pp. 578-79.

Contributor to Dictionary of the Bible. Edited by James Hastings. Revised Edition by Frederick C. Grant & H. H. Rowley. New York: Charles Scribner's Sons, 1963. "Glory (in OT)" pp. 331-32; "Isaiah" pp. 423-24; "Isaiah, Book of" pp. 424-27; "Jeremiah" pp. 465-70; "Poetry" pp. 778-80; "Sabbath" pp. 866-67; "Selah" p. 894.

Contributor to Encyclopedia Americana, 1966, Vol. 15, "Isaiah" and "Isaiah, Book of" pp. 407-09; International edition, 1973, pp. 484-86.

Contributor to Encyclopaedia Judaica. Jerusalem: Macmillan & Co., 1972. E.g. "Budde, Karl Ferdinand Reinhard," Vol. 4, col. 1455.

ARTICLES IN PERIODICALS

"The Son of Man in Daniel and The Ethiopic Apocalypse of Enoch," in JBL 79 (1960) 197-209.

"The Biblical Understanding of the Future," in Journal of Religious Thought 19 (1962-63) 99-108.

"What I believe it means to be saved," in USQR 17 (1961-62) 291-93.

"The Speech of Theophany," in Harvard Divinity Bulletin 28 (1963-64) 35-47. The Dudleian Lecture delivered on January 31, 1963.

"Abraham and the Nations. Blessing and World History," in Int 19 (1965) 387-98.

"Form Criticism and Beyond," in JBL 88 (1969) 1-18. The Presidential Address delivered at the annual meeting of the Society of Biblical Literature on December 18, 1968, at the University of California, Berkeley, California.

BOOK REVIEWS

1961 Johannes Hendrik Scheepens, Die Gees van God en die Gees van
     die Mens in die Ou Testament (JBL 80 [1961] 396).

     Walter Beyerlin, Herkunft und Geschichte der ältesten Sinai-
     traditionen (JBL 80 [1961] 383-384).

     H. N. Bream, J. M. Myers and O. Reimherr, eds., Biblical Studies
     in Memory of H. C. Alleman (USQR 17 [1961] 78-79).

     Gerhard von Rad, Genesis: A Commentary (Religion in Life 31
     [1961/62] 145-146).

1962 G. Ernest Wright, ed., The Bible and the Ancient Near East (Int
     16 [1962] 104-106) and (USQR 17 [1962] 243-244).

1963 Curt Kuhl, The Old Testament: Its Origins and Composition (USQR
     19 [1963] 156-157).

     Harvey H. Guthrie, God and History in the Old Testament (USQR 19
     [1963] 55-57).

     Walter Eichrodt, Theology of the Old Testament, Vol. I (USQR 19
     [1963] 49-50).

     Roland de Vaux, Ancient Israel: Its Life and Institutions (USQR
     18 [1963] 159-160).

1964 Klaus-Dietrick Schunck, Benjamin: Untersuchungen zur Entstehung
     und Geschichte eines israelitischen Stammes (JBL 83 [1964]
     207-208).

     Claus Westermann, ed., Essays on Old Testament Hermeneutics (TT
     21 [1964] 228-230).

1965 C. R. North, The Second Isaiah (Int 19 [1965] 360-364).

1966 Th. C. Vriezen, De godsdienst van Israël (JBL 85 [1966] 110-112).

     G. A. F. Knight, Deutero-Isaiah. A Theological Commentary on
     Is 40-55 (JBR 34 [1966] 253-257).

     J. D. Smart, History and Theology in Second Isaiah (JBR 34 [1966]
     253-257).

1967 Hans-Joachim Kraus, Worship in Israel: A Cultic History of the Old
     Testament (USQR 22 [1967] 276-279).

1971 Gabriel H. Cohn, Das Buch Jona im Lichte der biblischer Erzählkunst
     (Bib 52 [1971] 141-145).

     Otto Kaiser, Einleitung in das Alte Testament (BO 28 [1971] 213-215).

E DUE